RICHARD RHODES

Why They Kill

Richard Rhodes is the author of nineteen books. His *The Making of the Atomic Bomb* won a Pulitzer Prize, a National Book Award, and a National Book Critics Circle Award. He has received Guggenheim, Ford Foundation, MacArthur Foundation, National Endowment for the Arts and Alfred P. Sloan Foundation fellowships, and lectures frequently to college and professional audiences. Rhodes and his wife live in Northern California.

WHY THEY KILL

The Discoveries of a

Maverick Criminologist

RICHARD RHODES

Vintage Books

A Division of Random House, Inc.

New York

FIRST VINTAGE BOOKS EDITION, OCTOBER 2000

Copyright © 1999 by Richard Rhodes

All rights reserved under International and Pan-American Copyright Conventions. Published in the United States by Vintage Books, a division of Random House, Inc., New York, and simultaneously in Canada by Random House of Canada Limited, Toronto. Originally published in hardcover in the United States by Alfred A. Knopf, a division of Random House, Inc., New York, in 1999.

Vintage and colophon are registered trademarks of Random House, Inc.

The Library of Congress has cataloged the Knopf edition as follows:
Rhodes, Richard.
Why they kill : the discoveries of a maverick criminologist /
Richard Rhodes.
p. cm.
Includes bibliographical references and index.
ISBN 0-375-40249-7 (alk. paper)
1. Criminal psychology—Case studies. 2. Violent crimes—Case studies.
3. Criminal behavior—Research—Methodology. 4. Athens, Lonnie H.
I. Title.
HV6080.R46 1999
364.3—dc21 99-18920
CIP

Vintage ISBN: 978-0-375-70248-8

Author photograph © Marion Ettlinger
Book design by Robert C. Olsson

www.vintagebooks.com

146119709

For Ginger

I and the public know
What all schoolchildren learn,
Those to whom evil is done
Do evil in return.

—W. H. Auden

Contents

Why They Kill

PART I

THE MAN WHO TALKS TO MURDERERS

Which of us has known his brother? Which of us has looked into his father's heart? Which of us has not remained forever prison-pent? Which of us is not forever a stranger and alone?

—Thomas Wolfe, *Look Homeward, Angel*

Prologue

Why do they kill? Why do some men and women and even children assault, batter, rape, mutilate and murder? No question has so stubbornly resisted explanation. Religions, ideologies and every discipline or science that touches on human behavior have offered answers—theories invoking moral, supernatural, behavioral, social, neurological or genetic causes. None of these well-known theories credibly and authoritatively explains the violent crimes you and I follow in the news every day. It strains common sense to imagine that people are born to violence when rates of violence differ from group to group, culture to culture and age to age. It strains common sense to invoke brain damage to explain violent behavior when most people with damaged brains are not violent. Poverty, race, subculture, mental illness, child abuse, gender, are all disqualified, singly and collectively, as explanations for criminal violence by the sheer number of exceptions within every category that even a casual investigation reveals.

I have personal experience of violence, which is why it interests me. For two years, between the ages of ten and twelve, I was subjected to beatings, psychological and physical torture and near starvation at the hands of a stepmother whose amused malevolence substantiated the wicked stepmothers of folklore. When my older brother and I were removed from our abuser's dark precincts by an enlightened juvenile court and sent to a private boys' home to recover, I gained thirty pounds in three months. As a result of my extended personal encounter with evil, most of my books have examined human violence in one form or another, always for the purpose of discovering what causes such violence and how it might be prevented, mitigated or at least survived.

I encountered the work of Dr. Lonnie H. Athens, an American criminologist, almost by accident, scanning a catalog of books published by the University of Illinois Press. The catalog listed Athens's 1992 book *The Creation of Dangerous Violent Criminals* and explained that it was based on in-depth interviews he conducted with more than one hundred violent criminals. Compared to statistical studies of police records or CAT scans of criminals' brains, that approach seemed refreshingly direct, so I ordered a copy of the book. It surprised and fascinated me. Not only did it offer a credible explanation of the process whereby the violent criminals Athens interviewed learned to be violent, it also immediately helped demystify the newspaper accounts of violent crimes I read every day. (Violent criminals often brag about their crimes, for example—a seemingly self-defeating behavior that frequently leads to their arrest. Athens's work revealed that individuals who decide to use violence need the fearful respect of their intimates and seek it even at the risk of being caught.)

After due consideration I located Athens at Seton Hall University in South Orange, New Jersey, where he teaches, and proposed to write a book about him and his work. As I interviewed him, studied his work and extensively reviewed the criminological, psychological and historical literature of violence, I realized that his findings might have far wider application to understanding violent behavior.

Because Athens's personal experience of violence prepared him to find what previous investigators have missed, this book begins with his own story, moves next to his work and then tests his findings by examining whether they apply to well-known violent criminals whom Athens had not investigated, to violent behavior in other cultures and times and to the ordeal of violence in combat. Finally, it explores Athens's most recent work, which looks beyond violence to the construction and reconstruction of the human personality. It concludes by considering how Athens's discoveries might be applied to interrupt and thereby to prevent the development of violent criminality. Unfortunately neither Athens nor anyone else has found a way to reverse the process once it's complete.

CHAPTER ONE

Bring It On

The James River flows through Richmond, Virginia, like human time. Turbulent above, where the fresh Appalachian water breaks white across the rocky shoals of the fall line, it rushes purposefully past the old Confederate stronghold only to stall and forget itself and slacken to tidal meanders below. Life is contention, and violent homicide has troubled the passage of the river since aboriginal days. It pushed up from Jamestown in 1607 with English adventurers hunting for gold, darkened the bloody ground of civil war, spills through the drug-divided city today and always aggrieves with private murder. If murder is madness, why does its run reach so far? Why has violent death undone so many?

In Jamestown days homicide rates in the West were already declining. Contending human beings had murdered one another in medieval Europe at rates comparable to those in the most murderous American cities today. Urban and rural patterns reversed in that ungoverned age: Medieval cities were safer than the violent peasant countryside. In the seventeenth century new monopolies of state began sequestering violence in police forces and armies. A civilizing process displaced murderous disputes from the street to the courtroom; homicides declined dramatically to historic lows early in the twentieth century before the modern urban rise after the Second World War.

When Lonnie Athens remembers the river running through Richmond, he remembers the Manchester Cafe, his grandfather Lombros Zaharias's diner for mill hands, set on a narrow triangle of land wedged among paper mills and cigarette factories in southside Richmond, at the end of the Mayo Bridge. Athens's mother christened him with his grandfather's name, transliterating Lombros into Lonnie to shield him from the ridicule the rednecks heaped on Greeks in Richmond. More than anyone else Pop Zaharias steadied Athens's turbulent childhood.

The Manchester Cafe was an Edward Hopper scene. The mill hands called it a slop joint: big plate glass windows, separate entrances for whites and colored and divided service inside; marble countertops where burly tattooed men in undershirts leaned on their elbows drinking buttermilk; dark booths stained with sweat; a chalkboard listing the tabs that Pop let regulars run up between paychecks; a menu of hotcakes, hamburgers, salt herring, Pop's legendary bean soup, black coffee, orange Tru-Ade, apple wine and Richbrau beer; cigarettes and chewing tobacco for sale at the register; Hank Williams's "Lovesick Blues" or Woody Guthrie's "Philadelphia Lawyer" on the Wurlitzer jukebox; coal smoke from the mills billowing past like cloud shadows and Pop's flowers and fig trees taking refuge in the garden behind. "There was always plenty of good plain food to eat," Athens remembers, "colorful scenes to watch, humorous stories to hear and no blows to fear." No lack of colorful scenes at home either, but their auras signaled storms of family violence.

Violence might have come from that violence. Instead, partly because Pop knew how to keep the peace at the Manchester Cafe, Athens would eventually earn a doctorate in criminology at the University of California at Berkeley. A compact, handsome man with an explosive laugh, coiled and intensely focused, he would talk his way into prisons past hostile guards to interview convicted rapists and murderers, alone and unprotected, sometimes at the risk of his life. Searching the heinous narratives for the tracks of the beast, he would find the rude, brutal, informal and probably universal program that creates dangerous violent criminals. He would discover for the first time definitively what generations of his colleagues in psychiatry, psychology, sociology and criminology had glimpsed piecemeal but failed to comprehend: the malevolent logic of violent acts. He would publish two brilliant, original books. And then he would spend twenty years beating his head against the brick wall of professional resistance to his hard truths—truths that might inform strategies of prevention and guide the criminal justice system to identify and sequester violent recidivists.

Pop's sheltered daughter Irene married wild Petros Athens, who called himself Pete the Greek. Pete strolled into the Manchester Cafe in his army uniform one day near the end of the Second World War, ordered a beer and asked to talk to Mr. Zaharias. When Pop came over, Pete switched to Greek and told him he'd met his daughter at a church picnic. The young soldier was due for discharge soon; Irene thought her father might hire him. Bridling at the impropriety, Pop warned Pete not to speak to Irene again unless her mother was on hand to chaperone. He didn't need help in the café, but he believed in Greek helping Greek, so he agreed to try out Pete at the front counter.

Pete combed his thick, coal-black hair straight back on his large head. He was broad-shouldered and barrel-chested, with hard biceps and powerful forearms, but he was short in the leg. Pop thought he looked like Jim Londos, the "Golden Greek," the professional heavyweight wrestling champion of the world. Pete thought so too. Londos was one of Pete's heroes. The other was Rocky Marciano.

Pete married Irene and joined the family, but he didn't last long as Pop's front counterman, slinging hamburgers under the Dr Pepper clock. The mill hands called Greeks "flat-footed guineas" and ridiculed the sound of their language: *Quack-quack-quack, quack-quack.* "You weren't black," Athens explains, "and you weren't white. You were just some type of strange foreigner caught between two groups and marginalized." Pop shrugged it off as the price of doing business. He had started out in the 1920s with a pushcart selling doughnuts and coffee and expanded to a shack, and now he owned his own restaurant and a nice house on Byrd Park and had money in the bank.

Pete had a different program. Pete had a bold demeanor: *Bring it on if you want, and if you don't, fine.* He had grown up in Pennsylvania, where his father had been a brickyard worker and a professional wrestler—a brutal, hard-core, hand-to-mouth peasant from Sparta. Pete's mother had died in her son's arms, decapitated in a car accident. When the mill hands hassled Pete at the Manchester Cafe, he took off his apron, debouched from behind the counter and beat them senseless. "He threw one guy through the plate glass window," Athens says. "Unfortunately another guy he almost killed was the foreman at Standard Paper Company, and they boycotted my grandfather's café. So my grandfather told Pete, 'We're not here to beat up people, we're here to make money. I've had enough of this crap about Greek pride. If you have money you have pride. You don't have pride if you don't have any damn money. What the hell are you doing? You want to be a wrestler, become a professional wrestler.' So he let him go." Pete found a job at the Lucky Strike factory.

Lonnie's older brother, Rico, was born in 1945. Lonnie came along in 1949. There were sisters born before and after Lonnie and a baby brother later, but the two older boys and their mother carried the burden of Pete's domination. "Man, woman or child," Athens remembers Pete lecturing them, "it's up to you. I didn't tell you to disrespect me. You told your fucking self to do that. If you're big enough to disrespect your father, you're big enough to get what you get." He knew what he was talking about. Pete's father's hands had been callused from the brickyard, and when he had hit Pete he'd busted his lips. Pete told Lonnie they had almost starved to death the year his father had smashed another laborer in the head with a two-by-four and the brickyard had laid him off. Pete left home when his father took after him with a hot poker and almost killed him. He shined shoes at a hotel before he joined the army and shipped down to Richmond. He was big on respect.

Pete worked for Reynolds Metal after Lucky Strike let him go. "I'm a hardworking SOB"—Athens transcribes one of his father's monologues—"and I deserve some respect for it. I work a regular job, but I make my livelihood by working on the side too. I'm a natural hustler. I know how to talk to people. I was born with the gift of gab. I can sell anybody. I can go out there anytime and make myself some extra money. I don't need any college degrees or union cards to do it, either. I don't need to wait for payday every week to get my money. I can make it on any day of the week. Talk is cheap. Money is what talks in this world, and my mind is always on how to make a buck."

Early in the Eisenhower era, when Lonnie was three or four, Pete bought a diner from an uncle of Irene's in Washington, D.C. The Red Star Lunch became Pete's Snack Bar, thirteen stools and a counter, fish cakes, hot dogs, hash smokes, french fries, pies, icebergs, two big coffee percolators, breakfast all day. The growing Athens family moved to the second floor over the diner. Pete had been a drummer in high school; he made extra money in Washington after hours playing drums at the Friendly Tavern.

He kept an unlicensed gun in a holster nailed up under the counter near the cash register, figuring a robber would order him to open the register and then Pete would grab the gun and blaze away. The neighborhood was transitional—Athens thinks that's why his uncle sold the place to Pete—and becoming threatening. Two black men came in one day and ordered three dozen hot dogs with everything on them. Lonnie was there helping out. "We had little pieces of paper already cut, and we'd get the hot dogs from the steamer and put the stuff on and wrap them, wrap them, wrap them." They loaded a box with the hot dogs and put the drinks in: Rock Creek Colas. The order came to twenty-five dollars. Instead of paying, one of the men grabbed the box. Pete demanded his money. "They said, 'We ain't payin' you anythin'. This is the cost of doin' business here on H Street,' and they started toward the door. My father pulled out the pistol, shot over their heads and said, 'The first SOB goes through that door, he's going to be eating some lead with his hot dogs.' " Pete held his gun on them while Lonnie called the police. Declining to press charges, Pete had the police collect fifty dollars from the two hustlers.

Pete was no less violent at home. "He'd grab my brother and me by the hair and smash our heads together, bloody our faces," Athens says. "I'd hide under the bed. He'd pick up the bed, and I'd hold onto the springs so he couldn't get me. He was a barbarian, a peasant from a Greek peasant family, an extreme patriarch." Pete believed that the man is always right. He would fight anybody, Athens remembers. "He'd say, 'I don't care who you are or who you think you are, you could be a doctor, you could be a lawyer, you could be anything, but if you mess with Pete the Greek, I'll knock your fucking ass on that floor, and you may not be able to get back up again.' " Athens respected his determination. "He didn't go off every day. I don't want to give the wrong impression. But when he went off, he went *off*."

He went off one evening when Lonnie, four or five years old, was arguing with his mother about taking a bath. She wanted to wash his hair. He resisted, and she complained to his father. Pete came roaring in, grabbed Lonnie, picked him up and shoved his head down the toilet. "Flushed it two or three times. I thought I was going to die. I thought he was going to kill me in that toilet. It was humiliating. The water kept going over me, and I just felt filthy. I was frightened to death."

Pete put Rico in the hospital. Rico learned from Pete. When Lonnie was a baby Rico had attacked Lonnie in his crib with a hammer and smashed his baby bottle. More than once he'd tried to smother his little brother with a pillow. This time they were fighting, and Rico pushed Lonnie down the stairs. He wasn't hurt, but it knocked the wind out of him. At supper Pete asked Lonnie how he had fallen down the damn stairs, and Lonnie told him Rico had knocked him down. Irene rushed to Rico's defense, which made Pete all the madder. He picked up a plate and broke it over Rico's head. Rico had to be hospitalized for stitches and a concussion.

The streets of Washington were violent as well. Lonnie did not escape being victimized. He describes an early incident in one of his books:

> While I was walking home from elementary school, three teenage boys began calling me "short legs" and taunting me relentlessly about my small stature. After I thought they had walked a safe distance away from me, I made the mistake of yelling back at them.

They suddenly began running after me. I cut across a vacant lot in a vain attempt to escape them. Once in the lot, they began throwing rocks and bottles at me as I ran. I was able to avoid getting hit until I tripped on an empty tin can. Just as I got back on my feet, one of the boys ran up to me and bashed me in the head with a brick. As I wobbled backward and put my hands to my head, I saw stars, black splotches, and blood pouring all over my hands and down my shirt. Then I got dizzy and collapsed. I woke up in the hospital, thanks to the kind intervention of a woman who had seen me lying on the ground.

Another time in Washington, Irene left Lonnie in Rico's care while she checked into the hospital to deliver a new baby. Rico had trouble at school. He used the occasion of his mother's absence to load his air rifle with BBs and go looking for revenge; he positioned himself outside his school and shot out windows and shot at kids leaving the building. He had dragged Lonnie along with him. The principal threw both of them out of school. They ran away and holed up in a shack in the woods for three or four days, surviving on food they shoplifted from a nearby Safeway. The police were looking for them. Their adventure ended when someone came up behind them at the Safeway and grabbed them by the back of the neck. They thought it was the manager, but it was Pete. He busted their heads together.

Living with violence, a child as bright as Lonnie could hardly avoid studying it. Hypervigilance is in any case one price children pay for childhood abuse. Athens traces the beginning of his interest in criminology to the summers he loved when Irene sent him from Washington to vacation with his grandparents in Richmond. The Zahariases lived in the Greek neighborhood on the edge of Byrd Park, an urban forest west of downtown Richmond that descends southward to the James River shoals. Their front porch looked across to the fountain in the northern reach of the park and the boat lake beyond. One summer a child molester was working the park, kidnapping children. The FBI, which has jurisdiction in kidnappings, decided it needed a decoy, and the agent in charge chose Lonnie. He sent him to the lake to walk around, cautioning him to stay by himself, away from other people. With men stationed to intercept anyone who tried to drag the boy off, the agent watched with binoculars from the Zahariases' porch. Lonnie, seven or eight years old, enjoyed his decoy work. "I'd go there every day," he says. "I wasn't scared. After awhile it got boring, and I started hoping that whoever it was would grab me." The molester never turned up. But Lonnie was intrigued.

Back in Washington after his summer adventure, Lonnie was playing the pinball machine at Pete's Snack Bar one day when mayhem ensued. A man walked in to challenge Pete. Pete had kicked him out before and told him to stay away. They had words. "Pete said, 'I told you not to come back in here. Get out.' The guy said, 'Fuck you, motherfucker, I don't have to get out of here.' " The man brandished an empty bottle, Pete drew his pistol, the man threw the bottle and Pete started shooting. The bottle missed. Bullets flew. "Contrary to popular opinion," Athens observes, "when you're really excited it's hard to shoot straight." But Lonnie was almost in the line of fire. The confined explosions beat against his head: *Bam! Bam! Bam!* "I could hear the bullets hitting the plaster wall beside me. I crouched down and held my ears." He was so terrified he wet his pants. Running toward the door, the man took a bullet under his arm on the right side. The shooting was ruled self-defense, but Pete was convicted of illegal possession of a firearm and had to pay a fine.

Between gun battles and the changing neighborhood, Pete's Snack Bar was failing. Pete had the soul of a carny, florid with wanderlust and get-rich-quick schemes. When Athens saw Federico Fellini's film *La Strada*, years later in college, he couldn't believe how much Anthony Quinn's circus strongman and Giulietta Masina's blond, diminutive, long-suffering mistress reminded him of his father and mother; mentally he retitled the movie *Pete and Irene on the Road in Italy*. In the summer of 1959 Pete sold his snack bar at a loss and prepared to take his family on the road to Florida. "The famous trip south," Athens calls it, laughing now at the lunacy of it. "The big dream, south to Florida for gold and the fountain of youth. We bought this damned station wagon and loaded up everything. Pete buys a big, extra-size cooler, puts ice in it, bologna and cheese, milk in there for my sister Connie and the baby, Billy. We made the trip in July, no air-conditioning in the damned station wagon so we were burning up, going around Florida all summer looking for a new place, looking for a beachhead."

They lived in the station wagon, slept in the station wagon, lined up outside gas station rest rooms to use the toilet and to wash. For driving-around money Pete would organize a tent and a table at roadside, and they'd sell trinkets and souvenirs, Lonnie and Rico flagging down cars. They lived like dogs. Pete at least was happy. According to Athens, that was how his father wanted to live. " 'No bills,' he'd crow. 'No fucking bills. No water bill, no heat bill, no electricity, no fucking mortgage.' " They ate bologna and peanut butter every day. Pete tried to get a job as a chef in Boca Raton. Then he got a job running a small gas station. It was his big plan: "This is how we can make it. We don't have to pay any rent, we can live out of the car. Park the car in the back. Make Rico the pump boy." Lonnie and his mother set up the table with souvenirs, hung up a sign. They rang a little bell to get people's attention while Rico was pumping gas.

Going unwashed, eating bad food and hustling to survive was exhausting and humiliating, and finally Irene had enough. "I don't know what happened," Athens says. "He smacked her around for complaining, smacked us all. But school was coming, and she put on the pressure. 'We can't keep living like this. We've got to have a home for these kids. They've got to go to school. You're crazy. This isn't working.' So he relented. North to Richmond. So this was the famous idiotic trip to Florida."

Much later Athens would write scornfully of academic criminologists who present themselves as experts on criminal violence without ever having had personal experience of such violence or contact with violent criminals. Their usual rebuttal to his challenge, he noted, was that "one need not actually *have* heart trouble or some other terrible disease to discover a cure for it." That was true, he agreed, "but [one] must at least *see, touch, smell and examine* actual diseased hearts if he ever hopes to know anything about them." Athens had certainly seen, touched, smelled and examined more than enough violence in his tumultuous childhood to know what he was talking about.

Settled in Richmond once again, Pete found a job at the Standard Paper Company racking up cardboard, and rented a marginal house in the north end. Factory wages didn't put enough food on the table. Pop came around regularly to visit the kids and slip Irene some money. When he saw how badly they were living, he intervened, telling Pete, "You're not going to feed all these kids like that. You should get a restaurant. Find a place and I'll set you up." Pete found a place downtown called King Joe's Restaurant. It seemed to be a sweet deal, but in fact the neighborhood was once again transitional. Lonnie designed the sign, a majestic crown with "King Joe's" spelled out in glowing neon tubing. He worked there after school, rinsing beer glasses in blue water, filling beer boxes.

At King Joe's one day, lounging in a booth and looking out the big front window, Lonnie witnessed stark horror. An empty street. Afternoon light. A woman runs into view, panic on her face. A man appears, chasing her with a knife. She dodges into a doorway, scrambles to open a glass storm door, wedges herself in full view behind it pulling it against her by the handle, screaming for someone to let her in. The man smashes the storm door glass, gashes his arm, the wound spurts bright red in the afternoon light, the man raises the knife high, ignoring the blood gushing from his arm, and stabs and stabs the woman through the shattered door frame as Lonnie watches, petrified. Blood everywhere—the man's blood, the woman's blood. She slumps and collapses. A beat, then the man swivels around, looks across at Lonnie, bolts across the street, bursts into King Joe's bleeding and brandishing his knife, shrieking, demanding that Pete tourniquet his arm. Lonnie's eyes are wide watching as he trembles in the booth by the window.

Pete jumped to it; he'd been a medic in the army. He tied off the man's arm, and the man ran out. The police and an ambulance arrived on the scene while Lonnie frantically explained to his father what the man had done to the woman who was dying in the doorway outside. All these years later, telling me the story, Athens still shudders when he remembers what he saw.

King Joe's was another bust, another big dream that wasn't working. One day when Lonnie was there two black men came in. One of them was agitated. Abruptly he pulled a gun and put it to Pete's head. Pete was midway along the counter and couldn't reach his pistol holstered beside the cash register down at the end. The gunman started reciting all the reasons he hated white people. "You motherfuckers done us wrong. Why shouldn't I kill your goddamn ass? Blow your fucking brains out all over you. You been fucking us over for years. You made us slaves, you bred us like animals, I'll blow your motherfucking brains out." While he ranted he clicked the trigger at Pete. It made Pete's hands tremble and he started to sweat. Lonnie was terrified.

Pete needed his gift of gab that day. He said, "Man, I don't know what you're talking about. I'm not from around here. I'm Greek, man, we got nothing to do with that. We weren't even in this country back then. My people came over after the First World War. We haven't done anything to you black people. I'm just trying to run a business here and support my family." And then, thankfully, the second man took his side. "Put that gun away, brother. Don't kill this man. He ain't done nothing to us. Let him go. Drop it." Finally the gunman put his weapon away, and they left. Pete closed up for the day to recover.

They moved to a cramped three-bedroom brick house on the other side of Byrd Park from Irene's parents, across from University Stadium on Maplewood Avenue, another transitional neighborhood. A big, muscular redneck named McCahill, with a Ku Klux Klan tattoo, in his late twenties, lived next door on one side; an older redneck named Seal on the other. The Athenses still spoke Greek at home; Irene called her children to meals in Greek. The neighbors registered the exception and picked at it: *Quack-quack-quack, quack-quack.* "What're you talking about," Seal would taunt Lonnie. "*Quack-quacking* over there all the fucking time, talking that *quack-quack* shit? Let these fucking people in, and the next thing is, they draw niggers." McCahill would agree: "These motherfuckers didn't even fight in the fucking war. We didn't fight World War Two to have these motherfuckers come live in our fucking neighborhood. They didn't even fight on our fucking side. I don't know what the fuck these motherfuckers are. Some kind of Moslems or Muslims? What are you? Are you a fucking Muslim or a fucking Moslem? Don't tell me you're a goddamned Christian. I know goddamned well you ain't no Christian." Lonnie would say, "Greek Orthodox," and McCahill would sneer, "They ain't no fucking Christians. Some fucking type of Jew or Moslem." One thing led to another. Rico took offense. By then he was sixteen but small for his age, like Lonnie. He told Seal, "Fuck you, I'll kick your goddamned ass." Seal pulled a gun and fired a couple of shots at him. He missed Rico, who retreated to the house. Then all-out war started.

Three neighbor women knocked on the door one day. When Irene answered, they grabbed her by the blouse, spit on her, smacked her and tried to drag her outside. Rico happened to be home. He pulled his mother into the hall and chased the women off. "This was an upwardly mobile neighborhood for rednecks," Athens says. "They'd just crossed the transition zone. They thought they finally had their place in the sun. That's why they were hostile. They were xenophobic, full of hate. If you get around xenophobic people, it's dangerous. They want to prove they're tough, and they try to get you. I felt like we were being lynched there."

The Athenses' neighbors—McCahill on one side, Seal on the other—built low cinder-block walls capped with brick at the front of their yards to express their aspirations. Pete couldn't afford a full-scale wall. He laid a row of bricks and hooked them into his neighbors' creations. When McCahill discovered the encroachment, he knocked off Pete's bricks. Lonnie knew there would be trouble. It worried him that McCahill was a lot bigger than Pete and had fifteen years on him—Pete was in his forties by then. Pete came home and silently repaired the damage, hooking his wall back into McCahill's. McCahill saw what he was doing and came out. "I'm not going to put up with this shit," he told Pete. "I'll just call the police to settle this." Pete menaced him. "We don't need any fucking police to settle this. I'll settle this with you right now." McCahill backed down.

Extending the war zone from the family to the neighborhood overwhelmed Lonnie. Pete ridiculed him, calling him a "goddamned runt." "I used to cry all the time," Athens recalls. "I was getting it at school, getting it from the rednecks in the neighborhood, getting it at home. And one day I just couldn't walk. I wasn't faking it. I guess it was a hysterical reaction. I just froze. I told my family I couldn't walk, and I crawled to the bathroom. Pete didn't like to spend money on doctors. I used to go to doctors by myself when I needed medical attention. I'd go down the boulevard and look for the right specialty, go in and give them a false name and address, 'Lonnie Jones' and some big address over on Monument Avenue. I never had any trouble. Some of them must have known." He was brazen enough to ask for samples when the doctors wrote prescriptions.

His hysterical paralysis persisted. Pete tried mustard plasters, to no effect. Lonnie stopped going to school because he couldn't walk. When Pete had to carry his son around, he conceded the virtue of doctors. Lonnie told a parade of specialists that he had a pain in his back. The doctors told Pete, "We don't know, he just can't walk. Something's wrong with him we can't detect; his bones seem to be all right; it must be nerve damage." After about three months of consultations, the doctors recommended placing Lonnie in a state home for crippled children located near Byrd Park. "They took me to look it over," Athens says. "I was just a kid, and here were all these crippled kids. I'll be honest with you, it looked like Frankenstein to me. It scared me out of my wits. So they took me back home and decided to try one more doctor." The doctor examined him and whispered something to Pete. Pete gave Lonnie a look, carried him to the car, threw him into the backseat and drove home. When they got there Pete turned around and said, "You better get up and walk out of this car or I'll put my foot so far up your ass you'll wish the fuck you couldn't walk." Lonnie was cured. "That was the miracle cure. I got up and walked into the house."

When not even paralysis could protect him, Lonnie understood that he had to protect himself. Tired of being pushed around, he resolved to try belligerence.

CHAPTER TWO

Thoughts Filled with Ghosts

"In nature," wrote Emerson, "nothing can be given, all things are sold." Mice, rabbits, deer, even family pets defend themselves when no one else protects them. Why should brutalized children do otherwise?

Lonnie Athens worked a paper route in Richmond in his junior high school years. The route included his own neighborhood, west of Byrd Park. Farther west it extended into Windsor Farms, where the rich people lived behind walls in mansions set back among live oaks and magnolias on long, curved roads that led down toward the river. Windsor Farms was a different world, and it spooked Lonnie, riding his bike under the overarching trees in the half-light of early morning, throwing papers, the trees looming and the houses dark. Nearer home his next-door neighbor menaced him when he wheeled by on deliveries. "He called me a Greek runt. Sicced his dog on me—'Get that fucking Greek runt!'" McCahill's German shepherd was vicious. Lonnie prepared a defense. He sawed off a broomstick handle and set a nail in the end. The next time the dog attacked him he smashed it in the head, and it squealed and went down. McCahill ran out screaming, "Whadya do to my dog, you fucking Greek runt? I'll kick your fucking ass!" Lonnie, half the man's size, picked up a brick and, wonder of wonders, McCahill backed off long enough to let him escape.

Threatening McCahill with a brick had been Pete's advice. "My father called me Peanuts or Einstein because I had a little microscope set and tried to do some science experiments at home," Athens recalls. "He told me, 'Look, Einstein, if you ever steal or mess with any girls in the neighborhood, I'll kick your ass. But if you go out there and bust somebody in the head, even kill somebody, I'll be behind you all the way. Remember that, Peanuts. You're my boy. Don't be like Rico. I've seen Rico run. Don't ever run like Rico. You don't run, I'll come and help you.

I don't care if it's kids or what. You stand up, I'll come help you, but don't ever run.' "

Lonnie took notice. By eighth grade, things started exploding. Pete grabbed him by the throat one day and choked him. Lonnie clutched a chair and menaced his father. That was a standoff. Another day Lonnie was target-shooting in his backyard with a bow a friend had loaned him when Pete came out and told him to put the bow away. Instead he notched an arrow and took aim at Pete, telling him, "Don't ever mess with me. Don't ever put your hands on me. I'll kill you if you ever touch me." And strangely enough, although Pete beat Rico and Irene severely, after that he was leery of touching Lonnie. Lonnie had lost his fear. He would call Pete names and then lock himself into his bedroom. By the time Pete got the door unlocked Lonnie would be out the window. He would scream, "I'll kill you one day! One day I will kill you! You fuck with me, you dirty fucker, and one day I will kill you!" He was imitating Pete, who often told his son that he was going to kill him, even putting a gun to his head.

Athens respected his grandfather. Pop Zaharias wanted Lonnie to go into medicine—he paid for the microscope set and financed Lonnie's experiments. "Don't be like your father," he told his favorite grandson bluntly. "He doesn't have any sense." Pop despised Pete's violence. He thought it was ignorant. Pop was a peasant off a Greek sheep farm, but he was shrewd and pragmatically antimacho. "Fight for what?" he'd ask Pete. "You goin' to make any money fighting? It's stupid." Pop called Pete a "one-stop salesman." Pete dragged Lonnie along when he made the rounds of small towns in southern Virginia selling knickknacks and sexual aids. "He sold flints, lighters, sunglasses, can openers, cartons of handkerchiefs, breath fresheners, rabbits' feet," Athens remembers. "But he had a whole line of other products that he held back selling until he sensed that a customer would be receptive—rubbers, vibrators, nude pictures, penis extensions. He'd make up little bottles of what he called Spanish fly out of Coca-Cola syrup and liquid No Doz and put a ten-dollar price on them. He'd tell them, 'You know, I got some other stuff here, for adults. How're you and the old lady doing? You need some help? Let me help you.' Turn to me: 'Son, go get me that box, son.' I'd bring in the box. 'Son, we have some adult business to talk about here, best go on outside.' Like I didn't know. He'd go into redneck bars and sell them pictures of black women and then go into black bars and sell them pictures of white women, work both sides against the middle. He had a lot of guts."

At Christmastime Pete would pull on an old army jacket, pin on a Purple Heart, snap a black patch over one eye, take up a cane and make his rounds claiming to be a disabled veteran. "Palermo," he would say. "Battle of Palermo, lost a lung and an eye. Help a veteran for Christmas. I got a son right here. You know how many I got just like him?" Down the back roads of rural Virginia Pete would target a service station, note the owner's name in the window, ask for him by name. If the owner wasn't around, Pete would claim he had an order, deliver two gross of condoms, refuse to wait, convince the pump boy to pay him out of the cash register and take off before the owner showed up. He would make a week's wages on one trip, covering his tracks with a false address on the receipts he wrote. A year later he would go back to the same towns and bull his way through his previous customers' outrage and sell some more, but the one-stop salesman had sense enough to stay away from the service stations he had scammed.

Athens's grandfather, born in 1882, was an elderly widower by the time Lonnie reached junior high. Although Irene had hauled the kids to church earlier in the Richmond years, she came to be ashamed of Pete's increasingly poor reputation in the community where she had grown up, and eventually stopped attending. Pop would pick up Lonnie and take him along for company. Through the church another nonviolent mentor entered Lonnie's life. The dean of Saints Constantine and Helen Greek Orthodox Cathedral in Richmond was a literate, sophisticated North Carolinian, Father Constantine Dombalis, who had trained at Episcopal Divinity and Columbia and who made it a point to include the Athenses on his visitations. "I would go by the house regularly," Dombalis recalls today in retirement, "and the children would be there and we would talk. Irene was a very fine person. She really held that family together."

Lonnie smelled condescension in the way he and his family were treated in church. His grandfather was respected, but Pete the Greek was a black mark on the Greek community, so the Athenses were pariahs. Lonnie challenged Father Dombalis. "I went to him and I said, 'We're always in the back of the church. Nobody talks to me. What is this? You treat the doctors and lawyers better than you treat people like us. This isn't a Christian church, it's a country club.' Dombalis was very wise. He said, 'Listen, Lonnie, I'm Robin Hood. I have to take from the rich to give to the poor. Who do you think pays for all this? You're right, this is God's house. You've got just as much right to be here as they do. If anybody says you don't, tell them to come see me.' So I respected him. He told me the truth."

The public library gave Lonnie a safe haven away from home. The books he read there raised questions that he took to Dombalis. "You could sense when he came in that he wanted warmth," the priest remembers. "It was what he missed from his father at home. He always sat nearby, next to my desk. I'd continue my work, and we'd talk at length. Sometimes his thoughts seemed to be filled with ghosts, and his eyes were sad."

Dombalis's support extended beyond counseling. "He realized that money makes things turn," Athens says. "He always told people, 'Pray to God, but don't sit on your hands.' " Following Greek Orthodox custom, Dombalis visited his parishioners every year during the Christmas season to bless their houses with holy water. The child he invited to accompany him—a stand-in for the Christ child—traditionally received a gift of cash in return; Lonnie collected as much as five hundred dollars in the years Dombalis chose him, money that put food on the family table. Thirty years later, in the acknowledgments section of his second book, *The Creation of Dangerous Violent Criminals,* Athens expressed his gratitude to Dombalis along with Irene, Pop and Rico "for increasing the odds that I become the author rather than a possible subject in this book."

In the seventh grade, giving a lurid class report on a Tarzan novel, Lonnie attracted a lifelong friend whose family exemplified another non-violent alternative. "I was saying Tarzan pulled people's arms out of their sockets. The teacher kept telling me, 'Sit down,' and I kept saying, 'Wait, there's one more chapter,' and the kids kept saying, 'More! More!' I told them Tarzan broke people's necks, got them in headlocks and tore their heads off. 'Sit down!' I said Tarzan wrestled animals and broke their jaws apart and pulled his knife and cut them up." Lonnie retreated to the pencil sharpener after his bloodthirsty report. A classmate, Michael Markowitz, as undersized as Athens was, strolled over and complimented him. "He told me, 'You're the funniest guy I know.' " Lonnie started spending time at Markowitz's house. One of Markowitz's older brothers attended the University of Richmond. College was another planet to Lonnie. He thought Markowitz's brother was cool because he wore a university jacket and carried a university notebook. Markowitz's father clerked at the Richmond post office. Mrs. Markowitz worked for the city. "Both parents working and two cars, their kid had his own car, they had a kid in college—in the Jewish community it wouldn't have been much," Athens says, "but in our community they looked like successful blue-collar people. They showed me another side of life. I lived with them one summer after a big fight at home. Mike and I were the smallest guys in school. I walked to school with him. Actually he used me for protection."

If Lonnie was small—barely five feet three inches and 120 pounds—he was earning a reputation for ferocity, which put the bullies off. He was one of those tough little kids who won't stop fighting, forcing a potential attacker to commit in advance to serious violence or avoid confronting him. In the eighth grade he chased everyone out of the gym locker room with a baseball bat. In the ninth grade, walking home from school, a bully stepped on his heel once too often and Lonnie was all over him, beating him, until the bully's sister bashed Lonnie with her purse, cutting his eye, and he ran off to find first aid. In the tenth grade a Mohawk haircut he endured for thirty dollars' challenge money ponied up by the barbershop's patrons earned him a two-week expulsion from school. By then his brother had joined the Marines. "Rico was kicked out of all the public schools. That made it hard for me to come in because they stereotyped me as a hoodlum. I wasn't a hoodlum—neither was Rico, for that matter—but that's how they had me pegged. When they expelled me, I wasn't going to go back. I was going to join the Marines like my brother. Fortunately, he came home on leave and told me, 'Don't be an asshole. You'll get killed. They'll use you. Stay in school.' "

Lonnie's ferocity made people leery of him. "I didn't go around challenging people, but I didn't let anybody challenge me, so I could walk anywhere. Markowitz was different. He was a wiseguy. He didn't fight with his fists; he fought with his mouth. He had an uncanny knack for finding people's weaknesses. He'd say, 'Hey, horseface,' and laugh. He was Woody Allen. But then people would be after him. They'd threaten to find him after school. So he'd walk out with me. They'd come up and see me and walk the other way." Markowitz's friendship and family life in exchange for Lonnie's bodyguard services was a fair trade.

The Athenses moved to a worse house in a less turbulent neighborhood. Pete was working at whatever odd jobs he could find: service station attendant, tree surgeon, Lay's potato chip truck driver, beer truck driver, root beer truck driver, cement layer, brick man, Krusty Pie man. With Rico gone, Lonnie moved up in rank, the oldest son at home. When Pete hit Irene, the younger children would run to Lonnie for protection. "I felt self-contempt, not doing anything for my poor mother. So I went downstairs one night when he was starting in on her and told Pete, 'Try me. If you want to hit somebody, hit me.' And he pulled a knife on me. This is about two o'clock in the morning—he usually started late at night—and I got scared because it was dark downstairs. I ran out the front door and picked up a brick and called in, 'Come on out, come on out, bring out the fucking knife, come on out, I'm here. I'm not running any more.' He came to the door, but he didn't come out. He probably saw me with the brick. I ran to Markowitz's house and slept over there.

About a week later Pete grabbed me by the throat. He said, 'What I do with your mother is none of your goddamned business. You're the child. I'm the father. This is between me and your mother. You got nothing to do with this. Don't get in the way or you'll get yourself killed.' He started choking me hard, and I just grabbed him and choked him back. And then he stopped. I don't know why he stopped. He never stopped with my brother. He'd just beat Rico down and beat him into submission. But with me he stopped. The next day he bought me a watch. It was the only thing he ever bought me." After their confrontation Pete and his son both slept with their bedroom doors locked. They went weeks without talking to each other. It was a hard way to live.

Athens came to understand from such experiences that subjugation is selective within violent families and that violent people such as his father are not necessarily mentally ill. Pete had a set of rules that he universally enforced. "He wasn't illogical. There was a logic to his violence. His basic rules, his ten commandments, he repeated over and over again to us: 'Don't bring the cops to my house. Don't have teachers calling at my house about you. Don't ever touch a piece of food without finishing it. Don't mess with my car. Don't mess with my money. And nobody messes with my old lady.' And he never hurt the girls. In fact he was always puzzled by their fear of him. He'd say, 'What the hell is wrong with you? What are you crying for? I haven't done anything to you.' So I never really believed in the mental illness model of violence. I knew you could be mentally ill and not be violent. And I knew you could be violent and not mentally ill. There's no one-to-one correspondence."

Athens worked as a parking lot attendant near University Stadium during his later high school years. In a chapter explaining his interest in violent crime in his 1997 book, *Violent Criminal Acts and Actors Revisited,* he describes a violent scene he witnessed there:

After a game one night, two groups of intoxicated men and women engaged in an ugly argument as they returned to their cars. While one group was getting beer from a cooler in their car's trunk, a member of the second group ran over to them, cursing. Suddenly a member from the first group repeatedly gouged the eyes of the man from the other group with a can opener. I was so terrified by the incident that I can still recall the victim putting his hands to his face and screaming, "Oh shit, one of those dirty SOBs has gouged out my eyes. Help me, help me; I can't see, I can't see, I'm blind." While he screamed in terror, the police arrived at the scene.

Less horrific, but similarly unforgettable, was an attempted rape that Lonnie broke up. Since he didn't have a car, his romantic life depended on double-dating with classmates who did. At a drive-in one night, a classmate who fancied himself a lover was alternating between swigging at a fifth of whiskey and struggling with his reluctant date while Lonnie and his date necked in the backseat. Frustrated, the classmate started the car and roared out into the country, following a dirt road that led to a quarry lake. When Lonnie told him to slow down, he pretended not to hear. At the quarry he parked, locked the doors and went on the attack, grabbing at his date and then judo-chopping her. "At first I thought it was a joke," Athens says. "I didn't think he was really hitting her—who would do something like that? But she started screaming. I said, 'What the hell are you doing?' My date asked him to stop, and he smacked her. I told him to leave her alone, and he turned around and smacked me. Then he just started in on his date, knocking her around, started ripping her blouse off, ripping her clothes—he just went crazy. I was trying to fight him over the back of the seat, but I couldn't stop him. I said, 'Look, you bastard, get out of the car, I'm going to kick your ass.' I got out and he got out, but he grabbed the fifth and broke it on a rock and started chasing me around the car with the broken bottle. I shouted to my date to lock the doors, and we were running around, running around, and then I grabbed a broken tree branch, and he came at me and I whacked him across the chest, kind of baseball-batted him, and he dropped the bottle and collapsed. Passed out. The girls opened the door and I said, 'What are we going to do?' They said, 'Call the police.' I said, 'We're all going to get into trouble.' I told his date, 'I'm sorry he ripped your blouse off, but let's just put him in the backseat so we don't get accused of stealing his car and I'll drive you to my date's house. She can get you a blouse.' That's what we did." Lonnie left the two girls at his date's house, drove his classmate home, left him passed out in the car and walked away. On Monday the school counselor called Lonnie in. He went in warily—he thought the police were after him. The counselor told him she'd had a call. "She said, 'It was a very nice thing you did over the weekend.' I played dumb. I said, 'What are you talking about?' and she said, 'Best we not say any more about it.' " No one did; the classmate was never charged.

If the counselor thought Athens had done something nice, she chose not to allow his chivalry to improve her opinion of his prospects. His high school district ranged from a slum surrounding a state prison east of his own neighborhood all the way to Windsor Farms, throwing together poor, working-class, middle-class and wealthy. "It was awful," he recalls, "and the cruelty was unbelievable. People came to school with better cars than your parents', better clothes than your father ever had." Called to a counseling appointment for career planning during his senior year, he waited his turn outside the counselor's office hoping she might point him to a scholarship program. He listened as she directed his classmates to Randolph-Macon, William & Mary, the University of Virginia. He knew his grades were better than theirs and wondered where the counselor would advise him to apply. When she called him in, she said, "Well, Lonnie, you're a person who likes a lot of action. We know just what you need. Here's a pass. Tomorrow at sixth period the Green Berets are going to be here, and we've selected you." He was shocked. He looked at her, looked at the pass and said not a word. The next day he found himself facing the Green Beret recruiter with twelve classmates from the slum. The recruiter played a tape of the Green Beret song and invited them to sign up. Lonnie, incensed, marched home and confronted his mother. "You've never been to school for me," he told her. "You never went to PTA. I told you if you don't go to PTA I can't make A's. If you don't see the teachers I can't make A's because they know that nobody cares. This time do something. Get on the phone, call the principal and ask him why they aren't recommending me to college. Ask him why the hell they're trying to send me to the Green Berets." For once Irene came through. She called the principal and challenged him: "Why are you trying to get my son killed? I already have a kid in the Marines. Why don't you send the rich kids, why don't they go to Vietnam?" After the call the principal told Lonnie the counselor had misunderstood his interests.

Markowitz's mother gave Athens the support that his high school denied him. Markowitz was planning to follow one of his older brothers to the Virginia Polytechnic Institute on his way to a career in medicine (he is an anesthesiologist today). "His mother suggested I apply there. I sent away for the financial aid forms, and she helped me fill them out." Pete surprised him by agreeing to release his financial records. Athens qualified for financial aid. He and Markowitz went off to college together in the fall of 1967.

"I was so glad to be there," Athens remembers, "I worked hard. To me it was the highest privilege to be there, and you had a meal ticket: You could eat all you wanted. Virginia Tech was an ag school, so it had vast farms. You took this card and gave it to the cashier. The only restriction was that you had to eat at a certain time, seven to nine for breakfast, eleven to twelve for lunch. You could sit there and eat, finish up with three or four different desserts, until the place closed."

With unlimited access to nutritious food in quantity for the first time since his days at the Manchester Cafe, Athens grew three inches and gained twenty-five pounds during his first year at college. He believes his small stature as an adolescent saved him from the successful violent performances that he would later identify as crucial to the development of violent criminality. "I never had any serious major victory, never really seriously hurt anyone. It's fortunate that I never resorted to weapons, because I could hit people twenty times and never seriously hurt them. I was quick, but I never had hitting power. I couldn't knock people off their feet. I was lucky I wasn't challenged when I picked up the baseball bat. If I had been, if someone had called my bluff, I might have hurt them, might have been kicked out of school, charged with assault, sent to prison. I would have been on my way to bona fide virulence. I was stuck in between for a long time, belligerent, with minor violent performances but no major violence. It bought me time to grow mentally." College removed him from immediate danger. He soon made the dean's list. He was planning to become a lawyer when he realized that he had already observed more criminal violence in his first eighteen years than most people see in their entire lives.

CHAPTER THREE

How the System Works

Violence is the Minotaur; those who survive it spend their lives threading its maze, looking for the exit. In retrospect it is not surprising that Lonnie Athens became a criminologist; but criminology was a surprise to him.

He and Mike Markowitz roomed together during their first two years at the Virginia Polytechnic Institute, the big land-grant university where they matriculated in 1967. They made an unlikely pair, Athens says—"the shrewd diplomatic Jew and the stubborn Greek warrior"—but they complemented each other as well. To his and his roommate's surprise, Athens earned top grades, which temporarily strained the relationship: Markowitz was supposed to be the better student. They hung out together, dated together, razzed each other constantly about who was shorter and eventually joined an outlaw fraternity—Tau Sigma Chi—together. Along the way they debated the universal mysteries that keep undergraduates up late at night everywhere in the world.

"We had different conceptions of manhood and right or wrong," Athens recalls, "what you should try to do in life. Markowitz thought I was quixotic because I was idealistic. He thought searching for truth and justice was setting yourself up to be a lamb for the slaughter. He'd say, 'Lonnie, I wish the world were the way you want it to be, but it isn't.' He was going to medical school frankly to make money. He believed that was the bottom line in life. 'People don't want you if you don't have money,' he'd tell me. 'They only want you if you do. Then they know who you are, and they respect you. You never learned that, Lonnie. You live in a dream world.' And I would argue that people who compromised truth were the ones who should lose in life. We're still having the same debate today."

Athens started out in political science; then a sociology course introduced him to criminology. "I didn't know such a field existed," he admits. "I didn't know the difference between sociology, psychology, social work or political science. I was sitting there listening to the lecture, and I just snapped. I thought, Wow, I know about this! I've had firsthand experience with this. I could do something here. I've got something to contribute." When he told Markowitz he had decided to switch from political science to sociology and to concentrate on criminology, Markowitz thought he was crazy. Athens knew better. "I was always puzzled about violence," he recalls. "In my house. In my neighborhood. I wondered why it happened. I wondered why people did it. I wondered why no one did anything about it." Most creative people choose careers born of childhood preoccupations. Athens understood that his full childhood of violent experiences—the most detailed, intimate case study he would ever collect—was too valuable, and earned at too high a price, to waste.

If he questioned his sudden decision, his continuing encounters with family violence confirmed its warrant. Letters came from his mother telling him Pete was beating her. He traveled home to see her when Pete had put her in the hospital and found her with her head wrapped in bandages and a patch protecting one eye. "I was going to kick his ass at that point. I was older, and I was going to kick his ass." That was one of the times Pete pulled a gun on him. "He told me, 'You can't interfere, Lonnie. The best thing to do is just go out that door and never come back, because there's nothing for you here. There's nothing you can do to change things. These aren't your problems. Just leave.' I didn't know what to do. In a sense I hated my mother, too. I didn't tell her to marry him. What the hell did I have to do with all this?" Ironically Markowitz encouraged him to disengage from his family with the same argument Pete had offered: that it was not Athens's problem, that he could not protect his mother or his siblings, that he had to save himself. It depressed him, but he stayed away.

Choosing a major to which he could commit himself personally gave Athens focus. He quit the fraternity. He had been dating the fraternity sweetheart, a bright, beautiful fellow student named Marilyn O'Rourke, and they married and took an apartment together. "I ate and slept criminology after that," Athens remembers. "I got completely into it. It was fanaticism. Some of the professors took me seriously, and I started hanging out in their offices. They gave me a job. I joined the American Sociological Society. I took a lot of statistics. Statistical studies are one whole side of sociology, and I bought into it. VPI had a great statistics department because agriculture uses statistics, so to get ahead I took advanced statistics. I was enamored of positivism. I thought that was the answer, to make social science like physics. I thought there was a secret numen underlying every phenomenon, and the key was mathematics and statistics."

Criminology, the study of crime, is a subdivision within the broader field of sociology, the study of collective behavior. Rooted in the anxieties of conservatives in postrevolutionary France about the mechanisms of social control, sociology emerged as a separate discipline with aspirations to scientific authority only recently, in the first decades of the twentieth century. Case studies predominated in those earlier decades— detailed portraits of subcultures and institutions, factual narratives affinitive to the muckraking social novels of the day. By the time Athens entered the field, in the late 1960s, statistical studies had choked off narrative with forbidding thickets of graphs, charts and tables. For many sociologists numerical manipulation of data seemed to certify authoritative results that participant observation could never match. Athens, a passionate novice with a cast of mind that favored brutal clarity, signed on.

The obvious place to study criminals is prison. The barrier to such study is getting in. Prison administrators dislike allowing civilians to roam their institutions asking questions. On his first foray into sociological research, Athens decided to propose conducting a survey of prisoners' political orientation using a brief questionnaire. He knew that Father Dombalis ministered to prisoners and had contacts with state officials, so he turned to the Greek Orthodox priest for help getting into the Virginia State Penitentiary in Richmond, the old state prison in the slums east of the Byrd Park neighborhood where he had grown up. Dombalis cautioned him that penitentiaries were dangerous places and suggested that Athens first test his mettle at a lower-security institution, Suffolk State Prison Farm, near Norfolk. Admitted to Suffolk State at Dombalis's urging, Athens assembled a random sample of thirty-five inmates and asked each of them three innocuous questions about their political preferences.

Having confirmed that his protégé could handle himself, Dombalis next arranged Athens's access to the Virginia State Penitentiary, an ancient fortress that has since been torn down. Athens sat in the penitentiary reception center for five days in December 1969 asking his three questions of eighty-four felons, a third of whom had been convicted of violent personal crimes including rape, assault and homicide. It was the first time he had confronted violent criminals elsewhere than on the Richmond streets. Fifty-five prison guards also responded to Athens's questions on paper.

Back at Virginia Tech, Athens coded his data onto IBM punch cards, one for each participant. "I thought I was some big scientist," he dismisses his naïveté today, "carrying around this stack of cards, sorting it by answers. I used the countersorter in the sociology department and did univariate and bivariate analysis. Pressed my research on my faculty adviser. He humored me. He acted like I was doing the greatest study since Karl Marx." Not surprisingly Athens found that inmates and guards have different opinions about politics, race and almost everything else. By then the chairman of the VPI Sociology Department had offered him a graduate assistantship with free tuition and a salary of $345 a month. That was a further revelation. Why go into debt for law school when graduate school would pay *you*? Athens reconfirmed his commitment to criminology. He struggled unsuccessfully to work up his prison study for publication, hoping that publication while he was still an undergraduate might boost him into a top graduate school. "I just didn't have the capabilities yet," he laments, "to review the literature and do a complete statistical analysis." It hardly set him back. He wanted to finish a Ph.D. as soon as possible so he could start his research and his career. Graduating a semester early from Virginia Tech, he pushed to begin graduate school in January. That limited the schools to which he could apply, among them the University of Wisconsin.

The Wisconsin faculty included the distinguished criminologist Marshall Clinard, author of a number of investigations of crime and deviant behavior. Boldly Athens wrote Clinard, describing his survey of inmates and prison guards and adding: "Knowing that your major area of interest is deviant behavior, I would like very much to study under you. I realize that your time is valuable and that many compete for it; yet I wish you to know that I am earnest in this endeavor and would be honored to have your guidance." Not many graduate school applicants report independent work and ask respectfully for mentorship. Clinard responded generously that Athens's prison study was "unique"; he wrote the dazzled undergraduate that he was "very glad" that Athens was planning to enroll and looked forward to working with him. In November 1970 Athens learned that he had been accepted at Wisconsin and would be awarded a teaching assistantship that included tuition, a salary, medical insurance and a union card. He and Marilyn began packing. One memento he took along was a pledge he had printed out on a card and posted on his personal bulletin board when he had first become passionate about criminology:

Intellectual Contract
I totally pledge full-time scientific study

of the most problematic act within any
social milieu, past, present or future:
Homicide

"It's naïve," he disparages it in retrospect. "I was a fool." What bright poor boy wasn't naïve as an undergraduate? In dreams begin responsibilities.

Marshall Clinard, flamboyant, wearing a dark blue beret, struck awe in Athens when they met. Athens shocked Clinard. "He was taken aback," Athens recalls. "It was obvious. He'd been everywhere and done everything, and he could read me like a book. He seemed a little disoriented when I introduced myself, like I couldn't be who I said I was. He didn't say anything, but later, after we'd bonded, he told me frankly that I was the crudest student he'd ever seen." Athens as a fledgling graduate student—trim and muscular, not tall, handsome, with dark eyes and a square jaw, his voice a resonant baritone softened by a Virginia accent—wore his black hair long and dressed in jeans and boots, but the rawness Clinard saw emerged from the challenging and nearly menacing way he carried himself, from his blunt, still-ungrammatical speech and his explosive laughter.

Lounging in a warren of cubicles in a corner of the sociology department that first term, waiting for a classmate, Athens observed a woman leave the department, return frantically, search her nearby cubicle, glare at him and begin shouting that he had stolen her purse. "He's not a student!" she screamed. "Get campus security!" He had to prove his identity before the campus security officer would let him leave. Soon afterward Athens took the podium for an oral presentation in Clinard's deviant-behavior seminar. He had never spoken in front of a class before. He was lecturing on the French sociologist Émile Durkheim's theory of suicide when the students began laughing. He wondered what they were laughing about. The laughter spread through the room. He realized that they were laughing at him. He threw the paper down and challenged, "Who do you think you're laughing at, motherfuckers?" Suavely Clinard intervened. He said, "Time out. Time out. Let's take a break," and led Athens aside. "Listen, Lonnie," he told him, "these students have never seen a person like you. They don't know what you're about. They're ignorant. But *they* think *you're* ignorant. So I'd appreciate your forbearance. You'll just have to be a little patient. Just go on up there and finish the paper, and everything will be all right. No more cussing, okay? Go up and finish." He led the way and reintroduced his unusual graduate student.

"This is a very impressive paper," he told the class. "I'm impressed with this man's work. I know his background and I'm very impressed with him, and this is an excellent paper." That set the tone. No one laughed. Athens finished reading his paper. Clinard and his wife made Athens a project that first year.

Clinard had trained at the University of Chicago in the glory days when its Department of Sociology, the first such independent department in America, dominated the field. He was a star among the third generation to come out of Chicago; his teachers—leaders like Edwin Sutherland and Herbert Blumer, both in their turn president of the American Sociological Society—had learned their trade from such sociological pioneers as former newspaper editor and race-relations activist Robert Park, social anthropologist and theoretician William I. Thomas and philosopher and social psychologist George Herbert Mead. Mead's colleague John Dewey had been another important influence at the University of Chicago; Park, Mead, and Dewey had all been students of William James, and Chicago-school sociology was rooted in Jamesian pragmatism.

American sociology at the beginning of the twentieth century had to extricate itself from biology, to make a space for itself among the sciences. The scientific dogma of the day, particularly in psychology, held that human social life arose from biologically determined instincts, evolved through a Darwinian struggle for survival and was then genetically inherited, a Lamarckian model that left sociology nothing to explain. Sociologists countered the argument that biology determined behavior by seeking to demonstrate that behavior determined behavior—that meaningful human activity, not biology, generated human culture. (The debate, deep and basic—ultimately a debate about whether human behavior is predetermined or freely willed—continues to this day, the opposition now calling itself sociobiology or evolutionary psychology.)

The Chicago pioneers and their protégés introduced the case-study approach to sociology, disassembling the components of Chicago's rich stew of marginal and immigrant groups in such books as *The Gang, The Strike, The Ghetto, The City, The Polish Peasant in Europe and America, The Hobo, The Professional Thief, Shadow of the Plantation, The Pilgrims of Russian-Town, The Gold Coast and the Slum*. William Thomas, coauthor of *The Polish Peasant*, and Robert Park, coauthor of *The City*, were big, dynamic men who believed that direct investigation would reveal more about the rules that underlay collective behavior than whole volumes of databases and questionnaires. In the first important textbook of sociology, which Park published with his younger Canadian colleague Ernest W. Burgess in 1921, the former journalist emphasized the advantage of working from concrete experience rather than what he elsewhere called "musty stacks of routine records":

> It has been the dream of philosophers that theoretical and abstract science could and someday perhaps would succeed in putting into formulae and into general terms all that was significant in the concrete facts of life. It has been the tragic mistake of the so-called intellectuals, who have gained their knowledge from textbooks rather than from observation and research, to assume that science had already realized its dream. But there is no indication that science has begun to exhaust the sources or significance of concrete experience. The infinite variety of external nature and the inexhaustible wealth of personal experience have thus far defied, and no doubt will continue to defy, the industry of scientific classification, while, on the other hand, the discoveries of science are constantly making accessible to us new and larger areas of experience.

These arguments away from statistical manipulation of data were a revelation to Athens. The Chicago school had lost ground to quantitative sociology in the 1950s and 1960s; Wisconsin, which had the largest sociology department in the world by the time Athens arrived there, was heavily committed to statistical studies—one reason Athens had chosen it. Clinard valued what he called "techniques of more precise measurement of associations among social phenomena" and believed they had "helped to advance sociology as a science." But he also suspected that his colleagues were flocking to the new techniques partly because numbers veneered their investigations with the prestige of hard science. "To many sociologists," he had recently told the Midwest Sociological Society, ". . . to become known as a quantitative expert, a methodologist with mathematical overtones, or an expert with the new electronic computers is one of the short cuts to contemporary respectability." Students aped their betters, he complained: "The opportunities provided by graduate training for . . . firsthand experience appear to be decreasing rather than increasing. . . . Graduate research today all too frequently involves the use of secondary data and the manipulation and tabulation of punch cards. Occasionally there are opportunities for brief personal interviews or brief pre-tests. . . . Today's graduate students often seem reluctant or even embarrassed to become fully acquainted with the data to be investigated, or social phenomena in the raw, as was expected, for example, of all graduate students at Chicago twenty-five years ago." Clinard might have been describing Athens's undergraduate study of inmates and guards.

To encourage Athens to think about alternatives, Clinard pressed on his talented student the works of quantitative sociology's most articulate critics. Absorbing them was crucial to Athens's acquisition of the tools he would need to study violent crime.

A paper by the philosopher of science Alfred Schutz reviewed the basic philosophic debate between the two schools of social science: whether the social world is different from the world that physicists and chemists explore. The quantitative sociologists believed that it is not; the qualitative sociologists of the Chicago school believed that it is, and that it therefore requires different methods of study. Schutz defended the difference, pointing out that "the world of nature, as explored by the natural scientist, does not 'mean' anything to the molecules, atoms, and electrons therein." Social reality, by contrast, has meaning to the human beings who live, think and act inside its frame—and it was just those meanings that sociology proposed to explore. To do so, writes Schutz, sociology needed a different set of tools. It had to make room for subjectivity. Its theoretical constructs had to be "constructs of the second degree, namely, constructs of the constructs made by the actors on the social scene."

Athens, for example, was interested in understanding why some people act violently. The methods of natural science—measurement and experiment—borrowed by quantitative sociology could reveal many facts about such people: that they are most commonly young males, living in big cities rather than small towns, who begin their criminal careers at a young age, who don't do well in school, who drive recklessly, who show reduced anxiety rather than increased anxiety when exposed to violent images (as measured by lie-detector-like instruments) and so on. But none of these facts answered Athens's question about motivation, because motivation can't be measured that way. To find out about motivation he would have to observe violent people directly, interact with them, ask them questions, get answers, look for common patterns.

A book on method and measurement in sociology by a student of Schutz's, the sociologist Aaron Cicourel, carried Schutz's argument further. "Cicourel's point," Athens summarizes, "was that there's no isomorphic relationship—no one-to-one correspondence—between the properties of the real number system and of social phenomena. You can't measure love. You can't measure personality. You can count things and see how they distribute themselves. But you can't *scale* social phenomena."

A recently published book by sociologist Derek Philips, *Knowledge From What?*, particularly impressed Athens. Philips revealed the miserable results of sociologists' efforts to quantify social behavior, the dirty little secret of sociology. "While there are indeed literally dozens, if not hundreds, of generalizations abounding in the sociological literature," Philips wrote scathingly, "the vast majority are either unconfirmed in empirical research or else are of such minor magnitude in explaining any observable facts as to be of limited utility." Philips pointed in particular to quantitative sociology's statistical studies, which measured one "variable" against another "variable" to see if they correlated—to see, that is, if they varied together. If they did, then one was said to "explain" the other. He gave an example: "Thus, if mental health status [one variable] correlates highly with social class position [another variable], [then] mental health status is, at one level or another, [said to be] explained by social class position." Philips looked at tabulations of these "significant" relationships among variables and discovered that collectively "the average 'significant' relationship explained about 10 percent of the variance." (Compare weather prediction: a 10 percent chance of rain—would you even take your raincoat?) One tabulation he found indicated that most behavioral research accounted for, at best, "something like 13 percent of the variance. Clearly, an ability to account for only 10 or 13 or even 20 percent of the variance is not very impressive, and does not lead to a high degree of predictive ability." He quoted an investigator who had observed " 'a gentleman's agreement among readers and editors [of sociology research papers]' " not to ask how much variance a study accounted for, " 'perhaps because the measures of explained variance are so embarrassing to all.' "

Trying to comprehend living systems by searching for relationships among variables left their most fundamental characteristic unexplained, Philips argued. He underlined that fundamental characteristic in a paragraph that spoke directly to the ambition Athens had expressed in the "Intellectual Contract" he had posted on his undergraduate bulletin board:

> If we are to go beyond the accumulation of lists [of variables] to a concern with *how a system works,* we must enter into it more frequently than most of us do at present. Such participation is necessary to provide us with reactions of our own which will help us to

properly understand the reports and behavior of others. For only by becoming involved in what we are studying can we fix upon the thing itself, become aware of it, experience it, and obtain "knowledge of" as well as "knowledge about" it. Certainly if we sociologists are really interested in process and interaction, as we so often claim, and if we wish to study the construction of meanings and of social relations, we can only do so from more active involvement and participation.

Athens was impressed most of all with the essays of Herbert Blumer, Clinard's teacher and colleague who was now a senior professor of sociology at the University of California at Berkeley. Variable analysis left out the *life,* Blumer argued: "We can and, I think, must look upon human group life as chiefly a vast interpretative process in which people, singly and collectively, guide themselves by defining the objects, events, and situations which they encounter." To understand that process, Blumer insisted, a scientist had to gain firsthand knowledge, which might involve "direct observation, interviewing of people, listening to their conversations, securing life-history accounts, using letters and diaries, consulting public records, arranging for group discussions and making counts of an item if this appears worthwhile." Charles Darwin had been such a naturalistic observer, Blumer wrote, "one of the world's greatest." The scientist had to explore, he had to inspect, and then he had to see the social action he was studying

from the position of whoever is forming the action. He should trace the formation of the action in the way in which it is actually formed. This means seeing the situation as it is seen by the actor, observing what the actor takes into account, observing how he interprets what is taken into account, noting the alternative kinds of acts that are mapped out in advance, and seeking to follow the interpretation that led to the selection and execution of one of these prefigured acts. Such an identification and analysis of the career of the act is essential to an empirical understanding of social action—whether it be juvenile delinquency, suicide, revolutionary behavior, the behavior of Negro militants, the behavior of right-wing reactionary groups, or what not.

Blumer's approach was exactly what Athens needed. In his first work with inmates and guards he had felt straitjacketed. If he wanted to understand homicide, he now realized, asking questions he had made up in advance and then running statistical correlations on the answers was "worthless"—not least, he says, because under such strictures he could not use his own firsthand experience of violence, which should be invaluable both as a guide to his exploration and as a check on the results. As he wrote Clinard later, "After reading the works of the critics whom you suggested, I came to the conclusion rather suddenly that the use of quantitative techniques was nothing but 'pseudoscience.' "

Newly converted, Athens at first went overboard. "It got out of control. I became totally intoxicated with *qualitative* sociology. I was convinced that all my prior learning was wrong, completely wrong, that everything I'd learned before was useless, that it probably did me more harm than good. I started questioning the motives of the experts I was hearing in class. I didn't know how to be tactful. I would raise my hand and say, 'Why would you be interested in poverty? You've never been hungry, have you?' I questioned experts on women who were men, people studying blacks who were white, people studying lower-class people who were middle-class, people studying violent criminals who had never been a violent criminal or never suffered from a violent crime. I'd often ask the criminologists why they didn't study white-collar criminals, as Clinard did. What was their credibility? Why were they experts? It didn't ring true to me. It still doesn't."

Despite the common sense of Athens's argument, his questions in his classes predictably angered the faculty members he challenged. The Clinards hauled him off to their house again for advanced instruction in deportment. Athens was willing to take instruction in etiquette but not in logic. Rather than give up his questions, he called out the cavalry. He circulated a petition among his fellow graduate students to invite Herbert Blumer to Madison. "The idea was for him to give a talk and take on all the leading positivists. I went to Clinard and said, 'You know him.' He said, 'Yes.' I said, 'You believe in his ideas.' He said, 'Yes.' I said, 'Okay, we got up a petition, took it to the department chairman, and he said he'd pay the honorarium. So will you invite him? And Clinard said he would." Blumer came to Madison in May 1972. Athens was waiting for him.

CHAPTER FOUR

The Full, Ugly Reality

Herbert Blumer proved to be a tall, broad-shouldered, dignified man of seventy-two. A pipe smoker with thick salt-and-pepper eyebrows, he combed his blond-gray hair straight back above a wide Dutch face. To Lonnie Athens he looked like Alistair Cooke. He was a Missourian, a St. Louis native and a football All-American. After graduating from the University of Missouri in 1921, he had joined the faculty in sociology there while simultaneously playing professional football as a tight end for the Chicago Cardinals. Missouri incubated a particularly virulent culture of the Ku Klux Klan in those days. The young instructor's career in his home state ended when he tried to stop a lynching. The mob restrained him and carried out its murder, but the scathing lecture on crowd behavior that Blumer added to his sociology course so scandalized the Klan that it brought pressure to force him to resign. He took a leave of absence and used the occasion to move on to graduate study at the University of Chicago, where he worked with Robert Park and served as a research assistant to George Herbert Mead, earning his doctorate in sociology in 1927 and teaching there and at the University of Michigan for many years afterward. His specialty was methodology, the difficult and controversial discipline of *how* to do scientifically authoritative sociological research— exactly what Athens was exploring and needed to know.

Blumer made a triumphal entry into Madison in that upper Midwestern springtime. He spoke on his own version of qualitative sociology, which he called "symbolic interactionism" and had based on Mead's social psychology. He was direct and eloquent, as much preacher as professor, a forceful but graceful man who believed whereof he spoke. The quantitative sociologists on the faculty who had vowed to set him straight bit their tongues.

Athens tests people. When Blumer sat in on Clinard's deviant-behavior class, the brash young graduate student challenged him. "I'd been trying to understand Mead's concept of the 'I' and the 'me'—his terms for our individuality and our social conformity—and I couldn't figure them out. I told Blumer there were contradictions there, and we got into a big debate. Most professors didn't like it when you pointed out contradictions. Blumer welcomed the challenge. He wanted more." Blumer arranged to meet with Athens privately in a borrowed office, and they continued their discussion. At dinner that evening at Clinard's house, the two senior scientists reminisced about the glory days at Chicago. Athens was dazzled. Blumer returned the compliment. Before he left he told Clinard that Athens was one of the most profound students he had ever encountered. When Clinard passed the compliment on, a flattered Athens understood that he had found the scientific mentor he'd been searching for.

Athens had begun corresponding with Blumer even before the Berkeley sociologist came to Madison, and they continued their connection afterward. In one letter Blumer sketched a methodological path for Athens through the jungle of violent behavior, a trail Athens might blaze. "If I were handling your dissertation project," Blumer wrote,

> I think that I would direct my study to seeing how the individual *handled* his disposition to commit assault or homicide. This is really what is involved in Mead's thought of the "I" and the "me." And this is something that can be gotten at through empirical study. Focusing on any given subject, I would wish to find out how he handled his impulses toward assault and homicide over time; this would be equivalent to building up a life history of his experience with such dispositions. Such a study could be very revealing and valuable.

Clinard advised Athens to take the easy road to a master's thesis so that he could move on to his doctorate. The most celebrated criminologist in the United States at that time was Marvin Wolfgang, a professor at the University of Pennsylvania and a committed positivist. Wolfgang's best-known book was *Patterns of Criminal Homicide,* a statistical study based on police reports that broke out homicides according to such categories as age, sex, race, occupation and criminal record of the offender, time and location of the offense, type of weapon, degree of violence, motive. Clinard knew the Madison police chief. He suggested Athens do a Wolfgang-like study using Madison police reports—collect the data, computerize it, sort it by categories, write it up in a month or two and have a good chance of seeing it published. Athens wasn't interested; he had other ideas. Clinard had steered him to Blumer. Blumer said to sink yourself in the milieu. The milieu wasn't available in the records. Athens was determined to interview some violent criminals. Clinard thought his plan was far too ambitious for a graduate student, but Athens wouldn't budge. Eventually Clinard acquiesced and wrote Wisconsin Correctional Systems on his student's behalf.

A board of WCS clinical psychologists offered Athens a hearing. He started by talking about W. I. Thomas's *The Polish Peasant* and Nels Anderson's *The Hobo,* books that investigated and reported the lives of their subjects in rich detail. He told the board that he wanted to do a similarly detailed study of violent criminals. The board thought he was crazy, he remembers. "They said, 'Where's your questionnaire?' I said, 'There's no questionnaire. I know the questions. I memorized them. This is like an interview on Johnny Carson. You just memorize ten or twelve questions and then, depending on the guy, you ask the question when the time is right.' They looked at each other and one said, 'You don't even have a questionnaire, an instrument?' I said, 'I don't need an instrument. This is symbolic interactionism. We don't believe in instruments. Instruments prejudge the situation. They're damaging.' " The chairman of the board stopped the discussion and sent Athens out into the hall. When he faced them again after they had caucused, the chairman told him, "Listen, son. We've got an instrument already made up. It's fifty questions. We think you could get a good interview, so we're going to let you do it this way. You administer our instrument, and then you can add on five questions of your own." Athens was indignant. "I beg your pardon," he protested, "but I can't deviate from my study. Adding my study onto yours would ruin everything. The prisoners have to think I'm clean. I can't act like I'm working for the prison. How are they going to trust me enough to open up? I can't even be associated with you people. I'm sorry." Which ended the discussion. Clinard picked up the pieces. He told Athens there'd been hell to pay.

Doggedly Athens wrote prison wardens in Illinois and Iowa. To his surprise Iowa welcomed him. With a small grant from the National Institute of Mental Health, he made his way with his wife to Fort Madison, Iowa, an old Mississippi River town at the bottom of the state. The Iowa State Penitentiary hulked beside the river like a fortress, the oldest penal institution west of the Mississippi—"a crude place," Athens says, "almost a dungeon." The warden welcomed him and turned him over to a lieutenant, who set him up in an office and arranged for him to take his meals with the convicts. "Here's a guard," Athens recalls, "he hands me a tray, I follow him to the food line, he finishes loading his tray before I do and walks over to the guard table. I leave the food line to walk to the guard table and all the inmates start whistling. Wolf whistles." Athens at that point was fresh meat, twenty-three years old. Instead of showing fear, he performed—set down his tray, faced his audience, grinned and gave them three or four full bows from the waist. Accepting the acknowledgment, they stopped whistling.

Athens reviewed the Iowa inmate records and selected thirty candidates for interviews. Three refused to participate because their cases were on appeal; two claimed they'd gotten a bum rap. The other twenty-five he set to work interviewing, averaging four hours per interview and keeping verbatim notes, while Marilyn reviewed their case records. No one had ever collected so many and such chilling narratives before: violent criminals describing in detail what they thought and felt when they committed murders, rapes or vicious assaults. In his books Athens takes pains to reconstruct these unique monologues as realistically as his notes and memory allow. They make horrific reading—deliberately so, he explains: "I . . . believe that readers need to be confronted with the full, ugly reality of violent crime not only to enlarge their understanding of these offenses but to prevent them from romanticizing their perpetrators." He promised his subjects anonymity; the testimony he has published is identified only by case numbers, but this is one of that first Iowa group:

CASE 2: CRIMINAL HOMICIDE

X and I had been traveling together for over a month. This trouble had been building. I was getting tired of his loud voice, bragging and tough-guy attitude is what it boiled down to. I figured I would get sick of it sooner or later.

We stopped at this railroad yard and started shooting bennies. He was bragging and talking loud as usual about how many women he had laid, how good he could drive a car and how many guys' asses he had whipped. He wanted to boss me around, but I could see that he wasn't that much: He was just lying. He kept up the tough-guy attitude and a Casanova act talking about this and that bitch. I got to hate the sound of his voice; he talked so loud it ran chills up my spine. He started acting like he could squash me out. He took my shyness for weakness. Then he began his grabbing on me. I said, "Can't you talk to somebody without grabbing them?" But he kept on doing it. I don't know what he said after that because I stopped listening and was thinking that I'd like to show

him he wasn't so tough; show myself, too. I hated him. His referring to me as a little guy irritated me. I wanted to cut him down to
size. I said, "You put your hands on me again and I'm gonna shoot
you." He said, "You wouldn't shoot me." I didn't like his doubting
my word, and I figured he'd grab me again. When he did, I shot
him fast.

The Athenses used up the grant money, drove back to Wisconsin and
raised more, returned to Fort Madison, left, returned again. Two of
Athens's twenty-five subjects lied to him during their interviews, giving a
different account of their crimes from the account in their case records;
he tore up those notes, leaving him with twenty-three cases. Rapport
with those men was high, he judged; three who had denied their crimes
in court acknowledged them in their interviews. Case 9, forcible rape,
revealed the full, ugly reality:

I hadn't had any pussy for some time, so I felt horny as shit. Then I
started thinking about this girl I met at a party a couple of weeks
ago. She was built thin, but enough meat was on her to throw it up
to me good. She never acted interested in me, but I had heard that
her and the older woman in her building were giving up boatloads
of pussy. I was drunk and my mind was on pussy, so I headed for
their place. (I found out from a friend where they lived.) When I
got there, I noticed the older woman in her room with the door
wide open, so I went in and said, "Hi." She asked me what I
wanted. I said I wanted sex and decided to try to talk her into fucking first. But she said, "I'm not going to do anything like that with
you," so I knew then I was just going to have to take it. I said, "Yes,
you are," and beat on her, but she still wouldn't give open, so I got
the pipe . . . she had next to her door. After I busted her once
upside the head, she said, "Well, if that's the way you want to be
about it, then you are going to have to take my clothes off yourself." I pulled her panties down and said, "Now bend over and
spread open, before I bust you upside the head again, but even
harder." When she bent over, I saw her big old fat ass. I tried to
drive my dick into her dark, brown spot, but it was too tight. I kept
pushing and pushing, but my dick started going down on me.
While I was trying to stick my dick up her, the younger woman
that lived in the same building came home. The older woman said,
"What you need is a taste of that young stuff, not me." I thought,

She's right about that, 'cause her stinking, ugly old ass wasn't doing nothing for me.

That young girl's pussy was what I needed. I'd been dreamin' about fucking her skinny, bony ass for some time. I pulled up my drawers and headed straight for her room across the hall. I kicked her door open. As soon as I saw her, I got hard again. When she asked me what I thought I was doing, I said right out front, "I want to fuck you." She said, "Get out, get out of here." I got mad and grabbed her around the collar, but she started screaming, "Rape! Rape! Rape!" I told myself, I am going to do whatever I got to do to get that pussy. I started squeezing her neck and saying, "Shut up, shut up. All I want is some pussy; I don't want to hurt you." She broke away from me and went into the kitchen, where she got a knife and cut me. I finally knocked the knife out of her hand, but she slipped past me and got out the door. When I heard her run out the building into the street hollering at the top of her lungs, "Rape! Rape! Rape!" I thought, I am in real fucking trouble now.

What makes these crimes so heinous, Athens point out, besides their obvious brutality, is "their relative lack of provocation. . . . The provocation is grossly disproportional to the injuries inflicted upon the victim. . . . Most people dread becoming the victim of a heinous violent crime more than any other crime." Criminals who commit heinous violent crimes, he adds "are the most *dangerous violent criminals* in our society."

But Athens sought criminals' recollections not only of their crimes. He also asked them about their previous experiences, going back into their childhoods, and there he found what he had to find unless violent criminals are bad seed, genetic monsters born that way: He found frightened, angry children:

CASE 9

One night I was woken up by loud voices coming from my parents' bedroom. I got a drink of water from the bathroom so I could find out what was going on. As I walked to the bathroom, I heard my mother say, "No, I told you not to do that, I don't like it." I thought to myself, What could he be doing to her? I started listening as hard as I could. My mother said, "Please don't do that to me anymore, it hurts," but he said, "I don't care whether it hurts or not." I heard noises which sounded like scuffling and my mother screamed, "Please stop, it hurts, it hurts bad, please stop now, no more, stop, stop." She would cry for awhile, scream out in pain and then start crying again.

As I walked back to my room, I knew that he must be hurting her awful bad to make her scream like that. It got me so mad and angry that I wanted to kill him. I thought about going in there, pulling him off her and kicking his ass good, but he was too big for me to handle. I knew there was nothing I could do. I wished he would stop, but he wouldn't. As I heard her crying from my bed, I felt bad because I couldn't do anything to help her. I wanted to get him off her and hurt him, but I was too afraid. I kept telling myself that I was just a little sissy. Then I tried to fall back to sleep and pretend it was all a bad dream.

"When people look at a dangerous violent criminal at the beginning of his developmental process rather than at the very end of it," Athens has written, "they will see, perhaps unexpectedly, that the dangerous violent criminal began as a relatively benign human being for whom they would probably have more sympathy than antipathy." Case 9 is shocking evidence to Athens's point: The child pretending that his mother's sexual torture is a bad dream transvenoms into the brutal rapist perpetrating multiple assaults. What experiences drove frightened children to become violent adults? That was the mystery the young Wisconsin graduate student had yet to resolve.

After Athens had finished all twenty-three interviews, he had the problem of interpreting them. There were no experts on qualitative methodology at Wisconsin. His interviews were in hand, but what was he supposed to do with them? One professor complained that the case material was too repugnant to put in a thesis. Athens was properly indignant. "What do you mean, 'repugnant'?" he countered. "This is like in medical school when you autopsy the corpse." So his master's thesis was a catastrophe, and he knew his days in Madison were numbered. He wanted to work with Blumer. He set his sights on Berkeley.

Once again he was out of phase with the school year. He would finish his master's work in January, but the Berkeley sociology department, crowded with graduate students, only accepted new applicants in September. Blumer opened the way; on his recommendation the university was willing to squeeze Athens into its school of criminology in midyear.

The Athenses rented a truck, loaded their belongings, gave their ancient car to a graduate student friend and plowed the northern route to California in the dead of winter, sliding off a mountain into a providential snowbank along the way. They found an apartment in Berkeley. Marilyn took a job as a secretary at the law school. Since they didn't have a car, they bought a children's wagon with wooden stake-rack sides to haul their groceries home. Crossing the campus for the first time, Athens felt triumphant. It was a long way from Pete the Greek's house to doctoral study at Berkeley.

The achievement was freighted with irony. Before they left for Berkeley, the Athenses had returned to Richmond for Lonnie's older sister's wedding. Pete and Rico had brawled the night before the wedding and arrived at the ceremony with split lips and black eyes. At the reception afterward, at Pete and Irene's, Athens's father launched a bullying harangue. "His no-good sons," Athens recalls it. "A son who would hit a father is no good, a father has a right to kill a son who puts his hands on him because he brought him into this world and he can take him out of this world." At that point Pete wheeled the barrage around to Athens's grandfather. "You had me working twelve hours a day in your goddamned slop joint," he accused Pop, "paying me thirty-five dollars a week. You didn't treat me right." Pop was old. He was a proud man. He didn't dare challenge Pete, but he mustered a stern expression. Athens was concerned that his grandfather might have a heart attack. He told Pete, "Leave him alone. He's an old man." Pete kept on. Athens barked, "Shut up and leave him alone." Pete snarled, "Don't you tell me to shut up. I'm your goddamned father." Athens saw his grandfather tremble. He jumped up and attacked Pete where Pete was sitting, hitting him in the face. Pete shot out of the chair. Athens knocked him down, piled on top of him and started punching. People pulled him off. Pete got up and made a remark. Athens picked up a lamp and swung it at his father. Pete took a glancing blow, knocked the lamp aside and went off to get his gun to shoot his son. Family members pulled Athens out of the house into the yard. Rico drove Lonnie and Marilyn to Mike Markowitz's apartment—Markowitz was a medical student by then. He let the Athenses stay with him until they could get bus tickets. "Pete wasn't seriously hurt," Athens concludes. "He didn't have to go to the hospital, but he was humiliated because the whole extended family had witnessed the fight. He'd always menaced people at family gatherings, and everybody had always submitted, so he was completely and totally humiliated. So he announced that he'd kill me on sight. I decided there was nothing I could do but move on. I couldn't win for losing, and the best thing was never to come back." Later, analyzing his cases, recognizing similar turning points in the lives of the men and women he studied, Athens would find a name for what he had started that wedding day in Richmond: He called it a "violent personal revolt"—the violated turning on his violator—and understood he was lucky it had not been successful.

He was more than ready to work with Herbert Blumer now. Blumer helped him reorganize his abortive master's thesis into something acceptable. Before he finished graduate school, he would extract from the twenty-three Iowa cases his first signal insights into violent behavior in a paper titled "The Self and the Violent Criminal Act," an early reconnoiter of the new ground he was breaking. Passing routine courses by pretesting freed him for independent study, and he read through the social psychology classics: Mead, Dewey, Thomas, Charles Horton Cooley, Robert Park—a dream come true. In summer Blumer loaned him his office. He wrote up his Virginia prison study and saw it published. Most of the students at Berkeley in those days were radicals, which left him feeling isolated and sometimes lonely. "Why aren't you studying the Vietnam War?" they challenged him. "Because I'm not studying wars," Athens told them, "I'm studying interpersonal violence." Americans killing Americans on the streets, Americans killing Vietnamese, which was worse? More Americans died on the streets in the years of that war than died in combat.

He was eager to pursue more interviews. He had questions to ask now, after studying with Blumer, that he had not thought to ask before. "It was hard getting into prisons," he remembers. "They put you through the bureaucratic wringer. They try to stall you until you give up. I didn't give up. Blumer helped me. He kept writing letters, making calls. Finally I got approval from the California Department of Corrections, but it was subject to the approval of the various wardens. San Quentin was right across from Berkeley, but the warden wouldn't let me in. Corrections pointed me to the California Medical Facility at Vacaville. By now it was the summer of 1974. The psychiatrist at Vacaville tried to freeze me out. I couldn't interview mass murderers, he told me, he wouldn't give me a list of available inmates, I couldn't do lengthy interviews because it would interfere with inmate programs. I went up there to have lunch with him to talk it over, and he started telling me I didn't know what I was doing. That set me off. I said, 'If you psychiatrists know so much, how come all these people are in here? And after they get out of here, how come they end up back here if you guys know everything?' So that started a shouting match. I said, 'You don't own these inmates. I have a right to study them. *They* ought to get to decide who studies them, truth be told.' "

One of Athens's troubles, as usual, was that he didn't look the part of a scholarly graduate student. He wore his hair down to his shoulders, anchored with a headband. He wore striped T-shirts, jeans, Swiss hiking boots—substantially the same clothes the prisoners wore. After the argument the warden overruled the skeptical psychiatrist and allowed Athens access. Ironically the shouting match helped Athens with the prisoners. Convict cooks, waiters and busboys had overheard and thought Athens had taken their side.

In addition to Vacaville, Athens lined up access to the California Institution for Men at Tracy—the most violent prison in the United States at the time—the California Institution for Women at Corona and the Alameda County jail at Santa Rita. By then he had bought a used eggshell-white Volkswagen beetle. Santa Rita was nearby, south of Oakland. Tracy, near Stockton, was fifty miles inland from Berkeley; Vacaville, east of Napa, forty miles north. Corona, southeast of Los Angeles, was a long overnight away and expensive in motel bills. But he was in.

CHAPTER FIVE

Taking the Attitude of the Other

Interviewing violent criminals was hard, dangerous work. The prisoners made it dangerous; the prison administrators made it hard. Lonnie Athens had no protection in prison because he was not wanted there. Wardens cautioned him that meeting alone with inmates was risky and put him on notice that they could not guarantee his safety. He understood that if he complained he would be denied further access, which meant he was effectively on his own. Guards searched him going in to make sure he was not muling drugs and strip- and body-cavity-searched the inmates he interviewed before returning them to their cells.

If the hostility was unnerving, the searches worked to Athens's advantage, making it obvious to the inmates that their keepers didn't trust him. At one prison he interviewed a tall, thoughtful drug dealer, a man with a long record of serious violence, who approved of the study Athens was making and decided to protect him. He still has a snapshot the man gave him, inscribed "To little Lonnie, keep the faith bro—your brother [X]." Athens detected his invisible shield in the aftermath of a near assault. While he was alone one day at the prison preparing for an interview, three inmates pushed into the room where he was working and menaced him. They told him, "You know, you got pretty hair, you're a pretty boy. You're real pretty." One directed the other two, "Get on that side of him—get on the other side of him." Athens was sitting at a desk with a phone. Lifting the receiver would signal security to send a guard. Athens jumped up and warned the inmates, "You bastards better not bother me. You try anything, I'm going to fight. I'm taking this phone off the hook." Everyone was focused on the phone. Protecting yourself in prison,

Athens explains, requires taking a stance. His hand hovering above the phone, Athens laughed and waved his attackers off. "Get the fuck out of here," he jollied them. After they left he discovered he was white and shaking. His guardian sauntered by. His people had been watching the room. He said, "What's wrong, little Lonnie? What happened, man?" Athens told him. He said, "Don't worry, little Lonnie, everything's gonna be okay. Stay cool. Don't say nothing to nobody. You coming tomorrow?" Athens told him, "Yeah, I guess I'll come, but I don't want those bastards pulling that shit on me." His guardian said, "Don't worry about it. Go on with the things you gotta do. See you tomorrow."

The three men who had menaced Athens showed up at the door of his interview room the next day badly battered. Their heads were bandaged. They had been worked over, and they were scared. "Please tell them to take off the hit," they pleaded with him. "We don't want to die. We were just fucking with you, man. We didn't do nothing to you. What we were fixing to do we didn't do, you know. We die behind this shit, you don't want that on your head." They left. After a while Athens's guardian came around. He asked if there had been any trouble. Athens told him, "No, man, those guys were begging for their lives. I don't want them hurt any more. Let them go. I appreciate what you're doing, but I don't want any more done. It's okay. Let's just drop this now." His guardian said, "Don't worry about it." He let the three men live. No one else menaced Athens at that prison, and his guardian recruited six or seven other men for interviews.

The terms of Athens's unwritten contract with the men and women he interviewed were honesty and anonymity. He established that position at the outset, he writes:

> I usually saw the inmates privately and explained candidly to them what I was seeking to do. I told them I was a student and I was doing a study about people who committed violent crimes and how they came to commit them. I said that to get this information, I wanted to interview individuals who had committed violent acts and who would speak honestly about themselves and their violent experiences. Then I made it perfectly clear that I did not work for the Department of Corrections, the FBI, the police, and so on; that I would keep all their remarks confidential; and that I would not provide any information on them to the correctional staff, other inmates, or anybody else. After explaining this, I asked them whether they had any questions, and they usually did. The most frequent ones were what I was getting out of doing the study;

whether I was being paid to do it; if so, by whom; and how their participation was going to help them in the institution. I explained that carrying out a study was part of my graduate degree requirements and that their participation in it would not bear on their future in the institution one way or the other. Another question that often came up was whether I had a tape recorder in the office or in my briefcase. I said no and let them look in my briefcase, in my desk, and around the office.

He told them he would take notes; they could always deny their content. They trusted him, at least provisionally, but let him know that he was vulnerable. Late one night he woke at home in Berkeley to a roar of motorcycles outside. He found a message in his mailbox the next morning: "Dear Lonnie: Hope everything is okay. We got arms that reach everywhere. If you need anything, just let us know, and if we need anything, we'll let you know." It unsettled him until he thought it through. "I decided I was being straight with them, so they had no reason to go after me."

It was easier at the women's prison, though Athens did not underestimate the potential for violence. Violent women were just as dangerous as violent men. Some of them teased him by staging sexual encounters with their lesbian partners when they knew he would pass their cells. It shocked him at first; in sex at least his childhood had been sheltered.

Athens's most frightening experience nearly ended his prison research. At one institution he visited he regularly heard snide comments from the guard staff about student protest at Berkeley; the guards made it clear that they counted him among the damned. He had been assigned a small cell with a desk in it for interviewing. He was waiting in the cell for an inmate one day when a guard he didn't know looked in.

"Aren't you the guy from Berkeley who's studying violent criminals?" the guard asked him.

Athens said he was.

"There's a guy here you've got to interview," the guard told him.

Athens asked the inmate's name. It was unfamiliar, which surprised him. He thought he should have encountered it when he reviewed the files of violent offenders. "What's he done?" he asked the guard.

"Hell, he's done it all," the guard said. "Rape, murder, robbery, mayhem—you name it."

Athens doubted if he had overlooked anyone with a rap sheet that long. "Thanks for letting me know," he told the guard warily. "I'll check out his file and set up an interview later."

"Later?" the guard responded. "You can't interview this guy later. We're shipping him out of here first thing tomorrow morning. It's either now or never." He saw Athens's hesitation and dismissed it. "Don't worry about it. I'll cancel your next interview and bring him instead."

Waiting in the doorway, Athens pondered why a guard he had never seen before would offer to help him. Then someone turned up the background music. It filled him with foreboding. He walked down the cell block to the cell of an inmate he had befriended. "What's going on?" he asked him. "What's with the music?" He named the inmate the guard was delivering. "Do you know this guy?"

"You're being set up, Lonnie," the inmate told him. "Nobody's gonna help you. You got to hold up your own pants now. You best be ready to fight when they bring that motherfucker down to your cell. He ain't no for-real bad dude. He's just a shaker and a faker." Before Athens could decide if the inmate was putting him on, the guard arrived with the prisoner. Athens made another stab at postponing, hoping to buy time to check the man's record, but the guard insisted that the shift was about to change and there was no time to trade prisoners. As Athens followed the inmate into the cell, he heard the guard lock the door behind him. "Open the cell door!" he shouted. "Leave it open!"

On the other side of the door, the guard laughed. "Sorry," he said. "Regulations."

The cell was no bigger than an elevator. Athens looked across at the inmate coldly staring him down from the other side of the desk and felt acute claustrophobia. "What's your rap?" he asked him.

"Booty robbing," the inmate said.

Athens felt fear. "Booty robbing?"

"That's right, college boy, booty robbing. You know what that is?"

"I think I do," Athens said. Desperate to collect himself, he started firing off questions. "How long you been doing it?"

"As long as I can remember," the inmate sneered.

"How often?"

"As often as I can. I love taking booty—young, old, man or woman, it don't make a shit to me." He looked Athens over: "Tell me something, college boy: Has anybody ever had your booty?"

Athens's fear thickened. His informant hadn't been joking. The guards had set him up. He was on his own. He would have to fight. He braced himself, measured the room, measured the desk.

The inmate broke the silence. "You know, college boy, there are two ways you can get your booty taken, the easy way or the hard way. It don't make no difference to me, 'cause I like it either way. So the only real question is, which fucking way do you want me to take it, easy or hard?" He reached across the desk and grabbed Athens's shirt.

Athens shouted, "The hard way, the hard, hard!" and hauled up on the desk. It caught the inmate above the knees and then Athens pushed forward and rolled it completely over the man, driving him to the floor. Leaping onto the upended desk, pinning the man underneath, Athens yelled for the guards. The cell door flew open immediately, and the guard who had set him up and a second guard burst into the room and took control. The music volume dropped. When the desk was upright again and the prisoner removed, the guards offered to write the man up. Athens waved them off. They told him nothing like that would ever happen again.

"The fate that I had narrowly escaped that day," Athens summarized the incident later, "haunted me as I continued my interviews at this and other institutions. The stark realization that some correctional officers represented as much of a threat to me as some inmates was unnerving. Based on my past experience interviewing violent offenders, I was prepared for an inmate occasionally 'going off' on me, but I did not expect correctional officers to sic inmates on me. Feeling extremely vulnerable, I questioned the wisdom of continuing the study." So did Herbert Blumer when Athens alluded to the incident, which only isolated him further. He told Marilyn and pledged her to pursue an investigation if something happened to him. It wouldn't be an accident, he warned her. He did continue, partly because his decision not to file a complaint against the booty robber earned him further respect among the inmates not only at the institution where the attack occurred but at the other institutions where he was interviewing as well. When word got around that he was no snitch, more inmates volunteered to be interviewed.

What Athens basically wanted to know at this stage of his studies was what decision processes, if any, a violent actor went through in the course of his violent acts. He wanted to know if the decision process was different for a near-violent act, when a violent act was not carried through. He also wanted to know how the violent actor saw himself at the points in his life when he was violent—his self-concept, that is—and how other people close to him saw him at such times.

Athens based his investigation on the model of human functioning that the philosopher George Herbert Mead had developed and that Herbert Blumer had refined. Mead's name is not well known today, unlike that of his friend and colleague John Dewey, but Dewey once declared

Mead to be "the most original mind in philosophy in the America of the last generations," a judgment in which the philosopher Alfred North Whitehead concurred. Dewey added that Mead had been "the chief force in this country in turning psychology away from mere introspection and aligning it with biological and social facts and conceptions."

Born in 1863 in South Hadley, Massachusetts, George Herbert Mead was educated at Oberlin College, Harvard University and the University of Berlin. He taught philosophy and social psychology at the University of Chicago from 1894 until his death in 1931. He published very little during his lifetime—one reason for his obscurity—but significantly influenced qualitative sociology through his teaching and through the posthumous publication of edited transcripts of his lectures, the best-known volume being *Mind, Self and Society,* published in 1934. Charles Darwin's *The Origin of Species* had transformed biology by the time Mead began original work; following in the Darwinian tradition, Mead set himself the challenging task of understanding how an organism shaped by evolution could acquire a mind and a self. Psychology then and since has taken conscious thought and self-awareness for granted. Because they appear to be uniquely human attributes, Mead wanted to know how they arise, how they are organized and what their functions are.

These questions were not only interesting in their own right. They were crucial to understanding human group life. "Human society as we know it could not exist without minds and selves," Mead told his students, "since all of its most characteristic features presuppose the possession of minds and selves by its individual members." Human society is not insect society or a colony of seabirds, Mead explained; what makes it specifically human—all that we understand by the word "culture"—is its investment of bare nature with meaning. The human world is different from the natural world, and the difference is that human beings attach meaning to objects (including other human beings) and act on the basis of those meanings: Think only of what human beings have done to acquire quantities of the yellow metal we call gold, or to defend the pieces of the earth's surface their occupants call their homelands, or to preserve the bodies and mark the location of our buried dead. Such meanings, Mead pointed out, are basically arbitrary, devised through communication among minds and selves—yours, mine, and others', today and back through time.

Any attentive parent can see mind and self emerging in her developing child. It is demonstrably not the output of a stored program but a social process: Infants supported physically but isolated from human communication wither and die. At the outset, Mead observed, "young children experience that which comes to them, they adjust themselves to it in an immediate fashion, without there being present in their experience a self." In that regard they are no different from any other young animal. But the infant's babble, physical and vocal, begins to organize itself into imitation and absorption: turning toward a familiar voice and face, meeting gesture with gesture and smile with smile. The child does not yet know itself, but it has begun reading that information, so to speak, from its caregivers' responses. Acquiring language accelerates and enlarges the process; Mead proposed that language "is essential for the development of the self." He might better have said "languages," because he evidently meant something more than English or Spanish or French. Children learn expressive languages, for example—family traditions of stance and gesture; dance, formal and informal; the Frenchman's shrugs and winks; the Italian's ebullience. They learn languages of color and form that are characteristic of the culture into which they were born. More to Athens's point, they learn languages of attitude and value—vocabularies of behavior. All these they incorporate, not merely by imitation but by increasingly fluent exchanges of verbal and gestural conversation.

Crucial to Mead's self-building process is objectification. We learn to perceive *ourselves* as objects by looking back through the eyes of others—by seeing ourselves as others see us, a process Mead called "taking the attitude of the other." "Thus," Blumer explains, "individuals may see themselves as being male or female, children or adults, members of this or that ethnic or nationality group, as being sick or well, as belonging to this occupation or profession, as having an encouraging or dismal future, and so on in innumerable ways." These objects, these personae, are built up primarily in social transactions with parents, siblings, relatives and other people close to us, members of what sociologists call our "primary group." They are basically descriptions, but loaded descriptions, charged with attitudes and values—the attitudes and values of the members of our primary group with whom we negotiated them. We attach them to bodily sensations to make them our selves. In computer jargon our selves are simulations: dimensional self-descriptions animated, colored and chiaroscuroed with feelings, attitudes and values.

It is appropriate that our selves should be simulations, because for Mead, mind—thought—is internal communication. "The very process of thinking," he concluded, "is . . . simply an inner conversation that goes on." We think by setting our selves talking to themselves in one or more of the languages we have learned. "Mead saw the mind as a form of behavior," Blumer elaborates helpfully—"a form of behavior in which the human being points out things to himself and uses what he points out to himself to organize and direct his conduct." The function of thought is to organize, test and select among alternatives before acting. "Ideas," Mead aphorized, emphasizing their service in testing alternatives before we select a line of action, ". . . are simply what we do not do."

So both the self and the mind are social in origin and in function. "The self," Blumer specifies, "[enables] the human being to carry on a process of communication with himself, and the mind [is] the behavior that takes place in this inner conversation."

Selves are not given. They are constructed. They are built, modified, altered, refurbished, even replaced over time. I was a child, but now I'm a man. I was a son, and now I'm also a father and grandfather. I was going to be a preacher, but I became a writer instead. A shy young woman becomes Eleanor Roosevelt, Saul of Tarsus becomes Paul in an overwhelming experience of conversion, a little Indian boy becomes Gandhi—and a child frightened by the sounds of violence from his mother's bedroom becomes a brutal rapist. That our selves elaborate across our lives is obvious, but what process inscribes the track of those elaborations remains to be determined, because not every shy young woman becomes a charismatic humanitarian, and not every frightened child becomes a violent criminal.

We communicate with others as well as with ourselves. That was how we acquired our selves in the first place. "To become an object to oneself," Blumer explains, "one has logically and psychologically to see oneself from the outside. One has to get outside of oneself and approach oneself from the outside. How is this possible at all? Conventional schemes in the psychological and social sciences do not even see the problem, much less address it." Mead saw the problem and addressed it. Conventional psychology simply assumed that the self and the mind are built in, as the "soul" is built in, part of our original genetic (or theological) endowment. Mead, accepting the evidence of evolution that human beings are part of the animal kingdom, observing that self and mind are uniquely human characteristics, decided to look for a natural explanation. The explanation he found, Blumer summarizes, was "that the self and the mind are products of participation in group life," emerging "in the process of interaction which the young child carries on with other human beings." How do we get outside ourselves? Blumer defers to Mead:

Mead proposes an ingenious answer to the question. He declares that one gets outside of oneself by taking the role of another human being or set of human beings, by imaginatively placing oneself in the shoes of others, thus putting oneself in the position of approaching oneself or addressing oneself from the standpoint of that role. Simple examples are to be seen in childhood play as when a little girl "plays mother" and in doing so, talks to herself and acts toward herself like her mother does. The child may call herself by her name, reprimand herself as her mother has done, and order herself to do such and such a thing. In taking the role or part of the mother the child has put herself in a position to approach or address herself from the outside and thus to form of herself the kind of object that is represented by that approach.

A later stage in the process, Mead saw, is what he called the "game stage," when a child takes a role within a group. Mead's favorite example was a baseball team, on which each player has to anticipate the decisions and actions of the other players on the team—has to "take the attitude" of those others—in order to coordinate his own decisions and actions with theirs. And as with a baseball team, so also at school, on the playground, at church, in the band and the treehouse and the grocery store and wherever else children interact with the larger world—but most influentially within a child's primary group. Such social interaction eventually produces adults who are skilled (to various degrees) at fitting in to the multiple and complex relationships, organizations and institutions of human society. Born as animals, humans are civilized by being invested with minds and selves through social interaction. Which is why, Blumer points out, though insect and animal societies are identical within species and remained fixed across time (except as they change slowly through evolution), "human group life varies enormously from society to society and is capable of undergoing vast transformation from generation to generation within the same society."

Among the many consequences of possessing a self, Blumer emphasized three, each of them important to Athens's investigation of violent behavior.

First, possessing a self makes it possible for a human being to ascribe meaning to the objects in his world, including other human beings. We read and interpret each other and the world. "Shown only a face," writes a psychologist researching memory, "we are prepared to judge a person's emotional state, personality traits, probable employment and possible fate." A sociologist commenting recently on Mead's legacy points out similarly that "individuals . . . may use their abilities as selves to exploit or abuse others as well as to conform to others' wishes or to promote others' interests."

Second, possessing a self makes it possible for a human being to assemble a world of private inner experience. "This inner world," Blumer writes, "is one of genuine social experience for him, in which he may cultivate his impulses, develop his emotions and sentiments, form and revise objects of others and himself, brood or exult over his memories, develop and restrain his inclinations, cultivate his intentions and nurture and shape plans of conduct."

Third, possessing a self makes it possible for a human being to interact with the world rather than simply react to it. Mead, whose large bulldog used to accompany him on his walks around the University of Chicago campus, liked to illustrate this point by describing the encounters of dogs. Theirs was a "conversation of gestures," he told his students, rather than a conversation enriched with significant meanings. In a dogfight, Mead explained:

> The act of each dog becomes the stimulus to the other dog for his response. There is then a relationship between these two. . . . The very fact that the dog is ready to attack another becomes a stimulus to the other dog to change his own position or his own attitude. He has no sooner done this than the change of attitude in the second dog in turn causes the first dog to change his attitude. We have here a conversation of gestures. They are not, however, gestures in the sense that they are significant. We do not assume that the dog says to himself, "If the animal comes from this direction he is going to spring at my throat and I will turn in such a way." What does take place is an actual change in his own position due to the direction of the approach of the other dog.

The difference Blumer and Mead are emphasizing is the difference between operating out of an inner world of experience and operating by direct response to a stimulus. To clarify the distinction Blumer offers an example that contrasts directly with Mead's dogfight:

> In having a self, the person is put in the position of indicating to himself his own action as well as pointing out to himself features of the arena in which the action is taking place. He may pick out different items of his ongoing action and different items of the situation with which he is faced, analyze these items, discuss them with

himself and by virtue of this process of interaction shape a line of conduct to fit his situation. This is equivalent to saying that by virtue of having a self the human being comes to construct his action instead of merely releasing a response to stimuli. For instance, he may note an impulse such as being hungry, think about different kinds of food, look at his watch to see if it is time to eat, decide to eat, give thought to whether he should eat at this or that restaurant, examine his supply of money and, after reminding himself that he is on a diet, decide to postpone eating entirely.

Nor do human beings have a choice in the matter. Blumer adds: "The human actor is forced to be a participant in his own action." When you or I see other persons, we read them—their form, their appearance, their gestures, their words, their actions. Dogs do much the same thing (although it usually involves more sniffing). But we then also assign meanings to what we read based on our personal interpretations. Those personal interpretations come with feelings attached. The meanings you assign may be different from those I assign. If your background—social class, education, nationality, family experience—is different from mine, your personal interpretations almost certainly will be different as well. Women in short skirts, admired by men on the streets of Manhattan, risk being attacked or even arrested in some Muslim countries. Slurping noodles is an expression of gusto in Japan, a social gaffe in the United States. American midwesterners find northeasterners rude; northeasterners, in turn, find midwesterners suspiciously polite. Mead, the son of teachers, a child of the solid middle class, mistakenly assumed that within a given society, the interpretations people make are based more or less on a shared set of meanings. He called that collective understanding, awkwardly, the "generalized other." The flawed concept gave Athens years of grief until he found a way to improve and correct it.

That violent criminals decide to act violently based on their interpretation of a situation would be a radical discovery when psychiatry, psychology and sociology assign violent acts to unconscious motivations, deep emotional needs, inner psychic conflicts or sudden unconscious emotional outbursts. But Athens also quickly discovered that violent criminals interpreted the world differently than did their law-abiding neighbors, and that it was from those differing interpretations that their violence emerged. Violent acts, he began to see, were not explosions: They were decisions.

CHAPTER SIX

_____

Beautiful Narrative

Lonnie Athens did not ask the violent criminals he interviewed in Iowa and California why they committed their crimes. "If they knew why they did it," he told me, "then nobody needed me." Nor did he want the men and women he interviewed to tell him a story. They were adept at inventing explanations of their behavior. They made up explanations for the court, to prove their innocence or mitigate their guilt; for the prison psychiatrist, to participate in therapy; for the parole board, to win parole. Athens wanted to remove them from that mind-set, to open up a pure stream of consciousness, to hear what they actually thought and felt when they assaulted or raped or killed.

They were wary at first. "People give accounts that are acceptable to their group," Athens explains. "A rapist in prison doesn't go around saying he raped someone. He says, 'I didn't rape anybody. I just had sex with some fucking bitch.' That's an acceptable account in that subculture. Or a homicide: 'I just fucked up a son of a bitch who deserved to get what he got.' It's not acceptable in everyday life to ask people for their pure, primitive stream of consciousness." To free that stream he had to distract them into lowering their guard.

He put them off guard by putting them at ease. It helped that he spoke their language. "We'd start talking about anything. They loved to talk about sex and filth. Sports, they liked to talk about sports. Boxing matches." At Santa Rio, George Foreman was training directly across the street for his fight with Muhammad Ali. Athens would stop in and watch and talk about that. Women's liberation was in the news. "They'd say, 'What's this shit I been hearing, Lonnie? These bitches going wild now, ain't they.' " He laughed and joked with them.

When he sensed they were ready, he began asking questions. He wanted them to construct objects of themselves at each point where they remembered being violent or near-violent. He started with the offense that had sent them to prison, because that was the offense about which he had the most information. "What went down?" he would ask. Next he would ask how they thought of themselves at the time of the offense. Eventually they would run out of steam—that much intensity was hard to sustain. Athens would switch back to small talk. When he sensed they were ready for more he would say, "Okay, this is another thing I want to ask you about. Who were you hanging with then? Who knew you well? Women? Any men?" He wanted their self-concepts. When they told him how the people around them saw them, they would want to qualify and rebut. After they rebutted they would usually open up, and their self-concepts would emerge.

Then he would collect their violent careers, working backward in serial order from the offense of record. "I'd say, 'What about before that? Was there another one before that? What happened that time?' " He went over the near-violent situations as well, the times when they almost carried out a violent act but did not follow through. Going back through their careers had its problems. "A lot of these guys had done so much violence that before twelve or thirteen years of age they didn't remember what the hell happened. It made it look like they'd always been uniformly violent, which I realized later couldn't be true. The younger ones did remember deep into childhood, and I added more interviews with younger felons later, when I worked out the developmental process."

Critics of Athens's studies have complained that he had no way of knowing whether or not his informants were lying to him. On the contrary, he understood at the outset that prevarication would be a problem with some offenders and developed ways to recognize it. Starting his interviews with the inmate's offense of record gave him a litmus test, since he had reviewed the police reports for that offense and knew the facts. "Prison is full of bullshit artists who get off on lying to you," he says. "By starting with the major offense, if I picked up that someone was lying to me on that, then I cut off the interview immediately. I knew not to waste my time asking any more." He followed that procedure throughout his informants' accounts wherever he could check material facts, discarding the entire interview if he found significant discrepancies. Because he was eliciting personal responses, he writes, checking facts was a surprisingly rigorous validation method:

It is much more difficult than it may seem to falsify in a detailed and consistent manner the so-called subjective side of a situation, that is, one's perceptions and evaluations, while at the same time not falsifying any of its material, or objective, details. This, of course, is exactly what would have been needed for an offender to falsify deliberately this information to me and not have it detected by the validation procedure that I used.

Some of the offenders Athens interviewed acknowledged crimes they had denied at trial, another measure of truthfulness; between Iowa and California, he writes, a total of "seven inmates who had previously maintained their innocence admitted to me that they committed the violent crimes for which they had been sentenced."

By asking the questions he asked he was necessarily imposing a structure on the narrative he was collecting. "That was my job as a scientist," he points out. But he was not thereby predetermining the content. "I visualized it as windows. I cut out the windows, but I didn't know what I would then see through the windows. That was their job—the people I was interviewing. They supplied the view—the content and the internal form. The point is, I didn't know in advance what I was looking for. So I didn't want to analyze until later. I didn't have any preconstructed theory because there wasn't one. Nobody had ever done anything even remotely similar before. Blumer said, 'Get a full description. Complete the descriptions first, and then move to an inspection stage and inspect your descriptions.' That's what I tried to do."

Why should a description of an event yield scientifically valid data? That was a question Athens's quantitatively oriented colleagues asked later when he published his research. They were trained to accumulate data sets such as answers to a questionnaire or records of arrests, and they thought of those data sets in terms of samples, controls, numbers. Narrative descriptions, they complained, were "journalistic," "subjective." But Athens was not interested in the antecedents of violent acts that data sets might reveal; he was interested in the violent acts themselves *as the violent actors experienced them,* and short of being present when people were assaulted, raped or murdered (and of course he did have personal experience of such events), narrative descriptions were necessarily his primary data. "The fact that the people I interviewed were selected in a nonrandom and nonstandardized fashion was of no consequence for my study," he would write. "The conclusions that I sought to draw were not about the statistical distribution of characteristics of violent offenders or offenses; rather, they were primarily about the social psychological processes at work in violent criminal acts. Thus I was concerned only with finding people to interview who had committed substantially violent acts."

At the theater, reading a book, talking to another person, we all recognize narrative authenticity, whether factual or fictional: It raises the hair on the back of our necks. Confident that his validation procedure would sort fact from fiction, Athens's goal for his interviews, he says, "was just to get beautiful narrative. I didn't have any preconceived ideas, so I had to test what I was getting aesthetically. I was following Blumer's advice, which was: The better the narrative description you get, the more likely you'll find the answer you want. I was looking for an authentic story, and once they hit authenticity it was like a high for me. Because I *knew* when it was authentic." His subjects thought his enthusiasm strange. "They saw I was reacting to their naked story. They found that bizarre. They'd say, 'Man, what the fuck is wrong with you? You're sicker than we are, come in here every fucking day voluntarily, taking all these stories, what the fuck is your problem? You ought to be in here instead of us.' And I would laugh. But I see why it looked that way to them—the irony of it, that it was violence but that I responded to its authenticity." So did Blumer. "I would read to him sometimes and ask him what he thought. He'd just sit back and say, 'Yes, I think you're getting something there, Lonnie, I think it's very good.' "

The philosopher of science Michael Polanyi points out in *Personal Knowledge,* a careful exploration of the process of scientific discovery, that language is more than merely a medium of communication. It also embodies a theory of the universe:

In a library of a million volumes using a vocabulary of 30,000 words, the same words will recur on the average more than a million times. A particular vocabulary of nouns, adjectives, verbs and adverbs thus appears to constitute a theory of all subjects that can be talked about, in the sense of postulating that these subjects are all constituted of comparatively few recurrent features, to which the nouns, adjectives, verbs and adverbs refer. Such a theory is somewhat similar to that of chemical compounds. Chemistry alleges that the millions of different compounds are composed of a small number—about a hundred—of persistent and identical chemical elements. Since each element has a name and characteristic symbol attached to it, we can write down the composition of any compound in terms of the elements which it contains. This corresponds to writing down a sentence in the words of a certain language.

Changing the analogy, Polanyi compares language to the symbols on a map. The closer a map comes in size and detail to the area it maps, he points out, the more accurate it is. But a map the same size and equally detailed as the area it represents would be useless—"since it would be about as difficult to find one's way on the map as in the region represented by it." A language with a unique word for every object and event would be equally useless. So in order to be useful, a language needs to be of manageable size. Polanyi calls this requirement the "principle of manageability." It enhances our intellectual discrimination as effectively as does a microscope or a telescope: "In the most general terms, the principle of manageability consists in devising a representation of experience which reveals new aspects of it. This principle can be put into operation simply by writing down or otherwise uttering a designation of an experience, from which we can directly read off novel features of it."

Polanyi offers a simple example. A list of the names and geographic coordinates of the two hundred largest towns in England, he writes, would be comparatively useless. But arrange those names and coordinates on a sheet of paper in their approximate geographical position—make a rough map—and "immediately we can read off at a glance the itineraries by which we can get about from any town to any other, so that our original input of 400 positional data (200 longitudes and 200 latitudes) thus yields 200 times 200 ÷ 2 = 20,000 itineraries."

This enhancement of our intellectual powers is not a magic trick, Polanyi emphasizes. One of the ways in which animals and humans learn is by identifying patterns. When patterns are buried in data, they are harder to see. Maps, verbal or spatial, reduce the clutter while preserving the basic relationships. Athens's carefully framed narratives of violent actors, like Polanyi's map of English towns, increased the visibility of the information imbedded in the reality they abstracted and symbolized. Athens still had to find the patterns, of course, but in order to do so he first had to make the necessary maps. He drew the borders, so to speak, with the questions he asked; with their answers the men and women he interviewed marked in the towns—that is, selected those features from the totality of their experiences that they considered meaningful. Later Athens hoped to trace itineraries no one before him had tracked.

When he did, his quantitatively oriented critics would compare their single points of data, collected on thousands of cases—nationwide homicide arrests, for example—to his dense life histories of dozens of cases, and complain that he was short on data. In fact each of his narratives comprised tens of thousands of data points, with a potential for multiplying "itineraries"—for finding underlying connections—far greater than the minimal data sets that quantitative sociologists analyze.

Athens had read Polanyi and understood these methodological issues. He also understood that his own tacit knowledge of violent behavior was the sharpest tool in his kit. His childhood experience of violence prepared him to recognize the authenticity of his subjects' violent interpretations. That was why he "knew" when the offenders he was interviewing were producing authentic narratives. It was why he believed so strongly in firsthand experience. "Although one need not *be* a violent criminal to discover the causes of others becoming violent criminals," he would write later in defense of his methods, "it is only a matter of common sense that extensive direct contact with violent criminals is absolutely essential if one expects ever to achieve this goal." When he collected an authentic narrative, savage though it might be with malefic violence, he drove home tired but happy.

Athens continued his interviewing, accumulating narratives until they began to seem to repeat themselves. In qualitative sociology, saturation serves the same purpose as randomizing a sample does in quantitative work: It validates comprehensiveness. Athens included the distant women's prison in his itinerary even though it was expensive in travel and time partly because he suspected that the women's narratives would be different from the men's and might delay saturation. The women were pivotal—important differences did turn up in their narratives—but their accounts eventually also became repetitious.

By the time Athens finished his California interviewing, in 1974, he had accumulated a total of thirty-five cases; adding those to his Iowa cases raised the total to fifty-eight. They chronicled the violent careers of forty-seven men and eleven women. Almost all the offenders described multiple acts of violence, so the offenses for which they had been convicted represented a minimum. Those offenses alone totaled twenty-seven criminal homicides, twenty aggravated assaults and twelve forcible rapes (one male offender in his mid-teens having been convicted of both rape and murder). Three of the offenders were in their forties at the time Athens interviewed them, nine in their thirties, thirty-six in their twenties (as was Athens) and ten in their mid to late teens. They were black, white, Asian American, Hispanic and Native American; upper, middle and lower class; from both urban and rural backgrounds. "The cultural diversity of my subjects," Athens writes ironically, "prevented me from developing an explanation bound by class, race, gender or subculture."

His interview records consisted of handwritten notes charted with arrows and circles and numbered sequences. It was fortunate that he could read his own difficult handwriting, because he couldn't afford to have his notes transcribed. Having assembled them, he then had to "inspect" them, as Blumer called it—analyze them for the patterns of thought and decision they revealed. This process paralleled the process of accumulating cases. Athens would see a distinctive feature in one case—for example, that the perpetrator anticipated physical attack when he initiated a violent assault; start looking for similar anticipations in other cases; modify his idea (his "concept") to account for the differences among the similar instances; and keep on looking and modifying until his concept saturated—until further examination of cases no longer led to modifications. He had done some of this analyzing and sorting along the way while collecting cases, of course—noticing patterns is unavoidable—but he had worked hard to keep an open mind about what he was hearing: Prejudging the material could bias the collecting.

What he found in this first full round of research, he developed and refined across the years in scientific papers and in the first of his two books.

In the foreword to that book Herbert Blumer celebrated Athens's fundamental and original insights and pointed out their importance. Many people had studied violent crime over many decades, Blumer emphasized. "Such studies have yielded vast quantities of diversified data and have been attended by an abundance of theoretical schemes seeking to account for violent criminal behavior." Athens's discoveries almost completely contradicted all those previous theories in psychiatry, psychology and sociology:

> Dr. Athens's study of the violent actions of criminals is . . . truly a pioneering effort and a rewarding effort. [His] findings are of solid significance. They throw a great deal of light on matters that are either obscured or overlooked in conventional study. They suggest ways of exercising effective control of violent behavior. They point to lines of study that offer considerable promise of pinning down the elusive aspects of violent behavior. They make this book a very important book.

Athens called the book *Violent Criminal Acts and Actors.*

CHAPTER SEVEN

Conscious Constructions

Lonnie Athens emphasizes early in *Violent Criminal Acts and Actors* that the subject of the book is *"substantially* violent criminal acts and those who commit them."* By "substantially violent," he explains, he means:

> That . . . the victim was either (1) substantially physically injured, that is, nonaccidentally injured either fatally or to a degree that usually calls for a physician's attention, such as results from a shooting, stabbing, clubbing or relentless beating; or (2) substantially sexually violated, as in the case of coitus, sodomy, fellatio, or cunnilingus, under either the threat of the infliction of substantial physical injury or the actual infliction of substantial or less severe physical injury.

All fifty-eight offenders whom he interviewed, he notes, committed at least one substantially violent criminal act.

Violent Criminal Acts and Actors does not explore how these offenders came to be violent. (He would identify what he came to call the "violentization" process in the years after graduate school, when he was teaching in Michigan and Kansas and continuing his interviewing. *The Creation of Dangerous Violent Criminals,* published in 1992, reports those findings.) In this first analysis he examines fundamental questions about the dynamics of violent actions: whether violent people interpret the situations in which they commit violent criminal acts—that is, analyze, assess and make decisions about whether or not to act violently—and, if so,

---

* In 1997 Athens edited and partly rewrote this 1980 book into a revised and enlarged edition, *Violent Criminal Acts and Actors Revisited.* My discussion is based on the later edition, from which all quotations are drawn.

whether the interpretations they form account for their violent actions. In all fifty-eight cases, answering both questions, he found that they did. "Thus," he writes, "the data reveal that violent people *consciously construct* violent plans of action before they commit violent criminal acts."

That straightforward conclusion directly contradicts the prevailing "scientific" theories of violent criminal conduct. Before Athens describes his findings in detail, he cites several representative examples of such theories to illustrate the difference.

Psychiatrist Ralph Banay, for example, in a 1952 paper, "Study in Murder," in *Annals of the American Academy of Political and Social Sciences,* asserts that "the true nature of the psychological phenomena of violence which causes [sic] one human being to inflict death upon another will remain shrouded in mystery unless a detailed psychiatric study traces down the inner motivations."

Psychiatrist Emanuel Tanay, exploring "Psychiatric Aspects of Homicide Prevention" in the *American Journal of Psychiatry* in 1972, first observes that what he calls "ego-dystonic" homicide "occurs against the conscious wishes of the perpetrator" and then notes that "the majority of homicides are ego-dystonic"—in plain English, according to Dr. Tanay, the majority of people who kill people do so in spite of themselves.

Two psychologists, David and Gene Lester, reviewing the scientific literature on homicide in their 1975 book *Crime of Passion: Murder and Murderer,* conclude that "real murderers are not usually motivated by any long-range plans or conscious desires. Most commonly, they kill during some trivial quarrel, or their acts are triggered by some apparently unimportant incident, while deep and unconscious emotional needs are their basic motivation. Most murders occur on sudden impulse and in the heat of passion, in situations where the killer's emotions overcome his ability to reason."

Athens concludes this short list of examples, which could be multiplied many times in the voluminous medical and scientific literature on personal violence, by citing Marvin Wolfgang and his psychologist associate Franco Ferracuti, who contend in their 1967 book *The Subculture of Violence* and elsewhere that 90 percent of criminal homicides are "passion crimes," acts that "are unplanned, explosive, determined by sudden motivational bursts" during which the offender acts "quickly" so that "neither reasoning nor time for it are at his disposal."

These theories in psychiatry, psychology and sociology are widely known and widely believed; they echo in the stock phrases of media reports of violent crimes: "a senseless murder"; "no apparent motive"; "he just snapped"; "an explosive outburst"; "we will probably never know why." Athens's discovery that violent criminals know what they are doing when they decide to act violently means that murders are never senseless from the murderer's point of view; that motives, however "trivial" and "apparently unimportant" they may seem to psychologists, do inform violent criminal acts; that violent criminals do not "snap" but make decisions and act on them; that in every case where a violent criminal is willing to discuss his violent criminal acts honestly it is possible to know why he committed them. In other words, the discoveries that Athens reports in *Violent Criminal Acts and Actors,* which emerge from the uncoerced testimony of violent criminals themselves, constitute a complete reversal of the prevailing theories of violent criminality.

Athens found that the interpretations violent actors make of the situations during which they commit violent criminal acts evolve through a common series of steps. The perpetrator first assesses the victim's attitude—"takes the attitude of the other," in George Herbert Mead's phrase—and indicates to himself what he believes to be the meaning of that attitude. He then engages in a dialogue with himself, implicitly consulting the significant figures out of his past whose attitudes he has internalized, to decide whether or not the victim's presumed attitude warrants violent action. If he concludes that it does, then he initiates violence against the victim. Athens begins *Violent Criminal Acts and Actors* with the report of a young male murderer that vividly demonstrates this process:

CASE 55: THE ACT (CRIMINAL HOMICIDE)

A partner of mine said he might come over to my pad with some broads, so I hurried over to the liquor store right around the corner to get a case of beer. As I was walking across the parking lot of the store, this guy almost ran me over. I flipped him off. The driver and his partners jumped out of the car and rat-packed me. They knocked me down, and the driver pushed my head into the dirt next to the cigarette butts. Then they went into the store. I just felt, "What a low fucking thing to do to somebody. They are just a bunch of yellow motherfuckers." In my mind I suddenly thought, "I've got to get back at these dirty motherfuckers," and I ran back to my pad for my rifle.

I got back to the liquor store as fast as I possibly could and waited for them about twenty yards from the front door of the store. While I was waiting, I kept trying to decide whether I should shoot to wound the motherfuckers or kill them, and whether I should shoot only the driver or his partners too. Finally his two partners popped out the door. I said to myself, "Fuck it, I'll shoot all of them." I fired two quick, wild shots but missed them both, and they got away. I decided then that I better put the barrel to the chest of the motherfucker who I really wanted—the driver—and make sure that I didn't miss him. I had stone hatred for him, and I righteously couldn't wait to see the look on his face when I blew him away. As soon as he popped out of the liquor store door, I charged right up to him, rammed the barrel in his chest, and pulled the trigger.

It would have been hard for Case 55 to mistake the hostile and contemptuous attitude of the driver and his partners, since they acted it out violently against him—although their violence was minor compared to Case 55's response. His private dialogue is compressed, as it usually is: He decides their act is "a low fucking thing to do to somebody," and characterizes them accordingly as a "bunch of yellow motherfuckers." A nonviolent person might come to similar conclusions—and decide either to shrug off the insult or call the police. But when Case 55 mentally rehearses his possible responses with the significant figures whose attitudes he has internalized, he reaches a different conclusion, "suddenly" deciding that the appropriate response to such low behavior is violent retaliation. Having fetched his rifle, he then engages himself in further debate about the finer points of revenge: whether to shoot to wound the two partners who only knocked him down or to include them in his intended execution of the driver, who added insult to injury by grinding his face into the dirt. Seeing them again leads him to reaffirm his original violent resolution. His acts of attempted homicide and homicide follow.

Athens discovered four distinct types of interpretations in the interviews he conducted:

The first type he calls physically defensive. A violent actor forms a physically defensive interpretation in two steps: first interpreting the victim's attitude to mean that physical attack is imminent or already in progress and then indicating to himself that he ought to respond violently and forming a violent plan of action. "The perpetrator forms his violent plan of action," Athens explains the physically defensive interpretation, "because he sees violence as the only means of preventing another person from inflicting physical injury on him or an intimate. The key feature of all physically defensive interpretations is that the victim makes a gesture that the perpetrator designates to himself as foreshadowing or constituting a physical attack." Physically defensive violent acts constitute the criminal portion of the class of violent acts that includes acts of self-defense. Athens found that criminals who form violent plans of action only as a result of physically defensive interpretations view themselves as nonviolent, much as law-abiding citizens do who feel compelled to use violence in self-defense. In forming a physically defensive interpretation, the perpetrator's predominant emotion is *fear*.

Case 18, a male in his mid-thirties, describes an encounter that evoked a physically defensive interpretation.

CASE 18: CRIMINAL HOMICIDE

I was sitting at a bar drinking a beer when this guy sitting next to me went to play the pinball machine. When he came back to the bar, he said, "You've been drinking my beer. I had a full can of beer when I went over to play that pinball machine." I said, "I ain't drank none of your beer." He said, "You better buy me another can of beer." I said, "Shit no, I ain't." At first I didn't know whether he really thought I had drank some of his beer or was just trying to bluff me into buying him a can, but when he later said, "You're gonna buy me another fucking can of beer," I knew then that he was handing me that to start some crap, so I knew for sure that I wasn't gonna buy him any beer. He told me again to buy him a beer. I said, "Hell no." I figured if I showed him that I wasn't gonna buy him a beer, he wouldn't push it, but he said, "You better go on and buy me another fucking beer." All I said then was, "I don't want any trouble; I'm just out of the pen, so go on and leave me alone, 'cause I ain't about to buy you any beer." He just kept on looking. Then I started thinking he was out to do something to me. He pulled out a knife and made for me, and I shot him once in the arm. He kept on coming, so I had to finish him off. He was out to kill me.

The second type of interpretation Athens calls frustrative. A perpetrator forms a frustrative interpretation when he interprets the victim's attitude to mean that (1) the victim is resisting or will resist what the perpetrator wants to do—such as rape or rob the victim; or (2) the victim wants the perpetrator to cooperate in a course of action that the perpetrator rejects—such as allow himself to be arrested. The perpetrator concludes after internal debate that he ought to respond violently to this frustration and calls up a violent plan of action. "The perpetrator forms this violent plan of action," Athens explains, "because he sees violence as the most appropriate way to handle another person's potential or attempted blockage of the larger act that the perpetrator wants to carry out . . . or [he does so] to block the larger act that the other person wants to carry out." The perpetrator's predominant emotion in forming a frustrative interpretation is *anger* at the thwarting of his intentions.

Athens transcribes two perpetrators' descriptions of violent incidents, a rape and a homicide, to illustrate the two kinds of frustrative interpretations:

CASE 49: FORCIBLE RAPE

I was listening to the radio in my apartment when I got horny and started thinking about getting me some pussy. I thought that I'd go down to the ———— district and find a nice white broad to bust my nut in. I knew the area pretty good, and it was far enough away from my own house. So I went out and jumped the ———— bus. I rode it to ———— Street and then got off and started walking around. I got a good look at this middle-aged white broad walking around some apartments, and I said to myself, I'm going to get that pussy and enjoy it.

I followed her up to the entrance of an apartment building. She used a key to get into the main door, and I had to get to it fast before it shut. I barely got to the door in time, but I waited a few seconds before I walked in, since I didn't want her to see me. When I went in I heard her going up the stairs, and I followed her. As soon as I got to the top of the stairs, I spotted her walking down the hallway, and I crept up behind her. When she opened the door to her apartment, I put my hand over her mouth, pushed her through the door and said, "Don't make a sound." Then I shut the door behind me and said, "If you make one fucking sound, I'll kill your ass."

I didn't want her to panic too soon, so I threw her off base and said, "Do you have any money?" She said, "All I have is the ten dollars in my church envelope." I said, "Well, give it here." She took the envelope out of her purse and handed it to me. Then I said, "Take your coat off." I took a long look at her and thought, I'm going to drive this broad all night long.

I grabbed her by the shoulders and threw her to the floor. She started yelling, "What are you doing? What are you doing?" I figured that I better let her know that I meant business, so I jumped right on her ass and started smashing her in the face and saying, "Shut up, shut up." As soon as she did, I stopped hitting her. Then I pulled her dress up above her face and reached for her meat, and she started screaming, "Stop, stop, stop!" and stomped the floor with her feet. I just thought, I have got to shut her ass up fast before somebody hears her, and then I really cut loose on her with lefts and rights and said, "Shut up, shut up before I beat you to death." Finally she shut the fuck up, and I pulled her dress back up, tore her panties off her legs and pulled out my rod. I got on her and put my rod up to her meat. When she felt it going in her, she yelled, "No, no, stop, stop!" but I kept driving it on in her. I wanted to drive her all night, but I came. Although I came faster than I wanted, I busted my nut good. After I zipped up my pants, I said, "Don't move," and split out the door.

CASE 10: CRIMINAL HOMICIDE

I was low on cash and had heard about a good place to make a hit. About an hour later my friend and I were punching the safe when a real young cop came in with his gun drawn and said, "You're under arrest; put your hands up." The first thing I thought was Here is ten years, and I don't want to do any more fucking time. I decided then that I wasn't going to give myself up. The cop walked up closer to us, and I thought about getting his gun away from him, but I wondered where his partner was. He looked nervous, scared. I thought in the back of my mind that he would not use the gun, but I didn't care either. Then I figured he didn't have any partner and about hitting him. I had to get out of the situation. When he got right up to us, I hit him with the hammer.

Athens calls the third type of interpretation malefic, from the Latin word for evil, *maleficus*. Three steps lead to malefic interpretations. First, the perpetrator assesses the attitude of the victim to indicate that the victim is scornful, belittling or otherwise contemptuous of him. Second, the perpetrator concludes from internal debate that the victim's attitude means he is evil or malicious. Third, the perpetrator decides to counter such evil maliciousness with violence and calls up a violent plan of action. "The perpetrator forms his violent plan of action," Athens writes, "because he sees violence as the most fitting way of handling evil or malicious people who make derogatory gestures. The key feature of all malefic interpretations is that the perpetrator judges the victim to be extremely evil or malicious." The perpetrator's predominant emotion in forming a malefic interpretation is *hatred*.

Case 55, the young man rat-packed in a liquor store parking lot who fetched his rifle and shot the "yellow motherfuckers" who humiliated him, is an example of violence emerging from a malefic interpretation.

So is Case 2, the man who grows to hate his traveling partner's bragging, condescension and constant grabbing and finally shoots him. Malefic crimes often appear motiveless to outside observers such as forensic psychiatrists because the provocation, judged by conventional standards, seems grossly disproportionate to the response. Athens's emphasis on the meaning of the provocation to the perpetrator illuminates the discrepancy: Though most people would not agree that being subjected to bragging or condescension or even being forced to grovel in a parking lot justify murder, they probably would agree that evil should not be allowed to triumph.

The fourth and final type of interpretation that leads to violent acts Athens calls frustrative-malefic. As the name implies, this type combines features of the previous two. The victim's frustrating resistance or insistence leads the perpetrator to conclude that the victim is evil or malicious, which demands a violent response:

> The perpetrator forms this violent plan of action because he sees violence as the most appropriate way to deal with an evil or malicious person's potential or attempted blockage of the larger act that he seeks to carry out or as the most appropriate way to block the larger act that an evil or malicious person wants to carry out. The perpetrator views the victim not only as an adversary but as a particularly loathsome one as well. . . . The mark of all frustrative-malefic interpretations is that they start out as frustrative interpretations. Before the perpetrator mounts his violent attack, however, the interpretations become malefic, with pure hatred always displacing the anger that the perpetrator earlier felt toward his victim.

Athens offers testimony by a male in his early twenties to an assault and robbery as an example of violence emerging from a frustrative-malefic interpretation:

CASE 21: AGGRAVATED ASSAULT

I was at a neighborhood tavern drinking beer next to this guy who I knew was a homosexual. He was showing his billfold around, and I began to think about hustling him. We were in the bathroom together several times, and I tried to hustle him, but he acted sneaky [he didn't put up any money], so I punched him. He then left the tavern threatening to call the police on me. I thought, That motherfucking queer, I should rob him and bust his motherfucking head. So I followed him. He went home. I knocked on his door, but he wouldn't answer. I got mad and kicked his door open. Then this guy, his boyfriend, who was shacking up with him, comes up to me. His boyfriend being there got me madder, so I punched the boyfriend. The boyfriend took off out the front door. I then caught that queer standing there watching and staring at me. This got me madder. I figured this was a good opportunity to rob him and mess him up too. I've gone this far, so I might as well go all the way and do a good job on him. I'm in trouble as it is. You can get just as much time for doing a good job as a bad one. I wanted to fuck him up. I started beating him.

In his first round of interviews, in Iowa, Athens had not asked his informants to recount their violent careers for him. He also had not asked them to recall occasions when they prepared to commit substantially violent criminal acts but for some reason did not follow through. In California he asked those questions and learned much more about the dynamics of violence as a result. Both his Iowa and California cases divided into the same four types of violent interpretations, which appear to be basic and universal. But interpreting a situation, Athens found, did not necessarily lead to carrying through a violent response: "Far more violent criminal acts are begun than are ever completed." If the point seems obvious, it has not been so to criminologists. Since the prevailing theories of criminal violence define such behavior as unconscious, irrational, explosive and even unintended, they leave no space for a decision to act or not to act. "It was believed that if violent criminals really thought about what they were doing," Athens comments ironically, "they would never commit their violent crimes. This naive belief was and still is based on the false assumption that unless violent criminals think like professional criminologists, their acts are, ipso facto, devoid of thought." Though Athens generously attributes such naïveté to "middle-class bias," it looks more like an intractable lack of common sense.

Three possible developments, Athens found, determine whether or not a violent actor follows through to commit a violent criminal act.

Athens calls the first possible development a "fixed line of indication," a type of tunnel vision: "After forming a violent interpretation, [a perpetrator] fails to consider anything else in the situation besides acting violently. He either immediately carries out his violent plan of action or further nurtures it along . . . until he finally does carry out the plan of action."

But a second possibility is a "restraining judgment," an escape from tunnel vision. The violent actor *"redefines the situation and on the basis of his new definition judges that he should not act violently."* As a result he drops or shelves the violent plan of action he has formed. "The occurrence of restraining judgments," Athens writes, "dispels the old, but still surprisingly prevalent, belief that violent crimes are 'acts of passion' devoid of all reason." Athens found that violent actors formed restraining judgments because of a fear that a violent plan of action would fail; fear of legal sanction (as when the appearance of witnesses leads a perpetrator intending robbery or rape to judge himself at risk of being identified and arrested); fear that the action would damage or destroy the social relationship—friendship, marriage—between the violent actor and the intended victim; out of deference to another person (as when the armed, angry black man who was menacing Athens's father in Pete's Richmond restaurant relented, deferring to his friend); and, finally, because the intended *victim* changes his course of action (as when someone being robbed stops resisting). The same young male who had not hesitated to kill the driver coming out of the liquor store who had shoved his face into the parking lot restrained his frustrative violent plan on another occasion:

CASE 55: NEAR-VIOLENT SITUATION

I needed to score [drugs], but my money wasn't right, so I started thinking about where I could get the coin. I decided that I was going to have to go out and rob some fucking place. Then I started thinking about different places to hit. My mind first turned to this Dairy Queen, but I figured that it wouldn't be worth the trouble since there wouldn't be much money there anyway. Then I started thinking about this small supermarket, but I dropped that idea for the same reason. Finally a cleaners flashed in my mind. I figured that it would be the best hit since there would be enough money and only old ladies worked there. I put on my sunglasses, grabbed my .45, took off the safety clip and headed for the cleaners. I walked in the place, pulled out my pistol and pointed it at the old lady behind the counter. I said, "This is a holdup. I don't want to shoot you, so give me all the money out of that cash register fast." She walked over to the cash register but then just stopped and said, "I'm not going to give you this money," and stepped on a button on the floor.

I told myself I was going to get that money. I leaned over the counter and put the barrel of my pistol in her face and said, "Lady, now I'm going to kill you." But just as I was going to pull the trigger, she opened the cash drawer and said, "You can get the money yourself." I then told her to get away from the cash register, and she did. After I grabbed all the paper money, she smiled and said, "I guess I don't know much about you youngsters these days." I looked at her for a moment and thought that she was just a nice old batty grandmother. Then I split fast.

Athens calls a third possible development an "overriding judgment." Sometimes a violent actor breaks out of a fixed line of indication but returns to it later. In such circumstances, Athens explains, "he either momentarily considers restraining his violent plan of action or actually forms a restraining judgment but then redefines the situation and re-judges it as definitely calling for violent action." Reviewing the instances he had collected of completed violent actions, Athens found that "the primary reason individuals form overriding judgments is because they judge the victim's conduct to be intolerable." They move, that is, to a malefic interpretation of the victim's attitude. To illustrate an overriding judgment, Athens cites the testimony of a woman in her mid-twenties convicted of aggravated assault:

CASE 32: AGGRAVATED ASSAULT

We were partying one night in my rooms at the hotel where I lived and worked. Everybody there was a regular, except for this one dude who I had rented a room down the hall. He just kind of drifted in, and X said that he knew the dude, so it was cool. We were all drinking wine, taking pills, and having a mellow time when I overheard this dude asking X who I was and saying that I was a bitch. I said, "Hey, who's the bitch you're talking about?" and he said, "You're the bitch." I thought to myself, What does this dude think he's doing, coming to my party uninvited and then calling me a fucking bitch? I said, "Don't you come to my party and call me a bitch." He said, "You are a bitch; I was high and you shortchanged me out of fucking twenty dollars when I paid you for my room today." I said, "Man, you're crazy." He said, "Don't try to slick me, bitch; I'm hip. I'm an ex-con. I know what's happening, and X knows I'm good people, so don't try to run that game on me."

My friends were having a good time, I felt good, and I didn't want to spoil the mood for any problems behind twenty dollars, so

I thought that I'd just pacify the chump and give him a lousy twenty and end it. I said, "Look, man, I didn't shortchange you out of any money today, but just to show my good heart, I'll give you twenty dollars. How about that?" He said, "Well, since you needed it so fucking bad that you had to try to run a game like that past me, then you can keep it, bitch." Then I thought that motherfucker was just messing with me. He was trying to make me out as a petty hustler and call me a bitch right in front of my friends. I said to myself, Please, motherfucker, don't mess with me anymore. I finally said, "Mister, I'm warning you, don't you fuck with me anymore or I'll show you what a fucking bitch is." He just looked at me, laughed and said "I haven't seen the bitch yet who could kick my ass."

Then I told myself, This man has got to go, one way or another. I've just had enough of this motherfucker messing with me. I'm going to cut his dirty motherfucking throat. I went into my bedroom, got a twenty-dollar bill and my razor. I said to myself, The motherfucker wouldn't stop fucking with me, and now he's hung himself, and I walked out of the bedroom. I went up to him with a big smile on my face. I held the twenty in my hand in front of me and hid the razor in my other hand. Then I sat on his lap and said, "Okay, you're a fast dude. Here's your twenty dollars back." He said, "I'm glad that you're finally admitting it." I looked at him with a smile and said, "Let me seal it with a kiss." I said to myself, Motherfucker, now I'll show you what a fucking bitch is, and then I bent over like I was going to kiss him and started slicing up his throat.

"In short," Athens concludes, "in the completed violent situations that I studied, the subjects always either entered into a fixed line of indication or else formed an overriding judgment, whereas in the near-violent situations that I studied, the subjects always formed a restraining judgment."

Athens's pioneering typology and dynamics of criminal violence confirm from evidence what religion, law and common sense all assert about such acts: that they are volitional; that violent actors consider, decide and choose when and where to act violently—in other words, that violent criminals are *responsible* for their acts. Theories of violent behavior that attribute such behavior to genetic inheritance, to unconscious motivations or drives or to antecedent social conditions implicitly (and sometimes explicitly) deny such responsibility. As a result, for example, psychiatrists frequently argue in court that someone who has confessed to a violent crime, particularly one that the psychiatrists judge to be "meaningless," is not responsible for that crime because such violence *in itself* demonstrates mental illness. The tension between such "scientific" exculpations of criminally violent behavior and the legal requirement that guilt requires proof of intent is a basic reason why discussions of criminal violence in the courtroom and the media leave so many citizens frustrated and confused.

Athens sought to understand the interpretations violent actors apply to the situations during which they act violently. He found that violent actors interpret such situations much as you and I might—fearfully, angrily, even hatefully. Where violent actors differ is in deciding to act violently as a result of those interpretations. What is different about their decision-making process that leads them to such different conclusions? To answer that question, Athens had to come to grips with a problem that had nagged at him since his master's work at the University of Wisconsin: the vagueness and inconsistency of George Herbert Mead's concept of a "generalized other"—the "community of attitudes," as Mead also called it, which we consult to form our judgments. When Athens did so, he broke through to a fundamental discovery about the structure of human personality.

CHAPTER EIGHT

Phantom Communities

Understanding George Herbert Mead's model of self-interaction had thrown Athens into crisis at the University of Wisconsin, crisis so serious that he had briefly considered abandoning graduate school and criminology and returning to Richmond to find some other career. Whether Mead's "I," "me" and "generalized other" made sense was the question Athens had debated at length with Herbert Blumer in correspondence and in person. The question had been important to the young graduate student because he had needed a guiding model of self-interaction as he set out to interview violent criminals.

"My idea was this," he says. "Violent crime is one of the most studied topics in sociology and psychology—just thousands of books. But almost everything I read, or we discussed in class, didn't make sense to me, didn't square with my own firsthand observations and experiences of violence. I wanted to do something different, and I realized that no one had looked into the self-interaction of violent criminals, into what they *thought about* when they killed, raped and assaulted. So there weren't any markers, nothing to hang on to. That's why I studied Mead. I didn't want to work everything up from scratch. I didn't have the confidence yet. I didn't have the credibility, for that matter—didn't have the medals. It wouldn't have been acceptable."

Mead's model came ready-made, and it was the foundation of the interpretive approach Athens intended to use. But he saw almost immediately that it had problems. Worse, no one else seemed to have noticed. "Either Mead was wrong, or I didn't understand him. In those days I thought Mead's ideas about the self didn't make sense to me because I was intellectually inferior. Coming from an illiterate background among all these students from Big Ten schools, I just felt very stupid. That was the crisis. I went ahead anyway, but it took me twenty years to figure out what was wrong with Mead's 'generalized other' and to find the right replacement."

Mead postulated a "generalized other" to explain where people acquired their sense of the collective attitude of their community. Interacting with one other person, I can take that person's attitude directly; but how do I assess and incorporate the attitude of the group—the unwritten rules of a community—in order to interact socially, organizationally, cooperatively? "A person is a personality because he belongs to a community," Mead answered this question, "because he takes over the institutions of that community into his own conduct. He takes its language as a medium by which he gets his personality, and then through a process of taking the different roles that all the others furnish he comes to get the attitude of the members of the community." The "attitude of the members of the community," incorporated into the self, is what Mead meant by a "generalized other." Almost twenty years out of graduate school, when Athens finally felt that he understood Mead's model and published an essay reviewing its strengths and weaknesses, he quoted what he called Mead's "most translucent and sublime definition of his most original idea":

> A child acquires his sense of property through taking what may be called the attitude of the generalized other. *Those attitudes which all assume . . . become for him attitudes which everyone assumes.* In taking the role which is common to all, he finds himself speaking to himself and to others with the authority of the group. *These attitudes become axiomatic. . . . From the first, [the generalized other's] form is universal, for differences of the different attitudes of others wear their peculiarities away.*

This averaging process was a way to incorporate society's rules and expectations into the self, a process consistent with the one that constructed the self in the first place and one that allowed meaningful interaction between individuals. "When people take the attitude of a single individual," Athens elaborates, "they tell themselves what a particular individual expects of them; when they take the attitude of a single group, they tell themselves what a particular group expects of them; but when they take the attitude of the generalized other, they tell themselves what everyone in their community expects of them."

Unfortunately, Athens realized as he came to trust his judgment, Mead's concept of a "generalized other," however "translucent and sublime," was afflicted with a fatal flaw: It did not match reality. It explained conformity, but it failed to explain individualism. It explained agreement, but it failed to explain disagreement. Mead thought it was "the structure . . . on which the self is built . . . this response which is common to all." It constituted, he said, "just what we term a man's character." It gave that man "what we term his principles, the acknowledged attitudes of all members of the community toward what are the values of that community." (Mead's idea of a "generalized other" is similar in some ways to a more familiar idea: the Christian conscience, "This Deity in my bosom," as Shakespeare calls it, except that Mead's entity is rather "This community in my bosom"—not divine but collectively human.) Athens, however, was studying men and women whose character and principles were so at odds with the acknowledged attitudes of their community that they had been judged violent criminals by a jury of their peers and sentenced to years in prison. On what feral structure were *their* selves built?

Athens worked hard to find an answer. "Mead's problem was the 'generalized other,' " he says. "He thought people had to have a common conception of what they were doing in order to carry out joint acts. But people don't necessarily agree. They certainly don't always agree about resolving a situation with violence, for example. Blumer and I used to argue about this. Why do two people in the same situation indicate different things to themselves? I said it couldn't be just what's going on in the situation. People bring interpretations *to* situations—they bring different things to the table. You've got to allow for that. That's the irony in Mead's model: You really don't have a self if you're like everyone else. You lose all individuality. And that's not the way the world works. That's what he didn't see."

The violent criminals Athens interviewed were extreme examples of a barbaric individualism antagonistic to society, which is one reason so many people romanticize violent crime. Athens saw nothing romantic about violent criminals, but their extremity heightened the contrast with Meadian conformity and made it possible to visualize a more subtle and realistic model.

Eventually he proposed that another, more intimate community assembled in the shadows of the self around the "I" and the "me." There might be a "generalized other" even farther out, a collective set of attitudes that made Americans American and Chinese Chinese. But interposed between the individual and the broad collectivity of society were the significant others whose attitudes had shaped that individual— parents and other members of his primary group, the voices of his past experiences. Without such a portable, semipermanent bodyguard of past experience, Athens would argue, "we would be forced to reinvent ourselves with each new, succeeding experience," which would create "the absurdity of a biographical-less self." The internalized attitudes of our significant others were the "one constant in the self's ongoing operation," which made it possible "for people to have selves that endured beyond their immediate, passing experiences." The incorporated attitudes could be visualized as "phantom others," Athens decided, and together they constituted a phantom community.

We talk to ourselves, he elaborates. When we do so "we always converse with an interlocutor, even though it may deceivingly appear as if we are only speaking to ourselves. Everything that is said to us, including what we say to ourselves, some interlocutor tells us." Even when someone else is telling us something, "we must simultaneously tell ourselves what they are telling us in order to comprehend the meaning of what they are saying." (If that sounds mysterious, Athens remarks, it isn't; it is simply what we mean by the phrase "following what another person is saying.") One set of interlocutors, then, speaks for "the people with whom we are conversing while undergoing a social experience." But that is not the only set of interlocutors around. "We also converse with *phantom others*, who are not present, but whose impact upon us is no less than [that of] the people who are present during our social experiences."

The impact of the phantom others may even be greater than that of the people with whom we are interacting, because our phantom community is always with us. "The people with whom we converse face to face in a highly mobile society may come and go, for better or worse, with each new passing social experience. On the other hand, the phantom other customarily stays the same across our different social experiences as long as the self . . . remains intact. Thus the phantom other is omnipresent because it travels along with people wherever they may go, and usually without their knowledge."

The phantom other is the one and the many, a single and multiple entity, because "we can only normally talk to one phantom companion at a time during our soliloquies." We usually have more than one available to consult:

> The phantom other is both a single and multiple entity because the individual phantom companions, when taken together, comprise a *phantom community*, which provides people with a [multiple] but unified voice and sounding board for making sense of their varied social experiences. The phantom community is a whole greater than the sum of its individual parts because *phantom circuits* or relations inevitably emerge between the separate phantom compan-

ions. Thus, while the phantom community is definitely a conglomerate, it is more than a mere conglomeration.

We are not necessarily aware of our phantom companions as we go about our lives. We internalize them and come to take them for granted. We put our attention elsewhere:

> Most of the time we take their presence in our lives so much for granted that they lie far beneath our normal level of awareness; so that we are rarely aware of their existence in our lives. Their disembodied figures are "there," but they are hidden from our conscious purviews. "The human mind is indeed," Charles Horton Cooley . . . perceptively observed, "a cave swarming with strange forms of life, most of them unconscious and unilluminated." While remaining oblivious to us, our phantom companions influence the creation of our deepest thoughts and emotions. Thus, whatever harm or good our phantom community does us is usually done from behind our backs.

"It's 'where you're coming from,' " Athens adds. "When you ask where someone is coming from—they're coming from their phantom community."

If my phantom community is unconscious, if I am oblivious to it, what evidence is there that I have one? It emerges in times of personal crisis. "When you're in personal conflict, it starts decomposing. When you have a crackup, it's your phantom community that's cracking. The chorus separates, and you see those key figures, those ghosts in there. When those faces start popping up, you know you're having trouble. You get in a crisis and somebody is telling you to do this, somebody is telling you to do that—that's your phantom community. They don't have names, but you go here, you go there, you don't know what the hell to do. That's why you're in crisis. They're all in conflict, and you're paralyzed."

As Athens's vision of personal turmoil implies, the phantom community is a hidden source of emotion. Emotions—fear, anger, hate, love— are meanings we assign to constellations of bodily sensation. We assign meanings by talking to ourselves. If, Athens writes, when we talk to ourselves, we always consult our phantom communities, then it follows that our phantom communities "must be major contributors to our emotions." They are: "They tell us how an experience that we are undergoing will unfold before it actually ends, which can create in us a powerful self-fulfilling prophecy. Ironically, such self-fulfilling prophecies can stir such deep emotions in us that they can bring about the very experiences imagined." Athens's violent criminal subjects often created such self-fulfilling prophecies in consultation with their phantom communities by deciding that they should react violently to what their phantom communities, interpreting the attitudes of their victims, told them were fearful, angering or hateful situations.

The phantom community, Athens concluded, not the "generalized other," was where violent actors found justification for responding violently. "Although our conversations with other people with whom we are mutually undergoing an experience are absolutely essential for us to understand its emergent meaning, the ultimate meaning of a social experience cannot be ascertained without conversing with our phantom community." He clarifies: "You don't invent the world. You're sitting there judging the world. The phantom community doesn't tell you up front what the world is. You get feedback from the world and then start judging it from your phantom community."

Violent actors act violently not because they are mentally ill or come from violent subcultures or are brain damaged or have low self-esteem but because they have different phantom communities from the rest of us. That difference is the reason they attach different, violent meanings to their social experiences. Many people feel frustrated—most of us do at one time or another. Many people become angry—most of us do at one time or another. Many people hate—most of us do at one time or another. But only a small subset of all of us use violence to resolve those conflicts. How people come to be members of that small group would be the subject of Athens's second book, *The Creation of Dangerous Violent Criminals.* In *Violent Criminal Acts and Actors,* after he identifies the four distinct types of violent criminal acts (physically defensive, frustrative, malefic and frustrative-malefic), he turns to his subjects' self-images—that is, to the objects they construct of themselves. Looking for patterns in his collection of interviews, he was fascinated to discover that the self-images his interviewees held when they committed their violent acts matched up with the types of violent acts they committed.

Athens found three types of self-images among the men and women he interviewed. He called them violent, incipiently violent and nonviolent.

Violent self-images have two hallmarks: "First, the actors are seen by others and see themselves as having a *violent disposition,* that is, a willingness or readiness to attack other people physically with the intention of seriously harming them. Second, the actors are seen by others and see themselves as having violence-related personal attributes (such as being mean, ill-tempered, hotheaded, coldhearted, explosive, or forceful) as a *salient* characteristic." In *Violent Criminal Acts and Actors* Athens quotes two monologues to illustrate violent self-images, both monologues masterful epiphanies of character. One informant, convicted of aggravated assault, describes himself at the time of his crime as a "low rider" who "just liked to get loaded, ride fast and fight" and who believed "that you do whatever you want to do, when and how you want to do it and fuck everything and everybody else." The other informant, whom Athens lists as "Participant-Observation Case 1," is his father, Pete the Greek, whose monologue permanently echoes through Athens's own phantom community. It concludes:

> I'm a man, and I want to be treated like a man. Hell, I'm real easy to get along with just as long as people don't take me too light. I just don't play. When I tell somebody something, I mean it. I don't want to hear a whole lot of horseshit about who did what. I don't care who a person is or who they think they are, either; they better not play around with me. I'll show them who in the hell they're playing with. They'll find out fast that they aren't fucking with any boy when they fuck with me. I'll put my foot in their ass quick. Once I get started on them, I'll fix their ass up right. I've ruined more than one good man in my time, and Jack, I'll do it again too. That's the way I am, and that's the way I'll be until the day that I die. Everybody knows that's the way I am.

Incipiently violent self-images, the second type Athens identifies, share one hallmark with violent self-images: Such people see themselves and are seen by others as having salient violent-related personal attributes. "In contrast to people with violent self-images, however, these individuals are seen by others and see themselves as having an *incipiently violent disposition,* that is, *only* a willingness or readiness to make serious threats of violence, such as violent ultimatums and menacing physical gestures, toward other people." Athens had missed this category in his first attempt at a typology of violent actors, a paper he published while still in graduate school titled "The Self and the Violent Criminal Act," based solely on his Iowa interviews; there he had postulated only violent and nonviolent self-images. Incipiently violent self-images were deduced from the violent criminal women he interviewed in California. Those women, he found, often had not determined whether they were "definitely and genuinely" violent until they committed themselves to carrying out their violent acts. He had suspected that interviewing women might turn up differences from men—after all, far more men than women are violent—and had pilgrimaged on expensive overnights down to the women's prison at Corona for that reason.

Case 28, a woman who had been convicted of criminal homicide, held an incipiently violent self-image at the time of her offense. "I was a bitter and bad-tempered person," she described herself to Athens. ". . . I felt rejected and like a stupid fool for letting my husband mistreat me. I was getting fed up and easily angered by things. I made a lot of awful threats to people, but they thought it was mostly just big talk. Everybody thought that I would do little real action besides get drunk, scream and cuss, and throw things at people until I passed out."

Nonviolent self-images, the third and final type Athens identifies, were (not surprisingly) rare among his interview subjects. People with nonviolent self-images, he writes,

> are not seen by others and do not see themselves as having a vio-
> lent or an incipiently violent disposition. They furthermore are
> not seen by others and do not see themselves as having violence-
> related personal attributes as a salient characteristic. To the con-
> trary, in these self-images the people are seen by others and see
> themselves as having as their *salient* characteristics a blend of both
> positive and negative—although all nonviolence related—personal
> attributes, such as goodhumored or dour, outgoing or shy, lazy or
> industrious, personable or boring, obnoxious or polite, ugly or
> attractive, smart or stupid and so on.

Case 48, a woman convicted of aggravated assault who held a nonviolent self-image at the time of the assault, told Athens she "just wanted to have a family, be a mother and live a nice life. I felt like a lady and wanted to be treated like a lady, but my husband was getting crazy and then embarrassing me in front of everybody behind his jealousy."

The reason the self-images of violent actors match their violent interpretations, Athens proposes, is simply that all of us, whether violent or not, refer to our phantom communities to construct both our self-images and our interpretations of situations. The connection between the two in the cases Athens studied was consistent and universal:

> In the fifty-eight cases at hand, I discovered that the types of self-
> image that the offenders held at the time of their offenses were

always congruent with the types of interpretation that they formed of the situations in which they committed the violent criminal acts. More fully, individuals who held nonviolent self-images committed their violent criminal acts only in situations in which they formed physically defensive interpretations. Those holding incipiently violent self-images committed their violent criminal acts only in situations in which they formed physically defensive interpretations or frustrative-malefic ones. Finally, those holding violent self-images committed violent criminal acts in situations in which they formed malefic, frustrative, frustrative-malefic, or physically defensive interpretations.

To illustrate these differences, Athens reports three cases of domestic violence. The first, Case 5, a man convicted of aggravated assault, held a nonviolent self-image at the time of his crime. "My family thought I was a hard worker who provided exceptionally well," he told Athens. "They knew I was highly motivated, a person who wanted to learn. . . . I loved self-accomplishment. I was a perfectionist. I wanted to make it before I was forty, make it while I was young; that was what I tried to do. I thought I had done it. I had pride in myself." His interpretation of his conflict was physically defensive:

> X and I were getting a divorce, and my lawyer advised me to move out of the house. I went home to get some of my things out of the basement.
>
> I heard X coming down the steps while I was packing my stuff to leave and first glanced at her when she was in the middle of the steps. I figured she was coming down to talk, but when she didn't say a word to me, I stopped packing and turned toward her. I saw that she had a boning knife. I thought that she was trying to steal me—stab me on the sly—while my back was turned. I jumped over a box into the corner, and she started coming fast, fast, fast. I knew she was going to try to kill me. I took the gun from the bag that I had just packed and fired.

Action such as this, following a physically defensive interpretation, may be determined in a court of law to constitute self-defense. "Self-defense" is a legal term, however, with specific legal limitations: The defender is usually required to retreat if retreat is possible and to apply only sufficient force to defend himself. Case 5 exceeded those limits;

hence his conviction for aggravated assault. Athens's category of physically defensive interpretation encompasses a wider range of behavior
than the legal category of self-defense.

Case 57, a man in his mid-thirties, held an incipiently violent self-
image at the time of his crime. His wife, he told Athens, "said that I was
too rigid and bossy. She felt that I forced her to accept all my decisions
with threats about what I would do if she didn't. I know I sure frightened
her when I got mad, because I did let her know that she better damn well
accept my decisions and not complain about it too much." He thought of
himself as "a hardworking man, a good provider, and generous to my
family," but he "still had to let her know from time to time that she better
not take her crap too far." His homicide followed from a frustrative-
malefic interpretation:

> I was out of town, and I called my wife one night to check on what
> was going on at home. She told me that she had seen an attorney
> and was filing papers to divorce me. I asked her to hold off until I
> got back home and could sit down and talk it over with her, but she
> said, "No, this time I really mean it." After she told me that, I blew
> up and said, "You better not do that to me. If you do, you'll be
> sorry for it." She said, "I've had a restraining order placed on you,
> so if you come around here bothering me, the police will get you."
> I said, "If I really want to get you, the police can't save you." I
> thought that telling her that would scare her, but it didn't. She just
> acted calm and confident, like she had everything all planned out.
> That got me madder. I knew then that it was no use raising any
> more hell over the phone since it wasn't intimidating her. I figured
> that I had to get home and confront her face to face. I just felt plain
> mad. I hung up the phone and headed straight for home. I wanted
> to see if she would talk as brave about a divorce to me when I got
> home as she did over the phone.
>
> When I did get home three hours later, she was in bed, asleep. I
> woke her up and told her to get up, that I wanted to talk. I told her
> if she stopped with the divorce that I would promise to act bet-
> ter. . . . But she wouldn't buy any of it. I got angrier and angrier.
> Then she came out and said, "Look, please do me this favor and
> give me a divorce." At that moment I felt cold hatred for her inside
> me. I told myself that I better leave before I exploded on her, but
> then I decided the hell with it, and I looked her straight in the face
> and said, "Well, X, you better start thinking about those poor kids
> of ours." She said, "I don't care about them; I just want a divorce."

My hate for her exploded then, and I said, "You dirty, no-good bitch," and started pounding her in the face with my fist. She put her arms up and covered her face, so I ran and got my rifle and pointed it at her. I said, "Bitch, you better change your mind fast or I'm going to kill you." She looked up and said in a smart-ass way, "Go ahead, then; shoot me." I got so mad and felt so much hate for her that I just started shooting her again and again.

A third example, Case 29, concerns a woman convicted of aggravated assault who held a violent self-image at the time of her crime. She described herself as a "femme fatale." Many men, she told Athens, "were sexually attracted to me, and I was sexually attracted to many different men. The men that I knew saw me as a sweet, cute, and sexy woman who loved to party, and they knew that I was loose too." But she was also "unsure about myself. I was an emotionally unstable person. I would usually act nice and be sweet, but I could get really hateful too. Once I did get real mad, I blew it, and I would do anything to somebody. Some people realized that when I went crazy, I was dangerous." Her crime followed from a malefic interpretation of a breakup:

My boyfriend and I were bickering when he announced to me that he had decided to go back to his wife and was going to pack his bags and leave. He said that now that he had a job making good money, she would take him back, and that he thought that they could make it together. I said, "Then you better give me some money for living here the last two months free and pay me back all the money that I've loaned you too." He said, "I don't owe you a damn penny for living here, and I don't have to pay you back any of that money you gave me." I said, "You dirty SOB, you don't give a damn about me. You've just been using me all along, haven't you?" He didn't give me an answer; he just acted cool and ignored me. I said to myself, He can't get away with pulling this after all the things he has already done to me. He broke up my relationship with X; he lived here free, he took my money, ruined my car. . . . He has just done too much to me to get away with it. I said, "Don't think that you are going to get away with this that easy," and he just got up and said he was packing his things. Then I started thinking about what I could do to get him. Poison him? No, he's not going to want to be eating anything now. I guess I have to shoot him. Then I thought I better not because I'd get into a lot of trouble for it, but finally I told myself, Enough is enough; I'm going to do it. I don't care if I do get in trouble. While I was still worked up and had the nerve, I went and got the pistol that my old boy-friend had left in the house. Then I walked up to him and said, "You dirty, rotten SOB." He said, "Please don't shoot me." I said to myself, You yellow punk, you never stopped beating me when I asked you, and I shot him.

People with violent and incipiently violent self-images, Athens comments, "interpret a wider range of situations as calling for violence on their part than do those with nonviolent ones"—one reason they are more dangerous. Only people with violent self-images project violence from all four types of interpretations. Incipiently violent self-images seemed to be less stable across his informants' life histories than did violent or nonviolent self-images. Athens thought that made sense: "These individuals must either stop making threats and attempts to seriously injure or sexually violate other people or actually carry out these threats and attempts, because other people will probably challenge them to do so sooner or later. An individual can bluff people only for so long before his bluff is called."

Athens calls the bluff of a psychiatrist he cites, Emanuel Tanay, who postulates that the typical violent crime is "ego-dystonic" rather than "ego-syntonic," meaning unacceptable rather than acceptable to the ego. "If violent crimes were in fact ego-dystonic," Athens observes, "then the self-images of violent criminal actors would be at sharp odds with their violent criminal actions instead of being consistent with them." He adds a mischievous coup de grâce: "Although violent criminal acts may be ego-dystonic for psychiatrists, they are ego-syntonic for the people who commit them."

In the last third of *Violent Criminal Acts and Actors,* Athens explores the careers of violent criminals. He defines "career" in this context as "a selective life history in which are recorded the major changes that people make in their selves and actions over all or some span of their lives." He found that his interview subjects held different self-images at different periods of their careers (which means, of course, that their phantom communities changed over time, an important discovery) and that their self-images matched the kinds of violence they chose to perpetrate during those periods. Violent, incipiently violent or nonviolent self-images characterized substantially violent, unsubstantially violent or negligibly violent periods. "When the perpetrators held violent self-images," Athens elaborates, "they underwent substantially violent periods. When the perpetrators held incipiently violent self-images, they underwent unsubstantially violent periods. Finally, when they held nonviolent self-images, they underwent negligibly violent periods."

Athens's career-period typology is more complex than his self-image and interpretation typologies. Substantially violent periods obviously include acts of substantial physical injury or sexual violation. Unsubstantially violent periods count less violent acts (such as slapping, backhanding, pushing, mildly punching, choking or kicking) and threats but also include substantially violent acts that were victim precipitated (that is, the victim started the altercation). Negligibly violent periods include no substantially violent acts "and few, if any, unsubstantially violent acts that were not victim-precipitated." Victim precipitation, then, can escalate violence in people not otherwise inclined to such escalation.*

Athens offers a chilling example of a violent self-image held by Case 56, a murderer in his early thirties, who recalled a number of substantially violent acts he carried out during a substantially violent period that began when he was nine years old. He had been a bright child, "mature and perceptive beyond my years. . . . I was very mischievous but not offensive where grown-ups were concerned. My folks considered me to be a real good kid." But he recalled having had "a little temper too, and after my grandfather taught me how to fight, I was the cock of the walk at school." His grandfather had coached him, he told Athens, in these words: " 'It is worse to win a fight if you're wrong than to get your ass whipped if you are right. But if you are right, then no holds are barred. If fists don't work, then don't box. Pick up a rock, baseball bat, anything. A bully doesn't deserve a boxing match anyway, but anything he gets.' " (Athens must have heard echoes: Pete the Greek had coached him with similar logic.) Following his grandfather's advice, Case 56 at nine years of

---

* Criminologist Marvin Wolfgang notably investigated victim-precipitated homicide, but defined victim precipitation to include only those occasions when the victim was "the first in the homicide drama to use physical force directed against his subsequent slayer" (Wolfgang [1957], p. 2). "Words alone [are] not enough" to count as victim precipitation, Wolfgang insisted (Wolfgang [1969], p. 72). Based on the evidence of his interviews, Athens expands victim precipitation to include verbal and gestural threats. Limiting threats to physical force, he points out, "ignores the meaning of precipitation to the victim and offender," "leaves out far too many cases in which the victim *is* a genuine contributing factor in the offense and includes far too many cases in which the victim is *not* a genuinely contributing factor in the offense" (Athens [1997], p. 36).

age downed a bully who had been picking on him at school, "kicked him in the head and face good and hard and bloodied his mouth and broke his nose." At eleven, fighting with an older boy, he "picked up a large stone and . . . busted him in the head." At twelve he broke an assailant's arm with a steel pipe. At thirteen he stopped a boy his own age from throwing darts at the back of his house by smashing him in the face with a two-by-four. At fourteen, after his abusive stepfather hit his little brother once too often, he shot and killed the man in an act of violent personal revolt. A career of substantial violence followed, including a prison murder Case 56 reported to Athens from which, he told him, he "got away . . . clean."

Athens found escalating, stable and de-escalating violent careers. Case 56's career was stably substantially violent from the age of nine. Careers escalated, Athens deduced, because "the types of self-images the violent criminals hold over their lives become more violent as the kinds of violent acts they commit become more serious and the acts become more frequent." He reports from participant observation the fully de-escalating career of an acquaintance, a union leader in his late thirties who had been arrested at twenty for shooting a man and released on probation. Between the ages of fifteen and twenty-one, Athens's informant had been a gang leader with what he called "a bad-ass reputation." Substantial violence in adolescence declined to unsubstantial violence in his twenties, after his arrest and probation; by thirty-two his self-image had become nonviolent. Athens's acquaintance had cooperated fully, offering documents to corroborate his testimony. It was an important case because, like Pete, the man had never served time in prison. Since most violent offenders fall between the ages of fifteen and thirty, Athens observes, later in life "most . . . undoubtedly have either fully or partially de-escalating careers."

Violent careers change—escalate or de-escalate—in response to changing phantom communities. What causes phantom communities to change? If someone succeeds at violent action, Athens argues, that success "leads his present significant others to consider him more violent and to show him more deference than before. If he accepts their new, more violent definition of himself and enjoys the new, more deferential way that they treat him, then he will develop" a more violent self-conception and a more violent phantom community. "In the wake of this development, he modifies his social circle and may change his immediate corporal community so that it includes more violent members." If, on the other hand, a violent actor "loses the battle against his antagonist, or . . . does not act violently because he has formed a restraining judgment," then "his repeated failure to take successful violent actions in these situations has dramatic repercussions. It leads his significant others to consider him less violent and to act more boldly toward him than they had before." If he accepts that revised definition of himself and tolerates their bolder way of approaching him, then he will develop a less violent self-conception and a less violent phantom community—and will also modify his social circle to include fewer violent members. Here as everywhere in his work Athens replaces the mystifications of psychopathology with the comprehensible and testable dynamics of familiar human experience.

Besides his pioneering typologies, Athens draws several basic and important conclusions from his first full study of violent actors. Since individuals "will commit violent criminal acts *only after* they form violent interpretations of the situations confronting them," and since carrying out such violent interpretations "is always *problematic,*" with "*variable* outcomes," it follows that "violent criminal acts are not compulsive actions that, once started, can never be halted." That conclusion directly contradicts most previous theories about violent crime and supports with evidence the legal and reasonable assumption that violent criminals are responsible for their violent crimes. "Since human beings are normally aware of at least some of the contingencies that confront them in any situation," he elaborates, "they can always exercise some degree of control over their conduct. At bare minimum they can decide whether to pursue or avoid a particular course of action."

Athens concludes further that people who commit substantially violent acts have different phantom communities:

Those who hold violent self-images have an *unmitigated violent [phantom community]*—a [phantom community] providing them with pronounced and categorical *moral* support for acting violently toward other people. Those who hold incipiently violent self-images have a *mitigated violent [phantom community]*—a [phantom community] providing them with pronounced, but *limited,* categorical moral support for acting violently toward other people. Finally, those who hold nonviolent self-images have a *nonviolent [phantom community]*—a [phantom community] that does not provide them with any pronounced, categorical moral support for acting violently toward other people, *except* in the case of defending themselves or intimates from physical attack.*

The relatively small number of men and women and sometimes children who live among us who have violent phantom communities "are at the heart of our violent crime problem," Athens writes. "Not only do they commit the great bulk of serious violent criminal acts, but even as victims they often *precipitate* those that they do not commit. That is, after forming one of the offensive violent interpretations—a frustrative, malefic, or frustrative-malefic one—they make physically threatening gestures toward people with nonviolent [phantom communities] who then commit violent crimes as a result of forming physically defensive interpretations."

When he revised *Violent Acts and Actors* into *Violent Acts and Actors Revisited*, Athens added a section he called "A Second Look." When he wrote the first version, he confesses, he failed to realize that it in fact embodied "an empirically grounded, rudimentary theory of violent criminal behavior." Reviewing that theory, he identifies as its basic assumption the idea that "crime is a product of social *retardation*." By "social retardation" he means that violent people "guide their actions toward themselves and others from the standpoint of an underdeveloped, primitive phantom community, an 'us' that hinders them from cooperating in the ongoing social activities of their corporal community or the larger society in which it is embedded." He goes on to list several "brute facts" to which his theory conforms.

The first is that there are multiple types of violent criminal acts. This brute fact contradicts those theories according to which "all or most criminal violent acts are crammed into a single form" such as sociologist Erving Goffman's "character contest"—a testing of honor analogous to a duel. ("Show me where there's honor in someone beating his wife," Athens says of Goffman's character-contest model.)

The second brute fact is that there is more than one type of violent criminal. Athens divides violent criminals into three groups based on their phantom communities and their self-conceptions: marginally violent, violent and "ultraviolent." Ultraviolent criminals, he writes,

---

* Where I have inserted "phantom community" in brackets, Athens used Mead's "generalized other" in the first edition of this book. "I used the generalized other to fill the hole," he told me, "because I didn't have the phantom community concept yet. I knew it wasn't right, but I had to hold the place, so to speak, so I could work on it later, and it was at least in the neighborhood." In *Violent Acts and Actors Revisited*, Athens authorizes the substitution in the section called "A Second Look."

"inhabit unmitigated violent phantom communities and paint violent portraits of themselves." Violent criminals "inhabit mitigated violent phantom communities and paint incipiently violent self-portraits." Marginally violent criminals (that is, criminals whose violence follows from physically defensive interpretations) "inhabit nonviolent phantom communities and, naturally, paint only nonviolent portraits of themselves." Each of these types of violent criminals "stands on clearly different steps on a violence progression ladder."

The third brute fact to which Athens's theory conforms is that "different types of violent criminals are capable of engaging in quite different types of violent criminal acts." In the nomenclature of the social sciences, expressive acts are those carried out for their own sake, to express the actor's point of view. Instrumental acts are those carried out to accomplish some purposeful end. Athens establishes that only ultraviolent criminals engage in purely expressive acts of violence—that is, acts that follow from a malefic interpretation, acts motivated by hatred. Physically defensive and frustrative acts are instrumental rather than expressive; frustrative-malefic acts are mixed. That ultraviolent criminals use substantial violence not only to defend themselves or to push people around but also purely as a means of self-expression, with minimal provocation from the victim or even without provocation, goes a long way toward explaining why we perceive them to be so exceptionally dangerous.*

At the end of his first book, Athens concludes that understanding the phantom communities of violent actors is crucial to explaining violent crime. He proposes several possible lines of research. One of those lines—identifying the social process that leads to the development of a violent phantom community—he would carry through in the years to come while he struggled to make headway in his academic career against the tide of criminological fashion.

---

* Two other brute facts to which Athens's theory conforms concern violent communities, which I discuss later.

CHAPTER NINE

Academic Crackers and Cheese

Finishing his doctoral work at Berkeley, writing the dissertation that he would revise and enlarge into *Violent Criminal Acts and Actors,* starting to look for academic appointment, Lonnie Athens at twenty-six felt unfit for public consumption. He had talked almost exclusively to prison inmates for so long that he had nearly lost the ability to speak formal English, much less write it. Violent criminals breezed the way men do when they're laid back drinking beer, but the subjects of their casual conversation were rape and mugging and murder. It took its toll on Athens. Having immersed himself in the underworld of violence, he now found it hard to reemerge to the light. Job interviews were a struggle, and to make matters worse, Herbert Blumer was away in Illinois on a visiting professorship and not available to advise him. The doctoral candidate had already published two papers as a sole author, which put him well ahead of his peers. He assumed that his research, as he developed and published it, would establish his reputation. Not realizing how crucial his first tenure-track appointment would be, he accepted a two-year appointment as an assistant professor in the Department of Criminology at Wayne State University in Detroit, beginning in September 1975. It turned out to be a disaster.

"If you don't get tenure on your first job," he reflects, "it's the kiss of death and you may never make it again. You're stigmatized, just like a lawyer not making partner. I was naïve. I was a young, cocky kid. I thought I'd arrived. Nothing could have been further from the truth. This was an educational experience like none I'd ever had before. The system had now turned upside down. As a student your main obstacle was yourself—whether you had the discipline to study, what you could do. As an assistant professor your main obstacle was the chairman and the tenured professors. I learned that I was socially inept at white-collar work. I was Stanley Kowalski. I committed one social blunder after another. I was so inept I didn't even realize I'd blundered until I heard about it from gossip."

Attending the social gatherings organized to introduce the new faculty to the old—"academic crackers and cheese," he calls them—Athens discovered that his salary, which he had not realized he was supposed to negotiate, was two thousand dollars a year lower than any other new hire. He immediately cornered the department chairman to find out why. The chairman took offense, he says, and told him "maybe you weren't worth any more to us than that." He pressed for a chance to teach a graduate seminar in symbolic interactionism without realizing that graduate assignments were plums reserved for tenured faculty. He spoke up in faculty meetings when rookies were expected to be seen but not heard.

The chairman encouraged him to apply for government research grants, which paid a percentage to the university as overhead. "I told him, 'Qualitative researchers don't get grants, and if they do they're very small because we don't have big expenses, just interviewing. You must have known that before I came here.' But he was incredulous: 'You mean a person who studies violent crime isn't going to receive grants?' That's when I knew I was in trouble."

Athens was slow to adjust his wardrobe to his new position. He still wore his hair down to his shoulders, still wore a headband and jeans and boots. Students liked his style, and as he settled in to teach they gathered in his office. "One big black guy named Big House, a Vietnam vet who'd been in a street gang, would hang around my office. A white guy from a slum who'd been a heroin addict. Two or three others. We'd swap street stories, this and that, in there laughing. Every other word out of Big House was 'motherfucker'—'motherfucker' this, 'motherfucker' that. He wasn't mad; he was talking. I'd be laughing, asking them questions, talking about whatever. I started getting complaints that I had criminals coming around. I said, 'Wait a minute, what criminals are you talking about?' "

A mathematician on the faculty who taught night classes was murdered in the school parking lot. Athens also taught at night and started taking Watson, his big St. Bernard, to school with him, parking the dog in his office with its leash anchored to one leg of his desk while he taught a class. "One night I heard the dog barking and then all hell broke loose in the hallway—*boom! boom! boom! boom! boom!* Someone said, 'The dog's loose up there! Get campus security!' I ran up and my dog had the desk moving down the hallway, bashing up against the walls, people yelling and screaming and a terrified janitor down at the end—I guess he came to pick up the trash and the dog started barking and he got scared." The chairman banished Watson from the premises.

There was trouble on the publication front as well. A shorter version of *Violent Criminal Acts and Actors* that Athens submitted to the *American Journal of Sociology* was rejected because its peer reviewers thought its perspective was psychoanalytic. The *Sociological Quarterly* also rejected it. The *American Journal of Criminology* sent it to two nationally recognized experts on violent crime for peer review. "The first stated that it was the worst paper that he had ever reviewed for a journal," Athens wrote Blumer unhappily. "The other one stated that it did not meet the criterion of a scientific study but was instead a mysterious analysis of the 'stream of consciousness.'" On the other hand, a leading sociologist of deviant behavior, Howard Becker, author of the well-known study *Outsiders*, reviewed Athens's full book manuscript for a university press and enthusiastically endorsed it. "He's taken a topic on which a lot of nonsense has been written," Becker wrote, "and opened it up, with the help of a new kind of data, in an original and creative way. I think criminologists and social psychologists will find it very impressive." Despite Becker's endorsement, the press held the manuscript for six months without acting on it, until Athens requested its return. He revised it during his first year of teaching at Wayne State and over the summer.

If the chairman of the Wayne State Sociology Department found Athens delinquent, a senior professor in the department who had supported Athens's hiring, Frank E. Hartung, welcomed his young colleague. Hartung encouraged Athens partly because his own specialty was criminology theory. Ten years earlier, he had published a remarkable study, *Crime, Law, and Society*, which systematically and thoroughly demolished the psychiatric doctrine that many crimes were the product of compulsion or "irresistible impulse"—the "I couldn't help myself" excuse. Hartung traced the psychiatric theory of irresistible impulse to the most prominent and influential American psychiatrist of the nineteenth century, Isaac Ray, who identified murder, theft and arson as crimes typically triggered by such "compulsion." Ray even distinguished between social classes in his categories, Hartung notes: "Ray stated explicitly that the diagnosis of shoplifting as being kleptomania is indicated if the thief is a respectable, upper-class person"—a distinction extended today, as in the nineteenth century, even to rape and murder, for which lower-class defendants are far more frequently held responsible than middle- and upper-class defendants who claim mental illness. Ray, Hartung comments, "was by no means the last student who mistook the beliefs and values of his social class for scientific principles."

Hartung demonstrates that Ray derived the theory of the irresistible impulse and of the possibility of compulsive action outside intellectual awareness from nineteenth-century phrenology. Phrenology, the pseudo-science of reading character from the contours of the head, was based on the theory that our mental powers consist of separate faculties, or "mental organs," some thirty-seven in all, whose definite locations in the brain reveal their degree of development via the bulges and concavities of the skull. Phrenology's conviction that each faculty—"conscience," "benevolence," "reason" and so on—spoke its own language and functioned independently from the others became the basis for the curious psychiatric dogma, still influential, that it is possible to be criminally insane and at the same time perfectly reasonable. "While the reason may be unimpaired," Ray wrote in 1871, "the passions may be in a state of insanity, impelling a man . . . to the commission of horrible crimes in spite of all his efforts to resist." Change the jargon slightly, and Ray's assertion parallels, among many possible examples, Emanuel Tanay's "ego-dystonic homicide."

In 1862, having examined twenty-four murderers in the General Prison for Scotland at Perth, Ray reported that he found their "intellects" only "very slightly affected," so that "almost the only proof of insanity was the *act* itself, which was involuntary, impulsive, irresistible, and scarcely preceded or followed by any disorder of the intellectual functions." Hartung dismantles Ray's (and psychiatry's) faulty logic:

> The question is asked, Why do some people commit, for example, arson, larceny, murder [and] sexual offenses . . . ? The answer is, Because they have an irresistible impulse that forces (causes) them to do so. The further question is then asked, How do we know that they are in fact possessed by irresistible impulse? The answer is, We know it because they commit arson, larceny, murder [and] sexual offenses. . . . The reader will recognize in this the familiar vicious circle of logic, marked by a very small radius.

Contemporary psychiatry adds the idea of an unconscious to the idea of an irresistible impulse. The impulse becomes "unconsciously motivated." One distinguished practitioner cited by Hartung thus argues that the outstanding feature of modern criminal psychiatry is "the recognition of the emotional rather than the intellectual genesis of crime." Hartung found this triumph of recognition particularly offensive because it removed the criminal from responsibility for his crimes. Athens shares that revulsion. He also rejects as unscientific—as not based on the evidence and untestable—the notion that personality is divided into separate faculties, such as reason and emotion, which act independently. George Herbert Mead had pointed the way beyond that old dichotomy by demonstrating that reason and emotion both emerged commonly from the dialogues of the self. "Human beings *acting* toward one another," Athens would write, ". . . generate both thoughts and emotions. . . . During social experiences, the human organism and the social environment are united into an *indivisible* whole. . . . The failure to study social experiences explains why [traditional] theories are cast in such highly mechanistic and unrealistic terms that [they] often strain the credulity of laypeople, even if they do not strain the credulity of most professional criminologists."

Hartung's demolition of psychiatry's approach to crime supported the social-retardation theory of criminality Athens was developing. But Athens paid even closer attention to Hartung's exploration of the social psychology of motivation, underlining and annotating his copy of Hartung's book. Judging from his marginal notes, he found support in Hartung's work for some of the basic ideas he was refining as he revised the manuscript that would become *Violent Criminal Acts and Actors*. For example, Hartung challenged the assumption that violent acts develop too quickly for thought or planning. "The organization of [an] action," he pointed out, ". . . may be so rapid as to seem instantaneous, both to the actor and to a possible observer. The rapidity of an action does not by itself indicate the absence of cognition and reasoning. The temporal aspect of any human act is in itself no ground for concluding that interpretation, inference, and reason were absent from the act." Athletes, for example, frequently make split-second decisions that factor in complex judgments; so do people responding to emergencies. Why wouldn't murderers? Athens already knew from his interviews that they did.

Athens bracketed a paragraph in Hartung's book that summarized Mead's conception of attitude taking and labeled it "key statement." It included this central idea:

> [A person] identifies himself to himself as being a particular kind of object, which, in personal terms, means that he defines himself as being a particular kind of person. He then performs the role appropriate to the kind of person that he has identified himself as

being. The vocabulary of motives employed in the enactment of the role is part of this process of self-identification. One must learn to identify oneself differently in a variety of different situations, and to discharge the accompanying different roles, some of which may be in conflict with each other. One's statement to oneself of who and what one is determines the role that is played in a particular situation.

The last sentence in this paragraph is heavily underscored in Athens's copy of Hartung's book: "One's statement to oneself of who and what one is determines the role that is played in a particular situation." Here was support for his conclusion that a violent actor's self-conception determines the course of his violent decisions. "Self-conception as main determinant," Athens wrote in the margin.

But Hartung was leaving the department, and once again, as with Herbert Blumer, Athens found that he had hitched his wagon to a setting star. Although Athens enjoyed teaching and was judged "one of our most popular instructors" in a Sociology Department review, he was rejected for tenure in 1978. He filed a grievance with the American Association of University Professors that led to a final one-year terminal appointment.

During that terminal year, 1979, Athens's wife bore him a daughter, Maureen (she would be their only child). At Berkeley, Marilyn Athens had finished her interrupted undergraduate education and graduated with honors. She had found well-paid civil service work in Detroit with the Equal Employment Opportunities Commission. When she returned to her job, six weeks after her delivery, Athens took over child care by day and taught classes at night. *Violent Criminal Acts and Actors* was finally in production at an English press, Routledge and Kegan Paul, after a fortuitous encounter between Athens and the publisher, Peter Hopkins, at a meeting of the American Sociological Association. With a one-year-old daughter and a working wife, Athens scrambled to find another job.

An offer came from East Texas State University in Commerce, Texas. On inspection he liked the people and hated the place, but he needed the job and took it. He lived in a dormitory and sent money home. When he could—not often—he visited Marilyn and Maureen in Detroit. After a year in East Texas, Athens accepted an offer from Kansas State University in Manhattan, Kansas, in the wide buffalo-prairie country forty miles west of the state capital, Topeka. The visiting assistant professorship paid five thousand dollars more than he was making in Texas, and the department chairman hinted that a tenure-track opening might follow. Bracing himself for another year without his family, Athens moved to Manhattan in the autumn of 1981, but loneliness overwhelmed him and he decided to resign and move back to Detroit. More promises followed, he remembers—that the visiting position at Kansas State would last at least two years, that a tenure-track position would almost certainly open up. Athens and his wife decided to take a chance, even though Marilyn would have to give up her federal job and they would lose thousands of dollars on their house.

Settled again with his family in Kansas, Athens began preparing for another round of prison interviews. At the conclusion of *Violent Criminal Acts and Actors* he had pointed to the need to identify the social process that leads to the development of violent criminals. Now he wanted to carry out an investigation that might reveal such a process. He also wanted to study people whose violent careers had de-escalated, if he could find them. There were state prisons at Lansing and Hutchinson, Kansas, and a federal prison at Leavenworth. He submitted a proposal to conduct prison interviews to the Kansas State University Human Subjects Committee (which had to approve the use of human subjects for research), to the Kansas Department of Corrections and to the Federal Bureau of Prisons. While he was negotiating with the prison bureaucracies, the Human Subjects Committee decided that his prison interviews constituted a high-risk activity *to the prisoners*. Athens was stunned. "The chairman was a psychologist," he recalls. "He seems to have decided that since I wasn't a psychologist, I could injure these people psychologically. It was naïve. He didn't know what happens in prisons. These people have been through court. Even defendants who plead out have to go up and give a statement of admission in open court that they did in fact commit the crime to which they're pleading guilty. They have to summarize the acts they committed in doing the crime. That's already public; it's all public. They've been arrested, they've been arraigned, they've been strip-searched. In prison they're pressured into medical experiments, they're subject to being raped and beaten short of death—and this guy thinks I'm going to injure them by talking to them about their crimes." Athens appealed to the dean of the graduate school, concluding his letter: "The point has now almost been reached that it is virtually impossible to actually study criminals at KSU." Prison officials finally approved his proposal, and by October 1982 Athens could write his University of Illinois colleague Norman Denzin that he was "out in the field collecting data" as well as "teaching several big undergraduate classes."

The interviewing was hard work, as it always had been, but other than nearly being thrown off a tier at Leavenworth by a prisoner who resented the timing of his appearance ("You stupid motherfucker, why didn't you ask me about my life twenty-five years ago when I needed you?" his attacker had rebuked him), it advanced successfully. Since he was collecting entire criminal careers, this round of interviews ran seven to nine hours each, divided into two or three separate sessions over several days. He anchored his roster with a veteran group of eight ultraviolent offenders—men with at least three convictions for serious violent crimes. These he hoped to contrast with a younger group of thirty incipiently violent offenders who ranged in age from early to late teens. All had been convicted of a serious violent crime, and they also, Athens writes, "candidly admitted committing previous violent acts of varying gravity for which they were able to escape conviction or even arrest."

He assumed that the young offenders would not have completed the social process, whatever it was, that created violent criminals. Later, when he identified that process of "violentization" (a term Athens coined by combining the word "violent" with the classic sociological term "socialization"), he discovered that his assumption "was almost totally wrong." Even offenders as young as fourteen had fully completed violentization. That discovery made him question the uniqueness of the process he was identifying—was it significant but not unique to violent criminals? To determine if the process was unique, he interviewed half a dozen nonviolent criminals, men "who had no known arrests for violent crimes and had not reported to me ever committing any serious violent acts for which they had escaped arrest." The nonviolent criminals turned out to have undergone at least some of the social experiences he had found in the early stages of violentization. Athens had then to revise his understanding of violentization and to look further, "to find people who . . . *should* [have] become dangerous violent criminals, but who in all likelihood had *not* done so." The people he chose to study to check his findings were victims of domestic assault, "half a dozen recent women residents of a spouse abuse shelter, who had all been the victims of violent crimes, but who, with one important exception, had not reported committing any serious violent acts against others." The exceptional woman proved to have undergone full violentization, somewhat later in life than the young offenders he had interviewed. The other women had not. The crucial difference confirmed that the social process he had found was unique to violent criminals.

Before he came to that full understanding, however, his career collapsed. Unable to find a job in Kansas, Marilyn had made the best of the situation by starting work on a law degree at the University of Kansas in Lawrence. The Athenses moved from Manhattan to Topeka to shorten the driving time to Lawrence and to the prison towns where

Athens was interviewing, but his superiors in the Kansas State Sociology Department took his move as disconnection from their community. When a tenure-track position became available at Kansas State, it went to someone else. Jobless and broke, Athens retreated to Washington, D.C., lodged with his in-laws and made the rounds of congressional committees, lobbying groups and the National Institute of Justice, looking for employment.

An invitation to an interview arrived coincidentally from a large state university, which had solicited a list of black sociologists from Berkeley to comply with a consent decree. Berkeley had offered four candidates, including Athens, presumably because his colloquial first name led them to assume he was African American. On the phone with the department chairman his Virginia accent did not reveal his race, and he accepted the chairman's invitation to visit the university for an interview, hoping he could sell himself in person. The delegation that met him at the airport was shocked to discover he was white. He was not offered a job.

The Georgetown University Law Center had recently won a grant that required the preparation of a review of state habitual-offenders laws. Samuel Dash, then the director of the Law Center, chose Athens to conduct the study. Though he was only a hired hand, he had never earned more. Marilyn was admitted to George Washington University Law School, they took an apartment in Arlington and enrolled Maureen in day care. Athens liked his work. It was invigorating to be around brilliant, literate people. He befriended Heathcote Wales and Joe Page, both law professors who loved ideas and took them seriously. Athens added their names to his honor roll of white-collar coaches. But the grant came to an end after two years, 1983 to 1985, and despite the many grant applications Athens submitted, no agency was willing to fund him. He found himself out on the street again. "After that," he says, "it was a steep descent."

Marilyn's father, Jack O'Rourke, a self-made man, had started and built a successful company that sold and serviced commercial and industrial electric motors. "He was a mechanical virtuoso," Athens says. "He could fix anything. A big redheaded Irishman, a rough guy and a hard worker, he gave me a job as a rigger, loading and unloading these big motors for elevators and air-conditioning compressors off of a truck and onto the roofs of buildings. It was hard for him. He said, 'You've got a B.A., an M.A., a Ph.D. and no J.O.B., so I guess you'll have to work for me.' He was pissed. I'd failed his daughter. He wasn't enamored of the marriage in the first place. But he did give me a job. All the men knew I was a professor, and he was socially embarrassed. God bless him."

Rolling through federal Washington harnessed up in overalls and big leather gloves, invisible to the congressional staff and grant officers he had lobbied for employment or funding, Athens muscled heavy electric motors onto the roofs of the very buildings where the doors had slammed.

He somehow managed to continue studying and writing during this difficult period in his life. A paper he contributed to the *Sociological Quarterly* significantly challenged Goffman's "character-contest" theory of violent behavior. Goffman, one of the most original and successful American sociologists of the mid-century, had proposed that violent encounters were extreme examples of duel-like contests during which an individual gambles his character to "[display] to himself and sometimes to others his style of conduct when the chips are down." Goffman emphasized that mutual consent was a necessary preliminary to violent interactions, which he characterized as a "sport."

Goffman's theory, Athens wrote, had "provided a major source of ideas for explaining interpersonal violence." Athens objected to its facile logic. "On-the-spot agreements between conflicting parties to use violence in order to settle their disputes are *not* formed in most violent criminal acts almost as a matter of definition," he wrote. "In the case of forcible rape, victims do not agree to the use of violence in order to determine whether or not they will engage in sexual acts with their attackers. Similarly, in the case of robbery, victims do not agree to the use of violence in order to determine whether or not they will hand over valuables to offenders. . . . Mutual consent for the use of violence is absent from most violent criminal acts."

Athens stressed as well the *meaning* that violent actors assign to their acts. "A character contest presumes that people always commit violent criminal acts only in order to display a strong character and maintain honor and face or to avoid displaying a weak character and losing honor and face. However, this is not the meaning which the perpetrators of violent criminal acts often attribute to their actions." Such meaning depended on the circumstances, he explained, and included physically defensive and malefic interpretations that emphasized not honor but fear or hatred.

Athens called for a more inclusive, complex and exact theory of violent criminal behavior and offered a sketch of such a theory that anticipated the violentization process he was in the midst of identifying:

> Engaging in violence is not only a matter of having nothing to
> lose, but also a matter of having something to gain. People who

have a greater commitment to a violent social world than to a non-violent one *perceive* they have less to lose and more to gain by engaging in violence than do those who have a greater commitment to a nonviolent social world. The more committed a person is to a violent social world than to a nonviolent one, the more violent he or she will likely be.

From working as a rigger for Jack O'Rourke, Athens moved on in 1986 to an eight-month job as a probation and parole officer in northern Virginia. By then he had sent out a fair share of what would ultimately be more than seven hundred applications for teaching positions, with friends like sociologist Norman Denzin and law scholar Heathcote Wales supporting him with letters of recommendation. Nothing came of his efforts; in that decade of declining college admissions, sociology departments were downsizing all over the United States.

Working as a parole officer was "a nightmare," Athens recalls, "but I learned a lot about bureaucracy. All you did was push papers: urine tests, court costs, restitution fees, supervision fees, home visits, office visits. You had eighty-some people to check. Everything was superficial—what else could it be with that many people to follow? You'd go to people's houses quick, like a paperboy collecting. You had no idea what was really going on in these people's heads. The deputy chief's job was auditing your books. If you kept your books up, fine. You were just a human accountant." In spite of the system, he started writing detailed, penetrating reports that scotched more than one incipient plea bargain. Lawyers noticed his work and suggested he set up in business for himself. He did, writing Denzin in September that he had "started a small consulting practice from which so far I am earning a few needed dollars." He was limiting his practice "to individual criminal cases coming before the courts," he told Denzin, and not "conducting studies or grants which I have no stomach for. I am finally hearing what you have been telling me: You don't have to be an academic to be a scholar if you can [find] a way to manage. I hope that I finally have."

His penetrating parole reports led a Virginia state agency to hire him part-time to do sentence evaluations—background investigations and jailhouse interviews with convicted adolescent offenders to advise whether they should be imprisoned or placed under community supervision. He was bored, frustrated and deeply angry to have been cast aside despite the quality of his work. "As you may recall," he wrote an ailing Herbert Blumer in March 1987,

I was denied research grants by every granting agency in America at least a half dozen times. The research director at one government agency candidly told me that my work "resembled art more than science," to which I promptly replied, "good science and good art may have more in common than you realize." Then she suggested that I submit my application to the National Endowment for the Humanities. I tried it, but they, of course, responded that my work resembled science more than art.

He had decided to show the bastards, he told Blumer: "After years of hitting my head against the wall, I finally realized that I must either do my study with my own resources or not do it at all. Thus, motivated by the anger at their rejection, the rejection of academics and the desire not to be defeated by them, I embarked upon my analysis of fifty-odd cases. I have decided to complete my study in spite of everything."

He had written his English publisher, now renamed Routledge, the previous spring, enclosing a three-page outline of the new work; Routledge had responded with enthusiasm and offered him a small advance. His wife, now an attorney for the National Labor Relations Board, had agreed to carry the family. Writing Blumer in late March, Athens reported that the analysis for the book was "proving to be a difficult, but rewarding struggle. . . . The cases are rich and varied enough that I am confident that if I persevere, I will be successful." He knew that Blumer, eighty-seven years old, was gravely ill, and took the occasion to express his gratitude once more for vital mentorship:

I do not expect this book to be well received by most academics, as I naively assumed with my first book. The popular view by academics now is that genes, gonads, chromosomes, brain waves, etc., make people violent, not their social experiences. Since academics come from such bland backgrounds, it is easy to understand why they would believe violent persons could not possibly have any experiences which could make them violent. After I finish my study, I will have outlined a regimen which could make anybody into a violent criminal no matter what their biological makeup.

Your intellectual ideals, integrity and faith still inspire me as much as they did when I was in your classes. I still believe that social scientists who flaunt their knowledge of the social world but who have no first-hand knowledge of it are charlatans. You will always deserve great admiration for having the conviction and courage to say it louder than anyone else.

It may well have been the last tribute Herbert Blumer received. He died on April 13, 1987.

The Creation of Dangerous Violent Criminals turned out to be a deeply original book of barely one hundred pages. Routledge published it in 1989, when Athens was forty.

CHAPTER TEN

The Creation of Dangerous Violent Criminals (I)

To fix the reader's attention realistically on the subject of his book, Athens opens *The Creation of Dangerous Violent Criminals* with a grisly criminal monologue:

CASE 16: KIDNAPPING AND ATTEMPTED MURDER

James and I got the munchies and were walking to the grocery store to buy some cupcakes. In the parking lot of the store, we saw a fancy camper. I said, "Check out that camper," and we started looking in its windows. James said, "That's a bad truck, man." As we were walking away, an old woman walked by us with a big man pushing her grocery cart. She said, "Keep away from my truck." I said, "We were just looking at it." She said, "Keep your black asses away from my truck." After she told us to keep away from her truck, I got mad. After she added the part about our black asses, I got doubly mad and wanted to kill her old stinking ass on the spot. I said, "Kiss my ass, you old stinking bitch." The big grocery store man said, "Get out of here before I call the police." I said, "Fuck the police, they're not about anything. I'll kill that old bitch for talking about my black ass."

About ten minutes later we saw her truck again in a parking lot behind a building. I said to James, "Look, there's that same damn truck. Now I can get that old bitch." We ran out to the truck, looked around, and then busted open the back door. I told James, "When that old bitch comes back, let's take her out some place where I can stomp her ass. I'm going to fuck her up bad." James only laughed. I was still hot from her referring to our black asses and acting like we were dirt for her to kick around. I wanted to get her old stinking ass for saying that to us. I had hate for that old stinking white bitch. James wasn't as mad about her referring to our black asses as I was.

We sat in her camper eating the food she had gotten while we waited for her to come back. I couldn't wait till she saw us. When she came back to the camper, we pulled a knife on her and told her to start driving. She said, "I'll do anything you want, but please don't hurt me." As we drove off, she said, "I'm sorry for what I said to you at the grocery store, please let me go." We didn't say a word until we told her to pull the camper into a vacant lot we drove past. After she parked the camper, she started crying and slobbering, "Please don't hurt me, please don't hurt me, I'm sorry, please . . ." [Athens's ellipsis] I know the old stinking bitch was only lying. Seeing her slobber like that only made me madder and hate her even more.

I jumped out of the camper, grabbed her by the shoulders and threw her out of the cab. She landed face first in the dirt. She got up on her hands and knees and started yelling, "Help, police, help, police, help!" I said, "Shut up, you old stinking bitch," and kicked her in the stomach as hard as I could and knocked all the wind out of that old bag. She rolled up in a ball in the mud gasping for breath and I kicked her again, which straightened her out like a stick. I tried to lift her up by the clothes, but she was so muddy that she slipped out of my hands, so I grabbed her by the hair. James said, "Would you look at her ugly old face." After I looked at it, I got so mad, I smacked and backhanded her about twenty times. Then I threw her against the camper and she slumped down on the ground. James opened a can of pop and asked her, "Do you want some pop?" She said, "No, I only want you to let me go." I said, "I'm not going to let you go, you stinking old bitch, I'm going to kill you." I grabbed her by the hair again and slammed her head back and forth against the side of the truck until blood started running out from her hair and over her ears. Then I dropped her to the ground, kicked her over into the mud puddle and left her for dead. We got into her camper and drove off.

This malefic performance is certainly a heinous violent crime, Athens observes. It merits that designation because of the gross disproportion between provocation and assault: "The elderly victim nearly died as a result of the horrible injuries she sustained at the hands of her much younger male attacker." Criminals who commit such heinous violent crimes "are the most *dangerous violent criminals* in our society," Athens emphasizes, "with perhaps the lone exception of certain white-collar criminals whose actions jeopardize the health or safety of large numbers of people." The question he therefore proposes to address is: "*How* does a human being in our supposedly highly civilized society become the type of person who would commit these violent crimes without any apparent moral qualms or reservations? Or to put it more simply, What makes people become dangerous violent criminals?"

After reviewing the differences between his approach to answering this question and the traditional approaches of psychiatry and crimi-nology, Athens lists the "few simple assumptions" that have guided his study. One is "that people are what they are as a result of the social experiences that they have undergone in their lives." Most social experi-ences, however, are trivial; they pass in "an almost endless stream," quickly over and quickly forgotten. But some social experiences are significant—"consequential and unforgettable"—and those "have a last-ing impact upon people's lives and are remembered weeks, months and years" afterward, leaving "a permanent mark upon people regardless of their wishes." Among significant social experiences, he proposes to show, are those that make people dangerous violent criminals.

A second simple assumption that guided Athens's study is that "the significant experiences which make people dangerous violent criminals do not occur all at once in their lives, but occur gradually over time." Since "later social experiences often build upon earlier experiences," it is reasonable to conclude that "they must form some sort of developmen-tal process with discernible stages." He is not claiming that the process is rigidly deterministic, however. "This developmental process is probably not preordained. The earlier stages might make the later stages possible, but *not inevitable.* In other words, it may be that many more people start upon the process than finish it. They could complete some of the earlier stages in the developmental process without ever entering later stages."

The third simple assumption that guided Athens's investigation is that "it is far better to study fifty people in depth than to study 5,000 people superficially." Social scientists might not agree, he writes, but scientists in many other fields certainly would. He cites the authoritative text *The Art of Scientific Investigation,* by an English veterinary pathologist, W. I. Bev-eridge, which notes that "more discoveries have arisen from intense observation of very limited material than from statistics applied to large groups." Athens's material, of course, is his new round of fifty life studies collected in Kansas. His system of intense observation, he explains, is "the deceivingly simple, but time-proven method of constant comparison," which he applied to his cases for "what seemed like an endless time." That is, he "continuously compared the offenders' descriptions of their different social experiences [with] one another to try to isolate the nature of the social experiences which they had commonly undergone and the sequence in which they had undergone them."

Having done so, and having checked his tentative findings against the social experiences of nonviolent criminals and then domestic assault victims, he formulates a four-stage experiential process that he proposes to call violentization. He designates the four separate stages of violentization to be (1) brutalization, (2) belligerency, (3) violent performances and (4) virulency. "Each stage," he cautions, "describes the social experiences which people must completely undergo before they can enter the next higher stage of violence development."

Brutalization, Athens reports, is composed of "three more elemental experiences: *violent subjugation, personal horrification* and *violent coaching.*" All three "involve in their own way people undergoing coarse and cruel treatment at the hands of others that produces a lasting and dramatic impact upon the subsequent course of their lives." Who are those others? They are members of the subject's primary group, which Athens defines as "a group characterized by regular face-to-face interaction and intimate familiarity between its members, such as family, gang, or clique." (A "secondary group," in contrast, is distinguished by "the absence of the quality of intimacy, such as a large school's graduating class.")

Violent subjugation, one component of brutalization, occurs when "bona fide or would-be authority figures from one of the subject's primary groups use violence or force [the subject] to submit to their authority." Bona fide authority figures such as parents, would-be authority figures such as husbands or gang leaders, may expect not only obedience but also deference from those over whom they claim authority, and may feel justified in threatening to use or using extreme physical force to compel the subject's obedience and respect.

One kind of violent subjugation is coercion: The authority figure uses or credibly threatens violence "to force the subject to comply with some command (including to show respect) which the subject displays some reluctance to obey or refuses to obey outright." Once the authority figure begins battering the subject, he continues "until the subject signals submission by either obeying the command or loudly proclaiming an intention to do so quickly," at which point he stops. Although coercive subjugation is brutal, the subject retains a measure of control—submission ends the coercion. Athens sketches the dynamics of the experience from the subject's point of view:

> Prior to the onset of the battery and even [during] its early stages, the subject may act defiantly, but as the battery continues and becomes more severe, the subject's defiance erodes into fear. The subject's fear steadily heightens with the continuation of the battery until it finally erupts into full-fledged terror and panic sets in. The subject has now reached the point of breaking. The question which the subject always asks herself is: "How much more battering can I endure?" to which she sooner or later answers, "No more." The subject has now passed the breaking point, and submission appears to be the only way out. At first, submitting, and stopping the battery which it brings, provides a great sense of relief to the subject, but that relief quickly turns to humiliation with the realization that she was brutally beaten into submission. The humiliation from being brutally beaten down incenses the subject. Her burning rage becomes cooled only later, when it is transformed into a desire for revenge. The subject's desire for vengeance expresses itself in passing fantasies in which she batters, maims, tortures or murders her subjugator.

To illustrate coercive subjugation, Athens cites the recollection of a male in his mid-teens convicted of armed robbery:

CASE 19

I was sitting outside in a lawn chair one Sunday morning. My father yelled from the door, "Go get ready for church." I ignored him and kept sitting in the chair. I hated church. I couldn't stand listening to those sermons about sinning and going to hell. That kind of preaching got under my skin. I hated all those church people. Whenever they saw me, they would say, "Good afternoon, brother Tom." I couldn't stand hearing those church sermons and that dumb crap from those fools every Sunday.

When I didn't get ready for church, my father came back out and said, "I thought I told you to get ready for church." I said, "I'm not going to church." He said, "Oh yes you are going to church, now get ready." I said, "I'm not going to church anymore," and then he said again, "Oh yes you are" and went berserk on me. He started hitting me with his fists in the face and stomach. I yelled, "Leave me alone, stop hitting me, I am not going to church." But he kept on punching me, saying, "You are going to church." When I fell down on the ground, he grabbed me by the hair and started dragging me into the house, saying, "If I can't take you one way, then I'll have to take you another." I was scared he would pull all my hair out of my head, and my head and face were hurting bad, so I said, "Okay, okay, I'll go to church. Stop, stop, stop. Please stop." Then he finally let go of my hair, and we went into the house. As we walked toward the bathroom, he shoved me through the door and said, "Now get ready." When I looked in the mirror, I saw that I had a black eye, swollen face and fat lip. I was ashamed to go to church looking like that. I got so mad and angry thinking about it that I hit the bathroom wall with my fist. What he did to me was plain dirty. I wanted to get even with him for doing it. I wanted to kill him and kept thinking over and over again while we were sitting in church about shooting him.

A second kind of violent subjugation is retaliation: The authority figure uses violence to punish the subject for past disobedience recently discovered or for present disrespect. Retaliatory subjugation involves relentless battering, Athens explains, because the authority figure refuses the subject's offers of submission—denying her what Athens calls the "precious luxury" of choosing when to end the assault by submitting. "The battery is continued well beyond the point where the subject signals submission through such acts as pledging future obedience, begging for mercy or forgiveness or becoming completely hysterical." Retaliatory subjugation evokes responses in the subject different from those of coercive subjugation. At the outset she may feel dread rather than defiance. She may express outrage at the impending violence "and sometimes even her disdain for the subjugator." As battering begins and intensifies, fear overwhelms outrage or dread and thickens in turn into full-fledged terror. The subject asks herself, "How much more battering can I endure?" She answers, "No more," and offers to submit—but the cruel and relentless battering continues:

Once the subject realizes that the offer of submission will not be accepted, her feeling of terror changes into resignation. The subject bleakly concludes that nothing she says or does will cause the authority figure to stop the battering. As the feeling of resignation overwhelms the subject, her sense of time becomes greatly distorted, so that the battering may begin to appear to be taking place in slow motion. As the battery goes on for what seems to the subject an eternity, she lapses into an apathetic state. The subject, who has now become numb to the pain from the rain of blows, virtually stops all resistance and passively absorbs the punishment. While in this state, she experiences the battery almost as if it were happening to someone else rather than to herself. By the time the battery is finally brought to a halt, the subject has sunk into a stupor. As the subject slowly awakens from this stupor, humiliation at being mercilessly beaten down overcomes her, but the humiliation is only short-lived. As in coercive subjugation, it rapidly switches into a burning rage which is partly cooled when it is transformed into an intense desire for revenge against the subjugator. The intensity of this vengeance greatly exceeds what the subject felt during coercive subjugation. She has recurring fantasies about battering, maiming, torturing or murdering her subjugator long after this one episode of retaliatory subjugation ends.

Athens illustrates retaliatory subjugation with three cases—a stepfather and a son, a mother and a son, and a mother and a daughter—that demonstrate both male and female subjugators and subjects. When Athens interviewed the daughter, she was a young woman in her late teens serving a sentence for criminal homicide:

CASE 38

My mother came home from work and asked me where my little brother was. I said, "I don't know where he is." She said, "I told you not to let him run off." I said, "I didn't tell him to run off." She said, "You better find him; now get your ass out there and go do it." After we finally found him, she said, "Go to your room and take those clothes off. I didn't buy those clothes to beat on." I dashed up to my room and stripped.

She came into my room and said, "Take all your clothes off and lay across your bed." After I took my bra and underpants off, she started hitting me with an electric extension cord. I got so scared that I jumped under my bed, but she shoved the bed up. I tried to run out the door, but she blocked my way and drove me into the corner. She beat me all over with the cord—my ass, back, arms, legs and even my breasts. She hit me everywhere except for my crotch. It hurt bad, and I screamed and screamed, but it didn't faze her. She didn't seem to give a damn how bad she hurt me. I thought she might beat me to death. I said, "Please stop, please stop, I won't do it again, I won't do it again, I promise I won't, please stop." She said, "Bitch, I am going to teach you a lesson this time that your ass is never going to forget." She kept hitting me and hitting me while I was jammed in the corner with no place to run or hide. Since I realized then that she wanted to straight-out hurt me, I stopped begging, screaming and crying. I just looked at her while she beat me. She had a crazy look on her face. It seemed like she was determined to keep beating me as long as she could. It felt like I had been jammed in that corner for hours. I kept saying to myself, "When is she ever going to stop, when is she ever going to stop?" My body felt numb with pain. Then suddenly she stopped and said, "Bitch, you are going to school tomorrow with stripes." Thinking about it made me feel ashamed. After she left my room, I asked myself, "What mother would want to make her daughter suffer in agony like that for what I did?" I kept thinking I didn't deserve it.

As I was thinking about all these things, she called me down to wash the dishes. While I washed the dishes, I could see her in the living room listening to the stereo with her headset on. The anger started swelling up in me. I thought, I could just run in there with the knife I was washing and chop her head off and she would never know it. I would tell myself, "Do it, do it." Then, "Don't do it," then, "Do it" again.

Authority figures have different goals in mind when they choose coercive or retaliatory subjugation, Athens writes, which explains why one is more brutal than the other. Coercive subjugation seeks "momentary submission on the part of the subject and compliance with some present command." Retaliatory subjugation seeks "a more permanent state of submissiveness" that will ensure the subject's "future obedience and respect." They are not always successfully completed. The subject may escape, someone else may intervene or the authority figure may relent. Or the subject may forcibly resist, a special kind of violent performance that Athens examines in his discussion of the third stage of violentization.

Personal horrification is the second component of brutalization, the reverse of violent subjugation: "The subject does not himself undergo violent subjugation, but witnesses another person undergoing it." By "witnesses," Athens means sees or hears; hearing can be worse than seeing, since the subject "fill[s] out the unseen portion with mental imagery."

For personal horrification to occur, the person whose subjugation the subject witnesses must be a member of his primary group—"some close relative . . . such as his mother, sister or brother or a very close friend." People are much less traumatized by the death of a secondary-group member than the death of a primary-group member, Athens believes; similarly the violent subjugation of someone cherished "deeply personalizes this experience and ultimately makes it exceedingly traumatic for the subject." The violent subjugator is usually someone from the subject's primary group as well, but may instead be someone from outside that intimacy. Personal horrification is typically (but not exclusively) a byproduct of the distrustful, resentful and frequently violent reactions that develop in disordered families.

Witnessing the violent subjugation of someone close to him throws the subject into a classic double bind—damned if he does, damned if he doesn't. First, Athens writes, the subject feels apprehensive as he detects "a nasty altercation" in progress (or soon to begin) and worries that an intimate may be physically injured. Once the assault commences, his worst fears are realized. Apprehension "gives way to strong feelings of anger toward the intimate's subjugator." He focuses on the assault; time seems to lag; he feels every blow. He begins to ask himself the question, "How much more can I let the victim endure before I do something?" and he soon answers, "No more":

> The wrath rapidly building up in the subject climaxes in an urgent and powerfully felt desire physically to attack the intimate's subjugator. This desire expresses itself in passing thoughts and fantasies about battering, torturing, maiming or killing the subjugator.
>
> However, the reality of actually physically attacking the intimate's subjugator, as opposed to merely contemplating it, quickly leads the subject to restrain his mounting fury. The subject swiftly weighs the chances of successfully prevailing in a physical altercation with the intimate's subjugator and the consequences to the subject should he fail. After soberly reflecting upon the chances of success and the personal risk involved, the subject's fear for himself steadily begins to override [his] fear for the intimate. The subject now finds himself trapped in an excruciatingly cruel dilemma not

of his own making. He is afraid of what will happen to the intimate if he fails to intercede personally and of what could happen to the subject himself if he does not intercede.

The subject decides that he is powerless to stop the violence he is witnessing—a decision that does not relieve but only transforms his "great mental anguish." The second part of the double bind emerges: "The subject is now overcome by feelings of impotence which make the earlier feelings of anger return. But this time the anger is directed more toward . . . himself than toward anyone else, while before it was directed exclusively at the intimate's subjugator." He directs his anger toward himself because he blames himself. He concludes "that it was his impotence rather than the subjugator's wickedness which was principally responsible for the episode of violent subjugation which he only a few moments ago stood by and witnessed. No matter how right or wrong his reasoning, the end result is the same: He feels intense shame."

Case 9, the boy who heard his mother being assaulted in her bedroom and who "kept telling myself that I was just a little sissy," is an example of personal horrification. Another case also illustrates the violent subjugation and personal horrification of an entire family:

CASE 22

My sister and I heard my older brother and stepfather arguing and got worried. Although my stepfather never hit my mother or sisters, he would hit my older brother and me. When we went into the living room to see what was going on, my stepfather had an electrical extension cord in his hand and was shouting, "I'm sick and tired of your smart-aleck talk, I'm going to beat your ass good, you damned punk." Then he started lashing my older brother with the extension cord. As he lashed him with the cord, he kept saying, "You damned punk, I am going to beat your ass for talking smart to me." I couldn't understand why my stepfather was beating him like this. My brother was crying and screaming for help, but my stepfather wouldn't stop lashing him with the cord. I thought my stepfather had gone straight off and lost his mind. He was swinging the cord wildly, hitting my brother all over—arms, legs, back and face. I couldn't stand to watch him do it. It seemed like he was never going to stop, and I got scared that he was going to hurt my brother bad. I yelled, "Stop hitting him, you are going to kill him. Stop, stop." When he wouldn't stop, I felt the anger explode inside me. I wanted to kill my stepfather. I thought about picking up something and hitting him with it, but then I got scared. I was scared that if I didn't kill him, he would go off on me like he was on my brother. I was mad at myself for wanting to do something to my stepfather but being too scared to do it. I didn't know what I should do.

I knew somebody had to do something fast, so I ran out looking for my mother. After I found her, we ran back into the living room and she said, "Don't you do that boy like that, stop whipping him right now." But my stepfather still wouldn't stop, even though it already seemed like he had lashed him with that cord for more than an hour. My stepfather had totally gone off, and my mother had to grab ahold of him before he would stop whipping my brother. Afterwards, my little brothers and sisters, who were sitting together crying and shaking, asked me, "Will he do us like that too?"

People commonly think that personal experience has more impact than vicarious experience, Athens writes, but both violent subjugation and personal horrification are traumatic. "The worst part of *both* these odious experiences is the twisted feelings and thoughts which can linger on in a disordered state long after the immediate experiences which generated them cease. Thus, although the experience of personal horrification may be less traumatizing than violent subjugation from a *physical* standpoint, it is not less traumatizing from a *psychological* standpoint."

Brutalization, even of a child, is not identical with child abuse. "Abuse" is a normative term, a value judgment, and not all Athens's subjects considered their brutalization abusive. An authority figure can sometimes violently subjugate someone who has undergone personal horrification at his hands simply with threats, without physical harm. Nor is brutalization a process that occurs exclusively within families. Peer groups can brutalize, as gangs do; brutalization frequently occurs in prisons among adolescent or even adult offenders; and violentization, including brutalization, is often a part of combat experience, as we will see.

Violent coaching is the third component of brutalization Athens identifies: The subject is assigned the role of violent novice by someone in his primary group, usually someone older, who appoints himself to the role of violence coach. The coaching is usually "informal and implicit rather than formal and explicit," but its intention—"prompting violent conduct"—"is plainly obvious to all."

Because violence coaches are related to the subject, older or more experienced, they believe that they have the right and even the obligation "to instruct the subject as to how he should or should not conduct himself in conflictive situations." A violence coach may be the subject's "father, stepfather, mother, uncle, older brother, grandfather, or [one of his] older, more worldly close friends." The subject may have more than one coach simultaneously or serially. "Thus, for example, a father may be aided in his coaching by his wife or an older sibling, or a stepfather or older close friend may later take over this role for a natural father, often with zest."

Not every authority figure is an effective violence coach. To be effective, a coach must be credible. "Since many people," Athens writes, "particularly men, often speak as if they are much more violent than they actually are, most people's violent proclamations are usually appropriately treated as idle boasts by others. Unless novices believe that their coaches will attack or in the past have physically attacked people, the novices will not take their coaches' exhortations very seriously. Thus, subjects must perceive their coaches as being or having been authentic violent actors at the time of their instruction."

Coaching teaches novices what they should do when people provoke them:

> Novices are taught that they should not try to pacify, ignore or run from their protagonist, but should physically attack them. Further, novices are taught to use at least enough force to ensure that they will prevail in an altercation, even if it means gravely harming the protagonist. Violent coaching is based upon the stated or unstated premise that the world is inhabited by many mean and nasty people, both inside and outside primary groups, and the novice must be properly prepared to deal with these people when he meets them.

> Novices are always taught that taking violent action against a protagonist "is a *personal responsibility* which they cannot evade, but must discharge regardless of whether they are a man or a woman, young or old, large or small, or what their prior beliefs about hurting others may have been." They are seldom taught specifically how to discharge their responsibility. "The emphasis of violent coaching is not upon supplying the know-how for gravely harming people but is upon conveying the realization that grave harm should be done to certain people."

Athens contrasts violent coaching with "learned helplessness"—the perception of helplessness found in, among others, battered women who passively continue in battering relationships—which he calls its "direct counterpart." Violent coaching, in contrast to learned helplessness, teaches subjects "to operate upon the directly opposite assumption that they should be forceful, dominant and self-reliant whenever another person transgresses upon them."

Coaches use a wide array of techniques. Athens identifies five such techniques and pairs each with the teaching principle it manifests.

Vainglorification glorifies violence through storytelling. The coach tells personal anecdotes about violent acts—his own or those of relatives or close friends. "The plots in these anecdotes follow a predictable course," Athens writes. "A 'good' person becomes entangled in a physical altercation with an 'evil' person; then the good person subjects the evil one to a decisive and humiliating, but well-deserved, defeat." The coach, of course, or the violent actor he is glorifying, is the hero, the victim the villain. More cryptic anecdotes present violent feats "*as if* they are well known to everyone." The moral of such stories is that violence offers glory, which is there for the novice to claim. Vainglorification is the least punitive of violent-coaching techniques; its teaching principle is vicarious enjoyment.

Ridicule promotes violence through belittling and derision. Invidious comparison between the coach (or his exemplary surrogate) and the novice is the commonest form of ridicule. The coach not only boasts of his violent feats but also mocks the novice for having none to brag about. "The implication which novices draw from these comparisons is clear," Athens writes: "They are not as worthy a person as the coach and thereby they deserve the derision." The teaching principle embodied in ridicule is torment. "If people are subjected to derision or the threat of it long enough because of their failure to perform some action, then the point will finally be reached where they will prefer to take that action rather than suffer further derision." Athens illustrates ridicule and other techniques of violent coaching in action in the recollection of a man in his mid-twenties incarcerated for armed robbery:

CASE 2

My father told me that there were two things I better always remember: "If you ever get into it with somebody, don't ever run, but stand there and fight. If something is worth fighting about, then it's worth killing somebody over. If you get into a fight with anybody, try to kill them. I don't care who it is—a man or a woman—pick up a stick, board, rock, brick or anything and hit them in the head with it. That way you won't have to worry about having any trouble from them later."

One day my father brought home some boxing gloves and told me to put a pair on. I thought we were only going to play. He started punching me and telling me to punch him back, but I could never reach him. He said, "You ain't shit, you little punk, come on, hit me, you ain't shit. Anybody could whip your ass. I'm going to get your cousin over here to whip your ass. He's twice as bad as you are." I felt frustrated and humiliated and started crying. My dad kept grinning, laughing and punching at me and calling me a little punk. Finally my grandmother heard me crying and came in and asked my father what he was doing. He said. "I'm trying to make him become a man and not a punk. Since I'm his father, I've got a right to make a man out of him any way I want."

Coercion is coaching through coercive violent subjugation. "Some coaches," Athens explains, "threaten novices not with psychological punishment, as in ridicule, but with physical punishment. . . . The coach bluntly informs the novice that unless he physically attacks his protagonist, the coach will physically attack the novice with a vengeance." The seeming choice is in fact a predicament: "certain defeat and sure physical harm at the hand of [the] coach or less certain defeat and thus only possible physical harm at the hands of some protagonist." Coercion's teaching principle, Athens observes, is old, simple and effective: fear. A young woman in her late teens convicted of criminal homicide illustrates:

CASE 38

My mother taught me to take up for myself when people bullied me or talked shit to me. She told me not to take any shit from anyone, and she didn't care who it was, a man or a woman. She said, "If people are fucking with you, then jump on their ass. Don't ask your brother to do it for you; you've got to do it for yourself. It doesn't make any difference if you are a man or a woman. You've got to fight for yourself and not expect other people to do it for you. If it comes down to kicking someone's ass, I want you to do it right, understand? You go on and straight beat the shit out of them. If you ever come home crying because somebody has jumped on you, I am going to whip your ass bad. Do you want me to jump on your ass or are you going to jump on the person's ass who fucked with you?"

I heard my mother talk this shit since I was little, but I couldn't bring it into play until I was older, in my teens. It didn't dawn on me until then to actually do what she said.

Haranguing is yet another technique violent coaches use to train novices: "The coach repeatedly rants and raves to them about hurting other people without ever belittling or threatening them or appealing to their pride, as in the previous techniques." The teaching principle involved, Athens writes, is *"incessant melodrama:* if someone is told something often enough and with enough force and conviction, then it cannot fail but convince them eventually." The coach, the novice comes to understand, believes that there are kinds of people, including the novice, who should assault people who provoke them. "A man should not back down from anybody," a teenage boy convicted of armed robbery quoted his father to Athens. "You can't depend on a man," a young woman convicted of criminal homicide quoted her mother and grandmother to Athens. "A woman has to act, not just react, when people mess with her." Hearing harangues so often, Athens found, novices notice that their coaches "derive a perverse sense of pleasure" from ranting and raving. Novices may practice the same behavior in pursuit of that pleasure, mimicking their coaches' conduct, "without at first understanding the real meaning of their violent proclamations."

Finally, besiegement combines all these techniques except haranguing. The coach mixes a "potent combination of social penalties and rewards to overwhelm the novice and overcome any reluctance on his part to engage in violence." Novices "are forced to endure the pain and anxiety of ridicule and coercion if they refuse to attack their protagonists physically, while they are offered certain relief from this pain and anxiety, as well as the added pleasure of vainglorification, if they do successfully attack them." The teaching principle manifested is overkill. Haranguing is excluded, Athens surmises, either because it's less efficacious and possibly even counterproductive compared to besiegement, or because haranguing and besieging are mutually exclusive coaching predilections.

Coaches and coaching regimens may change. "A stepfather may take over the coaching of a novice from an older brother who, in turn, may have taken over from the natural father. The subject's new coach may prefer the technique of, say, vainglorification, whereas the previous one may have preferred coercion." A coach may change his coaching technique, especially if it seems not to be working. A subject may have more than one coach at the same time, each using a different technique or mix of techniques.

No matter how many coaches and techniques a novice endures, violent coaching is not sufficient by itself to propel him completely through the brutalization stage. All three brutalizing experiences are necessary to complete brutalization: violent subjugation, personal horrification

and violent coaching. They do not have to be experienced simultaneously, Athens emphasizes, although subjugation and horrification
usually occur in close proximity. Coaching is more often separate, and
may even precede or follow subjugation and horrification. Finishing
brutalization may take "weeks, months or years," but most people
who complete the process, males in particular, do so by early adolescence. Having undergone an "odious and traumatic" as well as "chaotic"
brutalization, Athens concludes, they are left "in a confused, turbulent
condition." That condition prepares them for the next stages of the violentization process.

CHAPTER ELEVEN

The Creation of Dangerous Violent Criminals (II)

Brutalization, stage one of the four-stage developmental process Lonnie Athens calls violentization, leaves its victim "deeply troubled and disturbed." The victim—the subject—asks himself again and again why he should have been singled out for such treatment. "At odds with both himself and the world," Athens observes, "the beleaguered subject becomes unusually reflective." He compares the social ideals of school and church with the reality of his personal experience and "concludes that there is a huge gap between the ideal and the real way in which people interact." But, given the subject's circumstances, philosophic speculation is a luxury and soon yields to the more immediate question of what he should do about his anguished predicament:

> Experiences as odious and traumatic as those undergone during the brutalization stage are not easily banished. . . . To the contrary, they leave a dark and indelible imprint upon the mind, an imprint with which the subject must come to terms. The need for the subject to take stock and come to terms with the brutalization experience is not any different from the need of most people to take stock and come to terms with other agonizing experiences, such as the death of a loved one, the dissolution of a long and previously happy marriage or a prolonged bout of unemployment.

So the subject begins once again to brood, but this time "his brooding is done with an explicit purpose clearly in mind. He wants to distill from these three experiences [violent subjugation, personal horrification and violent coaching] their larger general meaning for his *future* relationships with other human beings." Each experience contributes a characteristic perspective. Violent subjugation "generates relatively enduring emotionally charged thoughts that combine a barely repressed sense of rage with vague notions about physically attacking other people." The subject overgeneralizes from his experience of subjugation to conclude that the future is filled with risk—"that he may always be plagued by violent subjugation from one person or another." Personal horrification adds a sense of powerlessness, turning his feelings inward. Since he was not able to protect his intimates, he concludes angrily, he must be worthless. Violent coaching adds humiliation to his conviction of worthlessness. "The question which has been in the back of his mind for some time," Athens writes, "and which only now moves to the forefront is: Why have I not done anything to stop my own and my intimates' violent subjugation?"

In the belligerency stage of violentization, the subject redirects that painful question from Why have I not? to What can I do? His problem "finally becomes fully crystallized in his mind," Athens comments. The subject understands clearly for the first time that he must find a way to stop people from brutalizing him. He also understands clearly for the first time the full import of the violent coaching he has received. It strikes him with the force of a revelation. "It is *as if* the subject had earlier been partly deaf and has only now heard what his coach had been telling him all along: Resorting to violence is sometimes necessary in this world."

The brutalized subject resolves to do just that—to use serious violence—but with an important qualification: He resolves to use serious violence only if he is seriously provoked and only if he thinks he has a chance of prevailing. This first mitigated violent resolution represents the completion of the belligerency stage.

For the brutalized subject to determine for the first time in his life "to attack other people physically who unduly provoke him, with the serious intention of gravely harming or even killing them," Athens writes, is a "deeply emotion-laden resolution." It springs from "the volcanic blending of the wrenching experiences of violent subjugation, personal horrification and violent coaching" that pushed the subject "to come to terms with his brutalization experience as a whole." Athens cites four cases to illustrate the belligerency stage. Three are substantially identical to the testimony of this late-teen male convicted of aggravated assault:

CASE 9*

I was tired of people putting their punk trips on me, calling me a "punk" and shoving me around. I didn't like people treading on me, and I wanted to scream at them, "Don't tread on me, don't tread on me." I was scared that people would be treating me like a punk all my life. I hated myself for letting people make me a punk. I was ashamed that I was a helpless crybaby who couldn't protect himself or his mother. I was being stomped into the ground both mentally and physically. I knew that I had to somehow dig myself out. I finally came to the conclusion one day that I was going to have to kick people's asses like I had been hearing from my step-father. I was down and determined not to let my stepfather or anyone else make me out as a punk. I was going to make sure that no one treated me like a punk any way that I could. I was not out to make other people punks, but nobody better try to make me out as one either. I had had it. This was it, the end of being a sissy punk for me. I wouldn't have ever wanted to hurt people bad if it wasn't for this punk stuff. It was what made me turn mean.

But it takes more than a violent resolution to become violent, Athens cautions at the beginning of his discussion of the third stage of violentization: violent performances. "Intentionally injuring another human being gravely for the very first time in one's life is not as casual a matter as those who have not seriously contemplated, much less performed, such action might believe." Many people make threats. Such threats are usually expressions of anger, not of serious violent intention. They "sometimes give the false impression that anyone who gets mad enough can kill someone no matter how meek and timid [he] may be." Fictional narratives—novels, movies, television dramas—frequently depict such unrealistic transformation, probably because the people who produce them have little or no personal experience of violence and the people who consume them enjoy vicariously slaying enemies without exposing themselves to personal risk. In fact, Athens concludes from personal experience as well as extensive investigation, it takes courage to cross that portentous barrier, because attacking someone with potentially deadly force puts the subject's own "physical safety, freedom and psycho-

---

* This case is part of a different series from the one that included the rapist previously cited as "Case 9," who recalled listening at night to his mother being sexually abused.

logical well-being" at risk. So the question the brutalized and newly belligerent subject now asks himself, Athens writes, is, "When the time finally comes, will I be able to hurt somebody bad or not?"

Because the answer to this question is still in doubt, the subject is not willing to attempt serious violence unless he is seriously provoked. Athens defines four degrees of provocation: none, minimal, moderate and maximum, and found that the violent criminals he interviewed had responded in their initial violent performances only to the two higher degrees of challenge: to moderate provocation, which he defines as actions that "purposely and cruelly antagonize the subject to the point of tormenting him," or to maximum provocation, which he defines as actions that "place the subject or someone about whom [he] cares in imminent danger." Even sufficient provocation may not ignite the subject to violent performance if circumstances are unfavorable—if, for example, he decides that he cannot possibly prevail "and becomes paralyzed by fear," if a third party intervenes or if his protagonist backs off. For these and other, similar reasons, Athens concludes, "the subject's [initial] violent performance is always problematic no matter how much he might be provoked."

The immediate outcome of the subject's initial violent performance is as influential as the degree of provocation. Athens parses the grammar of violent conflict to identify a range of possibilities. A subject can win a violent confrontation. He can lose. In a major victory he "scores a clear-cut win and in the process inflicts grievous injuries upon the protagonist." A major defeat is the reverse of a major victory, made decisive if the subject sustains grievous injury. Or the conflict might come to no decision or to a draw. These outcomes may be more common than clear-cut wins or losses. No decision results when the altercation is interrupted before it is clear who won or lost. When the altercation progresses to the point of decision but no winner or loser emerges—when both combatants have struck decisive blows and inflicted grievous injuries—it is a draw. Athens cites the report of a male in his mid-teens, imprisoned for aggravated assault, to demonstrate maximum provocation and a major victory:

CASE 13

My little brother and I were walking down to the store when this older guy came up to us. First he looked at my little brother and said, "I need some money, punk, give me some." Then he looked at me and said, "Man, your brother better give me some money." I didn't want my little brother to get hurt, so I said, "Go on home now, Tom. I'll take care of this." After I said that, Tom broke and ran. The guy then got mad and said, "Man, you shouldn't have told him that. He was supposed to give me some money." I said, "That's between you two," and he said, "No, now it's between us two," and shoved me. I knew this guy could stomp a mud hole in me if I fought him using only my knuckles because he was a lot bigger and older than me. After he shoved me, I pulled out a knife and surprised him. Before he could do anything else to me, I sliced him across the chest. When I saw the blood running out of his shirt, I got scared. I thought to myself, Oh no, I cut him bad. He might die. I've got to get the hell out of here fast. I threw the knife down on the ground and blew in the wind. As I ran, I kept thinking, Oh no, now I've killed somebody.

In contrast, the report of another male in his mid-teens convicted of aggravated assault illustrates moderate provocation and a major defeat:

CASE 21

I was playing pickup basketball in the school gym. The same guy on the other side kept guarding me when I had the ball. Every time I dribbled or took a shot, he was pushing or shoving me. I got mad and said, "Get the fuck off me, man." He said, "Tough, that's the way the game is played here." When he kept on doing it, I knew he was trying to fuck with me on purpose. He wasn't guarding me close, but playing dirty basketball. When he later knocked me down from behind, I got mad and said, "Man, you better stop fucking pushing me." He said, "Fuck you." I waited for him to do it again. As soon as he did, I turned around and hit him four or five times in the face, which made him fall down. When he got up, he ran and grabbed a folding chair and hit me across the arms and face with it, which knocked me off my feet. I was laying on the gym floor almost knocked out with my face cut wide open and my eyes swelling up. I never really knew before how bad you could get hurt in a fight with somebody.

A violent personal revolt is a special kind of violent performance, with higher stakes and little room for no-decision outcomes or draws. "In these performances," Athens writes, "the protagonist is always a current subjugator of the subject or of a loved one of the subject. Since the subject is seeking to thwart either his own or a loved one's violent subjugation, his act is one of outright defiance against a perceived evil oppressor." If the subject wins, oppression may cease, but he understands that if he loses, "his oppression may become far harsher." Case 9 in this second series of cases, the late-teen male convicted of aggravated assault, who "was tired of people putting their punk trips on me," described attempting an unsuccessful violent personal revolt against his stepfather. The boy tried to pull a knife from his dresser drawer when his stepfather attacked him after an argument. His stepfather kicked the drawer shut on his hand and slammed him against the wall. "He knocked the wind out of me, and I fell down on the floor gasping for air," he told Athens. "He stood over me glaring and said, 'You had enough yet, punk?' I said real low, 'Yes.' He said, 'Are you sure you had enough, punk?' I got my wind back and said, 'No, I'm not.' He said, 'Do you want some more of me, punk?' I quickly said, 'No, no, no.' "

Draws and violent performances that come to no decision leave subjects in limbo, but victories and defeats have important consequences. Victory raises the possibility of moving on to a further stage of violence development. Defeat, "especially several major defeats in a row," jeopardizes the subject's progression in violence. "He may completely question the wisdom of his earlier resolution to be violent and come to the conclusion that since he has little aptitude for violence, it was a mistake . . . to have ever made this resolution." If so, he may resign himself to nonviolence and the continued subjugation that it almost certainly entails.

But defeat may instead strengthen the subject's belligerency. Not doubting his resolution, he may instead question his aptitude and decide that his tactics have been wrong, concluding that he should avoid physical confrontations by resorting to more lethal violence more quickly. "Thus, bitter defeats at the hands of protagonists can have the paradoxical effect of making the subject more determined than ever to be violent." Case 21, defeated previously while playing pickup basketball, illustrates:

My girlfriend and I were at a pizza parlor that had a pool table. I started shooting pool with an older guy who was there, and my girlfriend sat in a nearby chair smoking cigarettes and watching us. While we were playing pool, I noticed that this guy kept checking out my girlfriend. She was sitting in her chair backwards, and he was staring a hole through her pants. I knew what he was thinking—This is one bitch I want to fuck bad. I tried to get his mind off her and back on pool, but he kept staring hard at her pants and shaking his head. So I let him know that she was my girlfriend, but he wouldn't take the hint and kept staring at her ass and shaking his head. The next thing I knew he walks right up to her and straight out says, "You sure got a real nice big ass." When she didn't say anything back to him, he said, "You know, you ought to leave that little young asshole and go out with me." I was getting really pissed off now, but before I could say or do anything, he reached down and squeezed her ass. When he did that, she jumped out of her chair and said, "Get your hands off my ass." He said, "Fuck you, you dirty little rag," and she said, "Get out of my face."

I got mad as fucking hell then. First he won't stop checking out her body in front of me, next he makes the remark about her ass, then he squeezes her ass, and now he calls her a rag. After he called her a rag, that was it for me. He had now finally gone too far, so I grabbed a pool stick, tightened my grip around the thick part as hard as I could and swung it with all my might at his head. I broke the thin part of it across the side of his head, which knocked him off his feet. Then I quickly turned the stick around, jumped on top of him and started smashing him in the head with the thick end of the stick. I was fucking up the guy bad, blood was pouring out all over his head, neck and shoulders. Everybody in the pizza parlor then started screaming. "He's gone crazy, he's gone completely crazy. Call the police." My girlfriend started yelling at me, "Stop, stop, stop. You're going to kill him." I threw the bloody pool stick down on the floor, grabbed her by the hand and we ran out the door.

Successful violent performances may follow any number of draws and no decisions, minor defeats, even major defeats. But a notable violent performance will not *"by itself* have any lasting or significant impact" on the subject, Athens emphasizes. For lasting impact the subject needs to comprehend the full significance of his success. "The job of impressing the subject with the full significance of his successful violent action is gladly performed by other people who, for whatever reason, always seem to take a perverse interest and pleasure in violence—all the more so when they know the offender or victim."

The word goes out. Parents, brothers, sisters, neighbors, friends, acquaintances, school officials, police, prosecutors and judges all may become involved in assessing the significance of the violent performance. Primary group members have more influence than secondary group members, but the two groups' opinions reinforce each other:

The subject becomes conscious that other people's opinions of him have suddenly and drastically changed in the wake of his violent feat. . . . They see him as a very different person. Somewhat to the subject's amazement, he is now seen as an authentically violent individual, instead of a person who was not violent or only possibly capable of violence only a few short days or even hours earlier.

At least some of the people in the subject's primary groups see him not only as violent, but to his great astonishment, as *mentally unbalanced* as well. For the first time in his life, he hears people describe him in complete seriousness . . . as a "violent lunatic," "violent maniac," "violent crazy man," "madman" or "insane killer." . . . Such terms are not always pejorative, since acting crazily may only demonstrate that one has real daring and pluck, which, to members of some primary groups, is a positive rather than negative attribute.

Such opinions about his sanity may disturb the subject. He may also be puzzled to discover that members of his primary group (sometimes including his violence coaches) whom he took to be supporters of his acting violently "now suddenly begin hedging their support." They may do so—and label him crazy—because they believe he went too far.

People now begin to treat him differently. "People treat him as if he literally were *dangerous*. They act toward him much more cautiously, taking particular pains not to offend or provoke him in any way." When he approaches, they show apprehension. The emergence of that response "marks both the climax to the subject's experience of violent notoriety and the dawning of a new experience: *social trepidation*." Violent notoriety and the resulting social trepidation carry the subject to a critical point:

The subject must now decide whether to embrace or reject this personal achievement of sorts. The answer to this question presents the subject with a paradox. On the one hand, notoriety denotes being well-known for something bad. On the other hand, it is sometimes better to be well-known for something which most people think is bad and few think is good than not to be known for anything at all. Although the advantages may not be well recognized, being known as dangerous does have its advantages. The subject is afforded greater power over his immediate social environment. Since other people begin to think twice before provoking him, the subject can freely interact with other people without worrying as much about provoking them, so that for the first time he may feel liberated from the violent oppression of others. Moreover, painful memories of feeling powerless and inadequate originally aroused during his brutalization and later his belligerence experiences still linger in the back of the subject's mind. This cannot help but make his newly discovered sense of power almost irresistible. Thus, the subject's answer to the question of whether to embrace or reject the violent notoriety is virtually a foregone conclusion.

Athens does not use the word, but what he is describing here is a familiar phenomenon in contemporary America: celebrity. And as with celebrity in other lines of work, he proceeds to show, violent notoriety goes to the subject's head. The newly violent subject "undergoes a drastic change." He becomes "overly impressed with his violent performances and ultimately with himself in general. Filled with feelings of exultancy, he concludes that since he performed this violent feat, there is no reason why he cannot perform even more impressive violent feats in the future. The subject much too hastily draws the conclusion that he is now invincible." His notoriety at the same time makes it unlikely that others will disabuse him of that conclusion. He becomes increasingly pugnacious, "to the point where he will without the slightest hesitation strongly rebuke anyone who would foolishly criticize him."

He proceeds to make a new violent resolution, far more encompassing than his previous mitigated commitment: "He now firmly resolves to attack people physically with the serious intention of gravely harming or even killing them for the slightest or no provocation whatsoever." Such a resolution moves him from defense to offense. "The subject is determined not to tolerate any provocation from other people and, should the whim strike him, to provoke other people. He has suddenly been emboldened and made venomous at the same time." His new malevolence—not an inevitable outcome, Athens emphasizes, but a decision and a choice—is freighted with irony: "He has now gone full circle from a hapless victim of brutalization to a ruthless aggressor—the same kind of brutalizer whom he had earlier despised." Not that he notices, or that it would matter if he did. Moving to unmitigated violent resolution completes the last of the four stages of violentization: virulency. "The subject is ready to attack people physically with the serious intention of gravely harming or killing them with minimal or less than minimal provocation on their part." That is, he is ready to become an ultraviolent

criminal. The testimony of a male in his mid-teens most recently convicted of aggravated assault illustrates these transitions:

CASE 33

After I busted that dude's head open, the principal kicked me out
of school for the rest of the year. The students all spread around
that I had fucked up a dude real bad and sent him to the hospital,
so the principal had to get rid of me. Everybody, my people and
close friends, thought I had gone too far on the dude. They
thought he deserved an ass-kicking from me, but not to be put in
the hospital. They said, "You shouldn't have done him like that.
You went too far." It tripped me out as much as them that I could
hurt somebody that bad.

But nobody in the school or around my neighborhood would
fuck with me after that. People said, "James is crazy. Don't go
heads up with a dude like that because he will fuck you up." Most
people made sure that they gave me plenty of space and stayed
mellow around me. They paid me more respect and said "Hi" to
me when I walked by.

People may have thought I went too far on that dude, but I later
knew what I did was right. It must have been right because nobody
was giving me any shit any more. They didn't want to take a
chance of going up against me and having the same thing happen
to them. Before I put that big dude in the hospital, they would say
things like, "James talks a lot of shit, but I bet he is not really bad." I
showed them I was not all talk. I proved that I might not be big, but
dynamite can come in small packages.

The way people acted made me come alive. It swelled up my
head. I said to myself, "If I put that big dude's ass in the hospital,
then I could put any other dude on the street there too." If any
motherfucker out there talked or even looked at me wrong, I was
ready to walk right up on him and see if he wanted to give me
some. I was ready to throw down with everything I had. If a
motherfucker loses his teeth, then he lost some teeth. If he loses
his eye, then he lost an eye, and if he loses his life, then he lost a life.
It didn't matter to me. The way I looked at it was that is just one
less motherfucker this world will have to put up with.

The "proverbial violent outcast and loner" of American folklore
emerges in these late stages of violentization, Athens observes, because
the people close to him begin to avoid him to escape feeling physically

intimidated. He may remain socially isolated as a result, or he may find "that he is now a welcome and desired companion among malevolent groups for whom having violent repute is a social requirement."

Athens's four-stage violentization process is more immediately credible than other explanations of the development of violent criminality because Athens founded it on actual study of real social experiences. The causes of violence have become problematic in American society partly because psychiatric, psychological and other sociological explanations can be mysterious and often defy common sense. Juries have great difficulty believing that brutal murders might be manifestations of drug- or passion-induced temporary insanity or exculpated by a history of childhood abuse. If lack of personal exposure to violence or lack of knowledge of someone's personal history leads many Americans to credit the idea that people "just snap," many others are understandably skeptical of such attributions.

Violentization is an authentic developmental process, and unless someone has undergone it, Athens emphasizes, he will not become a dangerous violent criminal:

> The mere entrance into any one stage does not guarantee the completion of that stage, much less the completion of the process as a whole. The completion of each stage is contingent upon the person fully undergoing all the experiences that comprise that stage, and the completion of the process as a whole is contingent upon the person undergoing all the stages. . . . Any person who does ultimately complete the virulency stage, and consequently the entire experiential process, will become a dangerous violent criminal. This remains the case regardless of the social class, race, sex or age and intelligence level of people, as long as their degree of mental and physical competence is sufficient for them to perform a violent criminal act.

Immediately, seeming exceptions spring to mind—"good" children from "good" families, according to relatives, friends, neighbors or reporters, who "must have been bad seed" or who "just lost it." Athens avers to the contrary that "people who commit heinous violent crimes always have some violence-related experiences in their backgrounds, although [such experiences] may sometimes be deeply hidden from others and not apparent without a thorough and painstaking investigation of their biographies." Official records are notoriously inaccurate, he notes. People frequently lie to pollsters about such minor questions as whether or how they voted. Why would they be more likely to admit to official investigators or journalists that they have brutalized or undergone brutalization?

Unlike child abuse, which is almost exclusively identified with violence within families, violentization may develop in other primary groups, such as gangs, with little or no family participation. "Some very dangerous violent criminals," Athens writes, "refrain from taking violent action against their primary group members," and even within families, violentization is selective—Pete the Greek singled out Athens's brother Rico and Athens himself and spared their younger sisters violent subjugation, although the Athens girls experienced a full measure of personal horrification.

This selectiveness also explains one of the enduring mysteries of criminal violence: why so many fewer violent criminals are women than men. Besides their smaller average size, which makes the success of their initial violent performances more problematic, women are evidently discriminated against as candidates for violent coaching, if you will, just as they are discriminated against in other athletic, social and employment selection processes dominated by men, simply because they are female.

Violentization is transmitted experientially across generations, Athens observes, as the brutalized evolve into brutalizers, ensuring "that we always have a plentiful supply of new candidates to replace those who lose their lives, are sent to prison or possibly undergo maturational reform." But he emphasizes that transmission is not inevitable. The process from start to finish may take years or run its course in a matter of months (Athens calls such a compressed sequence, which his interviews support but do not directly demonstrate, a cataclysmic experience). It may be interrupted, sometimes for long periods. Women who become dangerously violent generally complete the process much later than men. The men whom Athens studied had typically entered belligerency "just prior to their teens, with at least some completing [violentization] before their mid or late teens." Nor does it always follow convention:

Just as people who have never read a physics book do not make earth-shattering discoveries in physical science, people who have never had any prior violence-related experiences whatsoever do not suddenly commit heinous violent crimes. Nevertheless, in crime as in science, people may exhibit real creative leaps in their thinking, feelings and conduct, although these leaps do not come entirely out of the blue because their past experiences make these leaps possible.

Athens emphasizes and reemphasizes that violentization is a social process, requiring interaction with others, and that as such it changes over time. Psychological processes are obviously involved in the conversion of a brutalized novice into a dangerous violent criminal, but these do not harden into enduring psychological traits:

> Psychologists have been caught up for over half a century in a rather vain quest to discover the psychological traits which distinguish violent and nascent violent criminals from ordinary people. This quest has been stymied in no small part because the psychological traits, or more precisely, psychological processes, which violent criminals manifest do not remain constant, but change as they undergo new social experiences over the course of their violence development.

Low self-esteem, Athens cites as an example, is frequently evoked to explain criminal violence. Subjects certainly suffer from low self-esteem during the early stages of violentization, he concedes, but "should they later reach the final stage, virulency, they will suffer from exactly the reverse problem—unrealistically too high self-esteem to the point of arrogance." To argue that such arrogance is merely a mask for low self-esteem is to deny the evidence to salvage dogma.

Not poverty or genetic inheritance or psychopathology but violentization is the cause of criminal violence. Athens offers abundant data but no numbers or control groups to support this conclusion because he is not pursuing statistical correlations (which can never, by definition, prove anything) but looking for universals—for processes that account for *every instance* of a phenomenon. His method—looking for what all his cases had in common that differed from what nonviolent cases revealed—used to be called the "method of universals" and has come to be called "analytic induction." Athens found support for using it, among other places, in the work of Alfred Lindesmith, a distinguished American sociologist best known for having used the same method to identify the unique social process whereby people become addicted to opiates, reported in his often-cited 1957 book *Opiate Addiction*.

Lindesmith defended analytic induction eloquently in a 1979 lecture.

"A cause must be thought of as a process," he argued—"not as a condition, variable, thing or event." To illustrate the point he reviewed the late-nineteenth-century discovery of the cause of malaria. In the jargon of quantitative sociology, Lindesmith tweaked his statistically minded colleagues, that historic and fundamental discovery would be simply "an instance of the verification of a non-quantitative theory by a 'soft' qualitative methodology," a merely "verbal" theory. Diseases, he reminded them ironically, are generally identified that way.

The discovery of the cause of malaria began in the observations of a French surgeon, Alphonse Laveran, working at a military hospital in Algeria. Laveran noticed that one of the crescent-shaped, pigmented bodies commonly seen under the microscope in the blood of malaria patients and previously believed to be a pathological product of the disease was wriggling and thrashing—was thus a living organism, a parasite. There was much debate about Laveran's observation, since the parasites did not always turn up in blood samples of malaria victims. More work was necessary to connect the parasite with its carrier, the female Anopheles mosquito. Eventually the complex causal process was sorted out: An infected female mosquito bites a victim and injects anticoagulant saliva to prevent the victim's blood from clotting. The parasites in the mosquito's saliva, called sporozoites, thus enter the bloodstream, quickly find their way to the liver and leave the blood to hide out there (which is why they do not always turn up in blood samples). In the liver they multiply repeatedly to form spores called merozoites. After nine or ten days the merozoites burst the liver cells and emerge to invade red blood cells and continue dividing, devouring hemoglobin and repeating the cycle. After several such cycles, some merozoites develop into male or female forms that invade red blood cells and wait for the next mosquito to bite. If ingested by a passing mosquito, they give birth to thousands of sporozoites. These offspring take up residence in the mosquito's salivary glands, ready to be injected into the next victim and carry the process on.

The parasite alone does not qualify as the cause of malaria, Lindesmith points out, because its presence alone does not always produce the disease—it doesn't produce the disease in the mosquito, for example. It can occupy the human liver for years without producing symptoms. And there are people with acquired immunity or protective mutations who can carry the parasite without suffering from the disease themselves. Rather than attributing the cause of malaria simply to the parasite, Lindesmith proposes, it would be more logical to think of the cause "as a unique, complex set of interactional processes involving very large numbers of essential conditions, factors or variables":

> In its initial stages such a unique set of interactions is commonly a non-obvious or subsurface one that has to be discovered. As the causal process in malaria runs its course it reaches a point where it is called the disease or a part of it. If this process is interrupted early, we say the disease has been *prevented;* if it is interrupted at a later stage, we say the disease has been *cured.* Since the cause continues during the disease and is a constituent part of it, it is not correct to say that the cause is simply an antecedent item in a sequence of events. There is no precise point at which one can say with assurance that the cause has given way to the effect. Physicians have suggested that a person has malaria [in the presence of the parasite] when his temperature first rises above 100 degrees, or, alternatively, when relatively large numbers of parasites first appear in his blood.

Laveran, Lindesmith points out in defense of analytic induction, "was *one* man seeing *one* parasite in *one* blood sample"—not a research team finding statistical correlations in thousands of data points in a database, with an equally numerous control group. For that observation he won a well-deserved Nobel Prize. Scientists do not find the causes of diseases—or of physical or chemical phenomena, for that matter—with statistics (although statistics may help narrow the possibilities). The critical factor in analytic induction as a scientific method is not the number of cases, Lindesmith concludes, but "what was learned from them and whether they are exemplary specimens of a specific kind or category of phenomena."

When Athens's quantitative colleagues discount his findings on the grounds that he observed only fifty or one hundred cases, they imply that some higher but arbitrary number of cases is sufficient for proof. Analytic induction, the method of universals, demands a far more rigorous standard of proof than does statistical correlation: *Every* case, every exemplary specimen, must demonstrate the same causative process. If a single case turns up that does not fit the pattern, then the pattern is inadequately derived. That rigorous standard of proof has a positive side. It allows science to learn by experience, to correct itself by adjusting for new evidence. Laveran's identification of a parasite as the "cause" of malaria when that parasite did not always appear in the blood of known malaria cases is a good example. The parasite theory had to be widened to account for the parasite's absence. Finding it hiding out in the liver explained why it was missing from the blood—and added an important new component to the theory. Athens was satisfied with his theory only when he had found what *all* his cases had in common that nonviolent criminals and individuals did not share. What all his cases had in common was a developmental process requiring brutalization, belligerency, violent performances and virulency: violentization.

But all Athens's cases are contemporary with his research. He has not reported other cases. Is violentization evident in cases outside Athens's review? Does it reveal itself in familiar cases such as that of Perry Smith in Truman Capote's *In Cold Blood*, or that of Lee Harvey Oswald? Does it apply to criminal violence in other times and places? Does it apply in cultures other than the contemporary United States? Is it, indeed, a universal explanation for seriously violent individual human behavior? After interviewing Athens at length and thoroughly exploring his work, I set out to answer these questions. I was astonished by what I found.

PART II

THE CIVILIZING
PROCESS

One of the most fundamental developments of Western civilization [is] the millennial transition from anomic violence to regulated violence, the passage from private vengeance, private warfare, and makeshift compromises devoid of guarantees, to a gradual acceptance of the king's justice as the sole locus of arbitral power which delivers his subjects from the scourge of the never-ending round of violence and private revenge.

—Alfred Soman, "Deviance and Criminal Justice in Western Europe, 1300–1800"

CHAPTER TWELVE

Cheryl Crane

To be universal, the four-stage violentization process Lonnie Athens extracted from his exemplary collection of cases ought to apply to other violent careers as well. But just as the causes of disease could only be identified when investigators asked the right questions and looked in the right places for evidence, so also does finding violentization in a specific case require an accurate and sufficiently detailed biography. People accused or even convicted of violent crimes do not often willingly provide such potentially compromising information. Even when they are prepared to be candid about their own experiences, they may choose to conceal or distort information about people close to them who may have been involved in their brutalization or their violence.

Fortunately, the available records of a number of well-known cases are sufficiently accurate and complete to support exploring them for evidence of violentization. Other cases with incomplete records may reveal at least some elements of the process Athens discovered. Examining such cases, complete or incomplete, tests the authority of Athens's theory and sheds light on violent actions that have previously seemed mysterious or unaccountable.

Cheryl Crane, one such case, was the daughter of the prominent mid-century movie actress Lana Turner and restaurateur Stephen Crane. In a notorious Hollywood scandal, when Cheryl Crane was fourteen years old, she stabbed to death her mother's lover Johnny Stompanato with a butcher knife. A coroner's jury found Crane's act of homicide justifiable; she testified that she had believed Stompanato was attacking her mother when she entered her mother's bedroom to defend her. In 1988 Crane published a memoir, *Detour: A Hollywood Story,* written with Cliff Jahr, in which she describes her childhood experiences in detail.

Turner, a platinum blond all-American beauty in the tradition of Jean Harlow, married and divorced frequently. Between marriages she took numerous lovers. "I am lonely unless I have someone to love," she once told an interviewer. She had been an impoverished, neglected child. Turner's mother, whom Crane called "Gran," was an Arkansas-born farm girl, one of twelve children, who eloped to Wallace, Idaho, two days before her sixteenth birthday with a blond Alabaman miner, gambler and bootlegger six years her senior named Virgil Turner. "Lana"—Julia Jean, called Judy—was born a year later. The marriage was turbulent; Gran regularly ran away from Virgil with Judy in tow, riding trains until she was broke and then calling Virgil to pick her up. She told her granddaughter she ran away because she was bored. When Judy was seven, her parents divorced in San Francisco. Gran became a beautician, Crane writes, and boarded Judy out "in a series of unhappy foster homes." The worst, in Modesto, was run by friends:

> On one of Gran's Sunday afternoon visits to Modesto, she discovered bruises and cuts on her daughter's body where she had been beaten with a stick. They both returned to San Francisco that day, ending two terrible years that Mother had endured in silence because she had been threatened with more beatings if she complained. "Your mother's coming," she remembers her foster parents saying. "Keep your mouth shut."

Judy's neglect also reduced her to begging for food when Gran was unemployed. Her father was robbed and bludgeoned to death on his way home from a crap game when she was nine. More foster homes followed, then an apartment Gran shared with the woman who owned the beauty shop where she worked. Eventually mother and daughter moved to Los Angeles—characters, Crane observes, out of Nathanael West's *The Day of the Locust,* "people who simply did not fit in anywhere else [and who] came to California in search of magic." The publisher of a Hollywood tabloid discovered Judy Turner at a soda shop in Hollywood when she was fifteen. She had developed early, Crane notes, with "thick reddish hair, gray eyes, pouty lips, fair skin and [a] perfectly proportioned figure." Fame and fortune followed, although the movie star always spent everything she earned.

Crane was Lana Turner's only child, born in 1943. Turner kept her distance from her daughter, raising her through nannies and governesses. Crane describes an early assault her mother herself recalled:

> She decided one Sunday afternoon, Nana's day off, to give me a bath. It was around the time of my first birthday and the very first time the two of us had ever been alone together. Nana had given her pointers, but the task both terrified and exasperated Mother. She remembers losing her temper in the struggle with a soapy squirming baby, when her hands slipped and all of a sudden she realized she was clutching me by the throat.
>
> "I gasped," Mother recalls in her autobiography, *Lana*. "I dropped [Cheryl] on a side table and, though she was sopping wet, pulled her up close to me, saying, 'Cherry, Cherry, I didn't mean it.' Almost like a grownup, [Cheryl] pulled away from me, then looked me straight in the face and laughed." The incident ended happily in hugs, but afterward Mother couldn't help feeling "as though I had been through a contest of some kind."

Denial of violent intention ("her hands slipped and all of sudden she realized") despite anger ("She remembers losing her temper") turns out to be an attitude Crane shares with her mother.

"By age four," Crane writes,

> when I sometimes began to be presented to her on sets or at home in the barroom, I knew the rules. I had been warned. As I was handed up for a careful hug and peck, lips never touched lips, skin hardly touched skin. It was for show, a "cocktail kiss" like a half-slide down the jungle gym. I knew never to touch pretty Mommy, her hair, her makeup, her dress. . . . "The hair," she would say flatly if it seemed I was about to forget. "Sweetheart, the lipstick."

Crane remembers "obey[ing] authority so readily that I seemed downright meek. To Mother's friends, I was an automaton child, shy, polite and solemn. 'Too grown-up,' they said. Photos of me after the age of two show an unsure little person who *never* smiled." She characterizes her childhood as "loveless."

In 1948, when Crane was five, Turner married a wealthy Easterner named Henry J. "Bob" Topping, heir to an industrial and tobacco fortune, who lived in Greenwich, Connecticut. Soon Crane had agreed to call Topping "Papa," though never "Daddy," a name reserved for her natural father. The Toppings eventually moved to Bel Air so that Turner could revive her flagging movie career. Topping's money, tied up in trusts, was not sufficient to sustain their extravagance, and Turner began supporting the household. The marriage soured. When Crane's father was badly injured in an automobile accident in Paris, Topping cruelly and vindictively informed his stepdaughter that "Daddy" had been killed. Word from Gran a few days later that Daddy was coming home sent Crane into hysterics.

She was obviously lonely and neglected. If her brutalization had not already begun at her mother's hands, Topping certainly began it:

> Papa had a low boiling point, and once I watched, aghast, as he beat with a cane the boxer dog he had given me. Another time he threw my poodle, Tinkette, against a wall. He and Mother had grown chilly with each other at cocktail hour, and recently I had been startled by the sound of a crash from downstairs. He had hurled a Baccarat decanter at [actress] Kathryn Grayson's head. Fortunately, he missed, shattering the bar mirror. The sound of fighting and slamming doors was increasingly common in their wing of the house.

These events qualify as personal horrification. It is unlikely that so incendiary a man would beat Crane's dogs and terrorize her mother without also violently subjugating her, but Crane chooses not to discuss that aspect of her relationship with her stepfather. Further horrification followed when Turner announced that she intended to divorce Papa Bob and that same night "swallowed sleeping pills and slashed two tendons in her wrist with a razor in a feeble attempt to kill herself." She survived, divorced Topping and took up with the B-movie actor Fernando Lamas, whom Crane remembers primarily for exhibiting himself to her one day and thereafter swimming naked in her presence when the two of them were alone.

Turner's next conquest provided Crane with extended experience of violent subjugation. Lex Barker, who had replaced Johnny Weissmuller as Tarzan in the late 1940s, courted and married Turner after she broke up with Lamas. He was a handsome, well-buffed Phillips Exeter and Princeton graduate from a socially prominent family in Rye, New York, divorced from a New York debutante, with two children of his own. Turner and Barker moved to London after their marriage to save on taxes, taking Crane and Gran along. By then Crane was ten years old and nearly as tall as her mother. When Turner proposed sending her to a

Swiss boarding school and sending Gran back to California with Barker's children, she rebelled. "If Gran leaves me here," she told her mother, "I will run away." Turner capitulated and allowed Crane to return to the United States with Gran, but on the way to the airport in Barker's Jaguar, Turner attacked her mother to punish her obstinate daughter:

> "Y'know, Mother," she suddenly said to Gran. "You've had it pretty soft all these years. I've looked after you, supported you—well, I've *had* it. You're not getting another dime from me. When you get back to L.A., you better get yourself a job."
>
> I spun around.
>
> "You just look straight ahead, young lady, and mind your own business."
>
> Gran burst into tears and covered her face as Mother harangued her all the way to the airport. Everyone solemnly studied the road. She accused Gran of using people, of taking from them and being selfish. I was screaming inside, *You're the one that uses and you're the one that's selfish—I hate you I hate you I hate you.* That moment I vowed to myself that I would never again call her Mommy.

Two days before Christmas 1953, the Barkers returned to Hollywood. Crane remembers withdrawing socially that winter because she "feared Mother's power to control me and exploit my adoration." She thought she struck people as "a pretty cold kid." Her classmates at school noticed the change in her; "some of them," she writes, "spoke to me as if we had never met before."

The following March, sitting alone beside the swimming pool at their Holmby Hills estate, Crane looked up to see Barker standing at the top of the garden steps wrapped in a towel, staring at her. "He was Tarzan, all right," she remembers thinking, "except for the sunglasses. At six feet four inches and 200 pounds, he dwarfed Uncle Fernando." He descended to the sauna room and invited her inside. "I want to show you something," he told her.

Inside he groped her breasts and her crotch through her bathing suit, exhibited himself (he introduced his penis as "Mr. Rabbit"), informed her that it was a father's duty to teach his girls about men and forced her to watch him masturbate. "I was growing rigid with fear," Crane recalls, "digging my nails in the bench. With his eyes fixed on my stomach, he began to pump away at himself, slowly at first, his mouth finally going twitchy and slack until, with a buck and a grimace and a moan, he ejaculated on the floor." She wanted to run. He cleaned himself with a towel, warned her to keep what had happened secret and walked out. She ran to her room and "put it from my mind. What had happened had not happened." She got out her dolls, including a handmade miniature of her mother, and pretended to have a tea party.

A year passed before Barker visited her again. This time he slipped into her bedroom at eight o'clock at night and raped her:

> "Remember Mr. Rabbit?" he asked. I squeezed my eyes shut. A hand tunneled under my nightie to wait between my legs. I stifled an urge to scream. Suddenly I felt a frightening jab. I sprang up, arms thrashing, my voice gasping to cry out, but he got his hand around my throat and threw me back. In another instant, the nightie was pulled away, my knees yanked wide, and with a bolt of pain he heaved his 200 pounds into the core of my loins.
>
> I choked. Was he going to kill me? I couldn't breathe. The pain was more than any I had ever known. Finally he released an anguished moan in my ear and collapsed.

Having taken her virginity, Barker then threatened her. " 'You know what they do to girls who tell, don't you?' he said. 'Girls who tell *anyone* what we just did? They take you away and you never see your parents again. They send you to a place called Juvenile Hall. . . . So if you ever want to see your mother again, or your grandmother, or your father, or your dog, or your goldfish or anything else, you'd better keep your mouth shut.' "

He raped her again a week later. She was humiliated and frightened. She had nightmares. "I was ten-and-a-half, going on eleven," she recalls. "I had never been able to make even the simplest decisions about myself, and now I realized that I had lost control of my body as well. I did not even own my insides. My stepfather did." Across the next two years Barker raped her about a dozen times. One particularly brutal assault followed their return from the hospital where Turner was recovering from a miscarriage. Sometimes he snatched at her genitals when her mother was in the room looking the other way: "He was so confident I wouldn't tell—and I wouldn't—yet part of me wanted Mother to spin around and catch us so I could face the terrible consequences and Lex would finally be stopped."

Crane whispered her horror to trusted classmates in the school where she boarded and learned from them that Juvenile Hall wasn't hell, and that even consenting sex with an underage girl was statutory rape.

Armed with that knowledge she tried to put off Barker's next attack with threats. He brutally escalated the assault:

> His forearm came up and smashed across my face. I blacked out for an instant, waking to feel warm blood in my mouth and hands choking my throat. "You're gonna show me, huh?" he yelled. *"You little bitch!"* And with that he plowed into me with a punishing anger. I fought not to black out again. What was happening was happening, and I was furious. I tried to scream, but he kept a hand grabbed around my throat and I couldn't breathe, even to gasp. *Is he killing me? Am I dying?* I wondered. My arms were useless as flippers, and I had no air, no voice, not even nails to scratch him. His orgasm brought an ecstatic hiss of rage that died off in waves. I breathed gulps of life as he rolled back and headed toward the door. "Remember—trap *shut*," he warned as he left.

Back at school she determined to tell Gran. Gran took her to her mother. Turner refused to believe her until she reported all the brutal details. The actress told her daughter later that she stood over her husband's sleeping form that night with her revolver in hand and came close to killing him—but restrained herself for fear of ruining her career. The statement qualifies as violent coaching, although Crane does not report how credible she found it. Turner did muster enough courage to throw Barker out the next morning. The following day he found mother and daughter leaving for a dental appointment and tried to stop them by holding on to the door of Turner's car; she hit the accelerator, dragging him along, hit the brakes to shake him loose and roared away.

Evidently Turner continued to suspect Crane of seducing Barker despite her daughter's detailed recounting. Drunk one day a few months after her divorce from Barker (who was never charged), she accused Crane of making a play for her new boyfriend, accused her further of having done so before and viciously slapped her. "She meant Lex," Crane protests:

> She meant that I had flirted with Lex, that I had seduced him! Had he not battered and choked and raped me bloody? But she did not believe me after all! And now she thought I was vying with her for Michael Dante! Sinking to a sofa, I wept as she stood above me and ranted. I was boy crazy, she screamed. I was running wild and bound to get a reputation. My denials were futile. I hardly had breath to speak.

On her way back to school by taxi, Crane decided to run away. After an evening on the streets she ended up in detention—at Juvenile Hall. Her mother retrieved her and raged at her some more. She retaliated that night by stealing a handful of Nembutals from Turner's nightstand, but fell asleep while waiting until her mother retired to take them. Ironically Turner was preparing that season for a major role in *Peyton Place*.

John Stompanato, a small-time con man, nominally the owner of a gift shop, made his living courting and bilking rich women. "He was handsome in an oily kind of way," Crane characterizes him, noting his "dark good looks, stealthy movements, watchful eyes and deep baritone." He was known around Hollywood, she says, "for the Academy-Award size of his phallus, which had earned him the nickname 'Oscar.'" He had recently divorced a B-movie actress, Helen Stanley, who charged him during divorce proceedings with attempting to strangle her mother for mislaying his handkerchiefs. This malefic paragon, an ex-Marine who had been one of mob boss Mickey Cohen's bodyguards, gave Crane a horse and taught her to ride in the course of seducing her mother.

While Crane practiced adolescent rebellion at a progressive private school in Ojai, Turner and Stompanato flew off to London for principal photography on a movie in which Turner would star with a new male lead, twenty-six-year-old Sean Connery. Stompanato wanted Turner to finance and star in a movie he hoped to produce; her refusal to countenance the possibility led to frequent arguments. When Stompanato heard rumors that Turner was sleeping with Connery, he hijacked her limousine, burst onto the sound stage at Pinewood Studios and threatened Connery with a gun. Connery decked him. "After he lost the confrontation with Connery," Crane reports, "his frustration with Mother boiled over." At home in Hampstead, in the midst of yet another argument, Stompanato attacked Turner, "knocked her around" and tried to smother her with a pillow. A maid who heard her screams may have saved her life. Her larynx was bruised in the encounter. When she went to work the next morning, Turner told an associate producer who was a friend about the assault. He alerted Scotland Yard, which deported Stompanato the same day.

Back in the States, Crane attended the premiere of *Peyton Place* before traveling to London for Christmas with her mother. "Two of the film's subplots," she writes, "might have been lifted right from my life. One concerned a man's repeated rape of his stepdaughter (who in desperation clubs him to death), while the other involved a youngish mother (Mother) and her rebellious daughter (played by Diane Varsi)." After the premiere, Crane says, "I couldn't get *Peyton Place* out of my mind." The movie mirrored reality so closely that it seems to have precipitated Crane's advance into the belligerency stage of violentization:

> As I watched Mother act with Miss Varsi some tiny membrane snapped inside me. They were all too familiar, those icy, dangerous looks Mother gave, the imperial manner and tight-assed way of crossing a room, the way she would turn and punch home a line.
>
> I had watched her act with a screen "daughter" before in *The Prodigal*. But that child was eight years old and their interplay was loving. Now, for the first time, I sat engulfed by her Cinemascopic image, watching her scold a tall teenager, one whose soft-voiced manner reminded me of me. With that snap came a moment of realization: the techniques Mother used to intimidate and control me came not from a well of feeling but from her bag of actress tricks. To her, life was a movie. She did not live in reality.
>
> If my love for her suffered with the slapping incident [when Turner accused Crane of flirting with her men], I now saw she was able to control me only because I fell for the acting. I let her control me. If she said yes and I said no, what could she really do? She lectured me endlessly on showing respect and obedience to one's mother, yet look how she treated Gran.

Despite these rebellious conclusions (or perhaps because of them), Crane reports that Christmas with her mother in London was "the happiest time" they had ever spent together. Turner was patching up her relationship with Stompanato during her daughter's visit, writing him passionate letters and taking his transatlantic calls. He rejoined her in Europe after Crane left. In the months to come, Crane writes, when the couple moved on to an extended holiday in Acapulco, "Mother says she lived in terror and just barely survived his physical brutality." Among other incidents, "he smashed a door, slapped her around and held a gun to her head, mainly because she refused to sleep with him." Turner resisted Stompanato by getting drunk. She disliked being seen with the man in public because of his gangster reputation, but there was talk that they might marry.

When they returned to the United States in March 1958 it was time for the Academy Awards. Turner had been nominated as best actress for *Peyton Place,* competing with Joanne Woodward for *The Three Faces of Eve.* Turner invited Crane and Gran to accompany her to the awards, pointedly not inviting Stompanato. Woodward won, but the nomination itself was a boost to Turner's career; movie-star mother and smoldering daughter returned afterward to the star's bungalow at the Bel Air Hotel and talked about moving Crane back home from boarding school. When Turner said goodnight and went to her bedroom, she found Stompanato there. They fought furiously. Crane, willing to challenge her mother but not yet prepared to defend her, retreated from this continuing personal horrification into fear, becoming, she says, "a fetal lump that lay as still as death. . . . I knew then what I had to do: Go-to-sleep, go-to-sleep, go-to-sleep."

By the time Stompanato next attacked her mother, Crane had found her resolve. Crane positions a crucial conversation between the two occasions in her memoir. Characterizing herself as simultaneously supportive and contemptuous, she makes it clear that she was finally prepared to respond with violence to her mother's indirect but effective violent coaching:

> "Baby, things aren't . . . good . . . between John and me," [Mother] said. "I don't know what to do."
>
> "Leave him, Mother," I said. "Make him vanish."
>
> "I can't, Baby. You see, the truth is I'm afraid of him. He threatened to hurt me if I try to leave him. He knows people he can hire to harm my face or even kill me." She let out a tiny shudder, then, hugging her bosom, she rolled her eyes so that they rested on my left shoulder. "Baby, what am I going to *do?*" she said plaintively. "You've got to help me. Please . . . will you?"
>
> She had played the lingering close-up well—now cut, that's a print. I swallowed hard because I believed she was in danger, but something inside me said that eighty percent of what she was doing at this moment was playacting. Screen art blurred into life. She was in a jam, it was clear to see, but at some level in her mind, she was already beginning to self-dramatize in order to manipulate an escape. She was—incredibly—reaching out for help from me, a fourteen-year-old.
>
> I had seen her do things like this before, unloading her personal problems onto others for them to straighten out. Until her M-G-M contract was dropped two years before, an army of service departments had made all her great and small worries go away. In addition, there were always her lawyers, agents, managers, maids, hairdressers, boyfriends and Gran to turn to before economies had to be made and the soldiers cut back. Now, raw recruit that I was, it was my turn.

In the Bel Air bungalow, Turner went on, Stompanato had slapped her, punched her and menaced her with a razor. "She broke down," Crane writes, "and I threw my arms around her. . . . I felt scared and confused and overwhelmingly guilty. To think that the very first time she needed me, I hid under the covers. Now here we were a second time. . . . Who was the parent here and who the child?" Turner fixes her daughter with an imploring look. "Baby, what am I going to do?" she asks—rhetorically, Crane implies.

So the stage is set for the fatal knifing, at a newly rented house in Beverly Hills. Turner learns that Stompanato has lied about his age, claiming to be forty-three; he is only thirty-three, five years younger than she. Beatings she can tolerate, but the implication that she is a fading beauty clinging to a gigolo is more than she can bear. She tells Crane she intends to get rid of Stompanato that night and does not want to be alone. Crane hovers in her room, watching television and trying to write a term paper on the vertebrate circulatory system. Stompanato arrives, the shouting begins—" 'You damn BITCH!' he screamed. 'You're not getting rid of me that easy. I'll cut you up first!' "—Crane runs back and forth from her room to the landing, assessing the danger. She has never seen Stompanato angry before. "He seethed. He clearly hated her. It was controlled anger, but his neck veins stood out and he breathed from one side of his mouth. He hunched his shoulders as though he were going to pull out a pair of six-shooters, while the hands at his sides clenched and writhed like a snake's tail in death. He never once looked at me, but burned his glare into Mother."

The fighting escalates. Turner breaks for her bedroom and locks the door. "Open up this motherfucker or I'll break it down!" Stompanato roars. Turner unlocks the door and allows him in. More shouting. Mother and daughter hold a conference in the hall. " 'Why don't you just tell him to go?' I said. 'You're a coward, Mother.' " Turner responds that she's afraid of him—" 'terrified.' "

The argument continues in Turner's bedroom. Crane advances and retreats, listening at the closed door. Stompanato's threats turn physical. He is going to cut Turner up. "And don't think I won't also get your mother and your kid," Crane reports him saying. "I don't even have to be there. I have people to do the job *for* me—and I'll *watch*." Crane runs downstairs "in panic. I have to do something. . . . I ran through the kitchen door. On the sink lay a gleaming butcher knife. Scare him, that's it. I grabbed the knife, ran upstairs, and laid it beside the door."

More threats and screaming. Crane picks up the knife. The door flies open. "Mother stood there, her hand on the knob. He was coming at her from behind, his arm raised to strike. I took a step forward and lifted the weapon. He ran on the blade. It went in. *In!* For three ghastly heartbeats, our bodies fused." Stompanato backs off the knife, collapses and dies.

Except that people don't run onto knives, especially people experienced with violent altercations. The eight-inch butcher knife penetrated his abdomen all the way to his spine, punctured a kidney, deflected off his backbone and sliced his aorta. Later, at the Beverly Hills police station, in the office of her mother's old friend Clinton B. Anderson, the chief of police, Crane gave a statement. It seemed Stompanato had not been raising his arm to strike Turner when Crane stabbed him; he had been holding his jacket and shirt on a hanger over his shoulder—on his way, presumably, to leaving the bedroom. "It was later reported accurately," Crane writes, "that I told Anderson that I did what I did to protect Mother. However, somewhere in the retelling, damaging words were put in my mouth that had me saying at the instant of thrusting the knife [*sic*], 'You don't have to take that, Mama!'—a phrase that would wrongly suggest premeditation." Her mother was sitting nearby during this unguarded confession. Anderson, Crane writes, specifically asked Turner if she had "heard [Cheryl's] version of this incident"; Turner acknowledged that "Everything she said is true." This testimony contradicts Crane's assertion that "words were put in my mouth." Other words she says she "was reported to have told Anderson" include (with Crane's ellipses): "I opened the door and went in . . . neither of them said anything. I didn't say anything. I just walked between them and . . . did it." And ("another misquote"): "I pushed the knife into his stomach with all my might." As if to emphasize that these statements were true despite her later denials, Crane writes of the coroner's inquest that "[a] verbatim transcript of the testimony I had given Chief Anderson in his office that night was read into the record. It was noted that although Mother had sat four feet away, I spoke with eyes downcast, with no prompting from anyone, and the account I gave in Anderson's office did not vary from the one given earlier [immediately after the murder] to Anderson in my bedroom." Crane offers an explanation for her denials. Without them, she explains, the "reading public might have imagined me to be a young Lizzie Borden."

Cheryl Crane clearly murdered Johnny Stompanato to protect her mother. If she "just walked between them . . . and did it," then the act was not physically defensive but frustrative-malefic, and Crane at fourteen was farther advanced in violentization than she presents herself to be in her memoir. Turner, an experienced manipulator of violent people, understood that her daughter was dangerous; why else would she have chosen Crane to protect her against the likes of Johnny Stompanato? The coroner's jury finding of justifiable homicide when the killer wielded a butcher knife and the victim was unarmed indicates that the jurors found it difficult to comprehend that the adolescent daughter of a woman of wealth and celebrity could be seriously violent. Lonnie Athens's study of the etiology of violence clarifies how and why.

Mickey Cohen, who had experience in such matters, saw the discrepancy in the jury verdict. He told the press afterward, "It's the first time in my life I've ever seen a dead man convicted of his own murder. So far as that jury was concerned, Johnny just walked too close to the knife."

CHAPTER THIRTEEN

Alex Kelly, Perry Smith, Mike Tyson

Alex Kelly, whom the press called the "preppy rapist," was carefully pro-filed in Sheila Weller's 1997 book *Saint of Circumstance* after his conviction that year for the rape of a Darien, Connecticut, schoolmate in 1986. Kelly came to press attention because he was a handsome, upper-middle-class, socially successful athlete who had jumped bail and spent almost a decade on the run as a ski bum in Europe before finally returning to face trial. Kelly was known for dating the most beautiful girls in his community, and many of his fellow athletes laughed at the idea that he might rape anyone. "Why would Alex have to do something like that?" Weller reports them asking. Though Weller was unaware of Lonnie Athens's work when she wrote *Saint of Circumstance,* her detailed account of the Darien rapist's childhood offers what I take to be persuasive evi-dence of his full violentization.*

Kelly was born in May 1967, the second of three sons of Joe and Mela-nie Kelly, a successful Darien plumber and real-estate developer and a Pennsylvania socialite. Stern, handsome Joe Kelly had grown up in a poor section of Stamford, Connecticut, and someone who knew his family then remembered that his father beat him. Joe continued the tra-dition with his sons. "People whispered about Joe Kelly's temper," Weller observes. A Darien attorney told her Joe was known to be a "strict disci-plinarian." On the testimony of "Jay Bush,"† a friend of Alex Kelly's older brother Chris, that euphemism stood for full-scale violent subjugation:

---

* My discussion of Weller's work is of course my interpretation of the material.
† At their request Weller assigned pseudonyms to many of the people she interviewed.

"Joe would come home from working hard, the three kids would be acting up, going off the wall—and he'd take off his belt. Or he'd slam Chris against the wall. I saw it. As kids, growing up, we used to see the kids getting beaten by Joe all the time. Belts were a popular way. Fists. Slamming them up against walls. In front of friends."

It appears that Joe violently subjugated Melanie Kelly as well, adding personal horrification to the boys' brutalization. Weller reports that Chris's friend Bush "used to be very troubled by signs that Chris was violent toward his girlfriends. Chris apparently tried to choke one woman and gave his last girlfriend black eyes.* Bush says, "I'd say: 'Chris, how can you hit a girl?' And Chris would say, 'I know it's not right, but it's like a reflex. My dad used to do it all the time to my mom.' " (Joe Kelly contends that he was never violent with his wife.) After Alex Kelly was arrested for rape, his parents separated for a time; Weller reports Melanie told a realtor who rented her a house "that she could no longer take Joe's 'mental and physical abuse.' "

Weller sought no evidence of violent coaching, but Joe's alleged brutality toward his wife appears to have set an example that Chris linked to his own abuse of women. Alex's focus on rape implies that he made a similar connection. The gulf in social background between Joe Kelly and the corporate executives who populated prosperous Darien may well have made him cynical and almost certainly fueled his rage at his sons' behavior. Later, the Kellys showed themselves to be sacrificially protective of their most violent child—they paid tens of thousands of dollars in restitution for burglaries Alex committed, encouraged and funded his flight to escape prosecution and forfeited hundreds of thousands of dollars in bail—implying that they discounted or minimized the extremity of his behavior, an important form of violent coaching.

Chris became a bully and an outcast. Alex at first directed his resentment and anger into athletics, where he got an early taste of the rewards of even minor violent performances. At nine years of age he was the terror of junior football: "The other parents were getting upset," a neighbor told Weller—"the little kids were getting beat up by Alex. He couldn't control himself. He *wasn't* going to lose." He continued to be extremely fearful of his father.

By twelve years of age, in junior high, Alex still panicked when his father threatened him. Weller describes an occasion when Alex had sprained an ankle and was on crutches wearing a cast. He was talking with friends outside a neighbor's house when his father came screeching

---

* Chris Kelly died of a heroin overdose in 1991.

up in his sports car to chase him home. " 'Alex went into a *fit* of panic,' [one friend] recalls. 'He *panicked*. He was choked up. He was crying.' " The frightened boy limped home. "And then: 'Mr. Kelly comes down the steps from the family room and *screams* at Alex, swearing at him. And he picks up an encyclopedia-sized book and he throws it—Alex is shrieking—at Alex's ankle: *right* at the cast, right at the injury.' "

At the same time that his brutalization was continuing at home, away from home Alex was discovering the social rewards of his good looks and bold manner. A friend, writes Weller, "noticed Alex grabbing girls' breasts and snapping their suit tops at Weed Beach. . . ." " 'He was starting to get the clout with the boys that would carry into high school,' a female contemporary says, 'because he could get any girl he wanted. He was definitely on the prowl.' " He was evidently also moving through the belligerency stage of violentization. When he was twelve, he invited a new girl in town, a twelve-year-old whom Weller calls "Jamie," to join him on a picnic in the woods behind his house. "We were just fooling around and stuff," Jamie told Weller, "and I was still a virgin and I had never really fooled around, and he wanted to keep going. I told him no. But he didn't stop. For a second I was worried. So I told him, again, to stop. And he stopped right away, and everything was fine."

But by ninth grade, when he was fourteen, Alex had clearly passed through belligerency into violent performances. Contact sports influenced his transition. A boy who played football with him remembered that he "was aggressive though he talked a bigger line than what he'd do. . . . He could hit pretty hard. He *liked* hitting people hard. That kind of thing would get him excited." Someone else remembered that "he used to spit on people during games. He used to growl." He was a particularly vicious wrestler, applying split scissors and stretching holds to the point of severe pain: " 'Alex,' one wrestling fan recalls, 'would put submission holds on his opponents to the point that they would give up.' But *he* would not quite give up.' And he'd just look into the stands and be smiling at the stands while these kids were yelling in agony.' "

That same ninth-grade year, at a party in the fall, Alex allegedly perpetrated his first known rape, an unprovoked attack on a small, preadolescent thirteen-year-old girl that established his signature pattern. He appears to have concluded that his father, who was still observed beating him well into his high school years, was too dangerous to challenge in violent personal revolt, but that women could be dominated and abused with little risk of retaliation. The alleged victim, "Margaret," described the previously unreported experience to Weller:

"It was cold, it was dark, the party was going on, the music blasting. He said, 'Do you want to go smoke a little pot?' And I'm like, 'Oh, I'll try some!' I was trying to act cool, because there was an older crowd there." The boy [whom she established later was Alex Kelly] led Margaret out of the party, across the street, behind a neighbor's house—into the woods. "We were going to sit down and smoke some pot. But we never got to the pot. He slammed me down—pushed me. And then he started kissing me. I was: 'No! I thought we were gonna smoke some pot!' " The next thing Margaret knew, the boy pulled his pants down and put his penis into her mouth. "I was like, 'No! No!' I was choking! I was in shock. I couldn't do anything with it in my mouth. I tried pushing him off me. He said, 'Don't say anything.'

"He ripped his pants down and then my underwear down. He held me down and covered my mouth so I wouldn't scream." The boy forcibly penetrated Margaret. He raped her. "Then he got up and ran away."

Margaret confided in an older sister soon after the rape. Fearful of being punished themselves, they told no one.

Yet raping a preadolescent girl, though an act of heinous violence from the girl's perspective, did not lead to violent notoriety or social trepidation and thus seems not to have had the "lasting and significant impact" on Alex that Athens has determined to be necessary to advance a belligerent novice into the virulency stage of violentization. Margaret did not attend Alex's school and therefore was not available to demonstrate fear in his presence, and he evidently kept quiet about the assault. But if its lack of impact denied him a clear-cut victory, neither was the alleged rape a defeat. Because Margaret failed to report it, it went unpunished.

According to the victim, Alex committed his next known attempted rape a full six months later, in spring 1982, shortly after he turned fifteen. He made a perfunctory assault on an old friend, "Julia," after she passed out at a keg party. She woke to find he had pulled off her sweater and was standing over her shoving his erection into her face. She pushed him away, managed to intimidate him verbally and generously drove him home while he furiously called her a "bitch" and a "prude." He stayed angry for days at school. At another keg party, this one truant at nine in the morning, he persuaded her to follow him into the woods to talk over the earlier episode. Julia told Weller:

"He grabbed me by the shoulders, pinned me down, into the sticks. Ripped my bathing suit. Violently! *Off!* . . . I was so taken aback, I started screaming: '*What* are you *doing?!*' He said, 'Shut up!' He was not attempting to kiss me or anything. He was pinning me down, he was groping me, he was trying to pull my bathing suit all the way off. And then—don't ask me what possessed me but—I punched him in the face!

"I'm sure it didn't hurt him, but it stunned him. Just totally stunned him. He sat back. Physically, he could have continued to do what he'd started to do, but my nerve in having punched him and the fact that I had big-clout friends among the upperclassmen must have made him stop. I had just enough over him that he couldn't continue. He said—in a voice so possessed, it was scary— 'Why am I doing this to you? I can't believe I'm doing this to you. I've known you for so long.' . . . He was steamed up. His eyes were almost misting. He said, 'I'm sorry; I'm sorry; I shouldn't be doing this to you.' I remember thinking: Why does he keep saying '*to you*'? Then I immediately knew. I just *knew it*: He had done this to other girls. And it was totally premeditated: the approach at the party, the walk into the woods."

Weller discovered no other rapes or attempted rapes following this clear-cut defeat until Alex Kelly was almost eighteen. In the intervening two years, however, he burglarized houses and pursued a violently abusive relationship with a girlfriend that extended to throwing chairs and cutting his arm badly smashing his fist through a glass window. He was arrested at seventeen, in June 1984, for burglary and larceny. Weller estimates that Joe and Melanie Kelly paid about one hundred thousand dollars in restitution for the silver and other goods their son stole from neighborhood houses and fenced in New York; the restitution spared Alex all but two months of a three-year prison sentence.

He returned to high school a dark hero. Now his peers accorded him the social trepidation that Athens finds crucial to advancing through virulency. " 'He was, like, a legend,' says then-freshman Ed O'Neill. 'I remember all kinds of people saying, "He's a bad, bad man," in an awed sense. And, "Wow, that kid went to jail for robbing houses." ' " Alex began dating the most beautiful girl at Darien High, Amy Molitor (who would stand behind him again at his trial). The following spring 1984 he took up raping with a vengeance.

The first victim, "Jillian Henderson," a fifteen-year-old, needed a ride home from a party. Alex offered to drive her. When he pulled into a cul-de-sac near his house, she was frightened and pleaded with him to take her home. "He put his hands on me and told me to 'shut the fuck up.' " He forced her into the back of the vehicle, the victim told Weller, lowering the seat to make a pallet, and attacked her:

> "He had one hand around my throat and my head was hitting against the station wagon door—he was really trying to jam my head into it. And he kind of thrust. It was real forceful and real quick and real vulgar. Then I started crying, and he told me to get the hell out of the car. And he made me walk home. It was about two miles from my home. . . . I walked all the way home, alone, in the middle of the night, crying."

Weller perspicaciously charts Kelly's advancing violent performances:

> Things were escalating for Alex. Whereas his post-alleged attack behavior with the earlier girls had been nonverbal (running out of the woods and leaving Margaret there, dazed) or verbally cutting but not angry (telling Julia he didn't want anyone to think he'd done anything with her), now, with Jillian, there was verbal anger ("Shut the fuck up!"). And now there was not a description of just a sexual attack but one also of a physical threat: the hand around Jillian's neck.

His experience of defeat at Julia's hands appears to have increased Alex's resolve and led him to change his tactics.

He now demonstrated what Athens calls the "feelings of exultancy" that follow from "violent notoriety and the trepidation which it generates in others": After that night, Jillian told Weller, "Alex would brush by me real close in the halls at school and say, 'Slut . . . ,' like he enjoyed intimidating me."

Vacationing at a Vermont ski resort during the Christmas holidays that winter, Kelly allegedly raped a seventeen-year-old virgin who resisted him after he met her in a bar and accompanied her to the house where she was staying. She was treated in a hospital emergency room after the assault. She reported it in March 1995, after Kelly returned to the United States from Switzerland, but an attorney dissuaded her from pursuing prosecution, and Kelly's judges disallowed testimony about his prior alleged sexual assaults.

Kelly's hometown paper hailed him later that winter as a young man who had been "rejuvenated" and "rehabilitated." He was a "model student-athlete," one of his classmates told the reporter. On February 10, 1986, the model student-athlete wrestled sixteen-year-old Adrienne Bak (her real name, which she voluntarily revealed after Kelly's trial) into the backseat of Amy Molitor's parents' Jeep Wagoneer and choked and raped her. This time, besides throttling his victim to stifle her screams, he threatened her: "He said I was going to make love to him or he was going to kill me." Driving her home afterward, he repeated his threat: "He just kept saying it over and over: 'If you tell anybody, I'll do it again, and I'll kill you.'"

Because of that threat, Bak's family reported the assault to the Darien police but delayed pressing charges while they considered what the consequences might be. Three days later, emboldened, Kelly assaulted another high school student who had accepted his offer of a ride home from a party. After raping her vaginally, according to the police report, "He then forced her to kneel and bend over while he sodomized her. . . . After the assault Alex Kelly threatened to kill [her] if she told anyone of the assault." The student told her mother as soon as she got home, her mother called the police and Kelly was arrested the next morning, February 14.

Out on bail the following August, Kelly allegedly raped a thirteen-year-old girl while vacationing with his family at a resort in the Bahamas. He fled the United States the night before his trial was scheduled to begin for the two February rapes, returning in 1995 to face trial when his attorney won agreement to separate the two charges. The first jury that heard the Adrienne Bak charge was unable to reach a unanimous verdict. The second jury deliberated for eight hours and found Kelly guilty. He was sentenced in June 1997 to twenty years in prison, to be suspended after sixteen but followed by ten years of probation. At his sentencing Kelly apologized to his victim and her family for his long flight from justice but made a point of not apologizing for raping her. In late 1998 he pled no contest to the rape of the high school student whom he was accused of having raped, sodomized and threatened to kill. In exchange for his plea bargain, the judge set his ten-year sentence for this second rape to run concurrently with his previous sentence. His victim testified in court that she hoped his punishment would "help save another girl from the wrecking ball that is Alex Kelly."

Perry Smith, the central figure in Truman Capote's celebrated narrative *In Cold Blood,* was a far more conventional violent criminal than Alex Kelly. Smith and his partner in crime, Dick Hickock, murdered all four members of a Holcomb, Kansas, farm family, the Clutters, strangers to them, during an attempted robbery on the night of November 15, 1959. Smith insisted later that he was solely responsible for the murders, although both he and Hickok were convicted of them and eventually executed by hanging.

Both men wrote autobiographical statements for Dr. W. Mitchell Jones, the psychiatrist assigned by the court to determine if they were capable of distinguishing right from wrong at the time of the crimes. Constrained by Kansas law, which required a yes-or-no conclusion, Jones testified that Hickock was capable of making such a distinction but that he had no opinion whether Smith was or not. (In fact, Capote says, Jones believed Smith to be severely mentally ill.) Capote reproduces the statements at length. Smith's statement reveals his violentization; Hickock's does not.

"I was born Perry Edward Smith Oct. 27 1928 in Huntington, Elko County, Nevada," Smith begins. His family—his rodeo-cowboy father, Cherokee mother, two sisters and a brother—moved to Alaska two years later:

> In Juneau, my father was making bootleg hooch. I believe it was during this period my mother became acquainted with alcohol. Mom & Dad began having quarrels. I remember my mother was "entertaining" some sailors while my father was away. When he came home a fight ensued, and my father, after a violent struggle, threw the sailors out & proceeded to beat my mother. I was frightfully scared, in fact all us children were terrified. Crying. I was scared because I thought my father was going to hurt me, also because he was beating my mother. I really didn't understand why he was beating her but I felt she must have done something dreadfully wrong.

Smith recalled another incident of brutalization in Fort Bragg, California, where his family had relocated, when his brother "had been presented a B.B. gun and shot a hummingbird." Perry asked to shoot the gun. His brother pushed him away, telling him he was too small. "It made me so mad I started to cry. After I finished crying, my anger mounted again, and during the evening when the B.B. gun was behind the chair my brother was sitting in, I grabbed it & held it to my brother's ear & hollered BANG! My father (or mother) beat me and made me apologize."

His mother and father separated around 1935, when he was seven. She moved to San Francisco with her children:

In Frisco I was continuously in trouble. I had started to run around with a gang, all of which were older than myself. My mother was always drunk, never in a fit condition to properly provide and care for us. I ran as free & wild as a coyote. There was no rule or discipline, or anyone to show me right from wrong. I came & went as I pleased—until my first encounter with Trouble. I was in & out of Detention Homes many many times for running away from home & stealing.

It is a curious conceit of authoritarians, which Smith echoes here, that delinquent and violent children lack discipline and do not know right from wrong. Athens's studies demonstrate to the contrary that violent actors are sometimes extremely disciplined and distinguish right from wrong all too fiercely, reading their victims' attitudes through a flame of indignation and moral fervor and laying claim to the judgments of Almighty God Himself—having learned their trade from their brutalizers.

Before the detention homes, Smith told Capote, his mother put him in a Catholic orphanage. There he was brutalized by the nuns. "The Black Widows were always at me. Hitting me. Because of wetting the bed. Which is one reason I have an aversion to nuns. *And* God. *And* religion. But later on I found there are people even more evil." Smith picks up the story in his autobiographical statement, describing repeated violent subjugation at the hands of his detention home keepers and his fantasies of revenge in response:

I remember one place I was sent to. I had weak kidneys & wet the bed every night. This was very humiliating to me, but I couldn't control myself. I was very severely beaten by the cottage mistress, who had called me names and made fun of me in front of all the boys. She used to come around at all hours of the night to see if I wet the bed. She would throw back the covers & furiously beat me with a large black leather belt—pull me out of bed by my hair & drag me to the bathroom & throw me in the tub & turn the cold water on & tell me to wash myself and the sheets. ["What she used to do," Smith told Capote, "she'd fill a tub with ice-cold water, put me in it, and hold me under till I was blue. Nearly drowned."] Every night was a nightmare. Later on she thought it was very funny to put some kind of ointment on my penis. This was almost unbearable. It burned something terrible. She was later discharged from her job. But this never changed my mind about her & what

I wished I could have done to her & all the people who made fun of me.

Hurried by the attending psychiatrist, Smith skips forward in his auto-biographical narrative to adolescence, chronicling his passage through belligerency into violent performances and virulency:

When I was sixteen [in 1944] I joined the Merchant Marines. In 1948 I joined the army—the recruiting officer gave me a break and upped my test. From this time on I started to realize the importance of an education. This only added to the hatred and bitterness I held for others. I began to get into fights. I threw a Japanese policeman off a bridge into the water. I was court-martialed for demolishing a Japanese cafe. I was court-martialed again in Kyoto, Japan, for stealing a Japanese taxicab. I was in the army almost four years. I had many violent outbursts of anger while I served time in Japan & Korea. . . . [Back in the States, discharged from the army, having committed a burglary] I was sentenced to 5 to 10 years for grand larceny, burglary and jailbreak. I felt I was very unjustly dealt with. I became very bitter while I was in prison. . . . [That led] to Kansas where I got into the situation I'm in now.

Capote quotes Dr. Jones's evaluation of Smith, the evaluation that Kansas law did not allow him to offer in court. Although couched in psychiatric jargon, Jones's evaluation unwittingly corroborates Smith's violentization. Smith's childhood, Jones writes, "was marked by brutality and lack of concern on the part of both parents." As an adult, his "orientation toward the world" is " 'paranoid,' " which Jones explains means that "he is suspicious and distrustful of others, tends to feel that others discriminate against him, and feels that others are unfair to him and do not understand him." As a result, Jones continues, Smith "is overly sensitive to criticisms that others make of him, and cannot tolerate being made fun of. He is quick to sense slight or insult in things others say, and frequently may misinterpret well-meant communications." The words "overly," "quick," "misinterpret" and "well-meant" in these sentences reveal Jones's professional and personal bias: He judges Smith's attitude taking from his own perspective, not from Smith's. Smith's past experiences gave him good reason to be suspicious and distrustful, though his decision to respond with violence was his own.

Jones at least describes Smith's decision process accurately: "In evaluating the intentions and feelings of others, his ability to separate the real situation from his own mental projections is very poor." Since the "real situation" is a product of our "mental projections"—how else would we know it?—the same could be said of us all. On the evidence of Jones's interpretations, one might equally conclude that *his* ability to separate Smith's "real situation" from *his* own "mental projections" is minimal.

Jones reports that Smith "not infrequently groups all people together as being hypocritical, hostile, and deserving of whatever he is able to do to them." This observation confirms Smith's virulency, which by the measure of the Clutter murders is ultraviolent. "Akin to this first trait is the second," Jones adds, "an ever-present, poorly controlled rage—easily triggered by any feeling of being tricked, slighted, or labeled inferior by others. For the most part, his rages in the past have been directed at authority figures—father, brother, Army sergeant, state parole officer—and have led to violent assaultive behavior on several occasions."

Of the Clutter murders themselves, Capote reports that Smith spoke candidly to an old friend from his army days, Donald Cullivan, who visited him in jail. "See, Don—I did kill them," Smith told Cullivan. ". . . Dick [Hickock] helped me, he held the flashlight and picked up the shells. And it was his idea, too. But Dick didn't shoot them, he never could've." Smith denied that he killed the Clutters to prevent them from identifying him. According to Capote, he told Cullivan, "It wasn't . . . the fear of being identified. I was willing to take that gamble. And it wasn't because of anything the Clutters did. They never hurt me. Like other people. Like people have all my life. Maybe it's just that the Clutters were the ones who had to pay for it."

Athens discredits these mystical protestations. He points out that Hickock and Smith drove all the way from Olathe, Kansas, to Holcomb, a distance of some four hundred miles, on a tip from a prison inmate who had worked for Harold Clutter that the farmer kept a large cache of money in his house, that they tortured and finally killed Clutter trying to force him to tell them where the money was hidden—that is, in anger and frustration—and that they were then faced with the awkward fact that the three other family members present in the house had seen and heard enough to identify them if they were caught. Having interviewed a phalanx of violent criminals and heard their unvarnished narratives, Athens is skeptical of romanticized explanations such as Smith's. In Athens's judgment there is no such thing as murder without a motive.

Cullivan was shocked to learn that Smith felt no remorse for murdering the Clutters. Smith sharply corrected that naïveté, administering a valuable lesson in real situations and mental projections:

"Am I sorry? If that's what you mean—I'm not. I don't feel anything about it. I wish I did. But nothing about it bothers me a bit. Half an hour after it happened, Dick was making jokes and I was laughing at them. Maybe we're not human. I'm human enough to feel sorry for myself. Sorry I can't walk out of here when you walk out. But that's all." Cullivan could scarcely credit so detached an attitude; Perry was confused, mistaken, it was not possible for any man to be that devoid of conscience or compassion. Perry said, "Why? Soldiers don't lose much sleep. They murder, and get medals for doing it. The good people of Kansas want to murder me—and some hangman will be glad to get the work. It's easy to kill—a lot easier than passing a bad check. Just remember: I only knew the Clutters for maybe an hour. If I'd really known them, I guess I'd feel different. I don't think I could live with myself. But the way it was, it was like picking off targets in a shooting gallery."

If the violent were genetically defective or mentally ill, we might spare them a measure of pity for their affliction. Athens's work reveals to the contrary that violent criminals pass judgments and make decisions much as the rest of us do. They differ from the rest of us in following through with private violence.

A case in point is former heavyweight champion boxer Mike Tyson. Boxing is a controversial sport, with many detractors as well as passionate fans. (I am a fan, particularly of professional heavyweight boxing.) Its proponents insist that its purpose is to demonstrate athletic skill; its detractors suspect, not without evidence, that its attraction in a society where violence is generally proscribed is the spectacle of one man beating another unconscious. All sports carry some risk of serious injury, but boxing is unique in producing injury even unto death by intention rather than misadventure. Provided that the perpetrator of even a fatal injury follows the rules, he is not considered legally to have battered his opponent; since the victim was a volunteer, both contestants are legally protected by a claim of self-defense. Boxing injuries and fatalities could be reduced by requiring protective headgear, as Olympic contests do. That such headgear is not required in professional boxing is one reason detractors suspect its purity of purpose.

Because boxing hews so close to private violence, it has attracted a share of seriously violent contestants, some of whom have achieved exceptional success. To do so, of course, they have had to limit their violence to what is acceptable within the rules of the sport. Tyson has not found such limitation easy to sustain. His biting mutilation of Evander Holyfield during their title bout in Las Vegas in June 1997 is a notorious example of an interpretation leading to a major violent performance and of the confusion such interpretation engenders among commentators, experts and fans.

Michael Gerard Tyson was born June 30, 1966, in Brooklyn, New York, the second son and third child of an unmarried registered nurse and a forty-two-year-old construction worker who abandoned the family when Mike was two years old. The abandonment forced Lorna Tyson onto public assistance and eventually, when Mike was nearly ten, into marginal housing in the violent Brownsville section of the borough. As a child Mike was undersized and soft-spoken, with a lisp; the Brownsville toughs, boys and girls both, who regularly robbed him and beat him up called him "fairy boy." His older brother, Rodney, continued at home the brutalization Mike encountered in the streets.

A year in Brownsville was enough to move Mike into the belligerency stage of violentization. He undertook his first successful violent performance at eleven, when a teenage bully confronted him on the roof of an abandoned building, tending the pigeons he kept there, and deliberately twisted the head off one of Mike's birds. Mike attacked the bully furiously and beat him to the ground. "He would admit, many years later, that he loved the feeling," writes Tyson biographer Peter Heller, "that he still relished the memory of it. It was the first time he emerged triumphant by using his fists."

More successful violent performances followed, and with them a steady widening of Tyson's violent resolution as he passed into virulency. He joined a street gang, the Jolly Stompers. He became a skilled pickpocket and neck-chain snatcher and served as bagman when his gang held up corner markets. He helped mug drunks and customers flush from cashing checks. Heller says Tyson's neighbors remember him as "a bad-ass kid," one woman who grew up with him characterizing him as "a devil. You can see the devil in his eyes. . . . I don't care how much money he makes, he'll always be a devil, he'll always be evil." Tyson understands that his delinquency was a choice. "I wasn't sucked in by anyone else," he told an interviewer once. "I wanted to be sucked in."

Tyson started carrying a gun when he was twelve. Brandishing it in stickups landed him in the Bronx's Spofford Detention Center, where he first saw Muhammad Ali when the champion came to visit, and first conceived of escaping the ghetto by boxing. From Spofford he was remanded to a juvenile prison, the Tryon School for Boys, upstate in Johnstown. There he threatened teachers and fought with other boys, beating one so furiously that two large guards struggled to subdue him. By thirteen he was no longer undersized; though he had grown to only five feet eight, he weighed more than two hundred pounds and he could handle ten repetitions bench-pressing 250 pounds. A counselor at Tryon, Bobby Stewart, a former national Golden Gloves light-heavyweight champion boxer, took charge of directing this fulminant manchild, passing him on to a semi-retired professional boxing manager, Cus D'Amato, who saw his potential and developed it. Tyson won his first world heavyweight championship, against Trever Berbick, in Las Vegas, Nevada, on November 22, 1986, when he was twenty. He became undisputed world heavyweight champion eight months later in Las Vegas when he beat Tony Tucker in twelve rounds.

Tyson was unwilling to limit his violent performances to the boxing ring, however, even during his years of success and increasing prosperity. He groped women in bars and subjected them to rough sex, got into fights, battered Robin Givens, the actress whom he married and divorced in the late 1980s, tore up hotel rooms and threatened people. He lost the heavyweight championship to Buster Douglas in Tokyo in 1990. His violence caught up with him in 1991 in Indianapolis, when he raped a young contestant in a Miss Black America pageant, Desiree Washington, fleeing town afterward when she went directly to a hospital emergency room and then filed charges. Between indictment and trial Tyson managed to allow himself to be caught on videotape at a news conference telling a member of his entourage, "I should have killed the bitch." He was convicted of rape and sentenced to six years in prison. Even in prison he threatened a guard.

Paroled in 1995 after serving three years, Tyson returned to boxing. In November 1996, heavyweight champion Holyfield stopped him in the eleventh round of a title fight. He convinced himself that Holyfield had won by cheating—head-butting, which opened a cut above his eye—and that the referee had chosen to ignore the offense. When Tyson met Holyfield for the rematch in June 1997, he was prepared to retaliate. The two fighters' heads clashed in the first round, once again cutting Tyson. In the second round, after a flurry of blows from Holyfield, their heads clashed again. Tyson protested, but the referee dismissed the protest, whereupon Tyson acted. Going into a clinch with Holyfield, he methodically mumbled his mouth onto one of his opponent's ears, bit a piece out of the crest and spit it onto the canvas. Holyfield reacted with something between horror and disgust, pulling away, pawing at his bleeding ear and gesturing to the referee while Tyson stood by, smirking righteously. With the crowd in an uproar, the referee conferred with the fight judges, concluding by penalizing Tyson two points and continuing the fight after Holyfield's cut man stanched the bleeding. The champion came out in the third round ready to punish his attacker. Tyson proceeded to sink his teeth into Holyfield's other ear. When the round ended, the referee and the judges disqualified Tyson and awarded the fight to Holyfield.

Tyson is familiar with conventional explanations of violent behavior. At a press conference the day after the fight, he was already speaking of having "snapped" after the referee ignored his protest. Immediately following the fight, however, in a hallway interview with sports reporter Jim Gray, he offered a detailed account of his attack that confirmed it was calculated and deliberate. "You bit him," Gray questioned Tyson. "Was that retaliation?"

"Regardless of what I did," Tyson answered, sweating in his fight robe with a towel around his neck and the cut still open over his eye,

> he's been butting me for two fights. He butted me in the first round, but then he butted me in the second round. Then, as soon as he butted me, I watched him and he looked right at me, and I saw him and he was going to butt me again. He kept coming up and charging into me. And no one warned him, no one took any points from him. What can I do? This is my career. I can't continue getting butted like that. I've got children to raise. And this guy keeps butting me, trying to cut me and get me stopped on cuts. I've got to retaliate. Look at me! Look at me! I'll go home and my kids will be scared of me.

"But you've got to address it," Gray insisted opaquely. "Why did you bite him?"

"I addressed it in the ring," Tyson answered honestly enough.

Immediately after Tyson assaulted Holyfield, fight announcer Steve Albert had pronounced what would become the standard explanation for Tyson's behavior: "Mike Tyson has apparently lost his reason, his rationale. He seems possessed right now." Ironically, so long as Tyson battered opponents within the rules of boxing, he was assumed to be acting rationally—acting, indeed, with exceptional perspicacity and skill. If he extended his battering beyond the rules, however, then people like Albert assigned his behavior to irrational impulses, even to (demonic) possession—presumably because breaking the rules lost him the fight.

But Tyson believed that Holyfield's behavior had challenged him to a different kind of fight, a street fight, with different rules.

At the press conference, after he claimed he "snapped," Tyson had said as much, explaining that when the referee had ignored his protest, he had felt that the contest was no longer a prizefight but had become a street fight. When we had watched the fight together the night before, Athens had accurately deconstructed Tyson's logic. "From Tyson's point of view," Athens had speculated, "if Holyfield won the fight by breaking the rules and Tyson lost the fight by following the rules, then Tyson would look like a punk. He thought Holyfield had reverted to street rules—use as much violence as you need to win—so he should revert to street rules too. He may have lost the fight, but by street rules he won— he scared Holyfield out of the ring."

"What's irrational," Athens added, "is putting violent guys in the ring together and expecting them to limit their violence to the rules."

As a result of Tyson's foul, the Nevada State Athletic Commission revoked his boxing license. To win it back he changed his management team and entered treatment with a Georgetown University Medical School psychiatrist, Richard Goldberg, who prescribed medication for chronic depression and diagnosed "issues related to his personality." A year later Tyson applied to the Nevada Commission for reinstatement. The athletic commission requested a psychiatric evaluation, which was conducted over a five-day period in late September 1998 by a six-man team of psychiatrists, psychologists and neurologists at Boston's Massachusetts General Hospital.

The evaluation of Tyson's mental status, conducted by two psychiatrists on the team, David Henderson and Ronald Schouten, illustrates the confusion about psychological traits connected to violent behavior that Athens discussed in *The Creation of Dangerous Violent Criminals*. The psychiatrists write in their report that Tyson began the evaluation by "express[ing] an interest in the professional books on Dr. Schouten's shelf, as well as an interest in social issues, especially the plight of the poor and victims of persecution. He expressed a desire to help the underprivileged and those who are suffering." Then, in one concise sentence, Tyson laid out the conventional explanation for his behavior and his own self-conception side by side: "I have no self-esteem but the biggest ego in the world."

Violent novices do suffer from low self-esteem, Athens confirms, "during the early stages of [violentization]," but "should they later reach the final stage, virulency, they will suffer from exactly the reverse problem—unrealistically too high self-esteem to the point of arrogance." Rather than accept Tyson's own testimony, however, the two psychiatrists pursued the matter further, insisting Tyson acknowledge the primacy of their theory. The unlicensed former champion, since his career depended on it, acceded to their mystification. "Upon further exploration," they paraphrase him, "he was aware that his inflated ego was a psychological defense to [sic] his poor self-esteem. He stated that he is uncomfortable with celebrity status, indicating 'I don't want superstardom.' "

After performing neurological and other examinations, the full evaluation team concluded unanimously that Tyson "should be engaged in a course of regular psychotherapy with the goal of building trusting relationships, understanding and managing his emotional responses to specific situations, and anger management skills." He had "deficits in executive control," which therapy would help him compensate for. The team did not believe he needed medicating. His ear biting "was the product of several factors: depression, impulse control problems exacerbated by depression, a sense that no one was protecting his interests, and a variety of social and financial problems." He was "mentally fit to return to boxing."

One month prior to his Boston evaluation, as his examiners well knew, Tyson had been riding as a passenger in a convertible driven by his wife (physician Monica Turner, whom he married after his release from prison) in Gaithersburg, Maryland. A security man was posted in the backseat. Stopped by congested traffic, the Tyson car was bumped from behind by a car driven by a man named Richard Hardick, which was recoiling in turn from being rear-ended by a third car driven by a man named Abmielec Saucedo.

According to a complaint that Hardick filed in Maryland district court two days later, when he stepped out to assess the damage, Tyson asked him "why I hit his car. I said something to the effect that the man behind me pushed me into his car." With his wife and his security man restraining him, Tyson approached Saucedo. "Despite being restrained," Hardick alleges, "Mr. Tyson hit the man in the face. I do not recall if the man fell to the ground. Immediately I got back into my car because I feared what Mr. Tyson would do next." Hardick powered up his window and locked his doors. Tyson's security man approached and signaled that he wanted to talk. Hardick lowered his window, whereupon the security man snatched his keys, warned him he was not going anywhere and asked for his driver's license. Dutifully Hardick passed the document out through his lowered window. Then he made the mistake of reverting to civilian rules:

I then thought that Mr. Tyson had calmed down and we could proceed with the exchange of information. . . . I got out of my car . . . and stood near the passenger door. Mr. Tyson then started toward me—he was in the medial strip. The woman driver and the same man who restrained Mr. Tyson previously did so again. Mr. Tyson was able to continue to approach me despite the restraint. When he got close, his arms, I believe, were being restrained, and he kicked me in the groin. I immediately doubled over in pain and fell to the ground. I stayed there until the police came.

Tyson and his wife had already left the scene when the police arrived.

Nevada restored Tyson's boxing license on October 9, fifteen months after it was revoked. At the hearing that preceded the decision, Tyson acknowledged and simultaneously denied responsibility for the Maryland incident. "I was irate, crazy, mad," he told the athletic commission. "I really said some bad things to those people. They were afraid of this big black guy using street vernacular. It was a big ugly scene. If he says I did it, maybe I was unconscious of doing it. I'm sorry." When one of the commissioners insisted that his attacks on Holyfield had been premeditated, Tyson implicitly acknowledged his culpability. "It's no one's fault but mine," he told the commissioner. "Some people are sheltered and protected, born with a silver spoon in their mouth. They don't know what it's like to be hungry and scared and have to have courage. They know who they are. I am no schizophrenic and no manic depressant. I'm just me. I represent people, pimps, whores, prostitutes. I always have to be strong, because I never know who's looking at me."

In the winter of 1998 Tyson prepared for his first fight since the Holyfield debacle, and the prospect of reestablishing his authority in the ring evidently cheered him. His handlers coached him to good behavior at a press conference he held in Hollywood on December 8 to announce his return to boxing. Since he could not complain about his legal situation, he confined himself to boasts that clearly displayed his violent self-image. "Everyone knows I'm on parole and trying to be very nice up here," he told the press with a smile. "If I appear to be something you're not acquainted with, understand my situation." Asked about the Maryland court case, he responded, "I'm not much for talking. You know what I do. I put guys in body bags." A question about another fight prospect prompted, "If the price is right, I'll fight a lion." The previous day, in an interview with the *New York Times*, he had sounded defiant: "If I went back to prison, it wouldn't be because I violated anyone. I didn't do anything to go back. If they send me back to prison, I can handle it. I'm not a wimp. I'm no chump. I'm not afraid of anything, except God." Of Holy-field, he told the *Times,* "He was butting me. Yeah, I bit his ears. He's lucky I didn't bite his throat. He's a boxer. He knew what he did was wrong." In Tyson's terms, Desiree Washington, Evander Holyfield, the two Maryland drivers and anyone else who stood in his way only got what they deserved.

The test of a good theory is whether it accounts for the known facts of the experiences it presumes to explain more efficiently and comprehensively than competing theories do. Violentization, and interpretations mediated by violent phantom communities, better explain the behavior of these three men—Alex Kelly, Perry Smith and Mike Tyson—than do conventional psychological explanations that invoke low self-esteem, irrationality, irresistible impulse or "deficits in executive control." All three men knew what they were doing when they committed violent acts. They did so because they believed in using violence to protect themselves, to take what they wanted and to express contempt for people they perceived to be evil. All three painted violent self-portraits and inhabited unmitigated violent phantom communities. All three, that is—despite their social, racial, economic and educational differences—qualify to be called ultraviolent criminals.

CHAPTER FOURTEEN

Lee Harvey Oswald

Some conspiracy theorists have argued that Lee Harvey Oswald was an ineffectual weakling incapable of mustering the violent malevolence necessary to conceive and carry out the assassination of President John Fitzgerald Kennedy. Few accused murderers' lives have been investigated so extensively as Oswald's. If brutalization, belligerency, violent performances and virulency are necessary to create a violent criminal, then the record of Oswald's life should provide evidence that he underwent such violentization. Evidence of violentization would at least confirm that Oswald was capable of assassinating President Kennedy, and would support Lonnie Athens's theory. Though it would not prove whether or not Oswald in fact assassinated Kennedy, or whether he acted alone, it would discredit one argument against his having done so.

Oswald's father died two months before Lee was born in New Orleans in October 1939. Robert Edward Oswald left his wife, Marguerite, Lee's mother, ten thousand dollars in life insurance, the equivalent of fifty thousand dollars today, but despite that security she sent her two older sons, John (Pic) and Robert, to an orphanage, hired baby-sitters for her infant and went to work. "She constantly reminded us that we were orphans," John remembered bitterly. "That she didn't have the money to support us." Money was an obsession with Marguerite Oswald, John and others would report, to such an extent that her sons recalled often going hungry. All three boys joined the service early to escape what Robert called her "outbursts" and Lee named "neglect."

Between baby-sitters in those first years, Marguerite's sister, Lillian Murret, who had five children of her own, often took care of Lee. Lillian's daughter Marilyn told the Warren Commission that the little boy was "adorable. . . . If you walked in the street with him . . . everybody stopped to admire him. He was a very pretty child, and very happy, very cute. . . .

He was very bright . . . very observant . . . not the type of child who if he didn't get his way would start screaming—never any of that. He was just a very pleasant child." A couple who baby-sat Lee for several weeks when he was two claimed otherwise. "Mother came home from work one day," Robert Oswald reports, "and found Lee crying and saw that he had big red welts on his legs. A neighbor told her that the hired baby-sitters had often mistreated Lee, whipping him to keep him quiet. She fired the couple on the spot. They told her that Lee was a 'bad, unmanageable child,' but Mother said a two-year-old baby couldn't be that bad. Aunt Lillian remembered later that Mother was terribly upset. She knew she had to work to support her children, but she said she'd rather quit her job than leave Lee with strangers." She had left her other two sons with strangers, of course. Lillian, a kindly woman, agreed to resume Lee's daytime care, and Marguerite moved nearby.

She was always a difficult person. "All her life I . . . heard my mother talking about conspiracies, hidden motives, and malicious actions of other people," Robert Oswald remembers. "While John and I were in the Bethlehem Home," he comments, "seeing Mother only on weekends and holidays, we didn't see many of her outbursts, but later on we saw plenty of them. I guess Lee learned at a very early age that Mother was *not* easy to get along with when she didn't get her own way." Even Marguerite's long-suffering sister would testify that "you just couldn't get along with her." The day after Christmas 1942, two months after Lee's third birthday, the sisters having fallen out, Marguerite shipped Lee off to the orphanage with his brothers.

She retrieved him a year later to move to Dallas with a tall, prosperous, Harvard-educated electrical engineer named Edwin A. Ekdahl, a man some years her senior, to whom she had become engaged. "His salary was over $1,000 a month," her sister says Marguerite told her, and he had "a bad heart; a very bad heart, I believe she said." Ekdahl was in fact recovering from a serious heart attack at the time of the move. John and Robert left the orphanage at the end of the school year to join the assembling family. Marguerite broke her engagement, bought a house, put the boys in public school, recommitted to marriage—"influenced in part by his substantial income," says the Warren Report—tried unsuccessfully to return her two older sons to the orphanage and finally married Ekdahl in May 1945.*

---

* Ekdahl was Marguerite's third husband. Her first was Edward Pic, a shipping clerk by whom she had John Pic, Lee and Robert's older half-brother. That marriage ended in divorce, which she blamed on John.

Lee loved his new stepfather. "He had white hair, wore glasses, very nice man," John testified. "I think Lee found in him the father he never had. He . . . treated [Lee] real good, and I am sure that Lee felt the same way [Robert and I] did, I know he did. . . . Because Mr. Ekdahl treated all of us like his own children." Ekdahl traveled extensively for a utility company. At the end of the summer, Marguerite sent John and Robert to a Mississippi military academy, which they liked, and she and Lee began accompanying Ekdahl on his travels. As a result of Ekdahl's traveling and a transfer to Fort Worth, Lee missed most of his first year of school.

Marguerite began fighting with her new husband soon after they were married. "She always wanted to get more money out of him," John believed. "That was the basis of all the arguments." The fights escalated over the three years of the marriage. Toward the end, it seemed to John that "they would have a fight about every other day, and he would leave and come back." After one of their longer separations, John recalled, in the summer of 1947, his mother and her husband stopped him on the street on his way home from work "and told me that they wouldn't be home that night, that they were going downtown to the Worth Hotel. This was one of their reunions. . . . So I went back and I told Lee and Robert, and this seemed to really elate Lee, this made him really happy that they were getting back together." Later that summer Marguerite caught Ekdahl in compromising circumstances with another woman and sent him packing. The following March 1948, when Ekdahl filed for divorce, he charged that his wife argued incessantly about money, flew into "uncontrollable rages" and threw cookie jars, glasses and bottles at him, endangering his already impaired health. Her "excesses, harsh and cruel treatment and outrages" made it impossible for them to live together. Marguerite testified that Ekdahl hit her, but the jury found her guilty of unprovoked "excesses, cruel treatment, or outrages," granted Ekdahl a divorce and awarded her only a fifteen-hundred-dollar settlement. "She lost," John summarizes. "He won."

If Marguerite was capable of "uncontrollable" rages during which she physically assaulted a husband with a bad heart, she was capable of violently subjugating her youngest son. She was a champion haranguer. No one testified that she physically assaulted Lee, but her assaults on his stepfather certainly constitute personal horrification, and as Athens learned from the violent criminals he interviewed, the threat of physical force by the same authority figure after personal horrification is sufficient for violent subjugation, making such subjugation possible even without physical assault. To that point Robert believes that Lee "was far more upset by their conflicts than we were. After all, we were miles away and he was right there to hear the quarrels. Besides, I think Lee was a lot more sensitive than any of us realized at the time. He kept his feelings to himself and didn't show how much he worried over the danger of losing the only father he had ever known."

Marguerite testified directly to violent coaching, the third leg of the brutalization triad, in a 1965 conversation with the author Jean Stafford:

I should say I'm very outspoken, I'm aggressive, I'm no dope. Let's face it, if you step on my toes I'm gonna fight back, and I don't apologize for that. That was my training along with Lee's father. . . . When my older boy [Robert] first went to school, he came home one day crying that the children had taken his pennies away from him. Mr. Oswald took his little hand and started teaching him how to fight back, and I listened and I thought it was a wonderful thing. I remember him saying "If you ever start a fight, you're gonna be whipped, but if they ever start a fight with you and you don't fight back, I'm gonna whip *you.*" Let me give you one little instance with Lee and the next-door neighbor boy. They were approximately the same age, and if not, they were the same height, and Lee had a dog. He loved his shepherd collie dog. It was named Sunshine. He used to romp in the backyard with his dog and took him every place he went, and this little boy was throwing rocks over the fence at Lee's dog. Well, my kitchen window had a view to the backyard. And I watched my son Lee for approximately three days telling the little boy over the fence he better stop throwing rocks at his dog. Well, I was amused, and I was just waiting to find out what happened. Finally one day when I came home from work the father called me on the phone. It seemed his son was very badly beaten up—in a child's way. My son Lee had finally taken it upon himself, after much patience, I thought, to confront the little boy enough to fight him, and the father didn't approve. I told the father what happened, and since the boys were approximately the same age and height, let them fight their own battles.

Marguerite does not say when this very bad beating "in a child's way" occurred, but a classmate of Lee's at Clayton Elementary School in Fort Worth offers a glimpse of him at eight, overage in the second grade. On the playground, Philip Vinson remembered, "when we were just turned loose and allowed to do what we wanted to, we would break down in little groups, and I remember the boys called them gangs. . . . There were . . . maybe three or four boys who . . . acted as leaders of these gangs . . . and I recall fairly vividly that Lee Oswald was one of [them]. . . . The other boys seemed to look up to him because he was so well-built and husky. . . . He was a little bit older than most of the boys, almost a year. The age makes a little more difference at that period than later on. . . . He was considered sort of a tough-guy type, although not a bully." In class, Vinson remembered, Lee "seemed fairly quiet. . . . He didn't brag or shoot off his mouth a lot." When a boy asked Lee "why he was so big and strong" he replied "in the manner of Popeye, 'I eat me spinach.' " But although Vinson knew most of the boys in the class, "to my knowledge, none of them ever played with him or went to his house for anything after school." Lee's leadership on the playground demonstrates that he was not yet a loner; he invited no one home because Marguerite banned visitors, keeping him isolated in order to control him.

The breakup of his mother's marriage to Edwin Ekdahl seems to have precipitated Lee's passage into belligerency. Between 1949 and 1952—from age ten to thirteen—he changed. Of the beginning of that period Robert remembers that Marguerite's "tirades" used to make Lee "upset. He would sulk and pout, but he never talked back. I could tell when he was upset because he would go off by himself and play with the dog or watch television. Sometimes he brooded for hours and went to bed still sulking. But he always recovered by the next morning." Later, a neighbor, Otis Carlton, recalled an evening at the Oswalds when he was startled to see Lee chase John through the living room with a butcher knife and throw the knife at his brother; it missed and hit the wall. "They have these little scuffles all the time and don't worry about it," Marguerite minimized the assault, as she had minimized Lee's beating the neighbor boy "in a child's way." (Minimizing violent behavior, a form of violent coaching, endorses it.) Hiram Conway, another neighbor, who taught John to play chess and whose daughter John dated, testified to Lee's transition across those preadolescent years, "the picture it built in my mind. . . . I have seen him fight with his half-brother and his brother and he would tear into them, and they would hold him off to try to keep him out of trouble, and he would try to kick their shins." But in Conway's building picture, Lee gradually revealed more intense belligerency, a striking contrast to Marilyn Murret's happy, adorable little boy:

> [Lee] was quick to anger and he was, I would say, a vile nature—he was mean when he was angry, just ornery—he was vicious almost, you might say, is the best word I can describe it. . . . John was a very genuine character, a fine boy. . . . Robert was much more spunky than John, but Robert didn't very often get into much trouble. . . .

He didn't walk up and down the street looking for children to throw stones at, like Lee did. [Lee] was a bad kid. . . . He would become angry with [children in the neighborhood] but . . . the children didn't fight with him much, they got out of his way. They would hide or move on, and it would be pretty hard to catch him in a fight because it would be pretty hard for him to have caught one of them.

Marguerite forced her older sons to leave high school to work to help support the family. After a year as a shoe stockboy, John rebelled, found a part-time job and returned to high school, signing his own report cards in defiance. Escaping his mother was more important to him than finishing high school, however, and as soon as he came of age, in January 1950, he joined the Coast Guard. Two and a half years later, after his junior year in high school, Robert also escaped by joining the marines. The following month, August 1952, Marguerite and Lee moved to New York City, where John, now married to a New York girl, was stationed on Staten Island. The Pics, who had a new baby, lived with Marge Pic's mother in her Upper Manhattan apartment; to accommodate Marguerite's visit, John's mother-in-law had gone to stay with friends.

Lee's new belligerency surprised John. "Lee was nearly thirteen," Robert Oswald reports, "an age when most boys rebel against their parents to some degree, but Lee's rebellion against Mother seemed total. He was often angry and slapped Mother more than once, John recalled. He had never done this when we were all together in Fort Worth." Lee's belligerency extended beyond his mother. "Lee enjoyed playing uncle" to the baby, Robert continues. "Marge said he was very gentle with the baby and could be genuinely helpful around the house, but she was alarmed by his rudeness to Mother. She spoke to him about that one day, and he gave her a sharp answer. After that, he treated Marge with contempt."

The visit dragged on for weeks, seriously inconveniencing Marge's mother. Marguerite talked of finding an apartment and a job but made no effort to do so, nor did she offer to pay for her and Lee's groceries. When John mentioned the expense, she harangued him. Marge bore the brunt of entertaining her freeloading in-laws. "Whenever there was an argument," John testified, ". . . my mother antagonized Lee toward hostility against my wife." The antagonism finally erupted in a serious confrontation—"the big trouble," John called it. As Robert reconstructed it, "One afternoon John came home and found the household in an uproar. Marge said Lee had pulled a knife and threatened her with it. He had been watching television, she said, and she had asked him to turn down the sound. He pulled out a pocketknife, opened the blade and moved toward her. She was frightened and moved away. Maybe she called for Mother. Anyway, when Mother came in and told Lee to put the knife away, he hit her."

John questioned his mother and Lee separately about the incident. Marguerite, he said, "attempted to brush it off as not being as serious as my wife put it. . . . Being as prejudiced as I am I . . . believed my wife rather than my mother." Lee "became real hostile toward me. . . . My wife . . . told them they [were] going to leave whether they liked it or not, and I think Lee had the hostility toward my wife right then and there, when they were getting thrown out of the house, as they put it." Marge had gone farther than John testified. When the FBI interviewed her for the Warren Commission, she described a serious threat; in FBI paraphrase, "Mrs. Pic stated that after the incident wherein Lee Harvey Oswald threatened her with the knife, she told Mrs. Oswald to either get out of the apartment or she would have her brothers come and have her thrown out, and this precipitated further immediate bitterness, during which Mrs. Oswald threatened to jump out of a window." John's siding with his wife put an end to his relationship with his younger brother. "I was never able to get to the kid again after that," he remembered. "He didn't care to hear anything I had to say to him." A social worker later paraphrased Lee's words to her: "that while Lee felt John was glad to see them, his sister-in-law . . . was unhappy about their sharing the apartment until they could find a place of their own, and she made them feel unwelcome. Lee had to sleep in the living room during this period although there were five rooms in the apartment, and he admitted that this made him feel as he always did feel with grownups—that there was no room for him." He did not tell the social worker that he had threatened his sister-in-law with a knife.

Marguerite found a basement studio apartment in the Bronx and went to work as a sales clerk. Lee hated sharing a single room with his mother; by January he had convinced her to move. At J.H.S. 117, a Bronx junior high school, his ditty-bop-talking classmates in pegged pants ridiculed his Louisiana accent and dungarees until he quit attending school. "He felt that they didn't want any part of him," a probation officer paraphrases him, "and he didn't want any part of them. . . . He felt he wasn't learning anything in school and that he had other, more important things to learn and do." Thereafter he hung out at the Bronx Zoo. He called a truant officer who picked him up there a "damn Yankee" and told a teacher who came to the apartment to coax him back to school that he would think about it.

Early in 1953 Lee was charged with truancy. Marguerite turned up alone in juvenile court at the time appointed for a hearing and told the judge her son had refused to appear. The judge was sufficiently astonished by such precocious civil disobedience to issue a warrant remanding Lee to a juvenile detention center to evaluate if he was mentally ill. At Youth House he was interviewed in succession by a psychiatrist and a social worker, and their reports confirm that he was struggling during this New York period of his life with what Athens calls the "conflicting thoughts and emotions," the "need to take stock and come to terms with the brutalization experience" and the "huge gap between the ideal and real way in which people interact" that characterize the belligerency stage of violentization.

The Youth House chief psychiatrist, Dr. Renatus Hartogs, told the Warren Commission that his diagnosis of "personality pattern disturbance with schizoid features and passive-aggressive tendencies" implied that Lee was potentially violent, but he did not find the boy to be mentally ill. His contemporary report incorporated Lee's own interpretation of his situation:

> He is a tense, withdrawn and evasive boy who dislikes intensely talking about himself and his feelings. He likes to give the impression that he doesn't care about others and rather likes to keep [to] himself so that he is not bothered and does not have to make the effort of communicating. It was difficult to penetrate the emotional wall behind which this boy hides—[but] he provided us with sufficient clues, permitting us to see intense anxiety, shyness, feelings of awkwardness and insecurity as the main reasons for his withdrawal tendencies and solitary habits. Lee told us: "I don't want a friend and I don't like to talk to people." He describes himself as stubborn and according to his own saying likes to say "no." Strongly resistive and negativistic features were thus noticed—but psychotic mental content was denied and no indication of psychotic mental changes was arrived at. . . . Lee is intensely dissatisfied with his present way of living, but feels that the only way in which he can avoid feeling too unhappy is to deny to himself competition with other children or expressing his needs and wants. Lee claims that he can get very angry at his mother and occasionally he has hit her, particularly when she returns home without having bought food for supper. On such occasions she leaves it to Lee to prepare some food with what he can find in the kitchen. He feels that his mother rejects him and really has never cared very much

for him. He expressed the similar feeling with regard to his brothers who live pretty much on their own without showing any brotherly interest in him. Lee has a vivid fantasy life, turning around the topics of omnipotence and power, through which he tries to compensate for his present shortcomings and frustrations. He did not enjoy being together with other children, and when we asked him whether he prefers the company of boys to the one of girls, he answered, "I dislike everybody."

Evelyn Strickman, the social worker, coaxed a similar story from Lee. He was apparently less guarded with her, since his belligerency is more exposed in her evaluation. "He . . . felt his mother 'never gave a damn' for him," she reported. ". . . Although his brothers were not as detached as his mother was, he experienced rejection from them too, and they always pushed him away when he tried to accompany them. They never met any of his needs. He said he had to be 'my own father' because there was never anyone there for him." He felt, he told her, "almost as if there is a veil between him and other people through which they cannot reach him, but he prefers this veil to remain intact." After he "agreed to answer questions if he wanted to, rejecting those which upset him," he "acknowledged fantasies about being powerful, and sometimes hurting or killing people." He claimed these fantasies never involved his mother, but he "refused to elaborate" on them. (Strickman also interviewed Marguerite and found her to be a total narcissist: "I honestly don't think that she sees him as a person at all but simply as an extension of herself.")

At this crucial time of transition in Lee's life, when he was undergoing the form of dramatic self-change that Athens calls belligerency, which includes "ponder[ing] the nature of humanity and more particularly whether or not civility exists other than in fictional accounts of social life provided in books and by schools and churches," New York City was in turmoil over the impending executions of Julius and Ethel Rosenberg for having passed atomic secrets to the Soviet Union, one of the darkest dramas of modern American political life. The Rosenbergs were scheduled to be executed on June 19, 1953, and supporters of clemency for the young Communist parents were passing out literature, holding public rallies and collecting signatures on petitions to President Dwight Eisenhower. Six years later, when Lee defected to the Soviet Union, he credited the Rosenberg events with alerting him to communism. "I'm a Marxist," he told journalist Aline Mosby. ". . . I became interested about the age of fifteen [*sic*]. From an ideological viewpoint. An old lady handed me a pamphlet about saving the Rosenbergs. . . . I looked at that paper and I still remember it for some reason, I don't know why." He remembered it because it catalyzed a crucial conversion.

Lee's exposure to the Rosenberg auto-da-fé almost certainly extended beyond reading a pamphlet. He had long been interested in world events, and this one was unfolding dramatically before his eyes, up to and through the crescendo of rallies and last-minute appeals and the double execution itself that made orphans of the Rosenbergs' two young sons. And the martyrs were spies! Lee's favorite TV program as a child had been *I Led Three Lives,* about an FBI informant, Herbert Philbrick, who posed as a Communist spy. "In the early 1950s," Robert Oswald recalls, "Lee watched that show every week without fail. When I left home to join the Marines"—a month before Lee and Marguerite moved to New York—"he was still watching the reruns." Robert thought Lee had picked up his "imagination and love of intrigue" from their mother. "She's always had a wild imagination, and I think it influenced Lee's view of the world. Even now, she still sees a spy behind every door and tree."

Seeing spies behind every door and tree was a form of violent coaching: cuckoo-clock counseling that the world was a dangerous place. To the question Athens says the brutalized subject always asks himself as he enters into belligerency—"Why did all this happen to me?"—Lee glimpsed in the Rosenberg story the possibility that he might find in communism a partial answer. In an interview with journalist Priscilla Johnson McMillan in Moscow at the time of his defection he hinted at the answer he found: "At fifteen [*sic*]," he told McMillan, "I was looking for something that would give me the key to my environment." The key— why all this happened to him—was, "My mother has been a worker all her life. All her life she had to produce profit for capitalists. She is a good example of what happens to workers in the United States." To the question Athens says fully crystallizes the brutalized and increasingly belligerent subject's problem—"What can I do to stop undergoing any further violent subjugation and personal horrification at the hands of other people?"—Lee saw in the Rosenbergs' espionage and martyrdom an inspiring model for direct, heroic and, if necessary, violent action to change the world.

Most accounts of Oswald's life locate his first investigation of communism in New Orleans after his return there from New York in 1954. But a report of one of his eighth-grade teachers at P.S. 44 in Manhattan, where he grudgingly began attending school again in September 1953, offers evidence that his disaffection with his country began in the summer of the Rosenbergs' execution. "During the past two weeks," the teacher wrote, "practically every subject teacher has complained to me about the boy's behavior. He has consistently refused to salute the flag during early morning exercises. In many rooms he has done no work whatsoever. He spends most of his time sailing paper planes around the room. When we spoke to him about his behavior, his attitude was belligerent. I offered to help him, he brushed out [sic] with, 'I don't need anybody's help!' " Refusing to salute the flag was not merely delinquency; it was Lee's first recorded expression of political protest. Corroborating his conversion at thirteen in New York City, when McMillan asked him in Moscow why he had become a Marxist, he included among his reasons "watching the treatment of workers *in New York* and observing the fact that they are exploited" (emphasis added). Further corroborating his early conversion, shortly after Lee and his mother returned to New Orleans in January 1954, he deliberately sat in the segregated section of the public bus he rode to school, which led to a fight. His family thought, comically, that his stay in the North must have erased from his memory the fact that the buses in the city where he was born and spent his first six years were segregated, but the gesture of solidarity with African Americans was one he would repeat (he sat in the Negro section of the New Orleans courtroom where he pleaded guilty on August 13, 1963, to disturbing the peace during a dustup with anti-Castro Cubans, for example), and another reason he gave McMillan for converting to Marxism was that he had "observ[ed] the treatment of minority groups in America: Communists, negroes [sic] and the workers especially."

The belligerency stage of violentization, Athens writes, "ends with the subject firmly resolving to resort to violence in his future relations with people." This personal resolution "is still a strongly qualified one; the subject is prepared to resort to potentially lethal violence, but only if he deems it absolutely necessary for the well-being of his body and mind and if he believes he has at least some chance of success." Oswald had formed such a mitigated violent resolution by the time he returned to New Orleans in January 1954, as the violent performances that followed make clear. Because of the coincidence of Oswald's identification of Marxism as the "key to his environment" with his passage through the belligerency stage of violentization, his escalating violent resolutions through the rest of his life would be highly colored by his deepening commitment to revolutionary politics.

The fight on the bus was one of several that people remembered from the period after Lee and his mother returned to New Orleans from New York. Marguerite immediately enrolled her son in Beauregard Junior

High School, a tough school located near her sister, Lillian Murret's, house. Beauregard's standards were so low, Lillian testified, that she had never considered sending her own children there: "They had a very bad bunch of boys going to Beauregard, and they were always having fights and ganging up on other boys, and I guess Lee wouldn't take anything, so he got in several scrapes." That Lee "wouldn't take anything" is further evidence of his recent mitigated violent resolution, as is a classmate's testimony that she remembered him well "because he was always getting into fights"—he had avoided conflicts before. Of the fight on the bus, Robert Oswald writes: "Several boys jumped on Lee and started punching him. People who saw the fight said that Lee seemed unafraid. His fists flew in all directions, but he was outnumbered and thoroughly beaten up." Marilyn Murret specifies that the boys "hit him in the mouth, and loosened his front teeth."

A second major defeat followed another brawl—this one at Beauregard—and led Oswald to consider a significant escalation. Edward Voebel, a classmate who befriended Lee, was an eyewitness:

Lee had a fight with a couple of boys . . . the Neumeyer boys, John and Mike. [Mike] was maybe a grade or two below Lee, and Lee was in a fight with John. . . . The fight . . . started on the school ground, and it sort of wandered down the street. . . . It kept going on, across lawns and sidewalks, and people would run them off, and they would only run to the next place, and it continued that way from block to block. . . . It was . . . on my way home, going that way. . . . I think Oswald was getting the best of John, and the little brother sticking by his brother, stepped in too, and then it was two against one, so with that Oswald just seemed to give one good punch to the little brother's jaw, and his mouth started bleeding . . . and when that happened, the whole sympathy of the crowd turned against Oswald for some reason, which I didn't understand, because it was two against one, and Oswald had a right to defend himself [but] the whole sympathy of the crowd was against Lee at that time because he had punched little Mike in the mouth and made his mouth bleed. . . .

The next day or a couple of days later we were coming out of school in the evening, and Oswald, I think, was a little in front of me [and] some big guy, probably from a high school—he looked like a tremendous football player—punched Lee right square in the mouth, and without him really knowing or seeing really who did it. . . . He passed the post on him. . . . That's when somebody walks up to you and punches you. . . . Someone passed the post on Lee. . . . I think this was sort of a revenge thing on the part of the Neumeyer boys. . . . I think he even lost a tooth from that. I think he was cut on the lip, and a tooth was knocked out.

Voebel, feeling "sympathy toward Lee for something like this happening," befriended his classmate. He came to know Oswald well enough to tell the Warren Commission that Lee "wouldn't start any fights, but if you wanted to start one with him, he was going to make sure that he ended it, or you were going to really have one, because he wasn't going to take anything from anybody"—precisely Athens's definition of a physically defensive interpretation.

Voebel liked Lee. The Oswalds lived above a pool hall at that time. On his way home from piano lessons, Voebel sometimes met Lee at the pool hall. Voebel gave Lee a tour of his uncle's collection of military weapons and learned that Lee "wanted a pistol. . . . I had heard so much talk [from Lee] about stealing and robbing . . . that it really didn't bother me until he did shock me one day when he came up with a whole plan . . . for a burglary. . . . He revealed the plan for stealing this pistol from a place on Rampart Street. . . . He had observed a pistol in this . . . show window on Rampart Street and his plan was to steal it." Lee proposed to cut the window with a glass cutter, steal the pistol and replace it with a plastic model of a .45 automatic he owned. Voebel went with Lee to see the display, hoping to talk his friend out of committing a crime, noticed burglar alarm tape framing the window and convinced Lee that cutting the glass would set off the alarm. Why would Lee want a pistol? Having recently suffered two major defeats, he had probably concluded that his tactics were ineffective—that he needed, in Athens's words, to "resort to more lethal violence and resort to it much more quickly than in the past. . . ."

Yet he allowed himself to be talked out of stealing the pistol, and a decade would pass before he resorted to lethal violence despite considerable provocation in his personal life. Why? At the time when he was evidently considering escalating to more lethal tactics, he was also immersing himself in Communist and Marxist literature—*Das Kapital* and *The Communist Manifesto*, which he found at the public library, and other works. His deepening commitment to revolutionary Communist ideology appears to have led him to form a restraining judgment where challenges in his day-to-day life were concerned. That is, although he would not take anything from anybody, he would not start fights either; he was contemptuous of the bourgeois culture around him and saw no reason why he should risk his freedom or his life for less than what he considered the highest ideals. (In this rational choice of time and place he validated Athens's insight that "The occurrence of restraining judgments dispels the old, but still surprisingly prevalent, belief that violent crimes are 'acts of passion' devoid of all reason. . . . The individual's perceived longer-term interest may permanently halt or merely temporarily delay his execution of [a] particular violent plan of action.") But revolutionary violence was a different matter. There Oswald soon demonstrated the full extent of his mitigated violent resolution. This stratified investment in violence is consistent with Oswald's identification with espionage, which he expressed clearly to the New York social worker Evelyn Strickman when he told her that he felt "almost as if there is a veil between him and other people through which they cannot reach him, but he prefers this veil to remain intact." Much later, in a journal Oswald kept after he returned to the United States from the Soviet Union, he described his stratified violent resolution eloquently:

> Resourcefulness and patient working toward the aforesaid goals are preferred rather than loud and useless manifestations of protest. But these preferred tactics now may prove to be too limited in the near future [and] they should not be confused with slowness, indecision or fear. Only the intellectually fearless could even be remotely attracted to our doctrine, and yet this doctrine requires the utmost restraint, a state of being in itself majestic in power.*

Oswald's restrained solution to the violence at school was to quit school, which he did in October 1955, shortly after his sixteenth birthday, and to try to join the marines. The recruiting sergeant concluded that Oswald was underage and refused to sign him up despite the false affidavit Marguerite supplied that claimed he was seventeen. A month later, Oswald bought his first gun, a clip-fed, bolt-action Marlin .22 rifle.

Evidence that Oswald had not abandoned his mitigated violent resolution where political issues were concerned emerged in December 1955, when he found work as a messenger for a dental laboratory and be-

---

* I have corrected Oswald's execrable spelling. The original reads: "resoufualniss and patient working towards the aforesaid goal's are prefered rather than loud and useless manifestation's of protest. But these prefered tactics now, may prove to be too limited in the near future, they should not be confused with slowness, indesision or fear, only the intellectualy fearless could even be remotly attracted too our doctrine, and yet this doctrine requirers the utmost restraint, a state of being in itself majustic in power."

friended a fellow messenger, Palmer McBride. Interviewed by the FBI eight years later, McBride told the following tale:

> Because we both enjoyed classical music I invited him to my home . . . and he did visit my home perhaps two or three times. I was living with my parents at that time and during his visits we would listen to records in my room. During his first visit to my home . . . the discussion turned to politics and to the possibility of war. At this time I made a statement to the effect that President Dwight Eisenhower was doing a pretty good job for a man of his age and background. . . . Oswald was very anti-Eisenhower and stated that President Eisenhower was exploiting the working people. He then made a statement to the effect that he would like to kill President Eisenhower because he was exploiting the working class. This statement was not made in jest, and Oswald was in a serious frame of mind when this statement was made.

It was Eisenhower, of course, who had refused to stay the execution of Julius and Ethel Rosenberg.

As soon as Oswald turned seventeen, in October 1956, he joined the marines, where personal violence is endemic. In boot camp in San Diego he qualified as a sharpshooter, meaning he could hit a ten-inch bull's-eye from two hundred yards in a standing position eight times out of ten. In Japan, where he worked as a radar operator, he endured considerable provocation at first—homophobic taunts, forced cold showers, verbal challenges—with the utmost "majestic restraint," walking away rather than retaliating. Eventually he joined the group to the extent of socializing, drinking, visiting prostitutes and defending himself. He became skilled at baiting officers who knew far less than he about world events. This "won the admiration of the others in the outfit," a fellow marine testified. He managed to shoot himself in the arm with a contraband .22 derringer, possibly to avoid picket duty in the Philippines that he considered imperialistic, possibly accidentally while trying to scare a gang of marines who had been baiting him. He was court-martialed for owning an unregistered weapon and began thinking about defecting to the Soviet Union. At a bar one night he poured a drink on a sergeant who had punished him with extended KP duty for the shooting incident and challenged the noncom to fight, but the MPs broke up the confrontation, and Oswald received a second court-martial. He withdrew from socializing after his weeks in the brig and began studying Russian.

Reassigned to a base in California early in 1958, Oswald began to follow the revolution then being fought between rebels under Fidel Castro and government forces under Cuban dictator Fulgencio Batista. A former U.S. Army sergeant, William Morgan, had made a name for himself fighting as a major in Castro's army. Oswald befriended a Puerto Rican fellow marine, Nelson Delgado, and talked of following in Morgan's footsteps—"lead[ing] an expedition to some of these other islands," Delgado remembered, "and free[ing] them too." When Delgado realized that Oswald was serious, he "started getting scared" and backed off.

Oswald finished his tour of active duty in September 1959 and almost immediately defected to the Soviet Union. His defection is well known, as is the fact that it failed. It was nonviolent except for a stagy suicide attempt at the beginning, when it appeared that the Russians might not admit him. From Oswald's point of view it was idealistic, the largest gesture he ever made toward putting violence behind him. It was extraordinarily naïve. The Russians did not celebrate him, did not even trust him. They sent him off to Minsk to work in an electronics factory and bugged his apartment. He concluded, as he had concluded before on the smaller stage of Beauregard Junior High, that his resolve was adequate but his tactics ineffective.

He came home, in mid-June 1962, an angry man, prepared to renew and extend his dedication to violence. His new Russian wife, Marina, testified to the change. "In general," she wrote after the assassination, "our family life began to deteriorate after we arrived in America. Lee was always hot-tempered, and now this trait of character more and more prevented us from living together in harmony. Lee became very irritable, and sometimes some completely trivial thing would drive him into a rage." She told the Warren Commission, "I did not know such a man in Russia." He had always slapped his wife around, as he had slapped around his mother before, but later in the year he began beating her. In Dallas in October, Marguerite noticed a black eye. Neighbors in the apartment building where the Oswalds lived heard Marina hitting the floor and saw a black eye and a bruised cheek. She told a Russian friend that Lee beat her when he caught her smoking, punched her for not drawing his bath and had threatened to kill her. He threatened to kill her more than once. He began raping her. She began to be afraid of him.

In the primary political arena of the world, that is—the privacy of an intimate relationship—Oswald for the first time achieved successful major violent performances and discovered the dubious rewards of being known as an authentically violent individual. Not only Marina came to fear him; so did her friends.* Overvaluing these experiences of violent notoriety and social trepidation, he now made an unmitigated violent resolution, firmly resolving, in Athens's words, "to attack people physically with the serious intention of gravely harming or even killing them for the slightest or no provocation whatsoever." At the end of January 1963, two days after he had fastidiously finished paying back the U.S. State Department for the money it loaned him to return to the United States from the Soviet Union, he ordered the first of the two weapons he would ultimately use during the presidential assassination—the .38 caliber Smith & Wesson revolver with which he murdered Dallas patrolman J. D. Tippitt. Given what followed, he was certainly thinking of using it for political violence, but he may not yet have decided on his target. Priscilla McMillan judges that Oswald decided to target Maj. Gen. Edwin A. Walker, a Dallas spokesman for the ultraconservative John Birch Society, after hearing about him at a dinner party with Russian émigrés on February 13. Shortly thereafter Oswald forced Marina to write the Soviet Embassy in Washington asking to be repatriated to the USSR, presumably to get her out of the way. He choked and nearly strangled her later that month when she had the temerity to throw a jewelry box at him in the middle of a fight.

Then, to Oswald's surprise, Walker left Dallas. McMillan speculates that the unexpected departure gave Oswald breathing space to plan more carefully and write a "justification for history." He let up on Marina. On March 10 he staked out Walker's house and took photographs. The photographs confirmed the advantage of a sniper attack, and on March 12 Oswald ordered a 6.5mm Mannlicher-Carcano Italian military carbine with a four-power scope, a rifle with low kickback and rapid bolt action that the FBI later judged "a very accurate weapon." The rifle and the revolver arrived almost simultaneously late in March, and at the end of the month Oswald had Marina photograph him with his new weapons in a black assassin outfit, holding dated copies of two of the Communist periodicals to which he subscribed—thus documenting his preparations.

When Walker returned Oswald attempted to assassinate the right-wing general on the evening of April 10 by firing through a window of his

---

* Alex Kleinlerer observed Lee humiliating and slapping his wife (for not completely closing her skirt zipper) while he was helping the Oswalds move in November 1962. He told the Warren Commission, "I was very much embarrassed and also angry, but I had long been afraid of Oswald and I did not say anything." Of discussions with Oswald about the comparative virtues of the Soviet Union and the United States, Kleinlerer testified, "I did not argue with him because he appeared to me to be dangerous in his mind, and I was frightened."

house into a room where he was seated doing his taxes. Walker survived with only a few bullet fragments in his right forearm because the wooden windowpane framing did not resolve within the depth of field of Oswald's scope; the unseen crossbar deflected his accurate shot so that the bullet only creased Walker's hair and shattered against the wall. When Oswald returned home at eleven-thirty that night, Marina asked him what had happened. Not knowing that he had missed, he announced that he had shot Walker.

"I told him that he had no right to kill people in peacetime," Marina testified. "He had no right to take their life because not everybody has the same ideas as he has. People cannot be all alike. He said that this was a very bad man, that he was a fascist, that he was the leader of a fascist organization, and when I said that even though all of that might be true, just the same he had no right to take his life, he said if someone had killed Hitler in time it would have saved many lives." When Oswald learned that Walker was alive, Marina recalled, "He said only that he had taken very good aim, that it was just chance that caused him to miss. He was very sorry that he had not hit him." In Athens's terms Oswald's attempt to assassinate Walker qualifies as a "no decision," a state of limbo that represented neither proof nor disproof of the strength of his renewed resolve. To achieve a clear-cut victory, he would have to strike again. To achieve recognition of that victory he would have to strike higher. "He had shot at the most famous man in Dallas," McMillan observes, "he had missed him by less than an inch, and the only newspaper coverage had been . . . three stories—and not a single one mentioned his name."

Yet the very fact that Oswald had attempted such a radical and forbidden act—and gotten away with it—emboldened him. Marina noticed how cocky it made him and knew why. She saw the result later in April in a confusing incident that she remembered as Lee preparing to assassinate Richard Nixon:

> It was early in the morning and my husband went out to get a newspaper, then he came in and sat reading the newspaper. I didn't pay any attention to him because I was occupied with the housework. Then he got dressed and put on a good suit, and I saw that he took a pistol. I asked him where he was going, and why he was getting dressed. He answered, "Nixon is coming. I want to go and have a look." I said, "I know how you look" . . . because I saw he was taking the pistol with him. . . . I didn't know what to do. I wanted to prevent him from going out. . . . I called him into the bathroom and I closed the door [on him] and I wanted to pre-

vent him, and then I started to cry. And I told him that he shouldn't do this, that he had promised me. . . . I held him [in the bathroom]. We actually struggled for several minutes, and then he quieted down. I remember that I told him that if he goes out it would be better for him to kill me than to go out. . . . It might have been that he was just trying to test me. He was the kind of person who could try and wound somebody in that way. Possibly he didn't want to go out at all but was just doing all this as a sort of joke . . . to make me feel bad. . . . At first he was extremely angry, and he said, "You are always getting in my way." But then rather quickly he gave in, which was rather unusual for him. . . . I told him that, "You have already promised me not to play anymore with that thing." . . . Then he said, "I am going to go out and find out if there will be an appropriate opportunity, and if there is I will use the pistol."

Marina was pregnant at the time of this incident; she told McMillan that Lee relented because she warned him she could lose the baby and if she did so, "You'll have killed your own child."

Nixon was not scheduled to travel to Dallas that day, but Vice President Lyndon Johnson was. The *Dallas Morning News* Oswald read that morning headlined Nixon, however: NIXON CALLS FOR DECISION TO FORCE REDS OUT OF CUBA. Was Oswald's dyslexia at work? Was he teasing his wife? Did she mix up Johnson's and Nixon's names? Only Oswald might answer these questions. The incident is important nevertheless, for two reasons: It demonstrates that Oswald was prepared to use lethal violence with very little provocation, and it reveals his renewed preoccupation with Cuba.

That preoccupation took him to New Orleans at the end of April, where he found a job and rented a post office box under the name A. J. Hidell: *A* for his Russian first name, Alik; *J* for James Bond, a role model; "Hidell" with a long English *i* for its purpose, to hide his real identity; "Hidell" with a short Spanish *i* to rhyme with "Fidel." (McMillan offers this decoding, but makes the short *i* Russian because Marina spied it out.) Marina joined her husband in New Orleans in mid-May and found him dry-firing his rifle in the evenings after dark on the screened porch of the apartment he had rented for them. "I asked him why," she testified. ". . . He said that he would go to Cuba." He told her, "Fidel Castro needs defenders. I'm going to join his army of volunteers. I'm going to be a revolutionary."

On July 1 he checked William Manchester's biography of John F. Kennedy, *Portrait of a President*, out of the public library. He also read *The Huey Long Murder Case* that summer. After he finished the Manchester biography, he began talking grandiosely to Marina about becoming president or prime minister in twenty years—when, McMillan notes, he would be forty-three years old, Kennedy's age at election. He went on that summer to read Kennedy's *Profiles in Courage*, which offered him the encouragement of Kennedy's well-known words, "A man does what he must—in spite of personal consequences, in spite of obstacles and dangers and pressures—and that is the basis of all human morality."

On August 9 Oswald activated his rogue New Orleans chapter of the Fair Play for Cuba Committee, apparently to build his bona fides for Castro. The following week he proposed to Marina that they hijack a plane to defect to Cuba. Interviewed that week on a local radio program, "Latin Listening Post," he said he believed that Cuba was now the only revolutionary country in the world.

In early September he read in the *New Orleans Times-Picayune* a report of an impromptu interview with Castro during which Castro asserted that the CIA was plotting his assassination (it was) and announced, "We are prepared to fight them and answer in kind. United States leaders should think that if they are aiding terrorist plans to eliminate Cuban leaders, they themselves will not be safe."

At the end of September, Oswald took a bus to Mexico City to apply for a Cuban visa. According to the Warren Report, "He engaged in an angry argument with the [Cuban] consul who finally told him that 'as far as he was concerned he would not give him a visa' and that 'a person like him in place of aiding the Cuban Revolution, was doing it harm.' " What had Oswald said that led the consul to conclude he was harming the revolution? Two separate sources—a secret letter to the Warren Commission from FBI director J. Edgar Hoover and a British journalist's impromptu interview with Castro in 1967—confirm that Oswald told the consul that he was considering assassinating Kennedy.* The British journalist Comer Clark quoted Castro directly in words the Hoover letter indirectly confirms: "The first time [Oswald visited the consulate during his trip to Mexico City]—I was told—he wanted to work for us. He

---

* Hoover's information came from an FBI informant, a member of the American Communist Party, who spoke personally to Castro. Journalist Daniel Schorr revealed the letter. Castro later denied having made these statements. His denial does not make them false, and their separate origins and the assassination itself support their assertions.

was asked to explain, but he wouldn't. He wouldn't go into details. The second time [he visited the consulate during the same trip] he said he wanted to 'free Cuba from American imperialism.' Then he said something like, 'Someone ought to shoot that President Kennedy.' Then Oswald said—and this was exactly how it was reported to me—'Maybe I'll try to do it.' "

On November 22, 1963, Oswald tried and succeeded. Cuba had refused him a visa because he appeared to be a wild man or a CIA agent provocateur. Frustrated by that, as well as by Kennedy's continued hostility to Cuba, hating Kennedy for his hostility and for his wealth, fame and power, Oswald found himself fortuitously in the right place at the right time—back in Dallas, working at the Texas School Book Depository along the route Kennedy's motorcade would follow—and carried out a frustrative-malefic murder. He murdered Patrolman J. D. Tippitt the same day, when Tippitt moved to frustrate his escape. After Oswald was captured, his brother Robert observed "how completely relaxed he seemed, as though all of the frenzied activity there in the Dallas jail and all over the United States had nothing whatever to do with him." To the contrary, Oswald was relaxed precisely because it did—because he had finally established himself as an authentically violent individual of historic dimensions. Dallas police detective J. R. Leavelle understood: "He struck me as a man who enjoyed the situation immensely and was enjoying the publicity and everything [that] was coming his way."

Dallas Police Captain J. Will Fritz, who interviewed Oswald at length after the assassination, saw clearly what Oswald was about:

I got the impression he was doing it because of his feeling about the Castro revolution, and I think that . . . he had a lot of feeling about that revolution. I think that was the reason. I noticed another thing. I noticed a little before when Walker was shot *[sic]*, [Walker] had come out with some statements about Castro and about Cuba and a lot of things and if you will remember the President had some stories a few weeks before his death about Cuba and about Castro . . . and I wondered if that didn't have some bearing. . . . I know a lot of people call him a nut all the time, but he didn't talk like a nut. He knew exactly when to quit talking.

Curiously, none of the many historians and self-appointed conspiracy experts who have written about Lee Harvey Oswald mentions the largest interaction between Kennedy and Cuba, the Cuban Missile Crisis of

October 1962, days after Oswald's twenty-third birthday, just when he began ramping up his personal violence and contemplating violent political action. We were all glued to our televisions that week; would Oswald have been otherwise? And would that apocalyptic nuclear confrontation not have reminded him of Julius and Ethel Rosenberg and his ecstatic early commitment to revolution that would revenge and transcend his brutalization?

Oswald prepared no routes of escape from his hastily improvised act of terrorism. His refusal to confess to the crime, his calm self-assurance and his care not to give Captain Fritz compromising information suggest that he expected to be tried—tried with the whole world watching, including Fidel Castro and the Cuban bureaucrats who had refused him a visa. He had acted as his own attorney at his second marine court-martial; he probably anticipated doing so again and making the trial a forum for his radical political views.

Oswald had not reckoned with the likes of Jack Ruby, however, a fully virulent violent actor, who shot and killed the man accused of shooting and killing the president two days after the assassination, on Sunday morning, November 24, 1963, when the Dallas police were moving Oswald into an underground parking garage to transfer him from the city to the county jail.

Ruby was a far less exotic specimen than Oswald. Born in Chicago in 1911, the fifth of eight children of an impoverished Jewish immigrant couple, he was brutalized by one or both of his violent parents: His alcoholic father was "frequently arrested because of disorderly conduct and assault and battery charges" according to the Warren Report; his mother was "severe with her children"—as one of her daughters had reported in 1937, "she was selfish, jealous [and] disagreeable." By eleven, when Ruby was judged "incorrigible at home" and interviewed for removal to a foster home, a psychiatrist found that he was "quick tempered" and "disobedient." The Warren Report summarizes the psychiatrist's findings: "He frequently disagreed openly with his mother, whom he considered an inferior person with whose rules he did not have to comply. Jack told the institute's interviewer that he ran away from home because his mother lied to him and beat him." The psychiatrist reported Ruby claimed "that he can lick everyone and anybody in anything he wants to do." He was interested in street gangs and was already sexually active.

At eleven, in other words, Ruby had already passed through brutalization and belligerency. Living afterward essentially on the streets, supporting himself and helping support his siblings by ticket scalping and other hustles, he was violent only in physically defensive situations until adulthood, but his quick temper earned him the nickname "Sparky." He was known from young adulthood, however, as someone who would fight ferociously if he heard insulting remarks about Jews or in defense of others who were being insulted or harassed.

He tried to dodge the draft during the Second World War but was eventually inducted into the Air Force. After the war he moved to Dallas, where his sister operated a nightclub, and went into the nightclub business himself. His escalation beyond physically defensive violence dates from that time. In 1950 he beat an employee with a blackjack. In 1951, when his guitarist told him to go to hell, Ruby knocked the man down, pinned him to a wall and kicked him in the groin (the guitarist responded by biting off the first two digits of Ruby's left index finger). In 1955 Ruby beat one of his musicians with brass knuckles, the wounds requiring numerous stitches. In 1960, in a wage dispute, he slugged one of his entertainers so hard he knocked out one of the man's teeth. In 1962 he beat his handyman severely enough to send him to the emergency room. In early 1963 he threatened to throw one of his cigarette girls down the nightclub stairs. He was arrested many times but never convicted. He was a friend of the Dallas police who staged benefits for police widows. He also loved his dogs. He was his own bouncer; "on about fifteen occasions since 1950," says the Warren Report, "he beat with his fists, pistol-whipped or blackjacked patrons who became unruly. At other times, he ejected troublesome customers without a beating. . . . However, many people stated that he employed more force than necessary, particularly because he often ended a fracas by throwing his victim down the stairs of [his club]." In 1958 he disarmed a man who had drawn a gun on him at one of his clubs, "beat him almost to death, put the gun back in the man's pocket, and threw him down the stairs." He knocked down a man six inches taller than he who outweighed him by fifty pounds and made the giant crawl out of his club. He "severely beat a heavyweight boxer who had threatened him." He was known at least once to have chased a man while brandishing his pistol.

He reacted intensely to the plight of persons in distress. After the assassination, he considered Jacqueline Kennedy and her children to be severely distressed and voiced particular concern that Oswald's trial would force the president's widow to return to Dallas. As he fired his .38 revolver point-blank into Oswald's abdomen, severing Oswald's main intestinal artery and aorta and shattering his right kidney, Ruby yelled: "You killed my president, you rat!" Jack Ruby murdered Lee Oswald malefically, hating him for what he had done.

Many have found it difficult to believe that Lee Harvey Oswald was capable of organizing and carrying out the assassination of John F. Kennedy. I believe the evidence that he did so is overwhelming; this book is not the place to review that debate. But Oswald's lethal trajectory from a brutalized childhood, through the cruel arena of the Rosenberg executions, to the murders of John F. Kennedy and J. D. Tippitt, should put to rest any claim that he was mentally ill. Lonnie Athens's warning in the opening pages of *The Creation of Dangerous Violent Criminals* bears repeating here:

> When people look at a dangerous violent criminal at the beginning of his developmental process rather than at the very end of it, they will see, perhaps unexpectedly, that the dangerous violent criminal began as a relatively benign human being for whom they would probably have more sympathy than antipathy. Perhaps more importantly, people will conclude that the creation of dangerous violent criminals is largely preventable, as is much of the human carnage which follows in the wake of their birth. Therefore, if society fails to take any significant steps to stop the process behind the creation of dangerous violent criminals, it tacitly becomes an accomplice in creating them.

We are culpable for these killers. A hand extended to that happy, bright, observant, pleasant child might have spared us Lee Harvey Oswald's terrible swift sword.

CHAPTER FIFTEEN

Murders with Motives

Lonnie Athens found no evidence that mental illness causes violent crime. Some of the violent criminals he interviewed had been diagnosed as mentally ill; most had not. They all had in common not mental illness but violentization. What, then, distinguishes violent individuals judged not guilty by reason of mental illness from violent individuals judged sane and therefore responsible for their crimes?

Technically many courts draw the distinction on the basis of the McNaghten rule, introduced in England in 1843, and its variants—the standards for judging legal insanity, which require either that an offender did not know what he was doing at the time he committed a crime, or that if he did, he did not know it was wrong. The McNaghten rule imposes a legal, not a medical, distinction, and mental health professionals have long sought to replace it with a straightforward psychiatric determination of responsibility. Not surprisingly, police, prosecutors and other criminal-justice professionals—and civil libertarians as well—have opposed granting to psychiatry the determination of criminal responsibility that has resided for five hundred years in courts of law, judges and juries of peers.

One reason for that resistance has been the obvious inadequacy of psychiatry's attempts to explain the cause of violent behavior. What distinguishes defendants judged insane from those judged responsible? What distinguishes John Hinckley, Jr., judged insane at the time he shot President Ronald Reagan and confined in a mental hospital, from Sirhan Sirhan, judged criminal for shooting and killing Robert Kennedy and sent to prison? Bizarre behavior might explain the difference—Hinckley had been a celebrity stalker before he attempted to assassinate the president—but then why was Jeffrey Dahmer, who ritually cannibalized his victims, not judged insane? An obvious difference is the one Wayne State University criminologist Frank Hartung found in psychiatric discussions of klepto-mania versus shoplifting: social class. Hinckley was the son of wealthy parents who could afford adequate representation, including psychiatric consultation, for their son; Sirhan and Dahmer were not.

Recall that Hartung traced modern psychiatric concepts of irresistible impulse to the work of the most prominent and influential American psychiatrist of the nineteenth century, Isaac Ray, and showed that Ray's theory was based on social-class distinctions, not scientific evidence. Ray distinguished kleptomania from mere shoplifting with a value test: "When the propensity to steal is manifested in a person whose moral character has previously been irreproachable, and whose social position and pecuniary means render indulgence in this vice peculiarly degrad-ing and unnecessary, his plea of having committed the larceny while deprived, in a measure, of his moral liberty, deserves to be respectfully considered." The pioneer psychiatrist added, even more explicitly: "If the object stolen is of trifling value, or incapable of being turned to any pur-pose of use or ornament . . . there can scarcely be a doubt that the plea should be admitted."

A parallel distinction—a supposed lack of motive—plagues one of the most influential psychiatric theories of violent criminality, a theory formulated in a study to which Truman Capote refers in *In Cold Blood* because the psychiatrist who evaluated Perry Smith consulted its authors: "Murder Without Apparent Motive: A Study in Personality Dis-organization," by Joseph Satten, M.D., Karl Menninger, M.D., Irwin Rosen, Ph.D. and Martin Mayman, Ph.D, four specialists affiliated with the Menninger Clinic in Topeka, Kansas (of which I am a trustee). The study is itself an attempt to wrestle with the difficulties of determining under what circumstances violent criminals should be held responsible for their crimes.

Dividing the "sane" from the "insane" murderer, Satten and his coau-thors claim (the ironic quotation marks are theirs), is uncomplicated "when rational motives are conspicuous (for example, when a man kills for personal gain) or when the irrational motives are accompanied by delusions or hallucinations (for example, a paranoid patient who kills his fantasied persecutor)." But dividing "sane" from "insane" becomes diffi-cult with "murderers who seem rational, coherent, and controlled, and yet whose homicidal acts have a bizarre, apparently senseless quality."

Proposing to define a specific syndrome that might account for such "psychopathology," the authors describe four men convicted of "bizarre, apparently senseless" murders. All four had undergone psychiatric examinations prior to their trials and had been "found to be 'without psychosis' and 'sane.'" The authors examined the men when their murder convictions were appealed. The examinations had been requested, the authors point out, because "a lawyer, relative or friend" of the murderers "was dissatisfied with the psychiatric explanations previously given, and asked: 'How can a person as sane as this man seems to be commit an act as crazy as the one he was convicted of?'" (Isaac Ray asked the same question of his morally irreproachable shoplifters.) "Crazy," as Athens notes, is what bystanders call people who use violence that they consider excessive for the circumstances; like "trifling value" or apparent senselessness, "crazy" is a value judgment. Athens's work demonstrates from evidence that people who commit violent criminal acts have reasons for doing so that they believe to be significant, not trivial or senseless—reasons they do not usually share with mental health professionals.

The cases of the four murderers, as Satten and his coauthors summarize them, immediately recall Athens's categories of violent interpretation, as well as his skepticism of the exculpatory tales violent criminals tell:

A.—Thomas: A 31-year-old chief petty officer in charge of a hospital, while talking casually to the 9-year-old daughter of one of his superior officers, suddenly grabbed the child, choked her and held her head under water long after she was dead. A discontinuity existed in Thomas' mind as to what happened; he could not remember the beginning of the assault, but "suddenly discovered" himself strangling his young victim.

B.—Adams: A 24-year-old corporal looking for a prostitute near a French town was approached by a 13-year-old boy who persistently asked him to change Army scrip into French currency; when refused, the boy seemed to mock or make fun of him, whereupon he struck the boy. Adams insisted he had no intention of killing the victim and did not recall the actual killing. When Adams "found out" what he was doing, the victim's body had been severely mutilated.

C.—Mason: A 20-year-old laborer and truck driver, frightened and angry following an argument with a friend, picked up a 14-year-old boy to whom he suggested homosexual relations. The boy refused, and kept "nagging" Mason to take him back home. Mason struck the boy, and began choking him. He said he didn't intend to kill the boy, but "found" the victim was dead.

D.—Elliot: A 43-year-old married Negro soldier lapsed into a dreamlike dissociative state under the taunting and mocking of a prostitute attempting to seduce him [sic] and get his money. He struck her with a tire jack, killed her and then mutilated and dismembered her body.

The authors comment of these four cases that the murderers themselves "were puzzled as to why they killed their victims" and that it was not possible to "reconstruct a rational motive": The murderers seemingly gained nothing by their killings, the doctors conclude, the murders were not escalations of some accompanying crime such as robbery, the victims were strangers or nearly so, and the methods of killing were "haphazard and impromptu." But surely the motive is obvious in three of the four cases: Adams, the corporal pestered while looking for a prostitute, hated being mocked; Mason, the laborer who made a pass at a boy he picked up, was angry at being rejected and hated being nagged; Elliot, the soldier resisting a prostitute, hated her taunting and mockery. Thomas chose not to explain or remember what prompted his anger or hatred toward the daughter of a superior officer. These are rational motives—who has not hated being mocked or felt anger at being rejected?—but the authors are unable to credit them because in their experience people do not commit murder for such reasons.

The authors further assert that "In all instances . . . the murder was unnecessarily violent, and sometimes bizarre." What book of etiquette the four doctors consult to determine when a murder is only sufficiently violent and when it is "unnecessarily" violent they do not explain, but they do emphasize that the murderers continued assaulting the bodies of their victims long after they were dead. Back in the days when vehicles were horse-drawn, such prolonged abuse of recalcitrant animals was so commonplace that it entered the language as a phrase: "Beating a dead horse." Everyone knew what such behavior meant; it testified to a mean temper—a full quota of rage, if you will—not to mental illness.

The doctors examined each of these four men in ten to twelve hours of clinical interviewing and five to six hours of psychological testing. They collected personal histories from the men themselves and from people who knew them. They conducted physical and neurological exams. Their findings offer pervasive evidence of violentization. Three of the men "had been frequently involved in fights which were not ordinary altercations, and which would have become homicidal assaults if not stopped by others." One (unspecified) of these three had been particularly violent, requiring "7 to 10 strong men to restrain him," had been "involved in sadistic attacks on children over a period of many years" and had admitted to "unnecessarily [*sic*] killing children and civilians while on duty in wartime Europe."

Working backward from this clear evidence of violent performances and virulency, Satten and his coauthors report that "All [four men] had been concerned throughout their early years about being considered 'sissies,' physically undersized, or sickly." Given these indications that the men were brutalized as children, it comes as no surprise to learn that all four experienced "extreme parental violence during childhood." For one man, "severe corporal punishment was something he took for granted as one of the natural phenomena of life"; another had "many violent beatings in order to 'break' him of his stammering and 'fits,' as well as to correct him for his allegedly 'bad' behavior."

One characteristic the four doctors mention seems on first inspection to contradict Athens's findings: "Despite the violence in their lives, all of the men had ego-images of themselves as physically inferior, weak and inadequate." Since all four men appear to have passed through full violentization, their crimes are compatible with violent self-images. The authors do not define "ego-image," nor do they quote the testimony that led them to conclude their subjects saw themselves as "physically inferior, weak and inadequate." I suspect "inadequate ego-image" is an earlier formulation of the current term "low self-esteem." Mike Tyson, in the opinion of his September 1998 psychiatric examiners, similarly feels sorry for himself, believing "that he has been betrayed by individuals close to him" and "that he is being used, victimized, and treated unfairly." In the best shamanistic tradition, the doctors consistently interpret by opposites. They follow their observation about ego images, for example, by noting that "to all [four men], adult women were threatening creatures" despite the fact that Adams was actively seeking a prostitute to service him when his victim interrupted him and Elliot beat to death, mutilated and dismembered a prostitute who dared merely to verbally abuse him.

Psychological testing confirmed that these men maintained violent self-images, revealing "manifestations of a bizarre, violent, and primitive fantasy life . . . in each of the men we examined. Repetitive dreams of violently killing, mutilating, burning or destroying others were seen; the brief TAT* stories of these men were filled with a quality of primitive, murderous hostility, in some cases glibly [*sic*] rationalized on the basis of the victims having 'provoked' their murderers, and in others precipitated by rejection or rebuff."

---

* Thematic apperception test, a psychological test during which the patient makes up stories about a series of line drawings of ambiguous situations.

Despite the unabashed devotion to violence expressed by the four murderers, despite the evidence that the men had extensive personal experience of violence as both recipients and perpetrators and thought about it constantly, despite the obvious (if minimal) provocation of the circumstances, the doctors conclude that all four murders were the result of "unconscious motivation." The men were "murder-prone" because they carried a "surcharge of aggressive energy" (whatever that is), or had "an unstable ego defense system that periodically allows the naked and archaic expression of such energy." As a result their "murderous potential" could "become activated . . . when the victim-to-be is unconsciously perceived as a key figure in some past traumatic configuration." Translated, I think that means they were easily angered, and the people they murdered reminded them of someone they'd had trouble with before: "The behavior, or even the mere presence, of this figure adds a stress to the unstable balance of forces that results in a sudden extreme discharge of violence, similar to the explosion that takes place when a percussion cap ignites a charge of dynamite." In other words, since the provocation the four men experienced seemed, to the doctors, not to justify committing murder, the murderers must have been ready to blow anyway and simply needed the right spark. Given their heinous crimes, the four murderers in the study may deserve being dehumanized to the status of sticks of dynamite, but substituting a metaphor for a brutal reality is bad science. One consequence of such misunderstanding, as the Menninger doctors report, is that "3 of these 4 murderers had conveyed their fears of losing control to legal officials or psychiatrists *before the murders took place*. The warnings were disregarded." So much for "unconscious motivation."

Curiously, beyond the diagnosis implicit in the title of their paper ("personality disorganization"), Satten and his coauthors never quite say that they consider their four murderers to be mentally ill. They do claim that the "hypothesis of unconscious motivation explains why the murderers perceived innocuous and relatively unknown victims as provocative and thereby suitable targets for aggression." Somewhere in the unexamined background of this claim is a vague awareness that people interact with primary figures out of their past—with their phantom community—to decide how to handle present situations. In Adams's case, the doctors observe, "the young boy he killed was a camp pet who ran errands for the soldiers, just as he himself had been a mascot for the men in his father's lumber camp." Unfortunately they conclude from this parallelism not that Adams learned from his childhood experiences that mocking adults has consequences, but that the boy he killed represented to him his "own hated self-image" and that the murder "appear[s] to have been a deflected suicide." This florid conclusion violates a basic principle of scientific inquiry, the law of parsimony, also known as Occam's razor (for the medieval scholar who formulated it). The law of parsimony advises that the simplest explanation consistent with the facts should always be given preference over more complicated explanations (thus shaving an explanation as closely as possible). I could make a case that the four murderers perceived their victims to be dangerous aliens disguised as innocent humans and killed them to save humanity (not so different from the case the doctors make), but angry frustration and malefic hatred are entirely adequate explanations given the murderers' documented virulency.

Lonnie Athens's research had not even begun when "Murder Without Apparent Motive" was published, and I do not mean to imply that Satten and his coauthors should independently have discovered violentization. No doubt their hearts are in the right place, but they reveal their naïveté and their condescension when they characterize the murders they report as "impulsive" and "senseless" and ascribe them to unconscious motivations. Their influential paper at least reaches the useful conclusion that murders of this kind "have grown out of a history characterized by extreme parental violence and early severe emotional deprivation." More to the point, the four cases offer further independent evidence that violentization is the cause of violent criminality.

Dorothy Otnow Lewis, a psychiatrist at Bellevue Hospital in New York City, has explored the antecedents to criminal violence in a series of papers and a 1998 book, *Guilty by Reason of Insanity*. Lewis and Georgetown University neurologist Jonathan Pincus, while colleagues at Yale University, studied a group of ninety-seven juvenile delinquent boys and found differences between those who were more and less violent. Uniquely, Lewis and Pincus were able to return to these earlier findings later to examine which characteristics differentiated nine of the boys who had subsequently been arrested for murder from twenty-four who had not been arrested for serious felonies in the intervening years. In 1986 and 1987 Lewis and Pincus also interviewed and examined fourteen of the thirty-seven juveniles under death sentences in the United States at that time.

Lewis's work is too extensive to review here in its entirety. In general her findings unwittingly support violentization as the cause of violent crime. Of the fourteen boys sentenced to death as adolescents, for example, all but one described childhood family violence and severe physical abuse, and five described childhood sexual abuse as well (the one exception denied experiencing physical, sexual or family violence; I would guess he wasn't talking). Pincus found that many of the boys had sustained serious head injuries and showed signs and symptoms of neurological damage—not surprising given their violent childhoods, but not in itself predictive, since many other people sustain neurological damage in childhood without becoming violent.

In the large group of ninety-seven delinquents Lewis and Pincus studied, Lewis reports that "the most striking difference psychiatrically between [more and less violent delinquents] was the finding that a significantly greater proportion of very violent children demonstrated or gave clear histories of paranoid symptomatology." Lewis explains earlier in the paper that she judged "paranoid symptomatology" to be present "if children had mistakenly believed that someone was going to hurt them and could provide several examples of this, or if they admitted to constantly feeling the need to carry weapons such as guns and metal pipes for their own protection in the absence of identifiable dangers." Since these juveniles were incarcerated in a correctional school in Connecticut serving "the most seriously delinquent children throughout the entire state" and had experienced violent subjugation prior to their incarceration, it is difficult to understand why Lewis judges their belief that someone might hurt them to be mistaken and their belief that they needed to carry weapons to protect themselves paranoid. To the contrary, their so-called paranoid symptomatology probably signaled that these more violent juveniles had passed beyond brutalization into belligerency and violent performances.

The more violent children, Lewis reports, "had been physically abused by mothers, fathers, stepparents, other relatives, and 'friends' of the family. The degree of abuse to which they were subjected was often extraordinary. One parent broke her son's legs with a broom; another broke his fingers and his sister's arm; another chained and burned his son; and yet another threw his son downstairs, injuring his head, following which the boy developed epilepsy." Pincus found that "almost 30% of the very violent children had grossly abnormal electroencephalograms . . . and/or a history of grand mal epilepsy, compared with none of the less violent sample."

In addition to this extensive evidence of violent subjugation, Lewis also reported evidence compatible with personal horrification: "The two samples also differed significantly in their exposure to violence. The fact that 76.8% of the more violent children were known to have witnessed extreme violence directed at others, mostly in their homes, compared with 20.0% of the less violent children, tells only part of the story." The rest of the story is the degree of violence they witnessed: "Several children witnessed their fathers, stepfathers, or mothers' boyfriends slash their mothers with knives. They saw their siblings tortured with cigarette butts, chained to beds, and thrown into walls. They saw their relatives—male and female—arm themselves with guns, knives, and other sharp instruments and, at times, use these weapons against each other. . . . Many children reported defending their mothers with pipes and sticks while their mothers were being attacked."

Lewis recognizes that these experiences have developmental consequences: "First, physical abuse often causes central nervous system damage, thus contributing to impulsivity, attention disorders and learning disabilities. Second, it provides a model with which to identify. Finally, it engenders rage toward the abusing parent, rage that can then be displaced onto authority figures and other individuals, against whom the child may vent this anger." Arguing that violence is "displaced" rage takes us back to the Menninger doctors' percussion caps and dynamite. Evoking a similar metaphor, Lewis implies that choosing to use violence to settle disputes is merely a "venting" of subterranean volcanic anger rather than a deliberate act. Such metaphors obscure the process Lewis is trying to understand and depersonalize the damaged children for whom she obviously feels compassion. The second and final of the developmental consequences on Lewis's list in fact parallel those Athens reports—violent coaching, the vengeful brooding of brutalization and early belligerency, the resolution to use violence that completes the belligerency stage.

When Lewis went on to compare nine of this large group who later were arrested for murder with twenty-four who had not been arrested for violent offenses in the intervening six years, she found that the nine were difficult to distinguish from the other twenty-four. She thought the nine showed more "psychotic symptoms" (Lewis lists "paranoid ideation," "illogical thinking," "bizarre, violent drawings," suicide attempts, "previous psychiatric hospitalization" and "visual and auditory hallucinations") and "major neurological impairment" and more frequently had close relatives who had been diagnosed to be psychotic. But, she writes, "neither early violence alone nor a history of abuse strongly distinguished the groups from each other." Since the twenty-four included fifteen who had been sent to the Connecticut correctional school for "serious violence, e.g., assault with a weapon, rape," it is unsurprising that Lewis had difficulty distinguishing them from the nine murderers—

at least fifteen of the twenty-four had evidently already moved into the violent performances stage of violentization and would have been developmentally similar to the nine murderers, if not yet fully virulent.

Lewis also judges the murders the nine committed to have been "mindless, impulsive, and unpredictable" and therefore "spontaneous rather than premeditated," showing that even such a determined and intelligent investigator as Dorothy Lewis has been misled by psychiatry's unsupported assumptions about motive and impulsiveness. As Athens writes of the corresponding conviction in the field of criminology, "It was believed that if violent criminals really thought about what they were doing, they would never commit their violent crimes. This naive belief was and still is based on the false assumption that unless violent criminals think like professional criminologists, their acts are, ipso facto, devoid of thought."

Some of the violent juveniles Lewis examined told her they heard voices. Auditory hallucinations are among the "psychotic symptoms" Lewis reports. Crime stories often mention that an accused murderer "heard a voice telling him to kill." In *Guilty by Reason of Insanity*, Lewis enlarges these reports into a theory that violent criminals are victims of multiple personality disorder. She acknowledges that "multiple personality disorder . . . has no laboratory test to validate its existence" (indeed, she notes, "very few mental illnesses can be confirmed by laboratory data"), but she reports meeting and talking to different "personalities" during her examinations of violent felons. "How these beings are created," she comments,

> no one really knows. It looks to observers as though certain chronically abused children self-hypnotize; they remove themselves from the situation. They see what is happening, but do not feel it. It is as if it were happening to someone else—someone else feels the pain and is strong enough to endure it. In time that someone else becomes a protector. Over the years, we have come to appreciate the ambivalent relationship that exists between protector personality states and the helpless children who created them. These protectors boast, "I took the pain." Then in the very next breath, they threaten to hurt, maim, even kill the "wimp" whose pain they endured. They are contemptuous of the child they saved.

Everyone hears voices, though not everyone names them as such. If that statement seems outrageous, bear with me. Some children have imaginary playmates with whom they converse. Particularly in times of crisis, many people acknowledge talking to and hearing from signifi-cant figures in their lives, such as a deceased parent or mentor, or God. Religious vocations commonly begin when God calls the suppliant to service. A fad of the 1990s found many Americans reporting angelic interventions—often disembodied voices—that they believed saved their lives. Most of us are familiar with the annoying experience of hearing a song lyric looping in our heads that we cannot seem to stop. More extremely, florid schizophrenics report being plagued by loud, incessant voices that are frequently critical, intimidating and so distracting that the schizophrenic finds it almost impossible to function.

(Sometimes the voices people hear at times of crisis are accompanied by visual hallucinations. People sometimes not only hear angels or aliens, for example, but also see them. Hallucinations, like voices, are commonplace in human experience. Under normal circumstances they occur during sleep, and we call them dreams.)

Although we might wish to believe otherwise, there is in fact no sharp dividing line in this spectrum of voices, from the faint to the florid. You may argue that normal people know the voices they hear are not "real," that when we hear from Mom or God or Eleanor Roosevelt we know we are really pretending to hear, to dramatize retrieving from memory Mom's or God's or Eleanor Roosvelt's useful advice. In normal situations we may stipulate that distinction to maintain the convention that normal people do not hear voices. People undergoing crises evi-dently feel justified in abandoning such stipulation. They testify in authoritative numbers that the voices they hear are real. And they are, though it is we who are generating them. They are the voices of our phantom companions, incorporated into our selves, advising us. We hear them with increasing urgency in times of crisis. Schizophrenics suffer from chemical imbalances that disable their volume controls; with medi-cation, the schizophrenic's voices fade into the quiet background where everyone's phantom companions ordinarily reside.

Everyone also self-hypnotizes—that is, narrows and focuses attention—most commonly during athletic performances and in the course of entering that state of alternative reality called sexual arousal. Many people dissociate—split, find themselves watching themselves—at times of social stress and particularly in emergencies, allowing a "protec-tor" to perform for the "wimp" who is uncomfortable or panicked. I vividly remember an occasion when my stepmother was beating my brother Stanley over the head with a mop handle from which a danger-ous bolt projected. I pretended to be invisible, hoping she would not see me and therefore would not attack me as well. (I remember the occasion because when I recalled it to Stanley forty years later, he corrected my faulty memory: It had been he who was watching and I who was being beaten. *His* recollection might be wrong, of course, but because he is older than I, I assume his memory of our common childhood experiences is more accurate than mine.)

As a writer, I have long been fascinated with where fictional characters come from. When I have written novels, my most vivid characters have seemed to emerge complete and entire—talking, thinking and behaving exactly as if they had been waiting in some unacknowledged mental greenroom to walk onto the fictional stage. One such character emerged for my novel *The Last Safari,* set in East Africa. A loyal, sensible, dignified, dryly humorous Somali assistant to the white hunter who was the main character of the story, Abdi appeared—seemingly unbidden— and all but dictated his dialogue. Only after the novel was published did I realize that he was a slightly disguised version of Tonto, the Lone Ranger's Indian sidekick, a character I knew intimately from listening to radio serials as a child. I have concluded from such experiences that writing fiction has affinities with improvisational acting, except that the writer expresses his improvisations in words. Both processes have obvious affinities as well with the production of "personalities."

Many of the violent criminals Athens interviewed told him that they heard voices in the course of committing their crimes. He saw nothing remarkable in that testimony. It simply confirmed his understanding that their decisions to act violently followed from a dialogue with their phantom communities—the "voices" were their phantom companions coming in exceptionally loud and clear. Lewis's "protected personality states," which threaten to kill and maim, correspond to the violent primary-group figures whom violent criminals consult in deciding how to interpret the behavior of their potential victims. Lewis unknowingly corroborated Athens's finding that the self incorporates phantom companions when she examined Arthur Shawcross, the Rochester, New York, so-called serial killer who murdered prostitutes. "Arthur Shawcross also experienced dissociative states," Lewis reports. "At these times he would hear his mother in his head, berating him and the women he was seeing. No one was good enough for Arty. They should die."

It is disappointing that Lewis should have diverted her exploration of violent criminality into the blind alley of multiple personality disorder (MPD). Significantly, she evoked her multiples' so-called recovered memories with hypnosis. "Once," she writes, "during a session in which hypnosis was used, Mr. Shawcross relived being sodomized with a broom handle, falling to the floor, and being unable to move. In his ordinary, conscious state he had no memory of this event."

The use of hypnotic suggestion to develop evidence of multiple personality disorder, family incest and supposed satanic ritual sexual abuse of children has been widely and justifiably discredited. In 1998, for example, John Jay College of Criminal Justice psychologist Robert Rieber reported reviewing old tape recordings of conversations between psychiatrist Cornelia Wilbur, who treated the famous "multiple" known as "Sybil," and author Flora Schreiber. The tapes, Rieber said, documented "the fraudulent construction of [Sybil's] multiple personality" by the implantation of "personalities" during hypnosis and Pentothal ("truth serum") sessions. "Sybil is a phony multiple-personality case at best," Rieber concluded. Wilbur and Schreiber's book, *Sybil*, published in 1973, began a fad of MPD diagnoses. Fewer than fifty cases of MPD were known before 1973; by 1990 more than twenty thousand had been diagnosed. I am not challenging the honesty of Lewis's work by drawing this comparison, only questioning its validity. Lewis retains enough skepticism to note that "material produced under hypnosis is always suspect, especially in a court of law."

Medical practitioners have been calling violent criminals crazy for at least the past two centuries. The criminal-justice system has strenuously resisted that interpretation. The conflict is partly a turf war, of course, comparable to the turf war medicine has largely won against religion by reinterpreting what used to be called sinfulness or diabolic possession as mental illness. If psychiatry drew its conclusions about violent behavior from scientific evidence, then it might have an argument, but Athens's authoritative scientific evidence that violentization is a developmental process rather than a psychopathology contradicts prevailing psychiatric theory, as I have tried to illustrate here. Psychiatric theory in this matter has little more basis in fact than the epithets people borrow from it to describe the newly fledged violent performer, as Athens writes, "for the first time in his life . . . in complete seriousness . . . as a 'violent lunatic,' 'violent maniac,' 'violent crazy man,' 'madman' or 'insane killer.' " Labeling violent people crazy does not make them so (although some of them, coincidentally, may be), nor has anyone found a treatment that can reliably deescalate a violent career.

Psychiatry is not to blame for the emergence of the late-twentieth-century fictional monster known as the serial killer, but the psychiatric concept of criminal violence as an unconsciously motivated explosion of rage bolsters the credibility of what is in fact a bureaucratic invention. "New views of serial murder," confirms historian Philip Jenkins in *Using Murder: The Social Construction of Serial Homicide,* "derived chiefly from the Behavioral Sciences Unit (BSU) of the Justice Department, with its headquarters at Quantico, Virginia, within the FBI National Academy. This unit had been established in the early 1970s, and rapidly developed an interest in 'profiling' violent offenders. . . . It was this group that popularized the terms *serial crimes* and *serial murder.*"

Ultraviolent criminals sometimes commit a series of murders, Athens points out; such serial homicides are enacted most commonly by violent drug dealers, professional murderers and armed robbers in the course of doing business. The BSU was originally concerned with the barriers to pooling information about such multiple crimes across city, county and state jurisdictions. Solving the problem offered the FBI a route to enlarging its authority, but local law enforcement resented federal intrusions into their jurisdictions. The notion of an irrational, predatory "serial killer" emerged in the early 1980s amid widespread hysteria about dangers to children from pornographers, satanic cults, lethal day-care centers and kidnappers, and the BSU encouraged it by cooperating closely with the media whenever a suitably baroque spree killer or multiple murderer happened to be on the loose. Jenkins identifies the 1983 hearings on child kidnapping and serial homicide of the U.S. Senate's Juvenile Justice Subcommittee, chaired by Sen. Arlen Specter, as the public forum from which emerged the popular notion of a multitude of predatory serial killers scourging the land; the hearings officially focused "on patterns of murders committed by one person in large numbers with no apparent rhyme, reason or motivation"—Satten and his coauthors' "murder[s] without apparent motive" again.

Specter's subcommittee estimated that there had been as many as 3,600 "random and senseless murders" in 1981; by the time the number had whispered its way around the circle of public discussion, it was inflated to estimates of 4,000 or 5,000 serial-killer victims per year (of about 23,000 total U.S. homicides). Jenkins discovers by looking closely at the official records that this large estimate was assembled by crediting "serial killers" with all homicides where the relationship between offender and victim was unknown, and with most cases where the offender was a stranger to the victim. In contrast, Jenkins writes, "current FBI estimates of the [so-called serial killer] problem suggest that the annual number of victims is closer to two hundred than four thousand," and the BSU's internal files ("based largely on news clipping services,"

Jenkins found) assign only about 50 homicides per year across the twentieth century to serial murderers.

More influential by far than congressional hearings in establishing the archetype of the serial killer was Jonathan Demme's 1991 film *The Silence of the Lambs,* based on Thomas Harris's best-selling novel of the same title, which glamorized the BSU even as it portrayed two colorful—but fictional and improbable—serial killers. In the 1990s the threat to American civilization, not to say women and children, of irrational, predatory serial killers was widely acknowledged, not least because it fit so many social, political, cultural and bureaucratic agendas, including those of family-value and law-and-order conservatives, antipornographers, feminists, homophobes, federal law enforcement agencies, child-victim advocates and Christian fundamentalists.

Far from producing accurate "profiles" of serial killers, the BSU has been criticized by professionals for reporting only its successful cases. "I mean, how many serial killer cases has the FBI solved—if any?" one FBI agent has asked publicly. Athens participated in the investigation of a series of rape-murders in Richmond in which the BSU was also involved, the Southside Strangler case. Because the BSU incorrectly profiled the perpetrator as a middle-aged white male, police passed over the young African American who actually committed the crimes, Timothy W. Spencer, when they raided a halfway house where he was a resident; he killed again shortly afterward. Spencer, ultimately convicted on DNA-matching evidence, became the first person executed in the United States for a DNA-based conviction.

The serial killer as deranged psychopath is a fiction, Athens concludes. Ultraviolent criminals may kill multiple victims within a short enough period of time to qualify for designation as "serial killers," but they know what they are doing and do it consciously, not compulsively and unconsciously. Even John Douglas, one of the best known of the BSU "mind hunters," concurs. "It strains credibility," he writes, "that multiple killers are so compelled to commit their crimes that they have no choice. Keep in mind that no serial killer in my experience ever felt so compelled to kill that he did so in the presence of a uniformed police officer."

If violentization is not mental illness but a developmental process, did it operate in the past as well as the present? Has it appeared in other times and cultures? If so, what is its function? What purpose does it serve? Athens's work opens the way to a consideration of these questions, which carry us across cultures and centuries into an alien, violent world.

CHAPTER SIXTEEN

Monopolies of Violence

Gian Lorenzo Bernini, the seventeenth-century Italian sculptor and architect, was a dangerous man. So was his younger brother Luigi. Their father, a Florentine sculptor who worked in Naples and Rome, had raised them in the family business and taught them their trade. Bernini was born in Naples in 1598 and died at the Vatican in 1680. Across his long life he perfected the Baroque style in sculpture in such well-known works as *The Ecstasy of Saint Teresa of Avila* and his bust of Louis XIV. He designed Saint Peter's Square and the Throne of Saint Peter inside the great cathedral itself.

In a review of books about Bernini and his work, James Fenton comments that the celebrated sculptor "was much feared for his anger" and illustrates why:

> One morning in 1638 Bernini saw Luigi leaving the house of his, Bernini's, mistress, who accompanied him to the door, [biographer] Charles Avery tells us, "in a suggestively disheveled state." Bernini, like most sculptors, was a strong man. He chased his little brother to their workplace at Saint Peter's and went at him with a crowbar, breaking a couple of his ribs. Then he pursued him home, sword in hand. When his mother closed the door against him, Bernini broke it down. Meanwhile Luigi had taken refuge in [the church of] Santa Maria Maggiore. Once again Bernini pursued him, but finally gave up beating on the door.

> Nor does the story end there. Bernini sent a servant to his mistress, Costanza Bonarelli, Fenton continues, "with instructions to disfigure her. The servant found Costanza in bed and slashed her with a razor." In the

meantime, Bernini, who had been "fiercely in love" with his mistress, cut her face out of a double portrait he had painted of her and him. He was fined three thousand scudi for his mistress's mutilation, Fenton reports—the price of one of his busts—"but the Pope waived the fine; the servant took the rap and went into exile." Luigi wisely absented himself awhile on another family project in Bologna.

Thirty years later Luigi violently assaulted and sodomized a young boy inside Saint Peter's itself. Luigi was supervising the construction of Bernini's Scala Regia, the elaborate arched staircase that connects Saint Peter's with the Vatican Palace; the boy was a member of his work crew. "The young victim suffered sixteen broken bones," writes art historian T. A. Marder of the assault. "Luigi was forced to flee to Naples upon threat of arrest and punishment, and his possessions were seized. The papal family was angry, the Bernini name fell into disgrace, and the great artist's future was endangered." Bernini was required to pay the boy's father a fine of two thousand scudi and an additional twenty-four thousand scudi to the public treasury, but the fine was eventually reduced and Luigi pardoned.

What world was this in which someone considered by his contemporaries to be not only Europe's greatest artist but also one of its greatest men carries a sword he is prepared to use, batters his brother with a crowbar and orders his mistress slashed? In which a servant severely wounds a woman with a razor on his employer's order? In which a man of prominence and mature years assaults and rapes a boy?

The civilian past was far more violent than the civilian present. The historical evidence of much higher rates of personal violence in past times is abundant and incontrovertible. Reporting agencies calculate murder rates as an annual total per 100,000 population. The murder rate in the United States in the last quarter of the twentieth century (when many Americans felt threatened by violent crime) varied from a high of 10.2 per 100,000 in 1979 to a low of 7.9 per 100,000 in 1983 and 1984. In 1994 the rate was 9. These numbers are high compared to modern homicide rates in Western Europe. In 1990, when the U.S. rate was 9.4, the British rate was only 1.5, the Netherlands 0.9, Sweden 1.5, France 1.1, Germany 1. (To anticipate one comment: The U.S. rate would have been high—4.8— even if African American offenders were excluded.)

Averaged into these national rates are higher rates for categories of people more prone to violence. Young U.S. black men were murdered in 1960 at the rate of 46 per 100,000; in 1993 their homicide death rate had almost quadrupled, to 167. The homicide death rate for all U.S. men fifteen to twenty-four years of age was 22 in 1987 and 37 in 1994. By contrast the rate for young British men in 1994 was 1.

But in thirteenth-century England, historians estimate, the national homicide rate was around 18 to 23 per 100,000. In fifteenth-century Sweden it ranged from 10 to 45. In London in the fourteenth century the homicide rate was 36 to 52 per 100,000; in Amsterdam in the fifteenth century it was 47 or more; in fifteenth-century Stockholm it was 42.5. These annual rates declined gradually until the eighteenth century, when they dropped rapidly to modern historic lows: 0.9 in England as of 1802, 1.4 in nineteenth-century Amsterdam, 3 in nineteenth-century Stockholm. Even the U.S. homicide rate declined to a comparable low of 1 per 100,000 in 1900 before beginning its war-fueled modern rise.

The violence of medieval Europe was personal violence. "Every day," complained an eleventh-century bishop of Worms, "murders in the manner of wild beasts are committed among the dependents of St. Peter's. They attack each other through drunkenness, through pride, or for no reason at all. In the course of one year thirty-five serfs of St. Peter's, completely innocent people, have been killed by other serfs of the church; and the murderers, far from repenting, glory in their crime." A cleric in an early chronicle found nothing romantic about a knight and his lady who terrorized the district:

> He spends his life in plundering, destroying churches, falling upon pilgrims, oppressing widows and orphans. He takes particular pleasure in mutilating the innocent. In a single monastery, that of the black monks of Sarlat, there are 150 men and women whose hands he has cut off or whose eyes he has put out. And his wife is just as cruel. She helps him with his executions. It even gives her pleasure to torture the poor women. She had their breasts hacked off or their nails torn off so that they were incapable of work.

Norbert Elias, the magisterial social historian of what he called "the civilizing process," writes of medieval Europe that "fear reigned everywhere; one had to be on one's guard all the time. . . . The majority of the secular ruling class of the Middle Ages led the life of leaders of armed bands. This formed the taste and habits of individuals. Reports left us by that society yield, by and large, a picture similar to those of feudal societies in our own times, and they show a comparable standard of behavior. . . . The warrior of the Middle Ages not only loved battle, he lived in it." By way of example Elias quotes a warrior's speech in a war hymn attributed to the minstrel Bertran de Born:

I tell you that neither eating, drinking nor sleep has as much savor for me as to hear the cry "Forwards!" from both sides, and horses without riders shying and whinnying, and the cry "Help! Help!" and to see the small and the great fall to the grass at the ditches and the dead pierced by the wood of the lances decked with banners.

"By my troth," boasts a king in a medieval *chanson de geste,* "I laugh at what you say, I care not a fig for your threats, I shall shame every knight I have taken, cut off his nose or his ears. If he is a sergeant or a merchant he will lose a foot or an arm." ("The fields which the *chansons de geste* describe," writes a French historian, "are littered with severed heads and scattered brains.") Compare these expressions of men with violent self-images with the violent self-image of Lonnie Athens's Case 35, a male in his early twenties convicted of aggravated assault:

I was a low rider. I loved to get loaded and drive fast or just kick back and listen to hard rock, drink wine, smoke dope and wrench my high-powered motor. . . .

When I got bored with all that, then I might go out scrapping. I was a quiet dude but enjoyed touching up a dude that was loud. If I heard a dude talking loud about a lot of shit, it upset me inside. Once that happened, I wanted to get it on, check out the dude's oil and find out if he was a quart low. I was not often ever scared of anybody or anything. I'd seen life come and go. . . . When I was hot, I was a mad animal, and even when I was cool, I still acted like a barbarian. . . .

The philosophy that I followed was that you do whatever you want to do, when and how you want to do it, and fuck everything and everybody else. This meant to me that you had the most balls, you did the most outrageous things; in other words, that you were one of the most terrible motherfuckers who ever walked the streets.

Did all these violent medieval nobles and peasants suffer from antisocial personality disorder or low self-esteem? A Dutch historian examining long-term trends in homicide advises otherwise: "We should not be led astray by the current assumptions of our time, according to which violent behavior is always destructive, 'dysfunctional,' and devoid of meaning. Such an unrealistic view of violence can only disparage our historical judgment of aggressive behavior in the past." Unless we are prepared to believe that violent behavior constitutes mental illness in one century but not in another, differing rates of violence at different times and places refute the psychiatric designation of violent behavior as psychopathology; and they refute genetic attribution as well.

Why was medieval Europe so violent? An Israeli historian studying crime in fourteenth- and fifteenth-century Paris concludes:

> Violence was the normative method of settling personal disputes in all classes of society [in Paris] in 1332, as it was in 1488. Aggression, both verbal and physical, was part and parcel of normal social intercourse. . . . The majority of cases concern brawls, street fights and casual violence. . . . While people resorted to violence with great ease, it was neither aimless nor detached. Emotionally motivated, it was based upon a variety of contacts and feelings. Propinquity, coprofessional loyalty, jealousy and revenge all played a role. It could occasionally stem from nothing more than rowdiness or drinking, while at other times it might be carefully planned and premeditated.

In thirteenth-century England, similarly, historian Ted Robert Gurr finds "a society in which men (but rarely women) were easily provoked to violent anger and were unrestrained in the brutality with which they attacked their opponents. Interpersonal violence was a recurring fact of rural and urban life." Nearly everyone carried a knife, historian James Given points out, as an eating utensil as well as a work tool: "Thus, when people quarreled, there was always the possibility that the participants might resort to knives, with lethal consequences." Given studied thirteenth-century English eyre rolls—records of sessions of eyres, which were county circuit courts convened by panels of royal justices. Of those cases where the murder weapon was listed (455 of his sample of 2,434 cases), he found that 30 percent of victims died of knife wounds. Agricultural tools served as weapons—axes, pitchforks, spades, mattocks, scythes. "Even if there was no sharp-edged tool at hand," Given writes, "people were ready to resort to whatever they could lay hold of. After knives, the most popular murder weapon was a stick of some sort, which accounted for 100 victims. Stones (fifteen cases), trivets (one), stools (one), and pieces of firewood (one) were all pressed into service at some time. Forty people were simply beaten or strangled to death, presumably with only hands and feet." Commoners committed these ad hoc murders and manslaughters; gentlemen and noblemen more often attacked each other with swords. "So common was violent death from homicide," another historian of thirteenth-century England, Barbara Hanawalt, found, "that in medieval London or Oxford the man in the street ran more of a risk from dying at the hands of a fellow citizen than from an accident. There were 43 percent more homicides than misadventures in London and 26 percent more in Oxford. In rural Northamptonshire the percentage of homicidal deaths was only 10 percent lower than accidental deaths."

The earliest depositions and indictments that I found available in published records date from the seventeenth century in England and Scotland, but they fully demonstrate the "violent anger" and "unrestrained brutality" these historians describe. For example, Henry Thompson, a laborer, was indicted for murder in Rotherham, in the north of England, on January 19, 1663:

> *Anne Ashmore, of Rotherham, spinster,* sayeth, that, upon the 30th of December, about eleven of the clock in the night, she being in her bed, in the almshouses upon Rotherham bridge, did hear one Henry Thompson, laborer, and then a dweller in the said almshouses, very violently fall upon, beat and strike one Margarett Hill, a poor old widow, with a rod or staff for almost an hour and a half together, in such a violent manner that the said Margarett Hill cried lamentably out, and said he would kill her; but still he laid the more on her, calling her witch, and said she had bewitched his mother, and gave her not over until he made her kneel down on her knees, and ask him forgiveness.*

Thompson's wife testified that her husband had taken offense when the widow had accused his sister of stealing apples. Margarett had died of the prolonged beating on January 18.

The York Castle archives, where Thompson's case is recorded, reveal as well the case of Margaret and Elizabeth Pinchbeck, a mother and her daughter, indicted for murder on October 29, 1671. Elizabeth told the coroner:

> That, about 8 or 9 o'clock in the evening on Friday last, this informant's father and mother being fallen out before their going to bed, after some ill words there was some strokes betwixt them, and her father took the stick from her mother, and several strokes was given. But this informant being in bed is uncertain who gave

---

* In this and subsequent transcriptions from old records I have translated dialect words and modernized spelling.

the more strokes, but she perceived her mother to bring an ax from under the cupboard, where it usually lay, and carry it to the bedside, and went into bed to her father, and seemed to lie very quietly, until this informant thought they had been both asleep; but, about 3 or 4 o'clock in the next morning, as she believes, she heard her mother rise out of bed and take the ax. This informant being amazed does not remember whether she had a candle or no; but this informant heard a great stroke given, which she believes was upon her father's head by her mother with the ax. And, upon the first stroke, her father gave a great shriek, and after that this informant heard a stroke or two more, but her father cry no more.

Margaret Pinchbeck then made her daughter get up, dress and help carry her dead father down the hill from their house to the brook that ran deep near the local mill. They dumped the body into the brook and returned home, where "her mother charged her that she should never tell to anyone that she killed her father, for, if she ever spoke of it to anyone, she would kill her." A passerby found the body the next morning, he testified, "with two dangerous wounds upon his head." A neighbor woman went to the dead man's house, where she overheard Margaret say, "Ah, Pinchbeck, thou hast sought to break my heart, but I live still, and hast thou put thyself away." Margaret herself confessed to the coroner at this inquest "that she did take the ax, and knocked her husband's brains out, for he had done her a great injury and did deserve it." Elizabeth was acquitted; Margaret was found guilty and burned alive.

A baron and his son, John and George Maxwell, were indicted for murder in Scotland in 1619. Since the crime involved a victim, John McKie, whom John Maxwell "in his politic and crafty manner" had induced to transfer to the baron "his whole worldly means and estates," the crime qualified as treason as well as murder—treasonable murder. "Thereby drawing [McKie] to his daily company and attendance," the indictment sonorously continues,

as well within his house . . . as other parts of the country where he made his repair and residence, [John Maxwell], moved by his avaricious and churlish disposition, loathing and wearying of the said John McKie his company, in the month of July, in the year of God 1618, to rid and relieve himself of his company, devised and concluded in his devilish heart the piteous and treasonable murder of the said deceased John McKie.

The baron and his son and their accomplices ambushed McKie "under the silence and cloud of night" as he returned unsuspecting to the baron's house one evening, "put violent hands on his person, bound both his hands and feet, and thereafter, in most cruel and merciless manner, playing the part of hangmen and executioners, with a hair halter [that is, a horse halter woven of hair], strangled and worried him to death" and dumped the body in a nearby bog. Father and son were convicted and sentenced to be beheaded in Edinburgh "and all their lands, heritages, tenements, annual rents, taxes, steadings, rooms, possessions, coins, cattle, furnishings, goods and gear to be forfeited" to the king. The English kept such good records, one historian remarks, because the king stood to profit from criminal convictions.

The most heinous crime I found preserved in these old records was one in a series of violent acts of revenge in a continuing feud between the Buchanan and MacFarlane clans in seventeenth-century Scotland. In 1623 a crowd of Buchanan fathers and sons presented a supplication defending themselves against an indictment for the murder of Andrew and Duncan MacFarlane, father and son, arguing that the killings were justified. Andrew, they explained, "during the whole course of his unhappy life, was known to be a notorious thief and rogue." He had "stolen some goods from certain of his Majesty's good subjects . . . some four or five years ago." William Buchanan, the father of one of the supplicants, "out of his true hatred and detestation of such thievish doings," had made inquiry and had searched out and found the stolen goods. Andrew had been forced to make restitution for them and pay damages. As a result he had "conceived a deadly hatred and malice against . . . William" and had "resolved, out of the pride and malice of his wicked heart, to be revenged upon him after the most detestable and cruel manner that the heart of him could devise." The manner Andrew devised—with his sons—was torture, murder and bestial mutilation:

> And knowing that the gentleman [William Buchanan] was accustomed at some times, for his recreation and pastime, to go to the hunting, in the moor above the Ducher [Brook], [Andrew] made choice and took hold of that occasion to do his turn: and having, by some previous means, been made acquainted with the gentleman's habit for his pastime, he, accompanied with his two sons, and seven or eight other lawless thieves, come to the said moor, and lay at await for the gentleman; and when he came there, about eight o'clock in the morning, without any company but four hunt-

ing dogs, they laid hands upon him and bound him fast, that he might not stir; and having consulted among themselves, after what form and manner they could dispatch him, they resolved, in the end, that his presumption in searching out the said goods required an extraordinary death, by torture; which they made him to endure, the space of ten hours, in manner following to wit: They bound him fast to a tree, at the said hour of eight in the morning; and every hour thereafter, till six at night, which made up ten hours, they gave him three cruel strikes with a knife, in such parts of his body as were not to bring present death; and having this way mangled him with three strikes, till the full number of ten hours were outrun, they then gave him the last deadly strike, at the heart; wherewith he fell dead to the ground! And having stripped him naked, because his tongue was the instrument whereby, as they alleged, he offended in searching out the former stolen goods, they cut his throat, took his tongue out of his head, slew his four dogs, cut one of their tongues out, and put it in the gentleman's mouth; and put his tongue in the dog's mouth: And not content herewith, but the further to satisfy their inhuman and barbarous cruelty upon the naked corpse, they slit up his belly, took out his whole entrails, and put them in one of the dog's bellies, after they had opened the dog's belly and taken out his entrails, which they put in the gentleman's belly: And so left him lying naked, and the four dead dogs about him; where he lay above the earth the space of eight days thereafter, before he was found.

Private violence served to prevent and settle disputes in a world where public means were limited or nonexistent. "The readiness of kinsmen to assist one another," Given observes, ". . . or to retaliate for an injury was undoubtedly a major factor in the regulation of conflict within the community. A man could not expect that he would be able to injure an enemy with impunity." As well as kin, he notes, servants also came to their masters' aid (just as Bernini's servant would do):

On September 25, 1205, William of Bramfield, subdean of Lincoln cathedral, was murdered by another cleric in front of St. Peter's altar. William's servants promptly cut the killer down. His body was hacked into pieces before being unceremoniously thrown out of the [cathedral]. Similarly, when Beatrice Swalwechine, an Oxford whore, stole books from the lodgings of some of the university's scholars, their servants beat her to death.

Historians attribute the gradual decline in private violence in early modern Europe to several simultaneous and interrelated developments. One was the consolidation of centralized power by emerging monarchies. "The greatest triumph of the Tudors," Lawrence Stone writes of sixteenth- and seventeenth-century England, "was the ultimately successful assertion of a royal monopoly of violence both public and private, an achievement which profoundly altered not only the nature of politics, but also the quality of daily life. There occurred a change in English habits that can only be compared with the further step taken in the nineteenth century, when the growth of a police force finally consolidated the monopoly and made it effective in the greatest cities and the smallest villages." By the time of Elizabeth I, English homicide rates had dropped to 6.8 per 100,000—a consequence, Stone suggests, of a "progressive shift of the burden of prosecution from the relatives of the deceased to some public authority." A similar "royal monopoly of violence" emerged in France with the consolidation of national power under Henry IV, Louis XIII and Louis XIV. Across his long seventeenth- and early-eighteenth-century reign, Louis XIV was even able to proscribe dueling among the nobility he required to attend him as courtiers at Versailles.

Monopolizing violence, Elias emphasizes, was not something monarchs pursued out of the goodness of their hearts; it was necessary to assure their income:

> The society of what we call the modern age is characterized, above all in the West, by a certain level of monopolization. Free use of military weapons is denied the individual and reserved to a central authority of whatever kind, and likewise the taxation of the property or income of individuals is concentrated in the hands of a central social authority. The financial means thus flowing into this central authority maintain its monopoly of military force, while this in turn maintains the monopoly of taxation. Neither has in any sense precedence over the other; they are two sides of the same monopoly.

Monarchs monopolized taxation and violence just as modern capitalists monopolized natural resources, Elias observes, and the emerging middle class depended on this double monopoly for its existence; control of violence was "the precondition for the restriction to economic, nonviolent means, of the free competition in which they [were] engaged with each other." But if not by violence, how did the emerging middle class resolve its quarrels?

Then as now, it sued the bastards. Access to courts of law was another important and interrelated development that slowly displaced violence as a way to settle disputes. "[Private] violence is only one means of settling disputes," Given comments, "and not a terribly effective one at that, since it is risky and involves dire and often incalculable consequences." For the emerging middle class, acquiring influence meant gaining freedom from such risk. Private and public justice had coexisted in medieval times, the French historian Alfred Soman observes, with private justice locally predominant. "Official justice was there in the background to deal with individuals who had crossed the threshold of community tolerance by the commission of a horrendous crime, or by an unforgivable number of deviant acts." Official justice came to be "increasingly adopted by the nobility, the prosperous bourgeoisie and throughout the ranks of officialdom as a not dishonorable way of resolving disputes."

Litigation, deplored today as presumptive evidence of *decreased* civility, in fact evolved as an alternative to violence, to *increase* civility. Observing that "most early modern homicides were outside the family," Stone discovers extrafamilial disputes increasingly being resolved through litigation as violence declined: "Thus in New England in the seventeenth century there were relatively few cases in the courts of conflict within a particular family, but 'an enormous quantity of actions between neighbors.' It is this extreme litigiousness that has caused historians like John Demos to describe the seventeenth-century village as characterized by 'an atmosphere of contention, of chronic and sometimes bitter enmity.' " (Violence *within* the family continued to be considered a private matter until very recent times; to some degree it still is, complicating the prevention and interdiction of child abuse.)

The third leg of this triad of developments followed from the other two. Elias calls it "the civilizing process." Soman observes that "the spread of education [in the early modern era] brought about far more than a spread of literacy; schooling in letters meant a schooling in manners." Gurr writes of a "cultural process of sensitization to violence." Stone notes that

the stress on civility, politeness and propriety spread down from intellectual aristocratic salons to wider sectors of society. The taming of upper-class violence by the code of the duel after the late sixteenth century was followed by the transformation of manners in the late seventeenth century, and then by the humanitarian ideology of the Enlightenment. First launched by intellectuals, lawyers, nobles and bourgeois . . . these new attitudes slowly penetrated all sectors of society, with the result that interpersonal physical violence has been on the decline in all areas of life.

Each of these historians is pointing out politely that people ape their betters; as the European upper classes were progressively constrained from violence across the early modern era, they made a virtue of necessity by adding personal restraint to their measures of social superiority, and the appraisal trickled down. Once violence is understood to be a behavior, not a pathology, the fact that it was responsive to social pressures no longer seems mysterious.

Paradoxically, the three centuries during which this historic decline in violence occurred were also centuries known for brutal public executions. If the spectacle of violence fosters violence, as modern critics of mass media claim, the opposite should be the case—public executions should have promoted violent behavior. Pieter Spierenburg, a Dutch historian, explores the paradox in his book *The Spectacle of Suffering*.

In the first place, Spierenburg observes, punishment is different from vengeance. Vengeance occurs among equals; punishment implies subordination, and "the emergence and stabilization of criminal justice, a process going on from the late twelfth until the early sixteenth centuries, meant the disappearance of private vengeance. Ultimately vengeance was transferred from the victims and their relatives to the state. Whereas formerly a man would kill his brother's murderer or beat up the thief he caught in his house, these people were now killed or flogged by the authorities."

Private vengeance had been enacted publicly; so was punishment. "Physical punishment was simply introduced into a world which was accustomed to the infliction of physical injury and suffering. In that sense it was not an alien element. . . . Urban and territorial rulers had to ensure that people accepted the establishment of criminal justice. But once they had accomplished that, they did not encounter psychological barriers against the full deployment of a penal system based on open physical treatment of delinquents." Which is to say: Spectacles of public violence did not *cause* private violence; private violence made such public spectacles banal. Indeed, public displays were valued as a form of advertising, proof that violence had come under monopoly:

When medieval rulers expropriated private vengeance and replaced it by criminal justice, they were drawn into display. It served a double function. It warned potential transgressors of the law that criminal justice would be practiced and it warned everyone to remember who practiced it. . . . During the late Middle Ages authority [in Europe] was mostly vested in the hands of rulers of cities and relatively small principalities. Their strivings toward a monopoly of violence in their territory were easily challenged; from without as well as from within. There was a relatively large amount of private violence and other forms of lawbreaking. The laws these authorities enacted had to be implemented visually through the public punishment of violators. The observable fact that punishments were indeed meted out constituted a necessary prerequisite for the preservation of a shaky position of authority. People had to see that "justice reigned" in a particular city or country. And the reign of justice implied the presence of persons powerful enough to catch and punish transgressors of the law.

So hangings, brandings, whippings, blindings, amputations, beheadings, garrotings, scorchings by fire, breakings with hammers, breakings on the wheel before or after death, throat slashings, drawings and quarterings—Spierenburg's partial list of the punishments he found in German and Dutch historical records—became dual-purpose public events: They reminded locals of who was in charge, while the resulting corpses, left exposed on gibbets (upright posts with projecting arms from which the bodies of executed criminals were hung by chains) along the roads leading into the district until they rotted away, offered a warning to strangers happening by.

"The idea that the display of corpses was to discourage potential criminals was often expressed," Spierenburg notes. In Strasbourg, where, exceptionally, corpses were removed from display, the city council in 1461 ordered a change of policy, explaining: "Up to now all the corpses of those hanged have been dropped, so that the gallows had stood entirely empty, as if no thief were punished here in Strasbourg. But we think that, if those executed remained hanging there, the sight of misery would produce anxiety and fear, so that many a person would refrain from stealing because of it, from fear of being hanged too." "Henceforth," Spierenburg adds, "only citizens would have the right to be cut down, if their families requested this."

Capital punishment for deterrence in the United States today clearly follows from these more robust early practices, and is also just as clearly vestigial. Less obviously, the resurgence of capital punishment in modern

America exposes the insecurity of U.S. authorities with the increase in violent crime, which challenges government monopoly of violence.

Violent public spectacles in Europe declined with the decline of private violence, another manifestation of the civilizing process, and disappeared with the consolidation of the modern nation-state in the nineteenth century. "The nation-state," Spierenburg comments, "because of closer integration of geographic areas and wider participation of social groups, was much more stable than the early modern state. And the liberal/bourgeois regimes, with their increasingly bureaucratized agencies, had a much more impersonal character. . . . Public executions were not only felt to be distasteful; they were no longer necessary." In contemporary states still operating insecurely along the old lines—Iran, Iraq, Zimbabwe, Saudi Arabia—public executions still occur, and the crowd still gathers to cheer them.

Historians examine historical events and postulate social forces to explain them. Changing behavior as complicated as personal violence is neither simple nor straightforward, however, as the long progress of that change in the West demonstrates. People did not simply decide to stop being violent because their governments were centralizing; the process was individual, gradual and presumably generational. If large social forces drove it, how did they impress their weight upon human communities and developing human beings? Where violence is concerned, what was the mechanism of the civilizing process?

CHAPTER SEVENTEEN

The History of Childhood

"Dominance is a social universal," Lonnie Athens asserts in a 1998 paper. The word derives from Latin *dominus,* meaning "master of the house." Human beings compete for dominance, which Athens defines as "swaying the development of social acts in accordance with one's preferences." Social acts are collective coordinations of the separate acts of individuals, and people dominate "when they impose their view of a developing social act on others." In the process, Athens continues, "in all communities, a dominance hierarchy invariably develops. People who occupy higher positions can make their identification of emergent social acts prevail over people in lower positions, which in turn sets off dominance struggles. Human communities differ from each other in many important ways, but in this critical respect, they are all the same." Athens proceeds to discuss the vexing problem of violent neighborhoods in modern cities—the paper's title is "Dominance, Ghettoes and Violent Crime"— but his analysis applies equally to the larger communities of Western Europe, within which personal violence declined across the past five hundred years.

"The norms that people use for settling dominance disputes," Athens proposes, "[are] the main source of a community's organization." Since the individuals who succeed in positioning themselves at the top of a community's dominance hierarchy determine those norms, "the individual type that predominates is the single most telling factor about a community." Predominant individual types have "their own relatively unique phantom communities, self portraits, patterns of action and insignia of dominance." Based on the individual types which predominate, Athens distinguishes three kinds of minor communities within the larger corporal communities of the modern United States. He calls them civil, turbulent and malignant.

A peaceful suburb might be a civil community; older neighborhoods in transition often include turbulent minor communities; bleak housing projects and inner-city ghettoes can be malignant. (From personal experience as well as professional study, Athens strongly rejects linking community malignancy with race. Violentization has nothing to do with race—or with poverty, for that matter.)

In civil minor communities the pacifist predominates, followed by the marginally violent person. The pacifist, Athens finds, "opposes taking serious violent action against others, even under life-threatening circumstances." He or she will not commit even physically defensive violent acts and paints an antiviolent self-portrait. A marginally violent person, the second most predominant type in civil communities, will only commit physically defensive violent acts and paints a nonviolent self-portrait. "Among the members of a civil minor community," Athens summarizes, "the prevailing norm is that disputes over dominance are settled nonviolently, such as by gossiping about, ridiculing, snubbing, deluding or temporarily avoiding rivals." In more extreme disputes in civil minor communities, rivals may be permanently purged from the group by firing, disowning, shaming, divorcing, ostracizing or shunning. Violent crimes may occur in civil communities, of course, because violent individuals may wander in or even try to settle in. Since the corporal (civil) community is at odds with their phantom communities, these violent intruders qualify as social misfits.

At the other extreme of Athens's spectrum of communities is the malignant minor community, where the ultraviolent person predominates, followed by the violent person. Ultraviolent individuals are prepared to commit the full range of violent acts Athens identified in his interviews with violent criminals—physically defensive, frustrative, frustrative-malefic and malefic—have unmitigated violent phantom communities and paint violent self-images, meaning they are willing and ready "to attack other people physically with the intention of seriously harming or even killing them for almost any dominative provocation."

Athens refracts his definitions of violent acts in this 1998 study through the lens of dominance competition. Physically defensive violence resists attempts at physical domination. Someone commits a frustrative violent act "to overcome other people's resistance to his domination or to resist other people's attempts to dominate him." Frustrative-malefic violent acts are designed "to resist people's perceived evil domination or to dominate people perceived as evil." Malefic violent acts punish people for degrading the violent actor (as his phantom community interprets it), because degradation "in effect denies his prerogative to dominate them by lowering his position below theirs in the community's dominance hierarchy."

Violent persons, the second most predominant type in malignant minor communities, have mitigated violent phantom communities and incipiently violent self-images. They are prepared to commit physically defensive and frustrative-malefic violent acts "under extreme dominative provocation."

In turbulent minor communities, Athens's third, intermediate category, no individual type predominates; a turbulent mix of all four types—pacifist, marginally violent, violent and ultraviolent—makes life chaotic. "Conflict arises," Athens writes, "not only over where one falls in the pecking order, but also over the appropriate means for securing a higher position. . . . Community members are not sure what to expect when disputes over dominance erupt between them." Turbulent communities are usually communities in transition toward either civility or malignancy. "Everything is loose and free," Athens quotes Robert Park about such places, "but everything is problematic."

Of malignant communities, Athens further observes:

> The prevailing norm is that physical violence is the most effective means of settling dominance disputes. Any time a serious conflict arises over dominance, it is presumed that one must be prepared, not only to use deadly force, but to receive it as well. . . . Thus, malignant minor communities constitute virtual combat zones where violent criminal acts of all types . . . occur with such depressing frequency that they become commonplace. . . . The commonplaceness of violence in malignant minor communities produces an unsurprising callousness toward violence among its members.

Athens's malignant communities recall Thomas Hobbes's contention in *Leviathan* that before the imposition of government, perpetual war was the natural condition of mankind:

> Whatsoever therefore is consequent to a time of Warre, where every man is Enemy to every man; the same is consequent to the time, wherein men live without other security, than what their own strength, and their own invention shall furnish them withall. In such condition, there is no place for Industry [or other constructive human activity]; and which is worst of all, continuall feare, and danger of violent death; And the life of man, solitary, poore, nasty, brutish, and short.

In malignant communities, people who are pacifist or only marginally violent are social misfits, which creates an excruciating dilemma for those who would encourage children in such communities to resist adopting violent ways. Without the protective training that violentization affords, they are vulnerable whenever they encounter dominance disputes.

Though Athens examines the social context of individual violence to explore the problem of violent crime in American communities today, his work has obvious application to the history of violence in the West. Turn his cross-section of modern minor communities ninety degrees, and it lines up historically with the progressive decline in personal violence from medieval malignancy to early modern turbulence to modern civility. Athens's modern turbulent and malignant minor communities then appear, as Spierenburg describes such places, as "unpacified islands" in which "serious violence today is concentrated. . . . The greater differentiation prevailing in the late twentieth century has led to the appearance of small islands within these [civil] societies where the pacification once guaranteed by the state has crumbled to some extent."

Medieval Europe was one vast malignant community. The feudal lords and the small knights at the top of the dominance hierarchy were at least violent and frequently ultraviolent men (and sometimes women) with violent self-images, who lived, as Elias observes, by "war, rapine, armed attack and plunder." So were the commoners whom they dominated— Henry Thompson beating a woman to death for accusing his sister of stealing apples, Margaret Pinchbeck ax-murdering her brutal husband in his sleep, Andrew MacFarlane and his sons mangling William Buchanan for ratting him out—people "easily provoked to violent anger," to quote Gurr again, "and . . . unrestrained in the brutality with which they attacked their opponents." If there were civil minor communities embedded in this larger malignant corporal community—*pacified* islands, as it were—they were religious retreats such as monasteries and nunneries, although there is historical evidence that monks at least could be as violent as the commoners who lived around them.*

---

* For example: "Sometime in the last half of the thirteenth century, the Cistercian abbot of the mother abbey of Fountains in Yorkshire paid a visit to the abbey's daughter house at Woburn in Bedfordshire. The servants of the two abbots fell to quarreling. The abbot of Woburn came with one of his monks, named William de la Graue, to stop the disturbance. William took a direct approach to the problem and hit one of the Yorkshire abbot's servants in the head with a hatchet. A man named John in turn shot the monk with an arrow, killing him instantly."

As monarchs, beginning in the late Middle Ages, moved to monopolize violence, they slowly, across several centuries, reined in the violent upper classes, which contested their authority. They were aided, Elias points out, by the increasing circulation of money that drove up prices and impoverished the lesser nobility, which subsisted on fixed rents. The monarchs collected taxes and therefore enjoyed an almost automatic increase in income as barter gave way to a money economy; and tax revenues allowed them to hire the legions they needed to monopolize violence.

The lesser nobility did not then go to jail; it came to the royal court—"forced by these circumstances," writes Elias, "and attracted by the new opportunities [to enter] the service of the kings or princes who could pay." At court, which was evolving through turbulence toward becoming a civil minor community, the knights—or their sons and daughters, grandsons and granddaughters—learned, gradually and often reluctantly, to behave differently, because different qualities were needed to succeed at court and different rules applied:

> [The prince] now possesses the monopoly of force. Owing to this monopoly, the direct use of force is now largely excluded from the competition among the nobility for the opportunities the prince has to allocate. The means of struggle have been refined or sublimated. The restraint of the affects imposed on the individual by his dependence on the monopoly ruler has increased. And individuals now waver between resistance to the compulsion to which they are subjected, hatred of their dependence and unfreedom, nostalgia for free knightly rivalry, on the one hand, and pride in the self-control they have acquired.

The story of King Arthur and the Round Table—Arthur contriving to limit the personal violence of his kingdom's knights by inspiring them to higher standards than personal glory and self-aggrandizement—is a fictionalized and idealized redaction of these real historical events.

The new restraint applies not only to the nobility, now becoming courtiers deploying skills of flattery and manipulation rather than physical violence (*needed* skills, by the way, as government enlarges its authority and more complicated organizations evolve). It applies as well to commoners. It diffuses out from centers of power in the form of professionals "legitimated by the central authority" (Elias)—soldiers, sheriffs, justices, police—but also in the form of social values legitimated by the increasingly pacified upper classes who dominate.

Elias demonstrates that process of diffusion with an amusing and profound excursion through Renaissance and early modern European books of manners. Erasmus of Rotterdam, for example, published a short treatise *On the Civility of Children* in 1530 that went through 130 editions across the next two centuries, indicating to Elias that "the problem of behavior in society had obviously taken on such importance in this period that even people of extraordinary talent and renown did not disdain to concern themselves with it." Erasmus's treatise is dedicated to a prince's son. It cautions the boy not to go about with snot on his nostrils, not to eat and drink without stopping to converse, not to lick his fingers at table, not to expose his private parts in public, to "replace [that is, cover] farts with coughs." More subtly, it advises him on dissimulation, a skill of courtiers, not of warriors. "A wide-eyed look is a sign of stupidity, staring a sign of inertia; the looks of those prone to anger are too sharp; too lively and eloquent those of the immodest; if your look shows a calm mind and a respectful amiability, that is best."

Outward propriety came first, just as it does with children; but just as it does with children, it moved inward and became habitual, "unconscious":

> Restraint on the instincts* is at first imposed only in the company of others, i.e., more consciously for social reasons. . . . This slowly changes as people move closer together socially and as the hierarchical character of society becomes less rigid. As the interdependence of men increases with the increasing division of labor, everyone becomes increasingly dependent on everyone else, those of high social rank on those socially inferior and weaker. The latter become so much the equals of the former that they, the socially superior, feel shame even before their inferiors. It is only now that the armor of restraints is fastened to the degree which is gradually taken for granted by people in democratic industrial societies.

And those restraints include, of course, restraints on personal violence. Elias reviews the history of manners because it demonstrates one

---

* For Elias, barbarism, including physical violence, is "instinct," a condescension inconsistent with his own argument. However, "There is no zero-point of all these data," he writes more perceptively in conclusion. ". . . The habits of self-constraint, the conscious and affective makeup of 'civilized' people, clearly differ *in their totality* from those of so-called 'primitives'; but both are, in their structure, different yet clearly explainable moldings of largely the same natural functions." We are all born as animals; how we are socialized determines how directly ("instinctively") we express ourselves—Elias's very point.

important mechanism whereby changing social values were diffused through the population. The process was holistic rather than merely rational:

> Civilization, and therefore rationalization, for example, is not a process within a separate sphere of "ideas" or "thought." It does not involve solely changes of "knowledge," transformations of "ideologies," in short alterations of the *content* of consciousness, but changes in the whole human makeup, within which ideas and habits of thought are only a single sector. We are here concerned with changes in the whole personality throughout all its zones.

Elias offers no psychic mechanism for this profound historical change of personality. Athens's conception of a phantom community, however, provides one.

So the malignant medieval community, dominated by an ultraviolent nobility, transformed with the increasing centralization of power and monopolization of violence into a turbulent early modern community. Voltaire even chose the French equivalent of the word Athens would choose two centuries later to describe the transition, remarking of France's Louis XIV, "The king succeeded in making of a hitherto *turbulent* nation a peaceful people dangerous only to its enemies." By the time of Napoleon, Elias concludes (and homicide rates confirm), the transformation from turbulence to a more or less civil corporal community was largely complete:

> Unlike the situation when the concept [of civility] was formed, from now on nations consider the *process* of civilization as completed within their own societies; they see themselves as bearers of an existing or finished civilization to others, as standard-bearers of expanding civilization. Of the whole preceding process of civilization nothing remains in their consciousness except a vague residue. Its outcome is taken simply as an expression of their own higher gifts; the fact that, and the question of how, in the course of many centuries, civilized behavior has been attained is of no interest. And the consciousness of their own superiority, the consciousness of this "civilization," from now on serves at least those nations which have become colonial conquerors, and therefore a kind of upper class to large sections of the non-European world, as a justification of their rule, to the same degree that earlier the ancestors

of the concept of civilization, *politesse* and *civilité,* had served the courtly-aristocratic upper class as a justification of theirs.

The sorry record of "civilized" colonialism demonstrates that civilized nations, though their violence is largely monopolized and sequestered, nevertheless deploy the same brutal potential as did their violent predecessors.

In modern societies made turbulent or even malignant by civil breakdown or by the withdrawal of colonial authority, emerging governments struggle, much as early modern Europe did, to control private violence and brigandry. They often find it necessary to buy off the military, which has assumed authority for the monopoly on violence that the previous government established it to enforce.

If Athens's types of minor communities turn out to have their precedents in types of historical corporal communities, communities similarly defined by the types of individuals who dominate them and determine their levels of violence, then the answer to the question with which I ended the last chapter—"How did those forces impress their weight upon . . . developing human beings?"—should now be apparent. They must have done so through changes in the socialization of children; specifically through a progressive decrease in the number of children undergoing violentization. This argument assumes that violentization, the process whereby modern violent criminals are created, was also the process that created violent medieval nobles and commoners. Is there evidence for such an assumption? And if so, did violentization decrease with the decrease in homicide rates across the past five hundred years?

The history of childhood has hardly been explored. The child may be father to the man, but most historians and anthropologists have chosen to neglect examining how children have been characteristically socialized in different times and places. The best-known and most-cited history, Philippe Ariès's *Centuries of Childhood,* is shockingly mistaken. Ariès finds medieval childhood free and innocent (because, he claims erroneously, the concept of "childhood" was unknown) and the change from then to now one of increasing brutality:

> Family and school together removed the child from adult society. The school shut up a childhood which had hitherto been free within an increasingly severe disciplinary system, which culminated

in the eighteenth and nineteenth centuries in the total claustration of the boarding school. The solicitude of family, Church, moralists and administrators deprived the child of the freedom he had hitherto enjoyed among adults. It inflicted on him the birch, the prison cell—in a word, the punishments usually reserved for convicts from the lowest strata of society. But the severity was the expression of a very different feeling from the old indifference: an obsessive love which was to dominate society from the eighteenth century on.

I hear echoes of romanticism in this proposition—"trailing clouds of glory do we come," and then "shades of the prison-house begin to close" upon us—but whatever its source in preconception, Ariès's argument is simply wrong, as wrong as his frequently cited notion that medieval artists "were unable to depict a child except as a man on a smaller scale," which he takes as presumptive evidence of "ignorance of childhood."

The truth is opposite and crueler. Its most authoritative historian in English is the psychoanalyst Lloyd deMause, who writes in his essay "The Evolution of Childhood" that

> of over two hundred statements of advice on child rearing prior to the eighteenth century which I have examined, most approved of beating children severely, and all allowed beating in varying circumstances. . . . Of the seventy children prior to the eighteenth century whose lives [that is, letters, biographies, autobiographies] I have found, all were beaten except one. . . . [A German scholar's] extensive survey of the literature on beating reaches similar conclusions to mine. . . . The beatings described in the sources were generally severe, involved bruising and bloodying of the body, began early and were a regular part of the child's life.

The history of childhood, deMause urges passionately, "is a nightmare from which we have only recently begun to awaken. The further back in history one goes, the lower the level of child care, and the more likely children are to be killed, abandoned, beaten, terrorized and sexually abused."

DeMause characterizes all this past violence against children as mistreatment. By modern civil standards it certainly was, but judging past behavior by present standards, whatever our natural sympathies, is anachronistic: It obscures the view. And in any case, as Athens emphasizes, brutalization and "child abuse" are not identical and should not be conflated; the violent criminals he interviewed frequently did not perceive their brutalization to have been abusive, nor was it necessarily administered by parents at home. Even deMause, despite his outrage, concedes, "All of this is not to say that parents didn't love their children in the past, for they did." And he observes, perspicaciously, that "for the parent in the past, expressions of tenderness toward children occur most often when the child is non-demanding, especially when the child is either asleep or dead." In malignant communities, to recall Athens's definition, "the prevailing norm is that physical violence is the most effective means of settling dominance disputes." Dominance is disputed not only between drunks in bars; it may also be disputed frequently between parent and child in the ordinary course of child rearing.

The custom of brutalizing children had biblical endorsement. "When one actually reads each of the over two thousand references to children listed in the *Complete Concordance to the Bible*," writes deMause, ". . . you find lots on child sacrifice, on stoning children, on beating them, on their strict obedience, on their love for their parents and on their role as carriers of the family name, but not a single one that reveals any empathy with their needs." Even Christ's admonition to "suffer little children . . . to come unto me," deMause argues, is a reference to the "customary Near Eastern practice of exorcising by laying on of hands, which many holy men did to remove the evil inherent in children."

DeMause explores at length brutality toward children in classical and biblical times, when infanticide was a common practice. Suffice it to point out that in ancient Greece it was the family's responsibility to seek vengeance for the murder of one of its members, much as it continued to be in early medieval Europe; while in Rome, according to Edward Gibbon in his *The Decline and Fall of the Roman Empire:*

> The exclusive, absolute, and perpetual dominion of the father over his children is peculiar to the Roman jurisprudence. . . . According to his discretion, a father might chastise the real or imaginary faults of his children, by stripes [lashing with a whip or scourge], by imprisonment, by exile, by sending them to the country to work in chains among the meanest of his servants. The majesty of a parent was armed with the power of life and death [that is, over his children]; and the examples of such bloody executions, which were sometimes praised and never punished, may be traced in the annals of Rome, beyond the times of Pompey and Augustus.

The historian James Given chronicles medieval child-rearing practices more thoroughly than does deMause, focusing on thirteenth-century

England; his summary of evidence comprehends violent subjugation, personal horrification and violent coaching:

> Medieval Europe believed firmly in the use of the rod and the staff as a means of moral correction and improvement. Thomas of Chobham in his *Summa* on penitence wrote that physical violence as a means of punishment and correction was permissible according to canon law and could be used by both laity and clergy. Parents were allowed to beat their children, masters their servants, teachers their pupils, and confessors their penitents. . . . Should someone accidentally die as the result of such correction, canon law held that the killer was not culpable of homicide, provided that he had not exceeded the customary measure in administering a beating.
>
> The use of corporal punishment was widespread within the medieval family. Men beat their wives and children. Indeed, the village community would on occasion punish women who had violated one of its regulations by ordering the errant woman's husband to beat her. . . .
>
> The received wisdom of the Middle Ages held that children, like all men after Adam's fall, were inherently prone to evil. Vincent of Beauvais in his tract on education wrote that "the feelings and thoughts of the human heart are prone to evil from youth. Therefore it is necessary to prevent the flowering of this evil in children, and to fight it and resist it with discipline." The punishment meted out to children could reach spectacular levels of brutality. Ralph, the son of Augustine the chaplain of Taynton in Oxfordshire, refused to learn his lessons. As a punishment, his father and his father's clerk tied him to the tail of a horse. Unfortunately, the horse escaped and dragged Ralph to his death. At the 1241 eyre Augustine was reported to have fled into Buckinghamshire.
>
> The rod was an indispensable instrument of education in medieval schools. The best opinion held that those who learned readily were not to be handled roughly. But those who were like "unbroken young colts" were to be taught good manners against their will by discipline. . . . Schoolboys were beaten regularly. The saintly bishop of Lincoln, Hugh of Avalon, who was not averse to cuffing his servants when they displeased him, remembered his childhood in a Burgundian monastery as a long string of beatings. . . .

Children and errant wives were not the only people likely to experience a beating. Physical punishment, administered publicly, was an integral part of the medieval church's penitential system. The church regularly imposed flogging as a penance for sexual derelictions. . . . In a period of one and a half to two months in May and June 1300, the court of the rural deanery of Droitwich ordered the beating of 79 people, 38 men and 41 women, almost all accused of either adultery or fornication. . . . Within the monastic cloister physical discipline was also customary. . . . The monks undertook to beat their novices even more severely than those who had made their profession. . . .

Thirteenth-century Englishmen were thus well schooled in violence. From childhood subjected to physical punishment by their parents and teachers, the witnesses of beatings administered to wives by husbands and to servants by masters, onlookers at the ritualistic floggings of penitents, they learned that a ready recourse to violence and the infliction of pain were a common, and necessary, part of adult life. These impressions were reinforced, and their skills at violence honed, by the popularity of violent games, from the exalted tournament to the lowly village wrestling match. A readiness to resort to aggression and violence was therefore a common character trait among thirteenth-century English peasants.

"One thirteenth-century law," deMause notes, "brought child beating into the public domain: 'If one beats a child until it bleeds, then it will remember, but if one beats it to death, the law applies.' "

Another scholar of medieval childhood, Mary Margaret McLaughlin, reports an unusual exchange between Anselm, the eleventh-century archbishop of Canterbury and future saint, and an abbot "who had complained to him of his difficulties in controlling the obstreperous boys in his charge, declaring that 'we never give over beating them day and night, and they only get worse and worse.' " Anselm, she says, responded by "pointing to the destructive effects of the use of force and 'injudicious oppression' upon the personalities of their young victims." His analysis anticipates Athens's analysis of the belligerency stage of violentization:

> Feeling no love or pity, goodwill or tenderness in your attitude toward them, they have in future no faith in your goodness but believe that all your actions proceed from hatred and malice

against them; they have been brought up in no true charity towards anyone, so they regard everyone with suspicion and jealousy. . . . Are they not human? Are they not flesh and blood like you? Would you like to have been treated as you treat them, and to have become what they are now?

In fifteenth-century Italy, a father, Giovanni Morelli, kept a diary. He lost his father in infancy; sent off to school at five, he recalled suffering "many blows and frights" from his masters. The arrival of his son Alberto delighted him: "And then when he was born, male, sound, well-proportioned, what happiness, what joy I experienced; and then as he grew from good to better, such satisfaction, such pleasure in his childish words, pleasing to all, loving towards me his father and his mother, precocious for his age." But precocious Alberto, reading Latin at nine, died before adolescence, and however loving a father, Giovanni Morelli excoriated himself for having "worn him out at school and with many and frequent harsh blows."

"It is only in the Renaissance," deMause finds, "that advice to temper childhood beatings began in earnest, although even then it was generally accompanied by approval for beatings judiciously applied. . . . Some attempts were made in the seventeenth century to limit the beating of children, but it was the eighteenth century which saw the biggest decrease. The earliest lives I have found of children who may not have been beaten at all date from 1690 to 1750."

Jean Héroard, a seventeenth-century physician to the child who would become Louis XIII, kept a diary, a unique record of childhood in transition. Héroard's extraordinarily detailed account of the life of the dauphin, or eldest son, of Henri IV, king of France, extends from the child's birth to his twenty-sixth year. Henri IV was assassinated in Paris in 1610, when the dauphin was eight; the boy immediately succeeded to the throne, but his mother, Marie de Médicis, served as regent until he exiled her in 1617 and rescued his authority. He died of tuberculosis in 1643, succeeded by his five-year-old son, the long-lived Louis XIV.

Héroard's diary reveals much that modern readers find shocking. Although the dauphin, as heir to the throne, was without question the most valuable child in France, his caretakers had difficulty nursing him sufficiently to keep him alive. They routinely and eagerly stimulated him sexually—manually and orally—and by the time he was five he was enthusiastically fisting the vaginas of his ladies-in-waiting and crawling into bed with them when they copulated with their husbands. What effect such instigations had on the dauphin's developing personality is not our concern here, but his physical discipline appears to have been transitional, a tug-of-war between the king and the queen, in keeping with the turbulence of the age.

"'The revival of religious asceticism," writes Elizabeth Wirth Marvick, a colleague of deMause who has studied Héroard's diary,

> worked its influence powerfully upon educated men and women in the early seventeenth century. It caused a change in educational approach. A deliberate effort was made to replace the traditional external threats and sanctions with inner controls established by the child himself. The new tactics were designed to heighten guilt rather than induce shame. This called for energetic and patient attention to children's behavior beyond anything that had been asked of adults before.

For the dauphin, the change meant occasional relief from violent subjugation. "Henri IV's rustic upbringing placed him in the 'spare the rod and spoil the child' tradition," Marvick continues. "He recommended frequent whippings for his son the dauphin and was not above administering *soufflets* [blows] in person. But the child's mother countermanded the king's orders whenever she could—secretly on occasion—and took the position that whipping was a last resort, signifying failure of those in charge."

Nevertheless the boy was whipped. The whipping began in his twenty-first month, four months before he was weaned. He was beaten on the buttocks with a switch. Another Héroard scholar, David Hunt, reports that "after the gravest offenses, the dauphin was compelled to expose his rear end so that the blows would fall on bare flesh." Hunt summarizes Héroard's explanations of why the future king of France was beaten routinely every morning and whenever necessary during the day:

> Various transgressions could lead to whipping: too much crying or carrying on, refusal to eat, unwillingness to show affection toward adults like the queen or, more frequently, the king himself. The most ubiquitous complaint was that the child had been *opiniâtre:* stubborn, obstinate, headstrong. Héroard wrote: "Awake at 8:00, he is obstinate, is whipped for the first time"—but not the last. Obstinacy comes up often in discussions of childhood. . . . The word (and its opposite, to be *sage*) acquired an almost cosmic sig-

nificance for children. Louis was told that men were placed in prison for obstinacy and that Christ went to the cross because mankind in general was *opiniâtre*.

The king humiliated his son—threw water in his face, whipped him, snatched off his hat when he refused to take the king's hand. But he usually held back from serious physical violence, perhaps to avoid injuring his heir, perhaps as a courtesy to the queen. "When he lost his temper with the dauphin," Hunt reports, "Henri recognized only one rule: the governess was to administer the whippings. Even this rule was ignored if the king's anger went completely out of control." The king worried that the governess, Madame de Montglat, was sparing the rod. He wrote her: "I have a complaint to make: You do not send word that you have whipped my son. I wish and command you to whip him every time that he is obstinate or misbehaves, knowing well for myself that there is nothing in the world which will be better for him than that. I know it from experience, having myself profited, for when I was his age I was often whipped. That is why I want you to whip him and to make him understand why."

October 23, 1604, was a dark day in the little dauphin's life, Héroard records. The physician prepares us: The boy loved his drum; "it was one of his greatest pleasures." His keepers controlled him with leading lines, like a little horse, pulling him along where he did not want to go. He is sullen on this October morning. Twice he is led to the king and queen and manages to be well behaved. The king goes off to hunt. When he returns he calls for his son. Héroard continues:

> So [the dauphin] went to find the king against his will, by force. The king says to him: "Remove your hat." He is reluctant to remove it, the king takes it off, he is irritated. Then the king takes his drum and drumsticks and things got even worse: "My hat, my drum, my drumsticks." To spite him, the king puts the hat on his own head: "I want my hat." The king hits him with it on the head. Now he is angry and the king against him. The king takes him by the wrists and lifts him in the air, stretching his little arms out to the sides: "Hey! you're hurting me! Hey! my drum! my hat!" The queen returns his hat, then his drumsticks to him. It was a little tragedy.

The king had injured his son's shoulder; the dauphin had to be carried away. Hunt finishes the story:

The rest of the day was filled with tantrums and whippings. During a lull, his [governess] tried to extract a moral: "Monsieur, you have been obstinate, you shouldn't, you must obey papa." Louis was incensed: "Kill mamanga [Madame de Montglat], she is bad. I will kill everyone! I will kill God!" He was finally put to bed at 10:30, slept unevenly, complained of pains in his shoulder and was unable to lift his arm or to hold what was put in his hand. . . .

Héroard remarked several times during the next months that the dauphin was afraid, still remembering the incident of October 23. . . . When the king used his glass, "he was very angry, but he controlled himself and calmly let it pass." The next day, "he wanted to cry but restrained himself out of respect for the king." Another time, "bursting with rage," he shouted at a nobleman: " 'I'm going to kill you, just wait, with my scissors!' then, repenting of the word 'kill' for which he had been chastised, 'I'm going to poke out your eyes.' "

For the next two years Henri IV withdrew from his son—whether as further punishment (they had often been affectionate and playful together before) or because the king felt it necessary to restrain his own violence, Héroard's interpreters do not say. When father and son interacted during that period of quarantine they did so formally, as master to servant. Then the king reentered the dauphin's life to begin preparing him for the throne. The preparation, Hunt makes clear, included violent coaching:

When the dauphin was about five, Henri began to get interested again in his chastened and increasingly dutiful son. The king undertook to instruct Louis in the virtues of audacity and courage: he forced the dauphin to flick out a candle with his fingers, saying "the one who wants to be papa's favorite has to snuff out the flame"; to fight with his older half-brothers; to jump a moat which was too wide for him. Henri told his son that he must not be afraid of anything and watched to make sure that Louis did not show any apprehension when, for example, there was a sudden clap of thunder. The dauphin also went to the hunt for the first time (in a carriage) and started to take riding lessons. Finally he began to attend sessions of the King's Council.

The regular beatings continued. "Scarcely were his eyes open when he was whipped," Héroard reports. The dauphin would get up early and hide or try to block the door. When he grew too big for Madame de Montglat to handle, the king ordered soldiers of the guard to restrain him for her. He passed over into the control of a "governor," Monsieur de Souvré, a court noble, when he was seven, but the beatings continued. He was whipped on the morning of his coronation, when he was eight. "I would rather do without so much obeisance and honor," he told Héroard that day, "if they wouldn't have me whipped." The beatings of the king of France continued until at least 1614, when he was thirteen years old and big enough to resist them. Even as an adult, deMause notes, "he still awoke at night in terror, in expectation of his morning whipping."

The available record of Louis XIII's life is insufficient to determine if he underwent full violentization. At twenty-one he led his army to battle to put down a Huguenot rebellion. Compared to medieval practices, his childhood experience demonstrates seventeenth-century moderation. In seventeenth-century France even the king frequently formed restraining judgments that deflected him from violently punishing his child.

In addition to using physical violence, the dauphin's keepers also put the fear of God into him by confronting him with retainers for whom he had shown fear—"a hunchbacked member of the guard," Hunt mentions, and "a mason in the king's service." DeMause, citing a variety of sources, finds this shift toward psychological rather than physical violence widespread. "As beatings began to decrease," he comments, "substitutes had to be found. For instance, shutting children up in the dark became quite popular in the eighteenth and nineteenth centuries." Terrorizing was another popular method of moral instruction. DeMause mentions scenes in a popular early-nineteenth-century didactic historical novel, Mary Sherwood's The History of the Fairchild Family, "in which the children are taken on visits to the gibbet to inspect rotting corpses hanging there, while being told moral stories." Most nineteenth-century readers did not realize, he says, "that these scenes are taken from real life and formed an important part of childhood in the past. Classes used to be taken out of school to hangings, and parents would often take their children to hangings and then whip them when they returned home to make them remember what they had seen."

One consequence deMause reports of this physical and psychological torment is "the enormous number of nightmares and hallucinations by children which I have found in the sources. Although written records by adults which indicate anything at all about a child's emotional life are rare at best, whenever discovered they usually reveal recurring night-

mares and even outright hallucinations. Since antiquity, pediatric literature regularly had sections on how to cure children's 'terrible dreams,'
and children were sometimes beaten for having nightmares." DeMause
finds all this brutalization of children inexplicable. Athens's work clarifies
that its purpose was violentization, to prepare children for an adulthood
where they would need to use physical violence to settle their disputes.

By the nineteenth century, when homicide rates in Western Europe had
dropped to near-modern lows, people were "civilized," more or less. The
dominant types in the larger corporal community were then, as they are
now in the Western world, the pacifist and the marginally violent person. Children were still, as they are now, being punished physically. Mrs.
Sherwood relied on the best Christian authorities when she counseled
her nineteenth-century readers that children were naturally evil, which
required for its correction "breaking the child's will." Regular beatings
were still part of that correction, British historian Margaret May reports,
but by then "appropriate methods for 'training the will' [had come to
include] isolation for varying periods in a corner, cellar or dark closet,
dietary punishments [bread and water], and keeping children in a fixed
position. Medical opinion was also divided, and while some counselled
mild treatment others still upheld shock treatment including beating or
immersion in cold water, especially for the constitutionally weak or
lazy." Modern horrors often turn out to be vestigial remains of old medical practices: Here in May's reference to nineteenth-century medical
opinion is the cold-water immersion that Perry Smith's detention-home
cottage mistress practiced on him a century later to cure him of bed-
wetting—and that contributed to his violentization.

An 1835 multiple-murder case exhumed by Michel Foucault and his
students at the Collège de France confirms the arrival of modern civility.
The detailed confession of a twenty-year-old farmer of the commune of
Aunay, on the Cherbourg Peninsula in northwestern France, begins sen-
sationally: "I, Pierre Rivière, having slaughtered my mother, my sister
and my brother, and wishing to make known the motives which led me
to this deed. . . ." Rivière told the examining judge at his first interrogation why he committed these parricides:

> I did it to help my father out of his difficulties. I wished to deliver
> him from an evil woman who had plagued him continually ever
> since she became his wife, who was ruining him, who was driving
> him to such despair that he was sometimes tempted to commit

suicide. I killed my sister Victoire because she took my mother's part. I killed my brother by reason of his love for my mother and sister.

Neighbors testified that Rivière's parents fought constantly; according to the mayor of Aunay, Pierre's father, Pierre-Margrin, was a man "of a very mild disposition, and those who witnessed his many quarrels with his wife always said she was in the wrong." A neighbor found it remarkable that "the father, very patient and very mild by nature, never beat [Pierre]." Pierre's chronicle of his father's abuse at his mother's hand is lengthy and exhaustive, contentious even in brief extract:

> They had no wedding banquet, and on their marriage night they did not bed together . . . and my mother said: He has only to get me with child and then leave, and then what will become of me?

> I was living with my father at Aunay. I was three or four years old, my mother came with her mother to fetch me . . . then without saying a word to anyone she took me and carried me off. As I cried out my father ran after her, and said he would not let her carry me away crying out like that . . . seeing which my mother said to her mother who was with her: Hit him, hit him. . . .

> My uncle was more prone to anger than my father, he could not bear all my mother said to him; when I hear her nagging like that, he said, she drives me too far, if she goes on I shall end by knocking her teeth in. . . . I was witness of all these quarrels, I can say that I was not greatly attached to my mother.

> My [grandmother] was growing feeble . . . but several persons report having seen my mother strike her and drag her by the hair. My father never struck my mother except for slapping her sometimes in the big quarrels with him she started. . . . She flared up in a rage at every trifle.

> [Throwing out a tenant she had told to stay, to plague him,] my father asked for the key of a loft, and when she refused, he took a chest which was in the house, my mother objected, then he held her while I loaded it. . . . As he held her she set to scratching his face and bit him in several places, my little brother Jules coming up, she told him: bite him, bite that wretch. . . . My father climbed

in a window to get into [the] loft, then she seized him by the legs and pulled him down, broke his watch-chain and tore his clothes, he did not strike her at all, but he said he would shut her up in a house to keep her quiet, he caught hold of her to carry her away, but her hands were free and she scratched him again even worse than the first time. . . . My sister joined in to stop my father and seeing that she was hindering him, I pulled her away and slapped her several times while my father took my mother off, she was shouting and so was my sister: Vengeance, he is murdering me, he is killing me, vengeance my god vengeance. . . . My father was so exhausted when he got to his house that he was spitting blood.

Pierre's mother set out then to run up enough debts to ruin his father. She largely succeeded, since Pierre-Margrin had no recourse in the law or the gendarmerie to protect himself. He was expected to discipline his wife himself, but he was evidently a pacifist in Athens's terms and unwilling to do so.

Pierre's confession reveals full violentization. His mother violently subjugated him and his father, which accounts as well for his personal horrification. A carpenter who knew the family implies that Pierre-Margrin violently coached his son, much as Lana Turner coached her daughter: "His father did tell me one day that the accused was more ill-disposed toward his wife than he was and if he had his son Pierre's character, Victoire Brun [Pierre's mother] would not be so easy in her mind." Much of Pierre's exhaustive narrative of his father's grievances could only have come from Pierre-Margrin.

The carpenter observed Pierre's passage through belligerency, at about the same age Athens would find to be common among twentieth-century violent novices:

I knew Rivière when he was a child, he seemed very eager to learn to read and write. When he was ten to twelve years old he did not seem the same anymore, he appeared to become an idiot, he displayed very great obstinacy, did not answer when called; he went to church alone and came back alone, he always looked as if he [was] ashamed, and almost never talked to anyone, he constantly held his head down and looked askance, he sometimes swore at his horse for no good reason; I sometimes felt that his father was distressed at his character, he used to say that he would never be able to make anything of him.

Minor violent performances followed. A neighbor's servant girl saw Pierre threaten one of his brothers with a scythe. "The child was weeping and crying out [and] said to me: Pierre said he wanted to cut off my legs." The girl also heard from her master's son that Pierre had "carried him into the manger where his horse was feeding, saying he was going to give him to his horse to eat; the child came back to the house in tears [and] had been so frightened that for a long time he did not dare pass Rivière's door." A farmhand found another of Pierre's brothers sitting in front of the fireplace on a chair with his feet tied to a pothook above "a flame that was drawing and would soon burn him; the child was already feeling the heat and was weeping [while] Pierre Rivière was walking round the room laughing heartily, a strange laugh, the laugh of idiots. . . . The child . . . told me that it was Pierre who had tied him up." Pierre himself acknowledged torturing animals. "I crucified frogs and birds, I had also invented another torture to put them to death. It was to attach them to a tree with three sharp nails through the belly. I called that enceepharating them, I took the children with me to do it and sometimes I did it all by myself."

The multiple murder was an extended violent personal revolt:

I loved my father very much, his tribulations affected me sorely. . . . I conceived the fearful design which I executed, I was meditating it for about a month before. I wholly forgot the principles which should have made me respect my mother and my sister and my brother, I regarded my father as being in the power of mad dogs or barbarians against whom I must take up arms, religion forbade such things, but I disregarded its rules, it even seemed to me that God had destined me for this and that I would be executing his justice.

Pierre decided to kill his mother and his sister because "they were leagued to make my father suffer," but in addition to his little brother Jules's love for his mother, he thought that killing the seven-year-old, whom he knew his father loved, would lead Pierre-Margrin to "hold me in such abhorrence that he will rejoice in my death, and so he will live happier being free from regrets." Napoleon was a model: "I conjured up Bonaparte in 1815. I . . . said to myself: That man sent thousands to their death to satisfy mere caprices, it is not right therefore that I should let a woman live who is disturbing my father's peace and happiness." So he "went to have my pruning bill [a bill hook, or hand scythe] sharpened on

Sunday May 24 at Gabin the Blacksmith's at Aunay, who was accustomed to work for us."

After several false starts—he was working up courage, and he wanted his father out of town—Pierre carried out the slaughter: "I seized the bill, I went into my mother's house and I committed that fearful crime, beginning with my mother, then my sister and my little brother, after that I struck them again and again." The cantonal judge of Aunay reports what he and the mayor, the doctor and the local health officer discovered when they were called to the house on June 3, 1835:

> We found three bodies lying on the ground [floor], viz. (1) a woman about forty years of age lying on her back opposite the fireplace at which she had seemingly been busied at the time she was murdered cooking a gruel. . . . The woman was dressed in her ordinary clothes, her hair in disorder; the neck and the back of the skull were slashed and "cutlassed"; (2) a small boy aged seven or eight, dressed in a blue smock, trousers, stockings, and shoes, lying prone face to the ground, with his head split behind to a very great depth; (3) a girl dressed in a calico print, stockings, no shoes or clogs, lying on her back, her feet on the threshold of the door giving onto the yard, pointing toward the south, her lace bobbins resting on her stomach, her cotton cap at her feet as well as a large fistful of her hair, which seems to have been torn out at the time of the murder; the right side of the face and the neck "cutlassed" to a very great depth.

The doctor reported further that Pierre's mother had been attacked so violently that her neck was almost completely severed, her head attached only by skin and muscles on the left side. Her skull was crushed and her brain nearly expelled; her face was "reduced to a mere pulp" from multiple blows; and she was six and a half months pregnant. He found "many blows" totally mangling little Jules, and so many billhook wounds to Pierre's sister's face that both her lower and upper jaws were almost completely severed.

Confirming the modernity of these violent crimes, Pierre was examined at length for signs of mental illness by one Dr. Bouchard, a "corresponding member of the Royal Academy of Medicine" in Paris. He noticed that Pierre was comfortable with what Athens calls the "sweet victory" of his successful violent personal revolt: "When reminded of his crime," the physician reports, "he speaks of it with a sort of tranquillity which is truly shocking." Ironically, considering the evolution of the idea of "irresistible impulse" that Athens's colleague Frank Hartung would later chronicle, Bouchard apologizes for his lack of familiarity with the latest psychiatric techniques: "I made no phrenological examinations, for this science has not yet made much progress, and I must admit that my acquaintance with it is too imperfect for me to venture to apply it in so serious a case."

The French physician found "no signs of mental derangement," but despite acknowledging the extended ripening of Pierre's concern for "his father's misfortunes" and the murderer's own admission that he had planned the crime for a month, Dr. Bouchard concludes that "the triple murder of which he was guilty can be ascribed, I believe, only to a state of momentary over-excitement brought on by his father's tribulation." *Plus ça change, plus c'est la même chose.*

"The basic assumption behind my theory," Lonnie Athens explains in *Violent Criminal Acts and Actors Revisited*, "is that crime is a product of *social retardation.* Social retardation exists when people guide their actions toward themselves and others from the standpoint of an under-developed, primitive phantom community, an 'us' that hinders them from cooperating in the ongoing social activities of their corporal community or the larger society in which it is embedded." The history of the civilizing process in the West strongly supports Athens's theory. Violentization is evidently a universal mechanism for shaping children to become adults prepared to survive in malignant communities. When the larger society itself was malignant, violentization was adaptive. Today violent and ultraviolent individuals are social misfits within our larger civil society. DeMause, exploring the history of childhood, comes to a similar conclusion. "Since some people still kill, beat, and sexually abuse children," he writes, "any attempt to periodize modes of child rearing must first admit that psychogenic evolution proceeds at different rates in different family lines, and that many parents appear to be 'stuck' in earlier historical modes." If the larger society civilized itself across the past five hundred years, further civilizing within violent families is surely possible. "Specific childhood experiences must occur to sustain specific cultural traits," deMause confirms, "and once these experiences no longer occur, the trait disappears."

CHAPTER EIGHTEEN

Primitive Violence

"Both men and women are volatile, prone to quarreling and quick to take offense at a suspected slight or injury. They are jealous of their reputations, and an undercurrent of tension, even latent animosity, accompanies many interpersonal relationships. Dominance and submission, rivalry and coercion are constantly recurring themes, and although the people are not lacking in the gentler virtues, there is an unmistakable aggressive tone to life." Medieval England or a malignant minor community in the United States today would both fit this description, but in fact it portrays the people of the New Guinea Highlands as one of the first anthropologists to visit that region, Kenneth Read, found them in the early 1950s.

Most indigenous societies were violent before Western contact and continued to be violent long afterward. For comparison the homicide rate among black males in Cleveland, Ohio, between 1969 and 1974—a notably violent population concentrated in a malignant minor community—was 141.2 per 100,000, fourteen times the U.S. national rate. But the Yanomamo of Brazil had a homicide rate of 165.9 per 100,000 between 1970 and 1974; the Murngin Aborigines of Australia, a homicide rate of about 330 per 100,000 in the early years of the twentieth century; the Gebusi of lowland New Guinea, a homicide rate of 683 between 1940 and 1962; the Hewa of New Guinea, a homicide rate of 778 between 1959 and 1968. Do these and other indigenous societies use violentization to prepare their children to cope with such malignancy?

The question would be easier to answer if anthropologists paid more attention to child-rearing practices, a neglect the psychoanalyst Erik Erikson lamented half a century ago in his landmark study *Childhood and Society*. "Even anthropologists living for years among aboriginal tribes," Erikson complained, "failed to see that these tribes trained their children in some systematic way. Rather the experts tacitly assumed with the general public that savages had no child training at all and that primitives grew up 'like little animals.' "

Some evidence exists. The best comes from New Guinea, because Western adventurers only began to penetrate that dangerous, luxuriant western Pacific island in the late nineteenth century, making possible modern observation of its native peoples in a nearly pristine state— among the Fore people, for example, cannibalism only stopped in the late 1950s. A major region, the Highlands, home to several hundred thousand people isolated by the rugged terrain into more than one hundred linguistic groups, remained sequestered in complete isolation until the 1930s. When Australians looking for the sources of placer gold (streambed wash) by following the rivers up into the mountains discovered fertile valleys improved with thatch villages and elaborate, flower-bordered gardens, the Highlanders were shocked to learn of a larger world beyond the thousand miles of divided cordillera that confined them. Carleton Gajdusek, a pediatrician and Nobel laureate virologist who lived among the Highland peoples for many years and greatly admires them, describes them in an essay as having been "stone-age cannibals" at the time of their discovery who were "unfamiliar with the wheel or textiles or ceramics or metal or grain crops."

New Guinea before the Australians pacified it existed in an almost Hobbesian state of perpetual warring malignancy, as Kenneth Read's description implies. Its reputation for head-hunting and cannibalism was such that Micronesians lost at sea would steer four times as far away—toward the Philippines—rather than south to New Guinea. Capt. William Bligh, cast adrift from the *Bounty* by his mutinous crew and desperate for food and water, similarly gave the island wide berth. Conflict in New Guinea was universal—a "long, relentless cycle of killing and being killed," Margaret Mead called it—and everyone constantly watched his back. The Fore, among others, considered the incessant warfare a curse, and welcomed Australian pacification, but other New Guinea groups, such as the Dani, cherished it.

An Australian anthropologist living among the Gahuku of the Eastern Highlands comments that "enemies seem to have been as necessary as friends for the satisfactions generally sought by the Gahuku. One obtained women from one's friends and also needed them for the prestigious, largely competitive activity of exchanging livestock and valuables. But one required enemies too, for warfare epitomized the highly prized qualities of strength and aggressiveness that brought most renown to groups and individuals alike." Such value-based arguments imply that

New Guinea indigenes killed each other merely for sport. A more objective source of conflict is revealed in the close match of population and territory between enemy groups: War was competition for resources, and it typically flared when one group gained some temporary material or numerical advantage over another and ceased when the advantage had been nullified. Personal violence was linked to group violence in these family- and clan-based societies; two cross-cultural surveys on motives and causes of war indicate in general that "the predominant motives for prestate warfare are revenge for homicides and various economic issues."

Violence within indigenous societies—what we call crime—also nullified advantage or deterred aggression. More aggressive men and women were more likely to be accused of sorcery, and losses from disease were often attributed to sorcerous malice. The remedy was murderous attack by the victim's kin: "crushing of genitals with stones," Gajdusek describes the Anga punishment for sorcery as he found it evidenced in victims he treated: "rupturing of kidneys with stone axes or hand-stones, breaking the femurs with stones, biting the trachea with the teeth."

L. L. Langness, an American anthropologist who studied the Bena Bena people of the New Guinea Eastern Highlands, has assembled a general review of Highlands violence, which he finds to be "characteristic of all Highlands New Guinea societies." Langness's evidence indicates that child rearing included brutalization:

> In the Bena Bena and environs children are encouraged to be violent and aggressive. Tantrums are frequent and are usually ignored. Boys are especially encouraged in aggressive behavior. Play is rough and unsupervised, and the weak suffer the strong. . . . Boys beat girls as well as smaller boys, and several children sometimes torment a single child. Likewise, the deformed or retarded are targets of derision and are subject to much teasing and abuse. Tiny boys are given sticks and encouraged to chase and beat girls, the adults urging them to "stick it up her vagina" or "go on, hit her hard." Children also hear the many stories men tell about fighting and about strong men of the past.

Adults violently subjugate children:

> Although rarely punished [sic], much violence is directed at children at certain times. If they are underfoot during adult activities, they are shoved roughly aside, slapped, or even switched, usually

quite hard. They quickly learn to stay out of the way. Castration threats are so frequent boys eventually learn not to fear them. Both boys and girls are threatened "in fun" with axes and knives and they often run crying in terror. . . . When adults are mourning a close kinsman, small girls regularly have a finger joint amputated. I know of one case in which a man was so overcome with grief that he bit rather than cut off a girl's finger. . . . On the rare occasions when an adult does punish a child, he or she invariably uses physical means.

Another anthropologist describes the punishments of the Mae-Enga, which Langness says would never occur among the Bena Bena:

A father early warns his children that the gardens are the mother's domain and must not be visited without her permission. A child who steals [from the garden] is lucky to escape with only a beating from the mother. Should she tell her husband, he is likely to punish the offender with great severity. He may slice the child's palm with a knife, lop off a fingertip, cut off an earlobe, cook it and make the child eat it, or smoke the culprit over a fire. At the least he will administer a sound thrashing.

Margaret Mead reports an extreme form of violent coaching among a group elsewhere in New Guinea:

It was considered necessary that every Tchambuli boy should in childhood kill a victim, and for this purpose live victims, usually infants or young children, were purchased from other tribes. Or a captive in war or a criminal from another Tchambuli hamlet sufficed. The small boy's spearhand was held by his father, and the child, repelled and horrified, was initiated into the cult of head-hunting.

"That the Tchambuli boys were 'repelled and horrified,' " Langness comments dryly, "could be merely a supposition on Mead's part."

Initiation ceremonies for boys, which may be ritual formalizations of violent subjugation and violent coaching, were brutal, Langness notes, "involving both force and physical pain." Those of the Bena Bena proceeded in three stages. At five to seven years of age, men took boys from their mothers for a day, pierced their ears with a sharp bone and feasted them with pig. At nine to eleven years of age, boys had their nasal septums pierced (men wore ornaments in their noses) and rolls of coarse leaves jammed up their noses to make them bleed in a male simulation of menarche; afterward the boys moved into the men's house, leaving mothers and sisters behind.* Sometime after twelve years of age, boys were secluded from women for at least a month, then subjected to major initiation, usually conducted standing in a cold mountain river: violent nosebleeding again, miniature arrows shot into tongue and urinary meatus—the opening of the glans penis—to make them bleed and forced swallowing of "bent lengths of supple cane which are worked down their throats, causing them to vomit." Eyewitnesses describe the boys' response to these indignities as rageful, and Langness comments that "New Guineans . . . are well aware of the painful and degrading character of their initiations" and make them an occasion to "explicitly point out to initiates their past failures and inadequacies." Men also use these occasions to coach boys "who they are, who their enemies are, what they must do to them and how."

Disputes among men and women resulted in violence ample for the personal horrification of their children. "Married women brutally fight with their co-wives or potential co-wives," Langness reports, "and in some cases, albeit rare, fight to the death." Widows cut off one or more fingers to mourn their husband's death. Husbands beat their wives and might wound or kill them for adultery. Lone women were targets for rape. Husbands in one society whose wives failed at blackmailing them into making more bride payments were allowed to kill them publicly by forcing a red-hot stone into their vaginas.

"The big men," said the Wangulam Dani, ". . . are those who kill. . . . The more people a man kills, the bigger he grows." Killing, Langness concludes, "is usually a prerequisite for leadership in the Highlands. . . . The limits of power, like justice and morality, were confirmed only by action—violent action."

Australian pacification efforts dramatically reduced at least intergroup violence in Papua and New Guinea before the two territories won independence in 1975 as Papua New Guinea. "They put on wigs and

---

* In a number of New Guinea societies boys were encouraged and expected to fellate older men. Semen was believed to be the male equivalent of milk; boys were told that the more semen they ate, the stronger they would grow. Some anthropologists call this custom "enforced homosexuality," but it was universal within the societies that practiced it, a normal part of growing up. Since contact with women was considered polluting and was kept to an absolute minimum—men bragged about how few strokes they needed to achieve ejaculation in intercourse with their wives—pederasty was evidently a valuable secondary sexual outlet for adult males.

red robes," Gajdusek told me, "and dispensed justice at periodic courts convened in the open air, and people accepted it because they loved ceremony and were tired of fighting all the time. The Australians should have been awarded the Nobel Peace Prize; they pacified the island without force or invasion." Behind the red robes, of course, were district officers and police patrols. But the monopolization of violence was minimal. Rather, it was what New Guineans call cargo—Western goods, wealth and obvious technological advantage—that encouraged them to desist, much as the monarchy and the upper classes with their wealth and prestige dominated the commoners in early modern Europe and led the way to civil societies.

Erik Erikson spent the summer of 1937 observing the Oglala Sioux—the Dakota—on the Pine Ridge Reservation in South Dakota. Despite his complaint against anthropologists, his comments on Sioux child rearing are limited and preoccupied with Freudian issues. Elements of violentization nevertheless emerge in his observations of the development of these fierce people. "Their cruelty was proverbial," Erikson observes, adding later, "What their cruel games with captives meant to them, it is hard to say. We know little about human cruelty except that it can manifest itself in 'peaceful' and even erotic entertainment as well as in the fury of battle."

Erikson was told of early violence which Sioux mothers visited on their infants:

> To be permitted to suckle, the infant had to learn not to bite the breast. Sioux grandmothers recount what trouble they had with their indulged babies when they began to use nipples for the first vigorous biting. They tell with amusement how they would "thump" the baby's head and how he would fly into a wild rage. It is at this point that Sioux mothers used to say what our mothers say so much earlier in their babies' lives: Let him cry, it will make him strong. Good future hunters, especially, could be recognized by the strength of their infantile fury.
>
> The Sioux baby, when thus filled with rage, was strapped up to his neck in the cradleboard. He could not express his rage by the usual violent motion of his limbs. . . . The companion [Sioux] virtue of generosity was fortitude, in Indians a quality both more ferocious and more stoical than mere bravery. It included an easily

aroused quantity of quickly available hunting and fighting spirit, the inclination to do sadistic harm to the enemy and the ability to stand extreme hardship and pain under torture and self-torture. Did the necessity of suppressing early biting wishes contribute to the tribe's always ready ferocity? If so, it cannot be without significance that the generous mothers themselves aroused a "hunter's ferocity" in their teething infants, encouraging an eventual transfer of the infant's provoked rage to ideal images of hunting, encircling, catching, killing and stealing.

This is minimal evidence, to be sure, though it hints of extremely early application of violent subjugation. Erikson is more revealing about boyhood, which included violent coaching by vainglorification and incitement to major violent performances:

> It fell to the older brothers . . . to introduce the small boy to the ethos of the hunter and to make loyalty between brothers the cement of Dakota society. Because of their exclusive association with the boasting older boys, the smaller ones must have become aware early enough of the fact that direct phallic aggressiveness remained equated with the ferocity of the hunter. It was considered proper for a youth to rape any maiden whom he caught outside the areas defined for decent girls: a girl who did not know "her place" was his legitimate prey, and he could boast of the deed.

Girls, for their part, were encouraged "to sleep at night with [their] thighs tied together to prevent rape."

Erikson also reports the results of TATs administered in 1942 to two hundred Pine Ridge children. He seems to assume that they reveal the breakdown of the premodern society he obviously idealizes, but what they in fact reveal is evidence of violent phantom communities, more probably aboriginal than responses to cultural breakdown:

> Dakota children . . . describe the world as dangerous and hostile. Affectionate relationships in early home life are remembered with nostalgia. Otherwise the world for them seems to have little definiteness and little purpose. . . . In the children's stories, action is mostly initiated by others, and it is mostly inconsiderate, untrustworthy and hostile action leading to fights and to the destruction of toys and property, and causing in the narrator sadness, fear and

anger. The narrator's action leads almost always to fighting, damaging of property, breaking of rules and stealing. Animals, too, are represented as frightening. . . . In the frequency of themes, worry about the death of other people, their sickness or their departure, is second only to descriptions of hostility emanating from people or from animals.

Marc Howard Ross, a political scientist, examined data coded from ethnographic reports of 90 preindustrial societies worldwide to see if personal violence correlated with a propensity for war. The data came from a standard cross-cultural sample of more than 150 societies that anthropologists have developed for such studies and recognize to be representative. Ross found that "internal conflict is a good predictor of the level of external conflict, and external conflict is an excellent predictor of internal conflict. . . . These results clearly support the argument that there is a 'culture of violence.' . . . Societies that are psychoculturally predisposed toward violence behave more aggressively both internally and externally."

By "psychocultural predisposition" Ross means that he found three variables that correlated with high levels of internal and external conflict in the societies he analyzed. One correlation was with harsh socialization practices, including inflicting severe pain, using corporal punishment, not indulging children, scolding them, handing them off to caretakers other than their mothers, stressing the value of fortitude and stressing the value of aggressiveness. The second correlation was with socialization practices low in affection, including less emphasis on the value of trust, less stress on honesty, distant fathers, less stress on the value of generosity, less expression of affection and valuing children less. The third correlation was with high levels of conflict over male gender identity. Ross summarizes:

> Our evidence is that gross differences between societies in their socialization practices on such questions as affection, warmth, punishment, aggression and gender role conflict are especially crucial for understanding conflict behavior. . . . Socialization provides individuals with a lens through which they see themselves and others, and . . . these perceptions are crucial in shaping their actions as adults. Dispositions learned early in life are not simply relevant on the perceptual level; they also involve specific behavioral patterns, such as how to respond to insults, the use of physical aggression, or whom to trust, which serve one throughout life.

Ross's general survey of indigenous societies throughout the world supports Athens's specific evidence from interviews with violent criminals in the midwestern and western United States. Ross also independently identifies violent actors' interpretations as the key to their actions. "Most conflict situations are highly ambiguous," he argues; participants easily invoke supposedly "objective" reasons for a conflict ("She, he, they, took my land, water, women"), but to an outsider what is striking is how often the same situation *does not* lead to violence. Thus, Ross concludes (as does Athens) that "objective situations don't cause overt conflict, it is the *interpretation* of such situations that is crucial." Since people learn from their primary groups how to interpret conflicts—in Athens's more encompassing terminology, arrive at their interpretations by consulting their phantom communities—what is important to know are the terms under which those intimate entities operate. Athens identifies violentization as the process that leads to violent phantom communities. Ross's examination of a large, representative sample of indigenous communities finds that some degree of violentization correlates highly in those communities with higher levels of personal violence ("internal conflict") and of group violence ("external conflict") as well.

Have I demonstrated that indigenous societies with high homicide rates violentize their children? Highlands groups in Papua New Guinea at least demonstrably brutalize their children, and the fact that high homicide rates follow that brutalization suggests that some members of those groups undergo belligerency, violent performances and virulency as well. Erikson's sketchy comments on the Sioux and Ross's ninety-society correlations fall short of full demonstration, but they support rather than contradict Athens's findings.

One phenomenon that deserves further study is what appears to be a widespread, socially approved encouragement of violent performances against girls and women—rape in particular—in the interest of advancing the violentization of boys and men. Given the limited resources of subsistence communities, one resource at hand that could be exploited to prepare males for warriorhood—for the support and defense of the community, that is—is their own (female) members, a more reliable and available supply of victims than prisoners of war and one that could be encouraged not to stall violentization by defending themselves. An additional benefit of such exploitation, explicit in the case of the Sioux, would be conditioning the females to dependency. Erikson reports just such an outcome: "The Sioux girl was educated to be a hunter's helper and a future hunter's mother. She was taught to sew, to cook and conserve food and to put up tents. At the same time she was subjected to a rigorous training toward bashfulness and outright fear of men." Vestiges of this primitive sexual economy survive in modern civil societies as tolerance for date rape, for the overlooked excesses of successful high school athletes, for some degree of spousal abuse and, modified by the civilizing process, for the chronic patronage of boys over girls. In such division of labor of violence training may lie the origins of the inequality of women.

Anthropologists continue to argue about what one calls "the importance of socialization, specifically the modeling of adult aggression via punitive child rearing and distant/authoritarian father-child relations," as a cause of violence. Athens's work offers a potentially fruitful, evidence-based recasting of the terms of that debate.

Anthropologist Bruce M. Knauft, for example, in a paper titled "Reconsidering Violence in Simple Human Societies," points out that socialization among the Gebusi, a lowland New Guinea society with an extremely high homicide rate,* "is affectionate rather than harsh." The Gebusi are affectionate toward their children, do not beat them, and allow them great freedom. The whole society of about 450 people, which is leaderless and egalitarian, works to maintain a mood of "good company," which Knauft says is the primary cultural value. "The opposite, negatively valued trait is *gof,* which connotes anger, hardness and violence. Violence and anger are considered antisocial and unbecoming, and individuals suspected of being upset usually go to great lengths to deny it."

Yet extreme violence is commonplace in Gebusi society, "a pattern of social life," Knauft writes, "that is generally peaceful and tranquil but is punctuated by aggression which, when it does occur, is unrestrained and frequently homicidal." Of 394 adult deaths Knauft recorded in a genealogical survey he conducted, "nearly one-third . . . were homicides." Gebusi killed other Gebusi primarily because they believed them to be sorcerers who allegedly caused someone else in the community to die of disease. "More aggressive, outspoken or assertive" men and women were "much more likely targets for sorcery accusations." When a Gebusi accused someone of being a sorcerer, there was "little collective

---

* As cited earlier, 683 per 100,000 between 1940 and 1962, which Knauft estimates dropped only to 419 per 100,000 *after* Australian pacification of the Gebusi, beginning in 1963.

opposition . . . no strong men or fight leaders to organize revenge killings, and no material compensation to forestall violence." As a result of this total lack of social prohibition, this open season for killers, "the violence that does occur erupts suddenly, is often devastatingly extreme and subsides with parties tending to act as if little had happened."

Imagine being a child in such a society, however affectionately cherished and unbeaten, with mothers and fathers and uncles and aunts regularly being publicly bashed to death out of the blue and no one stepping forward to intervene. (Husbands also, Knauft mentions in a footnote, "occasionally" beat their wives.) Why would your parents need to beat you to make you toe the line? They could violently subjugate you with personal horrification alone. They would only have to look at you sideways. Knauft confirms—unknowingly, because he is focused on physical rather than psychological subjugation—that such in fact is what occurs: "Any sign of adult anger or potential violence tends to inspire [in children] an emotional state *(abwida)* ranging from uneasiness, anxiety and embarrassment to extreme fright." And, confirming violent subjugation via personal horrification as the preferred Gebusi form, it turns out that "Gebusi openly encourage the use and display of *abwida* behavior to advertise vulnerability and encourage a return to good company." That is, Gebusi make sure their children experience plenty of *abwida* while they are growing up. Far from refuting socialization as the cause of Gebusi violence, Knauft confirms that socialization in the form of violentization occurs. Since his paper includes other "simple" human societies with extremely high homicide rates and seemingly affectionate childrearing methods—the !Kung Bushmen of Africa, the Central Eskimo— those groups probably also practice this more covert form of violent subjugation, consistent with the high value they place on hypocritical bonhomie. The children are not fooled.

Gajdusek, a romantic in the tradition of Rimbaud but also a first-rank scientist, who experienced living among indigenous societies, especially the Anga, at a level of intimacy few anthropologists ever pursue, regrets the modernizing of their cultures as a loss of knowledge. "The exotic, unique, now rapidly disappearing primitive cultures of mankind," he writes in an essay,

> far removed in their methods of child care and their practices of child rearing . . . present unparalleled experiments in the programming of the nervous system of the human infant and child. Our

mores and taboos, our religions and our ethics will not permit us to mimic nor even attempt to reproduce such experiments in the use of the developing nervous system once these primitive societies are gone.

In a private journal entry he engages the ethics of intervention more emotionally:

We cannot cure their yaws and ulcers, save their dying children, remove their arrows and treat their wounds without coming to them. We cannot come to them without bringing ourselves and our life into their horizon and to then refuse their request to see the outer worlds, or agree with those who would come and study them, observe them, and especially those who want to "help" or change them in any way (including to stop warfare, murder, fear, superstition, famine or pestilence) and who would yet "leave them as they were, primitive and picturesque" [would be] an insult to their human aspirations and intelligence and will never do. By coming we commit ourselves to the change and are agents of it. The change disturbs us for we know better than they do how pallid and barren and how unsatisfying the fruits of civilization can be at times.*

Elias also sometimes laments the paler cast of modern civilization compared to the florid medieval affect, a nostalgia his colleague Johan Huizinga made the starting point of his classic work *The Autumn of the Middle Ages:* "When the world was half a thousand years younger all events had much sharper outlines than now. The distance between sadness and joy, between good and bad fortune, seemed to be much greater than for us; every experience had that degree of directness and absoluteness that joy and sadness still have in the mind of a child."

But the evidence that violentization was widespread, if not universal, in the medieval and preliterate past and continues to smolder today in civil societies argues to the contrary that very few of the evolutionary coping strategies human beings have devised across the past two million years are ever really lost. We have our cannibals too (Jeffrey Dahmer

---

* Gajdusek experienced these conflicts personally. He informally adopted more than fifty children from indigenous Western Pacific societies and impoverished himself educating them in the United States. In 1996 he was arrested for sexually abusing one of his charges, however, and plea-bargained a short term in jail as a result.

comes to mind), our coprophiliacs, our hallucinators and berserkers and pedophiles, so relict in normal times that we consider them mentally ill. Would that our violent criminals were endangered species as well. To wish the primitive on the world again, however dithyrambic its emotional pitch, would truly be an insult to human aspirations.

In cases other than those Lonnie Athens personally studied, in documented patterns of historical change extending across centuries, in cultures other than Western and other than modern, violentization appears and reappears as a universal mechanism for creating seriously violent human beings. Is violentization also a special case of a more general (not necessarily violent) developmental process that most, if not all, human beings experience in the course of their lives? That was the next question Athens took up.

PART III

THE SELF AS A SOLILOQUY

Soliloquies supply the vital sustenance without which the self cannot live.

—Lonnie Athens, "The Self as a Soliloquy"

CHAPTER NINETEEN

Dramatic Self-Change

Works of art often emerge from significant, transforming experiences in the lives of the artists who create them. As it happens, so do works of science, particularly of theory. That should not be surprising: Creation in science and creation in art are close twins, though the artifacts that result are put to different tests and dressed differently for presentation.

After Routledge published *The Creation of Dangerous Violent Criminals* early in 1989, what Lonnie Athens calls his "steep descent" continued. He had hoped the book would change his luck, bringing grants and professional appointments. In his bitterness at the failure of *Violent Criminal Acts and Actors* to achieve recognition in criminology circles, he had jettisoned George Herbert Mead's and Herbert Blumer's jargon and written a spare, pure, paradigm-shifting analysis of the process that leads to violent criminality. Hardly anyone noticed, partly because the book was published abroad. (A paperback edition was published in the United States by the University of Illinois Press in 1992.) A few reviews appeared in academic journals. Several, by criminologists of the quantitative persuasion, savaged it—not enough cases, they complained, as if Athens had merely tabulated police records, and where was his control group? One review, in a symbolic interactionist journal, praised the book in terms it deserves: "My own research experience with over 500 violent men leads me to feel that [it] represents a profoundly creative and original theoretical contribution, on a par with any other criminological development this century."

Just as before with *Violent Acts and Actors,* Athens says, "nothing happened. The book failed. Everything failed. I was a failure. Things started coming unglued at the seams." He was still trying to find a teaching appointment, still sending out résumés, but his marriage was over. He

and his wife had separated before the book was published. Now a practic-
ing attorney with a government job, Marilyn was no longer willing to
consider moving. "Things had changed now," Athens paraphrases her.
"She'd done everything she could for me to be a success, and I'd failed.
Now it was her career. Her career was coming first. She was the captain
of the ship now, and that's the way it was going to be. There was a lot of
truth to what she said. I'd self-destructed. But I told her, Well, if you're
the captain of the ship, then I'm bailing out and that's the way it is. She
gave me seven hundred dollars, and I took the old car and threw my
things in the back and went off to Richmond." By then, his mother, Irene,
had divorced Pete the Greek. Athens boarded with her and continued
looking for work. He was forty years old.

Pete had moved to a trailer park and allowed his full circus-carny per-
sona to emerge. He was well on his way to becoming an outsider artist.
He made his living selling trinkets and homemade signs at flea markets
("THE DEVIL POWER OF MONEY BETWEEN MEN AND WOMEN," "THE OLD
CHICKEN HAS THE BEST BROTH," "WHEN I DIE, DON'T BURY ME, HANG MY
BALLS ON A CHESTNUT TREE," "BYE, BYE, BLACKBIRD"), called himself King
Kong Flagman, drove around in an old car gilded and decorated with
flags with a full-size stuffed gorilla as a fellow passenger and still carried
his gun. He was no less threatening and dangerous, but after an
encounter in 1984, when Athens had gone to see him, father and son had
come to a truce.

"He pulled a gun on me," Athens recalls, "and I told him, 'Go ahead
and shoot me, I don't care.' He put it away and kissed me. Said he
wouldn't hurt me. I don't know why he did it. I think just to check my
nerve." Then as now, Athens was left respecting his father. "Pete was
honorable in his own crazy way," he says. "He was consistent in his rules.
It was a peasant system of honor." (Petros Athens died—of natural
causes—on December 8, 1996. Athens's grandfather, Lombros Zaharias,
died at ninety-five in 1977.) Pete was part of Athens's phantom community, an important part, which was one reason Athens made his fellow academics uncomfortable. "Academia is a world where lying is
accepted," Athens frames the problem, much as Pete or Norbert Elias
would have; the difference is similar to the difference between the rude
candor of medieval knights and the diplomacy of the courtiers who succeeded them. Pete had a medieval's violence as well; Athens had chosen
not to be violent, but he still viewed his social and professional relations
through the prism of his archaic phantom community, which made him
direct and blunt and sometimes harsh. At some point during his steep
descent he went to see a counselor. The counselor diagnosed his pro-

blem as noble savagery. "There's nothing wrong with you," he told Athens. "You just belong in an Apache tribe. You'd be a hero. You'd be Cochise." But in the modern world, Athens says ruefully and with unintended irony, "they kill you."

He rekindled his friendship with Mike Markowitz, now a prosperous anesthesiologist. "Called him up, told him I was just visiting—I was ashamed to tell him I was out of work and going through a divorce. Hadn't seen him in twenty years. We met to eat, we ate, everything was fine. A couple of weeks later I called him and told him I had to talk to him. He said to meet him at the shopping center. We sat together in his sixty-thousand-dollar car. I told him my marriage was over. He sheepishly admitted his marriage was over too. I told him what had happened to me." They picked up where they had left off, best friends debating whose philosophy makes the best life, "the stubborn Greek warrior versus the shrewd, diplomatic Jew"—the archaic confronting the urbane again, mutually perplexed.

Irene sparked Athens's forensic career. She had been following the story of the Southside Strangler in the Richmond newspaper—the paroled burglar who was accused of the rape murders of a high school girl and three professional women and whose profile the FBI's mind-hunters misidentified. "She kept throwing papers at me," Athens remembers, "saying, 'Go on down there and help those people get this man—he's a bad man, do something.' " One of the murders was coming up for trial in Chesterfield County, a transitional urban-rural area that straddles the southern edge of Richmond. Athens contacted the county prosecutor, William W. Davenport, identified himself as a forensic criminologist and offered to help. Davenport, a calm, burly man with a moustache and a full head of dark hair who used to be an ironworker, warily agreed to see him.

"I figured they'd think I was a fraud," Athens says, "so I made a copy of my Berkeley diploma and took along my books." Davenport interviewed Athens in the company of his tall, top-gun chief prosecutor Warren von Schuch, a New Jersey–born former University of Oklahoma football star and a veteran of more than three hundred capital murder prosecutions. "They thought I was a plant coming in from the defense to find out what their case was," Athens confirms. They called his references, including Heathcote Wales at Georgetown. While they were checking up on Athens, to demonstrate his usefulness, he collected autopsy reports and case files and spent a marathon three days and nights developing a crime signature for the Southside Strangler, Timothy W. Spencer. He established that Spencer used the same grotesque technique in all four murders, binding his victims' hands and then slipping ligatures around their necks so that he could slowly choke them to death while he raped them from behind. The crime signature helped convict Spencer in cases that were otherwise circumstantial. "From that point on," von Schuch says, "we were pretty much sold."

Davenport hired Athens as a consultant to profile defendants in capital murder cases, but the work was sporadic. In September 1989 Athens joined the Chesterfield County Victim/Witness Assistance Program, which supported and prepared victims and their families and other witnesses for trial. A month after he took up the part-time position, the victim/witness unit got a new director, a thirty-one-year-old police captain's daughter from south Richmond named Elizabeth Bernhard, a vivacious single mother. The two bonded instantly. Bernhard had been widowed at twenty-eight when her husband was killed in a car crash and had recently been divorced after a brief second marriage, so she and Athens had much in common.

Bernhard assigned Athens to all the homicide cases and signed on to serve as the latest in Athens's series of white-collar coaches. She recalls the experience vividly:

> It took me about a day to realize that Lonnie was severely overqualified for the work he was doing here and I believe I flat-out asked him, "Why in the world are you here?" Eventually I realized that at that particular point in his life he didn't need a high-stress job. We got along famously. He has an unusual personality, as I've pointed out to him on numerous occasions. While I consider him a brilliant man, there's something of a lack of social skills in play. He frightens people. When you're dealing with serial killers, I would assume you have to present a very strong and forceful front. We're not dealing with serial killers. We're dealing with victims of crime. One of my personal favorites is Lonnie's habit of saying, "What do you mean by that? What do you mean by that?" "Lonnie," I'd tell him, "what I said was, 'Maybe it's time to go to lunch now.' What do you think I meant by that? I'm hungry and I'm ready to go forage for food." He has a tendency to become explosive, which is very effective in an interview process with an offender. It reinforces your control. But it scares the daylights out of your average victim.

If he was sometime combative, in the office he was funny. "He made me laugh. I would laugh and laugh. I found him vastly amusing. I called him the absent-minded professor. His necktie would normally be rolled up in a ball, shoved in his pocket in case he had to go to court. There were times when his socks didn't match, and I think he always wore the same shoes."

Remaking his life, Athens was reading Thomas Wolfe and working on a collection of short stories set in and around the Manchester Cafe, by then demolished and replaced with a small park beside the high concrete floodwalls that Richmond had built to contain the James River as it bent past the city. On her own time Bernhard typed his stories for him, old-fashioned stories with titles like "The Melting Pot Boils Over," "The Amorous Salesman," "Piggy Crenshaw Drops into the Manchester Cafe" and "A Mad Greek Comes to Rebeldom" that recycled Athens's childhood as slapstick and dark comedy.

But besides trying his hand at fiction, he was still wrestling with the problem of George Herbert Mead's taxonomy of the self, particularly Mead's confusing assignment of collective attitudes to a "generalized other." The generalized other had stuck in Athens's craw for twenty years, and for twenty years he had been grinding away at understanding it. He had tested Mead's ideas about the self in action, studying violent criminals, and now, opened to insight by the necessity of reorganizing himself, he found his way through. The result was two papers, "The Self as a Soliloquy" and "Dramatic Self-Change," which broadened the findings of his two books into an original and persuasive new general theory of human behavior.

Bernhard remembers debating Athens's word choices and typing endless drafts. "I was never embarrassed to tell him what I thought while I was trying to type it. I'd shout, 'Come here, pal!' He'd wander over. I'd say, 'This makes no sense at all. Either you've left out an insert or you just went brain-dead.' Some of his language we'd argue about. I'd always take the underdog position, sometimes not because I believed it, sometimes simply to irritate him, because I knew he'd explode. That can be a good thing. If you're too focused on too narrow a position, you may need shaking up. I wasn't professionally qualified to debate him. But I can tell whether something makes sense or not." The finished papers made sense. "He's an introspective and a very private man," Bernhard concludes. "But I think that when he decides you're a friend, it's a deep and abiding friendship."

Athens left Richmond before he finished the two papers. He had continued to follow university employment bulletins, and early in 1990 he learned that Seton Hall University, a Catholic college in South Orange, New Jersey, had openings in its Criminal Justice Department. He applied for a tenure-track assistant professorship. Seton Hall hired him. He started there in September 1990. In 1996 he won tenure as an associate professor.

The appointment seems to have plunged him into renewed despair, however. The summer of his tenure appointment he wrote a prose poem titled "Futility" that argued he had lived his life in vain. "I still feel like I am hitting my head against the wall," he wrote Norman Denzin. "I am approaching fifty and still have not made any real mark on my field. . . . I feel like the third or fourth best buggy whip maker in a world that hasn't needed buggy whips in a hundred years. Criminologists still routinely ignore my material on violence as do psychologists. . . . Although you would think that the more that you get rejected, the easier it is to take, the reverse is the case because you wonder if it will ever stop." Denzin, a loyal friend, responded by advising him to "stop feeling sorry for yourself. . . . You would not want to be recognized by this field as it stands now. . . . Your two books are giant mountains. . . . Get to work." Even as Athens was concluding he had lived his life in vain, he was teaching a full load of courses, revising *Violent Criminal Acts and Actors* for its *Revisited* reissue and spending summers in Richmond working up criminal profiles for Billy Davenport and Warren von Schuch. Mike Markowitz had introduced him to a pretty, unflappable, dark-blond recovery-room nurse named Jennifer Weatherford. He had proposed after a whirlwind courtship, Father Dombalis had officiated at their wedding, and they had bought a comfortable prewar brick house together in West Orange. If he still had nothing in the bank, he had a solid body of work that he continues to build on.

"I never did criminology for its own sake," Athens told me when we discussed his two general papers. "I found it interesting and colorful, but I always wanted to go back to general human action—to human nature, actually. I think that's one of the distinctive things about my work. It's hard to keep on the same problem, to build incrementally, because you've got to live with what you've done. You've got to transcend yourself all the time. It makes it very hard, but on the other hand, if you succeed, your work gets deeper and deeper and deeper. And that's what I think science is supposed to be about." "The Self as a Soliloquy" emerged from *Violent Criminal Acts and Actors.* "Dramatic Self-Change" emerged from *The Creation of Dangerous Violent Criminals,* although some of the drama was also Athens descending to rock bottom and coming unglued, the demolition and reconstruction of the self. When the two papers were peer-reviewed, anonymous reviewers predicted that they would become classics. They were published, finally, in 1994 and 1995 in the *Sociological Quarterly.*

CHAPTER TWENTY

Universal Processes

Soliloquy, from the Latin *soliloquium,* a word Saint Augustine coined, means talking to yourself. Most of us know the word from its theatrical imitation in soliloquies such as Hamlet's, where it mimics a process of thought with which audiences are intimately familiar while solving the playwright's problem of how to reveal a character's interior speech without resorting to the clumsy mechanism of an omniscient narrator. Stream of consciousness—a phrase William James popularized to describe our interior soliloquies—or internal monologue, a literary device whose invention is conventionally ascribed to James Joyce and Virginia Woolf, solved a similar problem in narrative fiction. That soliloquy is in fact interior speech is confirmed by modern studies of the self-talk of children, who typically soliloquize out loud until they enter school, when they learn to interiorize the process and go silent to avoid being overheard—literally keeping their opinions to themselves. Theatrical soliloquy works because it is inherently dramatic, not a speech to the audience but an implicit dialogue that we are allowed to overhear; well acted, it crowds the stage with unseen others debating the choices the character confronts and offering advice. In "The Self as a Soliloquy," Lonnie Athens makes explicit who those unseen others are.*

The problem he confronts in "The Self as a Soliloquy" is the ancient philosophic problem of the nature of the self. He starts with George Herbert Mead because, he writes, "Mead recognized more than anyone else that the self emerges and is sustained through soliloquizing. The virtue

---

* The discussion of soliloquy in chapter 8 concerning the "phantom community" appears there anachronistically, since Athens had not fully developed his analysis at the time he wrote *Violent Acts and Actors.* He revised that book in 1997 to incorporate it. I doubted if anyone other than historians of criminology would be interested in reliving his learning process.

of visualizing the self as a soliloquy is that anyone at any time and at any place can easily confirm that it exists by merely engaging in a moment or two of self-observation. People need only ask themselves: 'Do I talk to myself?' If the answer is yes, then they have verified their selves' existence." That parsimonious observation, Athens points out, establishes the provenance of the self without making it "a mysterious, metaphysical entity defying verification."

But Mead fell short of a full explanation. In the conversations that we conduct with ourselves—the soliloquies—that enable us to organize and negotiate our actions, Mead failed to identify a mechanism that might explain why we sometimes act in conformity with the attitudes of the community at large but at other times act in opposition. His "generalized other," Athens observes—the Greek chorus, as it were, that delivers the collective community opinion—explains conformity but not individuality, as I pointed out earlier. Nor did Mead's vision of the self as a process rather than a structure allow for the continuity of the self, the sense we have that we are who we are and have been that way persistently—at least since we became who we are now by growing up, or weathering a crisis, or undergoing a conversion or however we arrived at the self we presently call our own. What Mead's model needed was a stable component. "The self should be viewed as a fluid process," Athens continues, "that contains a critical, although mutable constant. . . . In my opinion, the self's fluidity must be seen as arising from our ever-changing soliloquies; while its constancy must be seen as coming from the stability of the 'other' with whom we soliloquize." And that "other" must account for both conformity and individuality.

To delineate this "other," Athens proceeds to identify thirteen basic principles that govern soliloquizing. Some he derived from Mead; some followed logically from one another; some emerged from introspection; all find support in the evidence of his interviews with violent criminals.

Principle one: People talk to themselves as if they were talking to someone else, except that they talk to themselves in shorthand. This principle, Athens says, may explain why it is so difficult to give directions. It may also explain why some people deny talking to themselves—because their soliloquy is different from their speech, highly compressed.

Principle two: When people talk to each other, they tell themselves at the same time what they're saying; otherwise they would not know. A corollary of this principle, Athens adds, is that people may talk to themselves silently while also echoing what they are saying to someone else, so that what they tell someone or what someone tells them is not necessarily what the speaker is thinking.

Principle three: While people are talking to us, we have to tell ourselves what they are saying. Unless we do, we do not know what they are telling us. Athens says we call this "following what the other person is saying," and it is more or less what Mead meant by his phrase "taking the attitude of the other." Principle two and principle three together, Athens points out, "demonstrate how the self is actively involved in both the transmission and reception of information to and from other people."

Principle four: "Soliloquizing transforms our raw, bodily sensations into emotions." We often identify and categorize bodily sensations so quickly that they seem to have originated as emotions. (For example, the sensations that arise in unfamiliar social situations—flushing, heart palpitations, nervous stomach—which shy people invoke as evidence of their shyness occur with equal intensity in people who do not describe themselves as shy.) At other times we have to work hard to explain our sensations to ourselves. Athens observes: "If it were not, in fact, for our ability to soliloquize, we would not experience the rich tapestry of emotions that both bedevil and enrich our existence. Instead, we would only experience a steady stream of vague bodily sensations, which undoubtedly would change in intensity, but not in general shape or form." Contrasting classifications like "thoughts" and "emotions," he adds, are categories that the self constructs, not separate entities. "In fact they occur together in experience."

Principle five: We always talk with an interlocutor when we soliloquize. "Everything that is said to us, including what we say to ourselves, some interlocutor tells us." One set of interlocutors is linked to the people we are conversing with; these go-betweens tell us what we are hearing by repeating what the other person says. Another set of interlocutors consists of phantom others. These virtual beings are not physically present, but they influence us at least as much as the real human beings who are. Indeed, their influence is greater than the real human beings in our lives, because people come and go, but our phantom others abide with us so long as our self remains intact. Nor are we normally aware of their presence.

Principle six: The phantom other is the one and the many. "It is a single entity because we can only normally talk to one phantom companion at a time during our soliloquies." It is multiple because more than one phantom companion is ready at hand. We need a council of phantom others for social flexibility, since different phantom others offer different expertise. Taken together our phantom others comprise a phantom community, a more or less flexible "voice and sounding board for making sense of [our] varied social experiences."

Principle seven: We soliloquize both superficially and profoundly. Superficially we self-talk ourselves through our daily experiences with people we are aware of and recognize. But ordinarily we are not aware of our phantom companions, Athens finds: "Most of the time we take their presence in our lives so much for granted that they lie far beneath our normal level of awareness. . . . While remaining oblivious to us, our phantom companions influence the creation of our deepest thoughts and emotions. Thus, whatever harm or good our phantom community does us is usually done from behind our backs." The phantom community emerges to awareness at times of dramatic self-change, as we shall see.

Principle eight: Our phantom others are the hidden source of our emotions. If we devise emotions by soliloquizing about bodily sensations (principle four), and if our phantom others play a critical role in our soliloquies (principles five and seven), then our phantom others must largely shape the emotions we devise. Our phantom others, Athens writes, "tell us how an experience that we are undergoing will unfold before it actually ends, which can create in us a powerful self-fulfilling prophecy." That prediction in turn can stir us so deeply that we will be moved to carry it out when without its powerful influence we might not have done so. Since our phantom others stand in shadow, we may well be unaware of their authority over us.

Principle nine: Talking to ourselves allows us to compose self-portraits. If we could not soliloquize, we could not describe ourselves to ourselves. Our self-portraits, however, are no more equivalent to our selves than an oil painting is equivalent to its living subject. That is, how I see myself is not necessarily how the rest of the world sees me.

Since who we think we are strongly influences how we act and what we do, Athens explores our self-portraiture in some detail. We compose our self-portraits, he observes, "during special soliloquies in which the main topic of conversation is ourselves." First we ask ourselves how our intimate acquaintances see us. Then we ask our phantom community how to assess those opinions. Only after filtering our intimates' opinions through our phantom communities do we arrive at a finished self-portrait. "People judge themselves from the perspective of their phantom community through, once again, literally telling themselves how their phantom community would likely think and feel on the whole about them in the light of their present individual intimates' thoughts and sentiments toward them." If our phantom community is fragmented—that is, if our phantom companions cannot agree—then composing a self-portrait may not be possible. We become a riddle to ourselves, a bundle of contradictions, a "divided self." Normally we take our self-portraits for granted. They become problematic at times of dramatic self-change. Except at those rare times, "the main topics of our soliloquies are events, happenings, occurrences, things and people other than ourselves."

Principle ten: The phantom community rules. It occupies center stage whether we are alone or with others. Talking to others about an experience we are mutually undergoing is "absolutely essential for us to understand its emergent meaning," but only in conversation with our phantom community do we determine its ultimate meaning.

Principle eleven: Since soliloquies are necessarily "multi-party dialogues," conflicts of opinion are always possible. Out beyond our phantom community lies Mead's "generalized other," which Athens describes as "the official voice of the community in which we live." He renames it "them" to make it consistent with Mead's "I" and "me." We may not always hear it in our soliloquies, Athens points out, and even if we do, it may or may not harmonize with what our phantom community—our "us"—is advising. If the "them" and the "us" are in close harmony ("perfect harmony being an impossibility"), the two entities may sound like one voice, and we may not be able to distinguish them. If they are sharply dissonant—"us" against "them"—we can usually distinguish them, but only if our phantom community, our "us," does not drown "them" out. We may, says Athens, be "all too painfully aware" of the dissonance—that is, of the differences between what our larger corporal community honors and values and what our phantom community honors and values. These are not imaginary entities, Athens cautions. They "operate in selves (although not always in the same ones) and selves operate in social worlds, not only in people's heads." If they are both screaming at us at once, "hurling contradictory directives," the conflict may paralyze or shatter us.

Principle twelve: Absolute conformists or absolute individualists are rare. Whether we act like one or the other in the course of a specific social experience depends on what our phantom community tells us. When our "us" (our phantom community) disagrees with "them" (our "generalized other"), we act like individualists, confounding "their" expectation; when "us" and "them" agree, we act like conformists, meeting "their" expectation.

Principle thirteen: Significant social experiences shape our phantom community. Athens improves on Thomas Wolfe to clarify this principle. In *Look Homeward, Angel*, Wolfe wrote of his characters that "each moment of their lives was conditioned not only by what they had experienced in that moment, but by all that they had experienced up to that moment." Wolfe's observation, Athens writes, is eloquent but imprecise.

There is no end to social experiences, but most are trivial and ephemeral. Significant social experiences, however, "are consequential and unforgettable." They mark people permanently. The social experiences from which phantom others arise "are unsurprisingly the significant experiences rather than the trivial ones."

In conclusion Athens proposes that "soliloquizing is the key to the self." The self feeds on soliloquies: "Soliloquies supply the vital sustenance without which the self cannot live." But our self is more than our soliloquizing; it is "I" and "me" but also "us," our phantom community. "While expressing itself during each new passing experience, the self endures beyond the immediate experience in which it was expressed." Four centuries earlier Montaigne anticipated Athens's crowded interior theater of consciousness. "We are all made up of fragments," the French essayist wrote, "so shapelessly and strangely assembled that every moment, every piece plays its own game. And there is as much difference between ourselves and ourselves as between us and others."

"Dramatic Self-Change" moves on from the taxonomy of the self to its dynamics. By "dramatic self-change" Athens means "changes in the self that are both drastic and abrupt," when (Athens quotes a fellow sociologist) " 'a person acts so differently that his friends and relatives have difficulty in recognizing him.' " Such changes, the sociologist continues, " 'are accompanied by a psychological reorientation in which the person sees himself and the world in a different light. He retains many of his personal idiosyncrasies, but he develops a new set of values and different criteria of judgment.' " The most recognized form of dramatic self-change is the conversion experience, which is a group or institutional adaptation of the process. "At minimum," Athens notes of conversion, "candidates must be placed under supervision of mentors, subjected to indoctrination and undergo rites of passage." But dramatic self-change usually occurs privately, without benefit of institutional support, in response to overwhelming and typically traumatic social experiences. Athens proposes not to restrict himself to conversion experiences but to identify the universals common to both private and institutional transformation. He distinguishes five sequential stages.

Stage one is fragmentation. To build a new self, the old self has to break apart. This stage, familiar to anyone who has undergone dramatic self-change, is usually "an excruciating experience," Athens comments, better appreciated in retrospect. That change is painful is one important reason why people do not like to change. Therefore "the ordeal of developing new selves will not be seriously entertained, much less embarked upon, until [people] are forced into it by the partial destruction of their former selves."

The self fragments in response to "a traumatizing social experience that is so utterly foreign" that it is incomprehensible. "Since people's selves and the social worlds that sustain them are not the same," Athens adds in a footnote, their response to adversity is idiosyncratic, but he offers a partial list of more or less universally traumatizing social experiences drawn from sociological or psychological studies of such events:

> Potentially traumatic experiences are myriad. They could include internment in a prisoner-of-war or concentration camp . . . the tragic death of a loved one . . . chronic illness, physical disfigurement, or invalidism . . . a natural disaster . . . the breakup of an intimate relationship . . . brutalization at the hands of intimates . . . demotion or a prolonged bout of unemployment, an all-consuming craving for alcohol or drugs . . . the later abstinence from their use . . . and sudden fame and fortune.

Such experiences are foreign because they contradict assumptions about the world that we have previously taken for granted. We are unable to assimilate them because our phantom companions do not agree and therefore cannot give us any clear, consistent directions on how to act. We are flooded instead to the point of immobility with conflicting thoughts and emotions. Since we cannot act, the pressure to act increases until the phantom community shatters. Our previous assumptions no longer serve to sustain us. We are divided against ourselves and left confused, "helpless and vulnerable in a world that seems to have suddenly turned upside down and become alien."

Stage two is provisional unity. If our former selves have fragmented, Athens writes, if we are "caught in the maelstrom of a self-crisis," at least we have been released by that disaster from the more insidious restraint of the assumptions we formerly took for granted. Thus released, we can now audit our formerly tacit assumptions by comparing them critically with the evidence of the new, foreign social experience that forced them to light. Through repeated audits we come to realize that our previous assumptions about the world were inadequate to comprehend our new reality.

Such realization is only the first step toward provisional unity, however. To develop a new provisional self we must also replace our old assumptions with new ones—that is, replace at least some of our former phantom companions with new ones—"which," Athens remarks, "can be an equally agonizing ordeal." New social experiences continue to bombard us while we pursue this remodeling, and while we may feel liberated by the splintering of our former phantom community, we probably also feel burdened and frightened by our loss of a familiar "us" with which to converse.

So, says Athens, we turn "for help and solace" to others whom we know or believe to have been there before us. Those others may simply be memories, "wisdom . . . merely whispered long before the present crisis ever arose but that only now makes sense." Or we may desperately search out people with experience "to plead for their counsel . . . now that the crisis is in its full throes." Lacking access to such people, we "may consider taking advice from whoever may offer it." Wherever we find our help and solace, we filter it before we take it. Rather than swallow it straight we use it as "a critical aid in finding [our] *own* ways. . . . People must always painstakingly work through their fund of advice determining whose counsel, if anyone's, is wisest to follow. . . . Thus, the solution finally arrived at is transformed through a circuitous process into a personal revelation." The process is personally apocalyptic because it involves incorporating new phantom companions into a new, provisional phantom community; anything less intense is not likely to inspire enough confidence to support testing it in the real world.

By the end of the provisional stage, we tentatively conclude that our new perspective comprehends the traumatic social experience that seemed incomprehensible before. Our self is whole again, if only provisionally.

Stage three, praxis, emerges in response to a newly fledged provisional's haunting question: "When I am confronted again with a social experience similar to the traumatic one that split apart my prior self, will my newly developed self meet the challenge of navigating me through this perilous experience?" In *praxis*, a technical term (from the Greek word for action or practice) Athens borrows from the work of the Swiss psychologist Jean Piaget, we put our new provisional selves to the crucial test of experience. With our new phantom community to guide us, we may successfully traverse an experience like the one that disabled us before. Doing so signals that our new provisional self is a successful reorganization, and "nothing breeds confidence faster in a person who is building a new self than passing this test." Repeated successes add further confidence.

But we may fail the test. Our new phantom community may be inadequate and we may not meet renewed challenge. "If nothing breeds confidence faster than success," Athens comments, "then perhaps nothing destroys it faster than failure." We may then conclude we need make only "minor but crucial adjustments" in our new provisional selves to improve our chances of succeeding. If we do then succeed, we may credit our previous failure with revealing inadequacies that we needed to correct, losing a battle to win the war. But repeated failure may force us to conclude "that the entire composition of [our self] must be completely altered," and that "all or most of [our] present phantom companions must be replaced." Such an outcome is disastrous. Not only have we abandoned our former self, but our new self is not working. All the time, energy and apprehension we invested in building a new self has been wasted. "Unless the fortitude can somehow be mustered to restart completely the arduous process of assembling [a] different unified [self]," Athens writes, "[the] present divided [self] will be kept." That act of desperation leaves the self in "a permanent state of disorganization, which, if prolonged enough, can culminate in psychosis."

If we neither pass nor fail the crucial test of experience, we are stuck in limbo:

> Depending upon how unusual traumatic social experiences similar to the one that shattered their prior selves are in their social world, people may or may not immediately get the opportunity to take the test again. Or a similar social experience may be undergone but not *fully* undergone. People may again undergo a similar traumatic social experience, but the experience may be interrupted before it reaches its apogee, so that although their newly unified selves face a test of sorts, these selves do not undergo a *crucial* test.

Until a crucial test of experience is undergone and passed, further consolidation is stalled. And this limbo, unlike Dante's original, has a trapdoor to hell: "Staying in limbo for a prolonged period may eventually generate enough anxiety in a person to produce an end result similar in nature, if not degree, to permanent disorganization."

Stage four is consolidation. When people achieve praxis, passing the crucial test of experience, "to their great amazement and personal satisfaction, not to mention pure relief, [they realize] they have finally successfully navigated a social experience very similar (if not the same) to that which brought about the fragmentation of their former selves." In consequence, "their new selves burst forth before their eyes, and more importantly, before the eyes of other people." With a still provisional but evidently competent phantom community in residence, "they can now organize their previously conflicting and disorganized thoughts and emotions . . . [merging] these thoughts and feelings into a viable, coherent plan of action that was all but impossible prior to their success." But permanence depends on how others respond. "No matter how personally amazed, pleased or relieved [people] may be with their success, only *others* can impress upon [them] the full significance" of having succeeded. Social recognition is crucial, and not recognition alone. "Other people must not only recognize our deeds or misdeeds, but they must also reflect this recognition in the concrete actions they take toward us. . . . It is the ripple that [our] success makes in [our] world of experience that creates a lasting impression upon [our] minds; the bigger the ripple, the more lasting the impression."

At this stage of consolidation, we still have to ask ourselves if we want to embrace our new persona—we still, that is, have freedom to choose. Usually we do accept our new selves, Athens writes, "for reasons that are easy to imagine." We have been through hell (and possibly limbo); if we now reject the person we are on the verge of becoming, not only would we be wasting that full measure of suffering, but we would also have to go through it all over again to take a different direction—or, alternatively, collapse into permanent psychological disorganization.

So people usually decide to embrace rather than to reject their new selves, for better or for worse, whereupon:

> A dramatic transformation takes place. The phantom companions, whose viewpoints they originally drew upon in passing the crucial test of experience, become quasi-permanent residents of their new selves. No sooner does this happen than people's newly found phantom companions begin to recede farther and farther into the shadows of their awareness. Finally, their phantom companions fall outside their conscious purview altogether. As their phantom companions vanish from consciousness, the prism [through] which they now refract their social experiences is simultaneously lost from sight. Thus, people once again take for granted the viewpoint with which they approach the world, as they did prior to starting the process of dramatic self-change. The vanishing of phantom companions from their conscious purview signals that their new selves have almost become fully consolidated. The only task remaining is for them to move out of the social groups in which they are not comfortable and into groups in which they will be at home with their new selves.

That final task, social segregation, constitutes stage five. Robert Park, Athens comments, "made great use of the notion of segregation. He defined segregation as a 'sifting and sorting process' through which, essentially, people gravitate to groups for which their background experiences best suit them." Social barriers complicate the process by challenging both exit and entry, a point Athens illustrates with two examples drawn from immediate personal experience as he worked on "Dramatic Self-Change" in Richmond and at Seton Hall. "The courts pass over true demons for the electric chair," he comments, "and, likewise, universities pass over creative geniuses." Despite barriers to social segregation, "people usually find themselves becoming fully accepted members of at least some new social groups with all the attendant social privileges and obligations," while at the same time becoming disenfranchised from some or all of the social groups with which they were formerly affiliated. Unless they do so, they may find it hard to sustain their new persona; "few people can thrive for long in a hostile habitat." Athens was undergoing dramatic self-change himself during the period when he worked out its stages; it is apposite that he published the two papers that resulted in a leading journal of sociology, reaching out from the more limited criminological community, which had been hostile to his work, to a larger social and professional group that has shown itself to be more willing to accept it.

Our biographies are histories of the dramatic changes we have undergone, Athens concludes; only in "the most insulated lives" is dramatic self-change a once-in-a-lifetime event. In the "open-ended book" of our existence, "we start a new chapter . . . each time we undergo dramatic self-change." If we succeed in developing a new, unified self, "it can later undergo fragmentation as well, beginning again the entire process."

The staging process of dramatic self-change obviously generalizes from violentization, although Athens drew on other evidence as well, including other sociological and psychological studies, autobiography and his recent grievous personal experience of divorce, unemployment and unrecognized achievement. In violentization, fragmentation follows from brutalization. Provisionality corresponds to belligerency, the belligerent novice finding new value in the advice of his violent coach and provisional unity emerging with violent resolution. Praxis for the violent novice consists of violent performances, which may succeed or fail or come to no decision. Success leads to consolidation, which corresponds to virulency and includes notoriety and social trepidation. Social segregation follows from achieving malevolence.

Dramatic self-change applies equally, however, to more productive transformation. Franklin Roosevelt's traumatization by paralytic polio forced him into dramatic self-change; after reconstructing himself he emerged as the deeper and more compassionate human being who guided the nation through depression and world war. But we retain some of our former phantom companions even after dramatic self-change, and Roosevelt's tragically limited response to the accumulating evidence of the Holocaust indicates that his phantom community was still partly class bound.

Martin Luther, on the evidence of Erik Erikson's classic study of the founder of Protestantism as a young man, experienced multiple episodes of dramatic self-change. When he was twenty-one, having just received his master's degree from the University of Erfurt, Luther responded to a panic attack during a thunderstorm by deciding to defy his domineering father's plans for him to become a lawyer and choosing instead to enter a monastery. "Luther himself never claimed to have seen or heard anything supernatural" during the attack, Erikson points out. "He only records that *something in him* made him pronounce a vow before the *rest of him* knew what he was saying." Phantom companions evidently shadowed young man Luther through that thunderstorm. Notice that Luther's description of his experience corresponds to what murderers sometimes say about what led them to kill—that something in them *made* them do it. "He had felt immediately afterward," Erikson reports, "that he did not really want to become a monk."

In the monastery Luther at least escaped continuing brutalization at the hands of both his father and his mother, a common experience for a child of the sixteenth century; it was his mother's brutality in particular, he would complain later, that drove him into "monkery." His phantom community, it would seem, advised him to take holy orders to escape further violentization. Since he was already a scholar, his superiors assigned him to become a priest. He celebrated his first mass at twenty-three. "Then," Erikson summarizes, "[he] fell into severe doubts and scruples which may have caused the 'fit in the choir.'" The fit in the choir was another breakdown following a failure of praxis—Luther did not want to spend his life in a monastery. A prolonged period of dramatic self-change followed, including a significant revelation when he was twenty-eight, after which Luther emerged fully transformed at thirty-two, when he nailed his ninety-five theses on the door of the castle church in Wittenberg and started a religious revolution.

Athens finds evidence of dramatic self-change in the autobiographies of Ray Charles and of Malcolm X. The pattern is visible in the youthful crises of Robert Oppenheimer, the first director of the Los Alamos laboratory where the first atomic bombs were built, and the Danish physicist Niels Bohr, both of whom emerged from periods of disabling self-doubt in graduate school to become charismatic leaders in theoretical physics.

By generalizing his findings from violent criminality to the full range of human experience, Athens demonstrates that they are first-order discoveries—true universals. "The Self as a Soliloquy" and "Dramatic Self-Change" make a new general theory* that encompasses not only Erikson's "identity crisis" but also the "cross-era transitions" in psychologist Daniel J. Levinson's landmark studies *The Seasons of a Man's Life* and *The Seasons of a Woman's Life*, which Gail Sheehy documented further in her well-known book *Passages*.

Niels Bohr once remarked that the goal of science is nothing so grandiose as universal truth. Rather, Bohr said, the modest but relentless goal of science is "the gradual removal of prejudices." It was a prejudice (which Copernicus helped remove) that the earth is the center of the universe, a prejudice (which Darwin helped remove) that humankind was separately created. One prejudice that has comforted us is that violent criminals are categorically different from the rest of us—mentally ill, or brain damaged, or monstrous, or anomic, or genetically or subculturally determined. Lonnie Athens demonstrates to the contrary that violent people come to their violence by the same universal processes of soliloquy and dramatic self-change that carry the rest of us to conformity, pacifism, greatness, eccentricity or sainthood—and bear equal responsibility for their choices.

---

* My wife, Ginger Rhodes, a doctoral student in clinical psychology, observes that Athens's work offers a basis for a new psychotherapy built on scientific rather than merely empirical evidence. An Athenian therapist would serve as an experienced source of help and solace to guide the client to reconstruct a more capable phantom community (and would presumably enter that pantheon as a new phantom companion).

CHAPTER TWENTY-ONE

The Gates of Mercy Shut Up

The gates of mercy shall be all shut up,
And the fleshed soldier—rough and hard of heart—
In liberty of bloody hand shall range
With conscience wide as hell, mowing like grass
Your fresh-fair virgins, and your flowering infants.

—William Shakespeare, *Henry V*

"War is the business of killing," S. L. A. Marshall contends in his seminal 1947 study *Men Against Fire,* adding that this "simplest truth in the book" is one "we are reluctant to admit." Our reluctance to observe too closely how our martial sausage is made is unsurprising, but it has obscured investigating how men are steeled to conduct the business of killing in war and what consequences follow from that grim, sacrificial duress.

Marshall Clinard, Lonnie Athens's first graduate adviser, wrote his former student after reading *The Creation of Dangerous Violent Criminals* to compliment him on the book, which he called " a most significant contribution," and to "wonder if you would exclude from [your] analysis the unprovoked brutal incidents that have characterized warfare generally, particularly in medieval times, but even today." Athens responded to the contrary:

Although I never originally intended for my theory to explain the atrocities that soldiers and terrorists commit under warlike conditions (which can be considered to be "quasi-institutionalized violent actions"), I would be willing to bet that the perpetrators of such acts have, in fact, undergone the "brutalization" experiences described in my book as part of their *informal,* if not formal, military training. Did either Ruth [Clinard] or you see the movie "Platoon"? . . . I think you will find that it confirms my theory. In fact, as I watched it, I kept thinking how my theory provides the basis for a systematic program designed to make people extremely violent either for the purposes of war or crime.

The monopolizing of violence by central governments required sequestering it in specialized military organizations—armies and police forces—which continue to be trained and psychologically conditioned to perform violent acts professionally. If governments had no such organs of control, ultraviolent individuals would quickly batter their way back to the top of the dominance hierarchy, as in fact they do when governments collapse. To what extent is violentization, or some institutional or quasi-institutional adaptation of that process, applied to preparing military forces to use violence? What relationship does violentization bear to military slaughters such as the notorious atrocities in Vietnam at places like My Lai? At minimum, military training invokes that specialized form of dramatic self-change known as conversion; but where, if anywhere, does violentization enter the picture?

Discussing violentization in the context of professional organizations that use violence under license from the state risks tarring brave and honorable men and women with the brush of so-called criminal mentality. I intend no such libel; it should be obvious by now that criminal mentality in the sense of a supposed mental defect that makes people violent is pseudoscientific dogma unsupported by evidence. As Athens wrote Clinard, the special form of dramatic self-change he found antecedent in violent criminals might also be applied to train professionals to use violence for more socially acceptable purposes. Indigenous warrior cultures do just that, as I have tried to show.

Yet professional organizations—armies, police forces—that train their members to use violence clearly have a problem, which is how to limit such violence to authorized protocols. Unauthorized violence domestically is criminal violence, and when police behave criminally we all have reason to fear. Unauthorized violence during war is slaughter and atrocity, and though international law that brands such acts criminal is still evolving, their effect on the soldiers who perform them is frequently devastating. Athens's work makes it possible to understand how organizations constrain unauthorized violence and under what circumstances accidents, incompetence or deliberate policy encourage its emergence.

Two recent observers of U. S. Marine Corps basic training—

Thomas E. Ricks in his 1997 book *Making the Corps* and Gwynne Dyer in his 1985 book *War*—independently recognize that military indoctrination is a conversion experience. "[Basic training] is, essentially, a conversion process in an almost religious sense," Dyer observes—"and as in all conversion phenomena, the emotions are far more important than the specific ideas." Ricks describes Marine Corps training as a "process of transformation [that is] more a matter of cultural indoctrination than of teaching soldiering, which comes later. . . . Before [recruits] can learn to fight, they must learn to be Marines."

In Athens's terms basic training is designed to induce dramatic self-change leading to a revision in recruits' phantom communities to incorporate new phantom companions whose values are military. Phantom companions are incorporations into the self of the attitudes of members of one's primary group. The deliberately isolated, deliberately disorienting, deliberately overwhelming experience of basic training fosters fragmentation during which the recruit bonds with fellow recruits and assimilates them and his drill instructors into his primary group. "Everything is taken away—hair, clothes, food and friends," a navy chaplain told Ricks at Parris Island, the Marine Corps boot camp in South Carolina. "It's a total cutoff from previous life." Illustrating fragmentation, he added, "That's why you get so much loneliness and so many suicidal tendencies." During the first part of the training phase the marines call "Forming," Ricks found, the drill instructors (DIs) verbally assault the recruits in the new platoon:

> This is the point when the drill instructors cut all those ties to the past and irrevocably establish the fact that they are in charge, entirely on their own terms, for the duration. . . . The five DIs appear maniacally angry. Shouting, pointing their fingers, raising a foot and slamming it to the ground, then whirling to scream at their next victim, they never stop moving—and never appear remotely pleased with the recruits' frantic execution of their buzz of orders. They manage to turn the inventory of the mundane gear the recruits have brought with them from Receiving into an extraordinarily intense, even excruciating experience. . . . It is a shocking experience, repeated for every new platoon on the island. It is one they will remember for the rest of their lives.

In case the roar of DI hostility does not completely drown out their self-talk, the recruits are required to chant what Ricks calls "a boot camp haiku": "Honor. Courage. Commitment. Kill, kill. Marine Corps!" Eventually, Ricks reports, this chant "will be tattooed on their brains, shouted almost every time they sit down for a class or mail call." Chanting and the DI clamor of orders are customarily explained as training to automatic obedience, but their more immediate purpose (in common with most institutional programs of conversion) is clearly to overwhelm and begin to revise the recruits' soliloquies. "I guess you could say we brainwash them a little bit," a DI admitted to Dyer. Dyer overheard a more candid explanation of the revision process from a marine captain lecturing recruits: "We're going to give you the blueprints," the captain told the new men, "and we are going to show you how to build a Marine. You've got to build a Marine—you understand?"

Military organizations encourage recruits to revise their phantom communities to incorporate military phantom companions partly to recreate the deep, basic trust that most people feel toward at least some members of their family—trust then put to use to mobilize action in battle. "There's a love relationship that is nurtured in combat," Capt. John Early, a Vietnam veteran who became a Rhodesian mercenary, told Dyer, "because the man next to you—you're depending on him for the most important thing you have, your life, and if he lets you down you're either maimed or killed. If you make a mistake the same thing happens to him, so the bond of trust has to be extremely close, and I'd say this bond is stronger than almost anything, with the exception of parent and child. It's a hell of a lot stronger than man and wife." Early, a combat junkie, may be romanticizing, though intense bonding between comrades is a commonplace of combat experience. U.S. Army Lt. Col. Dave Grossman, in his book *On Killing,* reports confirmation in "a tremendous volume of research" that "the primary factor that motivates a soldier to do the things that no sane man *wants* to do in combat (that is, killing and dying) is not the force of self-preservation but a powerful sense of accountability to his comrades on the battlefield." A nineteenth-century French officer and military theorist, Ardant du Picq, writes more pragmatically of "mutual surveillance." "When they tell you to get up," Ricks quotes a marine Vietnam veteran of the moment of truth in combat, "in the Marines you don't have to worry if the guys on your left and right is gonna get up."

Physically violent subjugation used to be a standard component of military training. "Just think of how the soldier is treated," Dyer quotes a 3,500-year-old Egyptian text. "While still a child he is shut up in the barracks. During his training he is always being knocked about. If he makes the least mistake he is beaten, a burning blow on his body, another on his eye, perhaps his head is laid open with a wound. He is battered and bruised with flogging." Military organizations in modern civil societies, which restrict violence even for military training, have had to devise psychological equivalents. The change has been complicated by the continuing evolution of the civilizing process. Brig. Gen. Jack Klimp, the commander of Parris Island when Ricks visited there, told him, "The kids I trained in '78, '80, were distinctly different" from today's recruits. "A lot of them back then were tough, hard kids—a lot more physically tough, less fragile than today's kids. . . . A lot of [today's kids] have never hit someone, or been hit." To condition recruits to physical violence, the U.S. Army and Marine Corps have added boxing in confinement and pugil-stick fighting to their training agendas.

Drill instructors function as violence coaches. Since they are usually combat veterans, they carry authoritative violence credentials. They talk killing and they teach killing. "You want to rip his eyeballs out," Dyer heard a lecturer on the use of mines tell recruits at Parris Island. "You want to tear apart his love machine, you want to destroy him, privates, you don't want to have nothing left of him. You want to send him home in a Glad Bag to his mommy!" A course in "combat hitting skills," Ricks reports—"essentially a series of boxing matches staged inside a three-sided padded wooden ring not much larger than a telephone booth"— begins the first week after Forming, along with pugil-stick fighting. "The pugil sticks themselves are really double-headed clubs about four feet long, with heavy green pads at either end." Recruits fighting with pugil sticks "are matched up in pairs," Dyer notes, "helmeted and gloved . . . and made to fight each other in a style that would certainly cause numerous deaths if not for all the padding." An instructor tells them: "You've got to be very aggressive! Once you've got your opponent on the run, that means you go on and strike with that first killing blow. . . . You don't cut him no slack! Don't give him room to breathe, stay on top of him . . . keep pumping that stick. That means there should be nothin' out here today but a lot of groanin', moanin', a lot of eyeballs fallin'—a lot of heads rollin' all over the place."

By the end of boot camp, Ricks found, most of the recruits he observed had internalized their DIs. "On the plane ride home from Charleston," he describes one newly fledged marine, "he dons his headphones and leans back to relax. 'I closed my eyes, and I saw Drill Instructor Sergeant Carey yelling at me.' (This vivid internalization is a common experience for members of [Platoon] 3086.)" A Samoan American private, Charles Lees, home on leave, "is surprised at how aggressive he can be. Showing off his marine uniform to old friends at Holy Cross, they go out for a beer. He gazes at a woman in the bar, not noticing that she has a man with her. Her male friend looks at Lees in a challenging way. Lees accepts instantly. 'What are you looking at, freak, you want to go outside right now?' he snarls. The man backs off. In retrospect, Lees is amazed at his own behavior. 'I opened my mouth and Sergeant Zwayer came out.' " Even Earnest Winston, Jr., whom Ricks describes as "a black recruit from the violent inner-city streets of southeast Washington, D.C.," though he found boot-camp violence training mild compared to his experience of violentization growing up in a malevolent minor community, nevertheless internalized his drill instructor. "It's funny," he told Ricks after he returned home. "I thought about him yesterday when my guys were out there smoking [marijuana]. I think he would have said, 'What are you doing, Winston?' He was the Truth. He could make it out here, even though he's white." When one member of the platoon later deserts, Ricks reports, "at night, Staff Sergeant Rowland and Sergeant Carey loom up in his guilty dreams. 'You got to go back,' the DIs tell him."

Basic training may move recruits to revise their phantom communities, but neither it nor the advanced training they receive afterward is evidently sufficient fully to prepare most combatants to kill unless they have already undergone violentization privately. During the Second World War, S. L. A. Marshall, then an army officer, conducted immediate post-combat interviews (individual and group) with about four hundred U.S. infantry companies in the Pacific and European theaters of war. He made a startling discovery:

> We found that on an average not more than 15 percent of the men had actually fired at the enemy positions or personnel with rifles, carbines, grenades, bazookas, BARs [Browning automatic rifles] or machine guns during the course of an entire engagement. Even allowing for the dead and wounded, and assuming that in their numbers there would be the same proportion of active firers as among the living, the figure did not rise above 20 to 25 percent of the total for any action. The best showing that could be made by the most spirited and aggressive companies was that one man in four had made at least some use of his firepower.

Nor did battle experience improve this ratio, Marshall adds.

Marshall's figure of only one man in four actually attempting to kill the enemy was vigorously disputed despite the authority of its evidence.

In a later edition of his book he noted in his defense that a U.S. Army infantry manual had cited his findings, making them official. Grossman reports more direct confirmations. "A 1986 study by the British Defense Operational Analysis Establishment's field studies division," he writes, reviewed "historical studies of more than one hundred nineteenth- and twentieth-century battles" and then recreated them in test trials, substituting lasers for weapons, to see if Marshall's revelation applied to earlier armies in earlier times. "The researchers' conclusions openly supported Marshall's findings, pointing to 'unwillingness to take part [in combat] as the main factor' that kept the actual historical killing rates significantly below the laser trial levels."

Closer to home Grossman investigates the Battle of Gettysburg during the American Civil War, fought with muzzle-loading muskets that were prepared for firing by tearing a paper cartridge of black powder, pouring the powder down the barrel, dropping in a bullet, ramming the bullet home with a rod, priming, cocking and raising the weapon to the shoulder to aim and fire. After the battle 27,574 muskets were recovered from the battlefield. "Of these," Grossman reveals, "nearly 90 percent (twenty-four thousand) were loaded. Twelve thousand of these loaded muskets were found to be loaded more than once [had more than one bullet in the barrel], and six thousand of the multiply loaded weapons had from three to ten rounds loaded in the barrel. One weapon had been loaded twenty-three times." Marshall's 15–25 percent firing rates arose in a war where soldiers were isolated in individual foxholes, so that their fellow soldiers were unable to see whether or not they fired. In the Civil War, however, soldiers confronted the enemy shoulder to shoulder in line, loading and firing in full view, so a man unwilling to fire had to pretend to load and reload—"possibly," Grossman speculates plausibly, "even mimicking the recoil of his weapon when someone nearby fired"—if his unwillingness was to remain undetected.

Marshall's counterintuitive discovery came as a complete surprise to the officers responsible for directing their men in combat, because the men fired their weapons whenever they were closely watched. That important distinction explains the apparent discrepancy between low firing rates and soldiers' avowals of bonding between comrades for mutual protection. Soldiers whose performance was visible—Ardant du Picq's "mutual surveillance"—performed. "Men working in groups or teams," Marshall confirms—machine-gun crews, mortar squads, sniper teams— "do not have the same tendency to default of fire as do single riflemen."

Why would soldiers choose not to fire unless closely watched? Perhaps they think that if they do not shoot at the enemy, the enemy will not shoot at them. Marshall found this commonsense explanation to be at least a secondary factor. "They were not malingerers," he prefaces his explanation of the primary reason for default of fire. "They did not hold back from the danger point. They were there to be killed if the enemy fire searched and found them." Despite their good intentions, their default of fire was "a result of a paralysis which comes of varying fears. The man afraid wants to do nothing; indeed, he does not care even to think of taking action." Marshall concluded that such paralysis originated in what Athens would call the soldier's "generalized other" and nonviolent phantom community, and what Norbert Elias would call the civilizing process:

> The average, normal man who is fitted into the uniform of an American ground soldier . . . is what his home, his religion, his schooling and the moral code and ideals of his society have made him. The Army cannot unmake him. It must reckon with the fact that he comes from a civilization in which aggression, connected with the taking of life, is prohibited and unacceptable. The teaching and the ideals of that civilization are against killing, against taking advantage. The fear of aggression has been expressed to him so strongly and absorbed by him so deeply and pervadingly—practically with his mother's milk—that it is part of the normal man's emotional makeup. This is his great handicap when he enters combat. It stays his trigger finger even though he is hardly conscious that it is a restraint upon him. Because it is an emotional and not an intellectual handicap, it is not removable by intellectual reasoning, such as: "Kill or be killed."

Marshall found evidence for his conclusion in studies by army psychiatrists of Second World War combat fatigue cases in Europe:

> They found that *fear of killing, rather than fear of being killed,* was the most common cause of battle fatigue in the individual, and that fear of failure ran a strong second.*

---

* "Battle fatigue" or "combat fatigue"—traumatic breakdown as a result of battle experiences—corresponds to the fragmentation stage of dramatic self-change. Such breakdown may be visualized as an unresolvable conflict between the soldier's civilian and military phantom companions.

It is therefore reasonable to believe that the average and normally healthy individual—the man who can endure the mental and physical stresses of combat—still has such an inner and usually unrealized resistance toward killing a fellow man that he will not of his own volition take life if it is possible to turn away from that responsibility. . . . At the vital point, he becomes a conscientious objector, unknowing.

As a result of Marshall's investigation the U.S. military revised its training program. From teaching men to fire their weapons accurately at fixed targets—the Second World War approach—it began teaching men to fire their weapons at pop-up targets under simulated battlefield conditions, a form of operant conditioning. More significantly, it began emphasizing killing rather than simply duty and courage—that is, it introduced explicit violent coaching into combat training. Marshall conducted follow-up investigations during the Korean War and found that the number of men firing their weapons had increased beyond 55 percent. Similar studies in Vietnam found a firing rate of better than 90 percent. Grossman, who cites these numbers, qualifies them significantly, however: He points out that they indicate only firing rates, not whether or not soldiers took aim. Soldiers unwilling to kill may well have substituted firing into the air, which Grossman calls "posturing," for withholding fire. Evidence that they may have done so is the high ratio of bullets fired to enemies killed in Vietnam. "Ardant du Picq," Grossman writes, "became one of the first to document the common tendency of soldiers to fire harmlessly into the air simply for the sake of firing." In nineteenth- and twentieth-century battles in which posturing was manifest, Grossman reports, bullet-to-kill ratios ranged from 13 to 1 to 252 to 1. In Vietnam the ratio of bullets fired to enemies killed was more than 50,000 to 1. Strategies of sector defense and covering fire with machine guns and M-16 automatic rifles account for some part of that high ratio, he says, but not for all of it. "One of the things that amazed me," a marine medic Vietnam veteran told Grossman, "is how many bullets can be fired during a firefight without anyone getting hurt."

Marshall's investigations imply that killing in combat requires violentization. The minority of combat soldiers he found who actually attempted to kill the enemy evidently came to military service already staged to some degree of violent performance which military training and combat experience completed. "Some of the most gallant single-handed fighters I encountered in World War II," he reports, "had spent most of their time in the guardhouse. . . . Company by company we found . . . men who had been consistently bad actors in the training period, marked by the faults of laziness, unruliness and disorderliness, with all . . . the virtues [in combat] of sustained aggressiveness, warm obedience and thoughtfully planned action. When the battle was over and time came to coast, they almost invariably relapsed again. They could fight like hell but they couldn't soldier." In addition to this minority of "bad actors" who may have been fully violentized before enlisting or being drafted, Marshall also found fighting men who were responsible rather than reprobate: "Fighting alongside the rough characters and taking an equally heroic part in the actions were an even greater number of men whose preliminary conduct had marked them as good soldiers. In the heat of battle these forceful individuals gravitated toward each other. The battle was the pay-off."

Faced with these differences in civility, Marshall was unable to identify any "feature of training" that could sort firers from nonfirers prior to combat. Marshall's "bad actors" were apparently further along in private violentization prior to joining the military than his "good soldiers," but both types appear to have become at least marginally violent (prepared to commit physically defensive violent acts) by the time they participated in active fighting. Nonfirers, in contrast, conform to Athens's description of pacifists (unwilling to use serious violence even under life-threatening circumstances).

Soldiers fight under conditions of mortal captivity. The enemy in front of them applies maximum effort to terrorize and destroy them. Behind them their own organization is prepared to punish them severely—even to kill them—if they dare to assay unauthorized retreat. Such duress surely relieves them of personal responsibility for authorized violent actions. Soldiers use violence because they are forced to do so, and Marshall's findings demonstrate how vigorously most men resist such coercion. "That the average man will not kill even at the risk of all he holds dear," Grossman observes, "has been largely ignored by those who attempted to understand the psychological and sociological pressures of the battlefield. Looking another human being in the eye, making an independent decision to kill him, and watching as he dies due to your action combine to form the single most basic, important, primal and potentially traumatic occurrence of war. If we understand this, then we understand the magnitude of the horror of killing in combat." Responsibility for making soldiers violent properly belongs to the government that orders them to war—that is, to all of us at home whose collective sovereignty the soldiers risk their lives to advance or defend. That they undergo trauma on our behalf, including violentization, is why we call their ordeal sacrifice—and why we honor them.

Most veterans return home from their experience of killing and take up normal lives in civil communities. "We live among millions of people who have killed fellow human beings with pitiless efficiency," Dyer writes, ". . . yet we do not fear these people. The overwhelming majority of those who have killed, now or at any time in the past, have done so as soldiers in war, and we recognize that that has practically nothing to do with the kind of personal aggression that would endanger us as their fellow citizens." Athens's work reveals the difference between killing in war and violent criminality to be narrower than Dyer seems to believe, but what *is* the difference? And why are some veterans unable to readjust to peacetime civility?

Ideally a military organization representing a civil community makes an ethical commitment to the men it requires to undertake killing on its behalf. It commits itself to limiting the direct, personal violence it will demand of these soldiers. Recall Athens's categories of violent interpretation: physically defensive, frustrative, malefic and frustrative-malefic. A physically defensive interpretation follows from the violent actor's conclusion that the victim "will soon physically attack him or an intimate" or that the victim "is already physically attacking him or an intimate." The key feature of a physically defensive interpretation "is that the victim makes a gesture that the perpetrator designates to himself as foreshadowing or constituting a physical attack, generating a grave sense of fear in him for his own or an intimate's physical safety." Of Athens's four categories, only this one allows the actor to sustain a nonviolent self-image. The ethical commitment that allows soldiers to return to nonviolent civilian life is a commitment to require soldiers to kill personally and directly only enemy combatants—armed opponents who by definition are threatening their lives or the lives of their close comrades, and against whom physically defensive violence is therefore justified. Limiting soldiers to physically defensive violence limits the degree of advancing virulency the men must undergo. This limit allows them to sustain a nonviolent phantom community they can take back home.

Which is not to say combatants must only fight defensively to be protected from advancing virulency. Athens's term "physically defensive" has nothing to do with whether battles are fought offensively or defensively. An ethically committed military may require its soldiers to attack the enemy or wait for the enemy to attack them. The enemy to be slain, however, must be a credible physical threat if the virulency of the soldier's experience is to be limited.

Historically, military institutions understood these limitations and tried to confine battles to combatants only, sparing civilians. The militaries of modern nation-states, since they are assembled from inducted civilians, have felt justified in carrying war to civilian populations, on the theory that the whole nation is at war and therefore culpable. Even so, ethically committed militaries have looked for ways to protect combatants from advancing virulency by distancing mechanisms, such as group responsibility within gun and aircraft crews and physical and mechanical separation from the victims. These institutional protections evidently prevent combatants from achieving clear-cut personal victories of violent performance, thus blocking their advance through virulency. They correspond to the practice, customary in executions, of multiplying the number of members in a firing squad or switches to be thrown in an electrocution so that the question of which individual actually accomplished the killing cannot be answered. In return for such protection, the military expects its soldiers to obey orders even at the risk of death, and not to use serious violence privately.

This ethical compact between a soldier and his military organization is essentially what military people mean by the word "honor." Such implicit agreements, evolved through long experience, are violated in modern war. For American combatants the worst violation by far was the Vietnam War. A Boston psychiatrist who specializes in treating combat trauma, Jonathan Shay, explored the consequences of that egregious violation in his 1994 book, *Achilles in Vietnam*.* Shay's insights are profound, but Athens's work sheds further light on the causes of the severe psychological damage many Vietnam veterans suffered, damage so extensive that Shay writes respectfully but grimly of "the ruins of character." At least a third of Vietnam combat veterans continue to struggle with combat trauma (now designated, somewhat inadequately, combat posttraumatic stress disorder [PTSD]), one manifestation of which is violent behavior. "More than 40 percent of Vietnam combat veterans sampled in the late 1980s by the congressionally mandated National Vietnam

---

* Shay found clear parallels between the experiences of combat and betrayal reported by the veterans he treats and those of the Greek and Trojan warriors in the *Iliad;* hence his title. The *Iliad* parallels, which I will not review here, offer further evidence that violentization is a universal process. Interested readers should consult Shay's book, published by Atheneum.

Veterans Readjustment Study," Shay writes, "reported engaging in violent acts three times or more in the previous year. We're talking about 300,000 men here. The percentage of combat veterans who reported averaging more than one violent act a month was almost five times higher than among the sample of civilian counterparts."

Shay has concluded from his work with veterans that severe, disabling combat trauma originates not in battlefield horrors alone but in horrors compounded by violations of the ethical compact between soldiers and the military. In ancient Greece the moral order was designated *thémis*. Shay names the modern military equivalent simply "what's right." "The specific content of the Homeric warriors' *thémis* was often quite different from that of American soldiers in Vietnam," he explains, "but what has not changed in three millennia are violent rage and social withdrawal when deep assumptions of 'what's right' are violated." In modern war, he adds, violation of "what's right" is even more common, because more people are in a position to betray soldiers in battle in ways that threaten their physical and psychological survival. "Veterans can usually recover from horror, fear and grief once they return to civilian life," he reports, "so long as 'what's right' has not also been violated." Betrayals of "what's right" remove or subvert the protection from advancing virulency that is the military organization's side of the ethical bargain. In consequence soldiers may be exposed to traumatic experiences of concentrated violentization.

"What's right," Shay observes, is not simply a matter of niceties of feeling. Fairness in war operates in a zone of mortal danger. "Walking point," he quotes a veteran—that is, leading a line on patrol—"was an extremely dangerous job. . . . The decision was made politically. . . . Most of the time politically. Certain people got the shit. Certain people didn't. Certain people on the right side of certain people." Whether the risk that results from violation of "what's right" puts the soldier in physical or only psychological danger, such betrayal by members of his military primary group is brutalizing. Shay found it evoked "indignant rage."

Shay confirms from his experience with Vietnam veterans "the mortal dependence of the modern soldier on the military organization for everything he needs to survive," which is "as great as that of a small child on his or her parents." Such dependence creates the conditions for destructive reorganization of the soldier's phantom community. "The vulnerable relationship between child and parent is a metaphor for the relationship between a soldier and his army. It is also more than a metaphor when we consider the formation and maintenance of good character. The parent's betrayal of *thémis* through incest, abuse or neglect puts the child in mortal danger." A veteran Shay quotes completes the parallel: "The U.S. Army [in Vietnam] was like a mother who sold out her kids to be raped by [their] father to protect her own interests."

Shay offers a variety of betrayals of trust in Vietnam. Many American career officers, for example, did not share the risks of combat. Those officers who did participate in combat were rotated in and out of combat assignments every six months, limiting their experience and increasing the risk to the men they commanded.

Inadequate equipment constituted a further betrayal. "My personal weapon . . . was the M-14 [rifle]," a veteran told Shay. "It was heavy, but at least you could depend on it. Then we got the M-16. It was a piece of shit that never should have gone over there with all the malfunctions. . . . I started hating the fucking government. . . . I started feeling like the government really didn't want us to get back, that there needed to be fewer of us back home."

So-called friendly fire was a particularly horrific betrayal. Shay transcribes one unexceptional example: "The first deaths in [X]'s platoon were caused by 'friendly fire' from adjoining sectors of the defense perimeter; the officer had neglected to inform them that he was sending men out on the berm. . . . [X] never head of any investigation or disciplinary action."

The most fundamental and devastating betrayal of trust in Vietnam followed from the U.S. decision to fight a war of attrition, to attempt to win by killing North Vietnamese army soldiers faster than they could be replaced. "Body count" corrupted the ethical compact by encouraging the unprotected killing of civilians whenever they could be construed to be participants or supporters or even when they simply could not be distinguished from participants or supporters. Greed for body count led ambitious superiors to encourage soldiers to seek revenge in further killing for the loss of a close comrade rather than supporting grieving. " 'Don't get sad. Get even!' was explicit advice given by officers and NCOs to weeping soldiers who had lost buddies," Shay reports. ". . . This apparently represented a conscious motivational technique by some in the American military during the Vietnam War. . . . Repeatedly, veterans have described their officers, comrades and even chaplains urging them to exact a price in blood from the enemy for their fallen friends—to get a 'payback.' "

Such heinous violent coaching precipitated in many soldiers what Shay calls "the berserk state," which is exactly Athens's "experience of malevolency"—the forming of an unmitigated violent resolution during

the virulency stage of violentization and the final development of malevolency. From that depth of hell, both Athens and Shay confirm, hardly
any man returns. "My clinical experience with Vietnam combat veterans," Shay writes, "prompts me to place the berserk state at the heart of
their most severe psychological and psychophysiological injuries." Based
on his experience, he concludes "that the berserk state is ruinous, leading
to the soldier's maiming or death in battle—which is the most frequent
outcome—and to lifelong . . . injury if he survives. I believe that once a
person has entered the berserk state, he or she is changed forever."

Men go berserk, Shay writes, when they become enraged, develop a
"manic obsession with revenge" and lose all restraint. He cites the
painful testimony of several veteran berserkers that clearly reveals the
violent self-images they formed:

> [After my closest buddy stepped on a mine] we looked and looked
> and looked. And the only thing that was left was, it almost looked
> like a wig. It was just his hair. Just his hair. And we put that in the
> body bag. And I was crying like a baby. . . . And I cried and I cried
> and I cried. . . . And I stopped crying. And I probably didn't cry
> again for twenty years. I turned. I had no feelings. I wanted to hurt.
> I wanted to hurt. And I wanted to hurt.

> After [my buddy] died, I was hurting, hurting bad. Then I went on
> a fucking vendetta. All I wanted was to fucking hurt people. All I
> wanted to do was rain fucking destruction on that fucking coun-
> try. If it fucking burned, I burnt it. I used more fucking ammo in
> the next three months than the whole fucking time I was there. . . .
> A lot of fucking air power, too. Before, I used Puff the Magic
> Dragon.* Puff was more efficient and human. . . . How could you
> say bullets are fucking humanized? But they were. [Afterward, I
> used napalm.] To see what napalm does—napalm was for *revenge*.
> Napalm would suck the air right out of . . . your lungs.

> [When an NVA soldier fired on me after I gave him a chance to sur-
> render] I emptied everything I had into him. Then I saw blood
> dripping on the back of my hand [from a grazing wound to the
> cheek] and I just went crazy. I pulled him out of the paddy and
> carved him up with my knife. When I was done with him, he

---

* A gunship capable of firing tens of thousands of rounds per minute that this man
was in a position to deploy.

looked like a rag doll that a dog had been playing with. Even then I wasn't satisfied. I was fighting with the [medical] corpsmen trying to take care of me. I was trying to get at [the enemy soldier] for more. . . .

I felt betrayed by trying to give the guy a chance and I got blasted. I lost all my mercy. I felt a drastic change after that. I just couldn't get enough. I built up such hate, I couldn't do enough damage.

Everybody'd get hit, and the hate'd build up, especially seeing what they [enemy soldiers] did to guys in the outfit they got hold of—cut off their dicks, cut off their ears. And I had to identify bodies at the morgue. It really fucked me up, them out in the sun all blown up like balloons. The stench—couldn't stand it.

Got worse as time went by. I really loved fucking killing, couldn't get enough. For every one that I killed I felt better. Made some of the hurt [go] away. Everytime you lost a friend it seemed like a part of you was gone. Get one of them to compensate what they had done to me. I got very hard, cold, merciless. I lost all my mercy.

I became a fucking animal. I started fucking putting fucking heads on poles. Leaving fucking notes for the motherfuckers. Digging up fucking graves. I didn't give a fuck anymore. . . . They wanted a fucking hero, so I gave it to them. They wanted fucking body count, so I gave them body count. I hope they're fucking happy. But they don't have to live with it. I do.

These narratives testify to the operation of unmitigated violent phantom communities that support taking pure malefic and frustrative violent actions. Shay's summary list of "characteristics of the berserk state," also derived from veteran testimony, demonstrates that violent notoriety and social trepidation as well as megalomania followed from these successful violent performances: "Beastlike; godlike; socially disconnected; crazy, mad, insane; enraged; cruel, without restraint or discrimination; insatiable; devoid of fear; inattentive to own safety; distractable; indiscriminate; reckless, feeling invulnerable; exalted, intoxicated, frenzied; cold, indifferent; insensible to pain; suspicious of friends."

"Betrayal of 'what's right,' " Shay points out, "is a conditioning event that prepares a soldier to go berserk. . . . I cannot say for certain that betrayal is a necessary precondition. However, I have yet to encounter a veteran who went berserk from grief alone . . . or from betrayal alone, if the betrayal did not cause a death or wound." Betrayal leading to death or wounding rises to the level of brutalization—of violent subjugation if directed at the soldier himself and of personal horrification if directed at his close comrades—and Athens's work confirms that it is indeed necessary, along with violent coaching, for violentization. In *The Creation of Dangerous Violent Criminals* Athens raises the "theoretical possibility" that "the entire process [of violentization] could be completed in a few months, producing what may be called a *cataclysmic experience.*" Shay's documentation of the creation of berserkers in combat confirms that cataclysmic experiences were all too tragically common in Vietnam.

Judging from their testimony and the testimony of their fellow soldiers, some of the men who participated in the notorious massacre of civilians at My Lai on March 16, 1968, which resulted in the deaths of some five hundred Vietnamese women, children, babes in arms and old men, had undergone cataclysmic violentization in their three months of combat experience in Vietnam prior to that atrocity. Other members of the U.S. Army Americal Division Eleventh Light Infantry Brigade's Charlie Company had arrived in Vietnam already violent. Yet others escaped violentization and consequently took no part in the slaughter despite being implicitly or explicitly ordered to do so. Betrayal of "what's right" was one significant influence on the men of Charlie Company who pushed through the undefended Vietnamese village that Saturday morning. My Lai was not the only massacre of civilians perpetrated by American soldiers in Vietnam—the same brigade's Bravo Company killed about ninety civilians at nearby Co Luy on the same morning—but it was the worst that has yet come to light.

In their prior three months in Vietnam, the men of Charlie Company had been sent out repeatedly to patrol for an elusive Vietcong battalion they never located. They began to feel isolated and alone, which bonded them to one another. One enlisted man, Michael Bernhardt, joined the company late and was always something of an outsider, but he still noticed the change. "We felt abandoned by anyone above us," he told two British videojournalists, Michael Bilton and Kevin Sim, many years afterward. "We were abused . . . they wore us down to nothing. . . . We were a small group isolated in a strange land. We had a company of men that all came from one country and we were dropped ten thousand miles away and felt close, because there was no one else to feel close to." A month before My Lai the company started to take casualties in the My Lai area from booby traps and mines—five dead, fifteen wounded, partly the result (by his own admission) of the carelessness of one of their officers, Lt. William Laws Calley.

Fred Widmer, another Charlie Company enlisted man, described to Bilton and Sim how his perception of menace gradually expanded from combatants to civilians as a consequence of the failure of the military organization to meet its ethical commitment to protect him:

> When we first started losing members of the company, it was mostly through booby traps and snipers. We never really got into a main conflict per se, where you could see who was shooting and you could actually shoot back. We had heard a lot about women and children being used as booby traps and being members of the Viet Cong. As time went on you tended to believe it more and more. There was no question that they were working for the Viet Cong. [So] at the same time we were trying to work with these people, they were basically doing a number on us—and we were letting them. So the whole mood changed. You didn't trust them anymore. You didn't trust anybody. Deep down inside, you had mixed emotions. You knew there was an enemy out there—but you couldn't pinpoint who exactly was the enemy. And I would say that in the end, anybody that was still in that country was the enemy.

As a response to this threat, some of the men in Charlie Company, violently coached by their leaders, began beating up prisoners, torturing prisoners, executing prisoners—began, that is, expanding their range of violent performances. "The voices of authority in the company," Widmer explains—

> the platoon sergeants and officers—acknowledged that [executing prisoners] was a proper way to behave. Who were the grunts to disagree with it? We supported it. . . . The first time I saw something really bad was the point at which we stopped taking prisoners. We had been there about a month and a half, or two months. There was one guy [whom] [Capt. Ernest] Medina had to shoot the prisoners. Instead of having everyone around and shoot them, they would walk them down toward the beach, or behind some sand dunes, and shoot them—a couple of shots and they were done. As time went by, things were done, ears cut off, mutilations. . . . The more it went on, the more you didn't trust anyone; you didn't believe anybody because you didn't know who was

who, you didn't know who the enemy was. As we went on, more and more prisoners would be executed. I would say it was a regular occurrence.

"It started with just plain prisoners," Bernhardt concurs—"prisoners you thought were the enemy. Then you'd go on to prisoners who weren't the enemy, and then the civilians because there was no difference between the enemy and civilians. *It came to the point where a guy could kill anybody*" (my emphasis). Medina chose not to stop these excesses. To the contrary, Bilton and Sim paraphrase their informants, "Medina's dislike of the Vietnamese was clear for everyone to see. GIs who showed kindness to prisoners were rebuked. According to witnesses, Medina himself beat up suspects during interrogation. A GI named Lloyd from the First Platoon remembered Medina had told them that if they captured a prisoner and didn't kill him, then they would have to guard him and share their food with him. Lt. Calley, who never pretended to like the Vietnamese, could be pushed to extremes of violence." Calley, for example, allowed one of his men to assault an old farmer during an interrogation and push him into a well, after which Calley shot him.

Besides abusing and executing prisoners, some company members also took the opportunity of patrols and search-and-destroy operations to rape women, with implicit command approval. "Rape?" an enlisted man named Varnado Simpson told Bilton and Sim. "Oh, that happened every day." Company members testify, the journalists report, that "a group within the company" had preyed on women "from the beginning of their tour of duty." If so, then it would seem that some members of the company had already been violentized before they arrived in Vietnam.

Successful violent performances expand a person's determination to be violent. "The more successful the performance or the bigger the violent feat performed," Athens writes, "then the more quickly the violent resolution of the person can be expected to deepen and widen." Charlie Company's Fred Widmer, for one, was honest enough to admit such changes in his perspective to Bilton and Sim. "I think if it ever occurred to me that things were getting out of hand . . . I suppressed it. It did creep up in my mind because you still have those values of what is right and what is wrong that you have been taught all your life. I think the frustration got to me but I also think I began to enjoy it. That's what is scary because at the time you did find yourself enjoying it. I guess you could term it the superiority we had over them." Feeling superior is a consequence of experiencing violent notoriety and social trepidation—of people treating the violent actor as if he were dangerous, which Charlie Company men such as Widmer had become. Enjoyment follows, in Athens's words, from "reveling in thoughts of his now proven courage and prowess."

The experiences that led up to My Lai developed virulency in some of the men of Charlie Company. But along with successful violent performances came failures and further losses. A few weeks before My Lai, Bilton and Sim report, the Eleventh Brigade's Alpha Company "came under heavy automatic and mortar fire originating in My Lai 4" for the second time that month. Two days later Medina inadvertently led his company into a minefield:

> Everybody was shaken. Three men were dead. Another twelve suffered ghastly injuries. Few could forget their own fear, or the screams of the wounded, or the gruesome task of loading the medevac helicopters. "When you have been through a minefield and put the remains of friends in body bags, nothing shocks you anymore," Michael Bernhardt recalled. For Widmer it was the first true experience of the horror of war, "the terror of seeing people blown apart." . . . Charlie Company's esprit de corps vanished without a trace. Morale sagged. . . . Although Medina [who skillfully handled the disaster] emerged from the catastrophe with his reputation among the men enhanced, rumors that the minefield had been laid by the Koreans—allies in the war—further undermined the company's faith that their officers knew what they were doing. But most of all, they blamed the Vietnamese—not the Viet Cong whom they could not see or find, but the Vietnamese of the villages who did not warn them of the minefields and the booby traps.

This defeat, a clear-cut loss, caused the leaders and some of the men of Charlie Company to conclude that their tactics were ineffective, that in Athens's words they "should resort to more lethal violence and resort to it much more quickly than in the past." "The idea that the villagers were 'definitely responsible,' " Bilton and Sim report, "filled the minds of the chastened and sullen company as they eventually pulled themselves free of the mines."

A few days before My Lai, a Mormon in Charlie Company, Greg Olsen, wrote a letter home describing the appearance of the berserk state—that is, of malefic violence—in men in his company:

One of our platoons went out on a routine patrol today and came across a 155-mm artillery round that was booby-trapped. It killed one man, blew the legs off two others, and injured two more. And it all turned out a bad day made even worse. On their way back to [the landing zone] they saw a woman working in the fields. They shot and wounded her. Then they kicked her to death and emptied their magazines in her head. They slugged every little kid they came across. Why in God's name does this have to happen? These are all seemingly normal guys; some were friends of mine. For a while they were like wild animals.

"Saturday," Olsen mentions later in his letter home, "we're going to be dropped in by air in an NVA stronghold." The "NVA stronghold" was My Lai.

Investigators never determined if the men of Charlie Company were ordered by their superiors to slaughter everyone in My Lai. Some swore they heard an order; others insisted the order was only implied. Without question they were encouraged not to grieve for their fallen comrades but to get even. Significantly, two men who refused to participate in the killing denied having been ordered to do so. Greg Olsen, the Mormon, was adamant that no such order had been given. So was Michael Bernhardt: "[Medina] didn't actually say to kill every man, woman and child in My Lai. He stopped just short of saying that." Whatever the orders, some of the men of Charlie Company refused to kill, confirming S. L. A. Marshall's findings and demonstrating that even under strong group pressure, individual differences in degree of violentization prevail.

"We started to move slowly through the village," Thomas Partsch, a compulsive diarist, stopped during the massacre to write in his diary, "shooting everything in sight, children, men, women and animals. Some was sickening. Their legs were shot off and they were still moving. They were just hanging there. I think their bodies are made of rubber. I didn't fire a single round yet and didn't kill anybody, not even a chicken. I couldn't."

Another enlisted man, Dennis Conti, although known to be an enthusiastic rapist, one of the group within the company that had preyed on Vietnamese women, also drew the line at malefic slaughter. Early in the attack Calley had found him forcing a young My Lai woman to fellate him by holding a gun to the head of her four-year-old child and had angrily ordered him to pull up his pants and rejoin his platoon. But later, when Calley ordered Conti and another man, Paul Meadlo, to line up a large group of men, women and children and kill them, Conti balked.

Carrying a grenade launcher, he stood behind Meadlo and Calley while they sprayed the unarmed civilians with M-16 fire, shooting off heads and tearing bodies apart with the high-velocity bullets. After Meadlo had loaded three magazines, he turned back to Conti weeping, passed Conti the rifle and told him, "You shoot them." Conti refused. "If they're going to be killed," he responded, "I'm not doing it." He gestured to Calley. "Let him do it." Calley did, while the two men watched. When Calley spotted a group of My Lai women and children in the distance running for the trees, he shouted at Conti to grenade them. "Conti waited until they reached the tree line," Bilton and Sim report, "before letting loose with his grenade launcher, firing above them into the top of the trees." The group escaped, and Calley let them go.

But other men in Charlie Company participated in the slaughter, and some of them took pleasure. Pleasure in slaughter is the darkest horror of virulent malevolence. Norbert Elias found it celebrated in medieval *chansons de geste.* "Neither eating, drinking, nor sleep has as much savor for me," the warrior minstrel sings. "The greatest joy a man can know," Genghis Khan is recorded to have said, "is to conquer his enemies and drive them before him. To ride their horses and take away their possessions. To see the faces of those who were dear to them bedewed with tears, and to clasp their wives and daughters in his arms." "Rapine, battle, hunting of men and animals," Elias explains—"all these were vital necessities [in medieval society] which . . . were visible to all. And thus, for the mighty and strong, they formed part of the pleasures of life." For the mighty and the strong at My Lai, not only straightforward killing smirched the soft morning. "Several [men] became 'double veterans,' " Bilton and Sim report,

> GI slang for the dubious honor of raping a woman and then murdering her. Many women were raped and sodomized, mutilated, and had their vaginas ripped open with knives or bayonets. One woman was killed when the muzzle of a rifle barrel was inserted into her vagina and the trigger was pulled. Soldiers repeatedly stabbed their victims, cut off limbs, sometimes beheaded them. Some were scalped; others had their tongues cut out or their throats slit or both.

How could such acts be pleasurable? Violent phantom companions advise their perpetrators to enact them because they know from experience that the intense trepidation of the victims will evoke equally intense feelings of superiority. A murderer in prison told C. Fred Alford, a political scientist investigating the nature of evil, "I didn't care whether I killed the guy or not. I just wanted to be his God for a little while. . . . No, that's not enough. I wanted him to know it." Shay found godlike exaltation to be one marker of the berserk state. "I felt like a god, this power flowing through me," a veteran recalled of a berserk frenzy. "Many Vietnam veterans I see in the clinic," Shay adds, "swing painfully between a crushed, tainted mortality and its nostalgically longed-for, but dreaded, godlike opposite." Investigators in a number of different disciplines concur that the berserker's powerful surge of joy reverses his previous sink of terror. Not merely sexual, as calling it sadism implies, it is existential, relief fountaining up like a spring from the cave of being where the brutalized novice cowered in mortal fear.

To be like a god is to escape, at least momentarily, human contingency; no wonder berserk, malefic violence feels ecstatic. "All of our virtues come from *not* being gods," Shay discredits the illusion: "Generosity is meaningless to a god, who never suffers shortage or want; courage is meaningless to a god, who is immortal and can never suffer permanent injury, and so on. Our virtues and our dignity arise from our mortality, our humanity—and not from any success in being God. The godlike berserk state can destroy the capacity for virtue." Athens concurs. "With this last development," he writes, "the experience of malevolency, the ultimate irony surfaces in the subject's life: he has now gone full circle from a hapless victim of brutalization to a ruthless aggressor—the same kind of brutalizer whom he had earlier despised."

When they came home, betrayed, malefic veterans such as these carried their violence with them. They had pushed beyond Gwynne Dyer's "overwhelming majority of those who have killed" who return to civility when they return to their families. They had descended from physically defensive violence into full malefic virulency, with violent self-images, unmitigated violent phantom communities and excruciating, conflicted memories of the taste of ecstatic slaughter. Shay transcribes the testimony of one such veteran at length, a man who did three Vietnam combat tours in tanks:

> I was eighteen years old [when I went over there]. And I was like your typical young American boy. A virgin. I had strong religious beliefs. For the longest time I wanted to be a priest when I was growing up. . . . I was just a typical American boy. . . . Sure, I wasn't

no angel, either. I mean, I had my little fistfights and stuff. It was, you're only human. But evil didn't enter it 'till Vietnam.

I mean real evil. I wasn't prepared for it at all.

Why I became like that? It was all evil. All evil. Where before, I wasn't. I look back, I look back today, and I'm horrified at what I turned into. What I was. What I did. I just look at it like it was somebody else. I really do. It was somebody else. Somebody had control of me.

War changes you, changes you. Strips you, strips you of all your beliefs, your religion, takes your dignity away, you become an animal. . . . You know, it's unbelievable what humans can do to each other.

I never in a million years thought I would be capable of doing that. Never, never, never.

This veteran, Shay explains, went berserk after the death of his closest comrade "and remained in that state for two years, until his behavior became so extreme that his own men tied him up and took him to the rear."

It was like two years I was like that. I remember re-upping [signing up for another combat tour]. I definitely remember. I wanted revenge. I didn't get it out of me. I wanted it, I wanted it, I wanted it. . . . It was unbelievable, the revenge never left me for a minute. . . . They took . . . my life. Somebody had to pay them back for that. And it was me [who had to do it], because it was my life. That's how I looked at it. I couldn't get enough. I could have had my hands around ten gooks' throats a day and it wouldn't be enough. . . .

I carried this home with me. I lost all my friends, beat up my sister, went after my father, I mean, I just went after anybody and everything. Every three days I would totally explode, lose it for no reason at all. I'd be sitting there calm as could be, and this monster would come out of me with a fury that most people didn't want to be around. So it wasn't just over there. I brought it back here with me.

Yet even in the grip of such extremity, many of these veterans struggled to restrain or at least to sequester their violence. One veteran who consulted Shay described roaming the appropriately named Combat

Zone—Boston's shabby red-light district—as a self-appointed vigilante to evoke the berserk state he craved without totally overstepping civilian boundaries:

> I never tried to kill myself, but a lot of the time I just don't care. For years I used to go down to the Combat Zone after midnight and just walk the alleys. If I saw someone down an alley in the dark, I wouldn't go the other way, I'd go down there thinking, "Maybe I'll get lucky." I'm amazed I wasn't killed. I guess I wanted to be killed. Once I came on a guy raping a hooker. She was screaming and screaming, and it was easy to tell he was hurting her bad. I yelled at him, and he turned around and started reaching behind his back. He was carrying. I ran on him so fast and had his elbow before he could pull out his piece, and I pounded the shit out of him. That felt so-o go-o-od. I don't know what happened to the woman. I guess she screwed [ran away] while I was doing him. After that I started bringing a meat fork to the Combat Zone. You know like from a carving set with two—what do they call them—tines. I sharpened them real good. I didn't want to kill anybody, and I figured you could only stick that into somebody just so far before it stopped. When I went to the Combat Zone I never went with a gun.

A clue to what these veterans were experiencing is Shay's report that " 'I died in Vietnam' is a common utterance of our patients. Most viewed themselves as already dead at some point in their combat service, often after a close friend was killed." What died? What was left of their nonviolent self "died" when betrayals threatened them or killed their close comrades and they heeded the drumbeat of violent coaching and launched themselves into malevolence. When they returned home they faced almost unbearable pressure to reverse that violentization, to convert themselves back into the civilians they had been before. But to do so—to abandon the violent phantom companions they acquired in combat— appeared to be their own betrayal of their lost comrades or the brutalization they had violently resolved to avenge.

The testimony Shay reports offers evidence for this explanation, which supports Athens's theory that we incorporate important primary-group members into our self as phantom companions. "I think I don't have long to live," Shay quotes one veteran, "because I have these dreams of guys in my unit standing at the end of the sofa and blood coming down off them and up the sofa. I wake up screaming and the sofa soaked with sweat. It seems like if the blood reaches me I'm going to die when it does. Other nights I dream of guys calling to me from the graveyard. They're calling to me, 'Come on, come on. Time to rest. You paid your dues. Time to rest.' " One veteran in his program, Shay writes, "conversed regularly with a guardian angel while on long-range patrol in enemy territory. These dialogues became part of the shared life of his team, with his men asking him what the angel had said. . . . Guardian angels, imaginary companions and personal patron saints to whom one appeals *in extremis* are probably considerably more common and 'normal' than mental health professionals care to admit."

Trapped between the community of war and the community of peace, believing that undergoing further dramatic self-change to reverse their violentization means abandoning their cherished war-zone phantom companions (and thus themselves, because the phantom community is part of the self) to the merciless enemy, many combat-traumatized veterans collapse into Athens's "permanent state of disorganization." Sometimes they understand they are safe at home, Shay illustrates with a composite of veteran testimony; sometimes they believe they are "In Country":

> I haven't really slept for twenty years. I lie down, but I don't sleep. I'm always watching the door, the window, then back to the door. I get up at least five times to walk my perimeter, sometimes it's ten or fifteen times. There's always something within reach, maybe a baseball bat or a knife, at every door. . . .
>
> It wasn't any different when I was working for ——— before I lost it and they put me in the psych hospital. I remember the company doctor putting Valiums in my mouth, and they strapped me to a stretcher. I was screaming, and I thought the gooks had overrun us and were pouring through the place. Everyone I looked at looked like a gook.

> I haven't spent a complete night in bed with my wife for at least ten years. . . . I'd do this crazy shit at night. I once threw her out of bed so hard it broke her shoulder. I thought there was an NVA [grenade] come in on us. Another time I thought *she* was a gook, and I had my hands around her throat before I woke up.

> At Christmas I try to make it perfect for the kids . . . but I'm like watching them through a dirty window. I'm not really there and they're not really there. I don't know which is which. Maybe none

of us is real. I'm wrapped up in some kind of transparent cocoon and everything gets to me kind of muffled.

"These," Shay reminds us, "are the voices of men as they are today, more than twenty years after their war service. About three-quarters of a million heavy combat veterans from Vietnam are still alive today, of whom a quarter of a million are still suffering in this manner." Nor does Shay hold out more than the slimmest of hopes for their recovery. "The character damage of a trauma survivor," he concludes, "can be understood as a reflection both of his or her radical aloneness and of the continued presence of the perpetrator in the victim's inner life."

If preventing war in the first place proves impossible, limiting it to confrontations among combatants reveals itself in this analysis to have practical and humane benefit as well as moral distinction: Abiding by such traditional limits helps protect our fathers and sons and brothers from descending into malevolence. Tragically, war by its nature tends to exceed such limits, especially with modern technology; under such Hobbesian conditions there will always be incompetent leadership and friendly fire and the emergence of malefic individuals, which one military psychiatrist calls "the natural dominance of the psychopath." But wars of attrition that clamor for body count undermine the very values for which our wars are supposedly fought. "If war goals, operational methods and military culture were so unjust," Shay says in indicting the war whose veterans he struggles to salvage, "that the Nuremberg principles loomed over every Vietnam combat soldier, we must recognize that the blood is on our hands too." This indictment parallels Athens's indictment of a society that tolerates the creation of dangerous violent criminals and thus, he writes, "tacitly becomes an accomplice in creating them." The urgent final question, then: What can be done to prevent or interrupt violentization?

CHAPTER TWENTY-TWO

Strategies of Prevention and Control

Lonnie Athens's evidence of the cause of violent criminality, the types of violent acts and actors, the progression of violent careers and the hierarchies of violent communities establishes for the first time a solid scientific foundation on which to build programs of violence prevention, interruption and control.

Hundreds of such programs—federal, state, regional and local, under both public and private auspices—operate in the United States today, supported by hundreds of millions of dollars of public and private funds. Though none draws explicitly on Athens's work, effective programs almost certainly incorporate elements of Athens's findings derived independently from practical experience. Practical experience is better than bad theory (there is plenty of that out there), but good theory shaped from evidence is better than practical experience alone.

In the last chapter of *Violent Criminal Acts and Actors Revisited*, Athens briefly explores some of the policy implications of his work. He proposes a program fitted to community needs that would blend "general prevention, selective rehabilitation and selective incapacitation" to control violent crime.

The place to prevent or interrupt violentization, Athens believes, is the school. "Although the community cannot guarantee a good family to every child," he writes, "it can guarantee them a good school," and "a good school can go a long way in making up for a bad family." Child abuse is obviously an evil that communities must address, but brutalization is not synonymous with child abuse. Separating abused children from their families does not necessarily prevent their brutalization, which might begin or advance in substitute settings such as foster care or group homes. Detention centers in particular are notorious for advancing violentization. Brutalization by peers, especially in street gangs, also escapes programs that focus on families. School-based prevention programs overcome these limitations.

Family violence still needs to be addressed, of course. Although brutalization and child abuse are not synonymous, serious child abuse is always potentially brutalizing. Thus, social-welfare policies that make keeping families together their first priority are likely to promote rather than prevent violentization. Athens's studies verify that caretakers who deliberately injure children to the point of requiring medical attention have undergone violentization themselves, believe in using violence to maintain dominance and settle disputes and will almost certainly cause further injury to, or even kill, children left in their care. Giving such violent caretakers second chances, as social workers and judges frequently do, with the best of intentions—attributing their violence to poverty or racial prejudice and propping them up with counseling, household helpers and other resources—cannot reverse their violentization. To the contrary, such endorsement implicitly authorizes further violence and makes the state complicit with the violators.

The function of a school-based prevention program, Athens proposes, would be to foster the development of nonviolent phantom communities while thwarting the development of violent phantom communities. It would do so directly by teaching children not only how to read, write and compute but also "how to fulfill their general duties and obligations as community members." In malignant minor communities especially, Athens writes, "a broad-based, community-oriented education program would always include specific instruction about the laws that govern using both deadly and nondeadly force in general, as well as those that govern using any force whatsoever, particularly in sexual relations. There is a dire need to counteract the ideas circulating in the community about people's right to act violently toward one another."

One often overlooked support for violence against children Athens does not engage is conservative Christianity. "Spare the rod and spoil the child"—the old dogma that the child is inherently evil and requires violent subjugation to chasten—still persists as a tenet of fundamentalist and evangelical belief. (Since the Bible was written in a barbaric era, when physical violence was the primary means of settling disputes, it unsurprisingly endorses violent subjugation.) The historian Philip

Greven examines the continuing enthusiasm for this dogma in the modern United States in his 1991 book *Spare the Child.* "The focal point of evangelical and fundamentalist Protestant childrearing," he writes, "always has been the emerging wills of children. Breaking the child's will has been the central task given parents by successive generations of preachers, whose biblically based rationales for discipline have reflected the belief that self-will is evil and sinful."

Greven reviews such Christian best-sellers as psychologist James Dobson's *Dare to Discipline,* Larry Tomczak's *God, the Rod, and Your Child's Bod: The Art of Loving Correction for Christian Parents* and Larry Christenson's *The Christian Family.* These self-appointed authorities generally advocate "breaking the will" of children—punishing them to the point of "unconditional surrender," unqualified obedience—beginning in infancy, before the child can talk. "If the punishment is of the right kind," Christenson asserts, "it not only takes effect physically, but through physical terror and pain *[sic]*, it awakens and sharpens the consciousness that there is a moral power over us, a righteous judge and a law which cannot be broken." J. Richard Fugate, a Christian school administrator, specifies the dimensions of the legendary weapon in his contribution to the canon: "The rod is to be a thin wooden stick like a switch. Of course, the size of the rod should vary with the size of the child. A willow or peach tree branch may be fine for a rebellious two-year-old, but a small hickory rod or dowel rod would be more fitting for a well-muscled teenage boy." Dobson favors a leather belt.

Punishment, these authors advise, may continue to the point of raising welts if necessary, and in no case should last less than ten or fifteen minutes. "Making stripes on a child is not the objective of chastisement," Fugate rationalizes, "but parents must reasonably expect them to be a necessary by-product of the child's rebellion on some occasions." According to Dobson, crying, beyond "genuine release of emotion," is a form of further rebellion: "Crying quickly changes from inner sobbing to an exterior weapon. It becomes a tool of protest to punish the enemy. Real crying usually lasts two minutes or less, but may continue for five. After that point, the child is merely complaining. . . . I would require him to stop the protest crying, usually by offering him a little more of whatever caused the original tears." As Greven observes, none of these authors specify when enough is enough. "Chastisement" is supposed to persist until the child unconditionally surrenders—"if the child repeatedly disobeys," Dobson comments, "the chastisement has not been painful enough"—and failure to attain that goal is claimed to risk the child's soul.

"Discipline" carried to the point of violent subjugation can lead to the creation of another violent individual. The evangelist Oral Roberts, for example, recalls in his autobiography an occasion when he and his brother, Vaden, were lying on a pallet at an open-air revival listening to their father preach. Another boy hassled them by jerking on the pallet. "Vaden said, 'If you touch our pallet again, I will cut your ear off.' " The boy told Vaden he lacked the nerve. "He didn't know Vaden like I did," Roberts comments. Soon "Vaden had his knife out and was cutting the little boy's right ear off" while Roberts restrained the victim. Their father heard the boy scream and rescued him from mutilation. "When he got us home he took down his big razor strap. It was made in two pieces. When he got through with us, we believed it had a thousand pieces." Athens's work exposes the ugly irony at the center of Christian "discipline": that it serves not to prevent violence but to further its production. It survives as a vestige of the child-rearing practices Lloyd deMause discovered in the history of childhood. In communities where religion continues significantly to influence child-rearing, church and Christian school leadership toward moderating physical punishment in the spirit of Christian charity would contribute to violence prevention.

Besides serving as centers for community crime prevention, Athens proposes, schools should also direct belligerent students to community rehabilitation programs while rehabilitation is still possible. "Since violent people usually develop mitigated phantom communities at least by the time they leave middle school," he writes, "teachers are in a strategic position to identify them based on their misconduct [minor violent performances] at school. This identification is vitally important because the opportunity for rehabilitation can [then] be made available to these individuals while they still have a real chance to benefit from it." Athens remembers being painfully stigmatized for his belligerence in school, which only increased his isolation. Most public schools today typically expel disruptive students, dumping them onto the streets without rehabilitation.

Good science is not political. Athens's work supports some aspects of both liberal and conservative positions on preventing and controlling violence (which implies that both are partly right and partly wrong about the cause of violent criminality). Only full passage through all four stages of violentization creates a dangerous violent criminal, Athens emphasizes. "The mere entrance into any one stage does not guarantee the completion of that stage, much less the completion of the process as a whole. The completion of each stage is contingent upon the person fully undergoing all the experiences that comprise that stage, and the completion of the process as a whole is contingent upon the person undergoing all the stages." It follows that only people who complete violentization through the virulency stage, "and consequently the entire experiential process," will become dangerous violent criminals. "This remains the case," Athens writes, "regardless of the social class, race, sex or age and intelligence level of people, as long as their degree of mental and physical competence is sufficient for them to perform a violent criminal act." The requirement for full passage through violentization explains why only some children in violent families, some members of violent gangs, some soldiers exposed to violence in combat become dangerously violent.

For liberals concerned with prevention, then, Athens's work supports timely intervention anywhere along the way to and through violentization. Efforts to reduce family violence, to reduce school violence, to offer nonviolent coaching such as training in negotiation, anger management and conflict resolution, to discourage bullying, to offer (nonviolent) mentoring of children at risk, to discourage violent coaching of school athletes, to improve child welfare, to counsel belligerent young people, to support gun control, to dissolve or pacify street gangs and many more such antiviolent initiatives should be effective.

Once violentization is complete, however—once someone has committed serious physically defensive or frustrative-malefic violent criminal acts and possibly serious malefic or frustrative acts as well—Athens's work locates them, he writes, "outside the reach of any presently devisable long-term rehabilitation programs, much less short-term ones." At that point, he argues, supporting conservative views, "the community can no longer safely afford to look away and to forgive either these individuals or their violent criminal acts. If these violent criminals were allowed to escape the harsh punishment that they deserve for their crimes, it would undermine the larger corporal community's legitimacy in the eyes of its nonviolent members." Neither prevention nor rehabilitation can succeed under such circumstances:

> The predatory violent actions of ultraviolent criminals will either prevent the educational and rehabilitative programs from realizing their goals or negate any gains that may be achieved through their implementation. . . . Community members will have little faith in education or rehabilitation programs when they and their neighbors are daily subjected to the threat of murder, rape, robbery and

assault. . . . The success of these . . . programs will hinge on the removal of ultraviolent criminals from the community.

Rather than encourage wholesale incarceration of criminals, however, Athens joins many legal experts* in proposing the pragmatic alternative of applying the resources of the criminal justice system selectively to apprehending, convicting and incarcerating dangerous offenders:

> The telltale sign that a member of the community is an ultraviolent criminal is his commission of either a pure frustrative or malefic serious violent criminal act. By carefully considering the details of the incident in which a violent crime occurred, a police officer, district attorney or judge could determine whether a pure malefic or frustrative violent crime was committed and thereby whether the suspect or defendant is an ultraviolent criminal. On the basis of this determination, they would then target his case for more stringent handling. More specifically, police officers would target him for special investigation and arrest, district attorneys would target him for the severest possible prosecution and judges would target him for the harshest possible sentence.

Athens's work disproves the conservative argument, which has found support in criminology theory based on only quantitative data, that all criminals are equally dangerous. In fact some criminals are demonstrably more dangerous than others, which justifies applying a greater share of limited community resources to targeting and incarcerating them.

Civil communities need prevention and rehabilitation programs as much as do turbulent and malignant communities, Athens emphasizes, to maintain and endorse nonviolent values. People move in and move out of all communities. Some of those people are violent and reproduce their violence in their children, so even civil communities must sustain programs of crime prevention, just as they sustain programs of disease prevention even when incidence is low. Fear of punishment— deterrence—may encourage some violent criminals to form restraining judgments some of the time, Athens writes, but "people are more likely to refrain from violence out of preference for a nonviolent existence than they are to do so out of fear of punishment."

---

* See, for example, Mark Moore, Susan Estrich, Daniel McGillis and William Spelmon, *Dangerous Offenders: The Elusive Target of Justice* (Cambridge, Mass.: Harvard University Press, 1984).

Athens's work does not support the conclusion that media depictions of violence cause violent behavior. Quantitative research funded with millions of taxpayer dollars has identified marginal correlations between televised violence and immediate post-program aggressive behavior, which is unsurprising as well as unenlightening: All of us feel aggressive from time to time, but only people who have been violentized commit serious violent acts. The fact that most children watch many hours of television, while few children grow up to become violent criminals, disqualifies media violence as a cause. Homicide rates were far higher in the Middle Ages, long before electronic media, than they are today, and they declined across centuries when children attended public displays of *real* violence for moral uplift. Violent people may find affinity in public violence; banning such displays would mean banning not only the programs and music that censors dislike, but also news reporting, professional contact sports, war, the death penalty, Shakespeare and the Bible. Blaming stories and images for the problems people cause is, and has always been, a way of suppressing dissent while avoiding serious issues and hard choices.

Athens's work explains why rates of violent crime are higher in the United States than in other industrial democracies when rates for other crimes, such as burglary, are the same or even lower: because more Americans undergo violentization. The explanation is not a tautology but a revelation. Scholars and social scientists have sought the causes of American violence almost everywhere else: in our diversity, in poverty, in racial difference, in urban conditions, in regionality, in masculinity, in our avidity for guns.

Violentization subsumes all those categories. The social segregation that follows from American diversity opens the way to multiple minor communities, some of which become turbulent or malignant, attracting and generating violent criminals. Our diversity results from diverse immigration, and violentization has resisted the civilizing process longer in the lower-class and peasant cultures whence many of our immigrant forebears came. Poverty and urban conditions reflect social segregation as well. The African American community, once violently enslaved, has depended for its survival partly on conservative Christian values that encourage physical punishment, and has been segregated by racial prejudice into impoverished turbulent and malignant minor communities where policing is both sporadic and more punitive. (According to the political scientist James Q. Wilson, adult black male homicide rates were declining in the late 1990s much faster than were white rates, a development he attributes among other possibilities to "social progress" and "residential relocation.") The South, statistically the most violent region in the country, combines poverty, enthusiasm for military service, conservative Christian values and social segregation as well. Indeed, so-called black violence may well be a subset of southern violence, since African American culture derives directly from the southern culture in which it was originally embedded before the great migration of African Americans to northern cities.

Not testosterone per se but the patriarchal preference for subjecting males to violentization, and their physical advantage in achieving early successful violent performances, explains why men are much more likely than women to be seriously violent. Gun ownership paradoxically indicates some degree of violentization, as higher homicide rates in homes where guns are present attest. People who feel they need a gun at hand, after all, do so because they intend to use it to settle disputes.

Set programs in place to help prevent violentization, rehabilitate partly violentized young people and selectively incarcerate ultraviolent criminals and American rates of criminal violence, which ultimately measure American social retardation, would decrease toward the more civilized, uniformly low levels of Western Europe and Japan. Easier said than done. Control of human violence is essentially a public health problem, directly comparable to the problem of controlling epidemic disease. The industrial democracies at least have advanced a long way toward meeting the challenge of preventing and containing such biologic violence in the twentieth century; fully half the population of the United States, for example, who would otherwise have died before reproducing or never have been born, is alive today because of twentieth-century improvements in public health. Man-made violence continues to fester, its treatment stalled in part by inadequate knowledge of its etiology. Athens's work supplies that missing knowledge, at least where personal violence is concerned. I suspect, but can't prove, that it casts light as well into the shadowy precincts of group and institutional violence. Any discipline, without exception, which concerns itself with human violence has lessons to learn and apply from Athens's seminal work.

Achieving greater social control of violence means spending money, of course, but we do that anyway on ad hoc programs ill-informed by scandalously inadequate research. Preventing and limiting violence means protecting children from brutalization in a country where physically punishing children continues to be acceptable behavior. It means mobilizing support for belligerent children rather than isolating and rejecting them. It means making schools the social and moral centers of their communities. (School violence is in fact declining in the United States, despite occasional sensational shootings; with active, informed programs of violence prevention, the day might come when security gates and backpack searches join duck-and-cover nuclear war exercises in the archives of human folly.) Preventing and limiting violence means focusing programs of social support and police protection on turbulent and malignant minor communities rather than building more prisons.

Psychiatry should abandon its failed mental-illness model of criminal violence, replace it with Athens's evidence-based symbolic-interactionist model and get out of the disreputable business of helping violent criminals avoid taking responsibility for their crimes. After Athens it is possible to argue that some people are violent *and* mentally ill, but it is no longer defensible to argue that people are violent *because* they are mentally ill.

Prevention programs have not taken advantage of Athens's work because it has not won the hearing it so obviously deserves. It has not won a hearing partly because it discredits the currently fashionable but demonstrably sterile quantitative/statistical social-science paradigm. Although quantitative criminologists have only clues to what causes violent criminality, too often they are willing, like astrologers, to crank out endless and unenlightening charts of influences. Unfortunately the gate-keepers of journals and research grants and program funding over-whelmingly embrace just such cookbook "science," which would be merely Swiftian (I'm thinking of Gulliver's Laputans, whose clothes were ill cut because in their fondness for "Mathematicks" their tailors took measurements with quadrants and compasses) if something less destructive of people and resources than criminal violence were at stake.

Athens is the criminological equivalent of Robin Warren and Barry Marshall, the two Australian pathologists who discovered in the early 1980s that a bacterium, *Helicobacter pylori,* causes chronic gastritis and stomach ulcers, which could therefore be cured with a straightforward course of antibiotic therapy rather than merely controlled, not always successfully, with a lifetime of expensive antacid drug treatment. The prevailing medical theory held that stress (somehow) caused stomach ulcers, and so much was at stake for the medical establishment, which had hardly investigated alternative explanations even though ulcer victims died in considerable numbers down the decades from bleeding perforations, that it required ten years and Marshall personally ingesting *H. pylori* cultures and developing gastritis before the two physicians' evidence would be grudgingly accepted and treatment protocols revised to include antibiotic therapy in addition to antisecretory drugs. The criminological establishment's studied indifference to Athens's work similarly invites skepticism and suspicion, even contempt. Criminological research receives millions of dollars in public funds, with very little return on the investment. Athens funded his breakthrough work almost entirely out of his own pocket.

In 1996 Ginger Rhodes and I published *Trying to Get Some Dignity,* a collection of interviews with seventeen Americans who survived childhood abuse and who had contacted me after I published *A Hole in the World,* my own memoir of childhood. Many of these men and women, myself included, had experience of brutalization. None had completed violentization. They had exceptional personal resources as children, including intelligence, but what seems to have saved every one of them was timely intervention, almost always private and voluntary. Someone saw their suffering and had the courage or simply the generosity of spirit to intervene. They were not necessarily rescued, but they were supported, or given reason to believe that they were valued, or shown alternatives to violence—nonviolently coached, Athens would say. In my case my older brother Stanley bravely went to the police after one too many beatings. One woman whose mother physically tortured and sexually abused her survived on the strength of the casual response of strangers who singled her out for attention because she was an unusually beautiful child. Another woman, whose aunt punished her and her sisters by forcing them to stand fourteen hours a day on a hot interior stairway without touching the walls, clung to the praise of her artwork by a police-officer artist who visited her school. Since most interviewees grew up before social welfare took notice of child abuse, teachers had been their lifelines.

All the official programs in the world cannot replace personal witness to civil values; it is by personal witness, after all, that civil communities maintain their civility and the civilizing process proceeds. Athens's work discredits protestations that violence persists because of the poverty, race, culture or genetic inheritance of "those people over there" and has nothing to do with you and me. Criminal violence emerges from social experience, most commonly brutal social experience visited upon vulnerable children, who suffer for our neglect of their welfare and return in vengeful wrath to plague us. If violence is a choice they make, and therefore their personal responsibility, as Athens demonstrates it is, our failure to protect them from having to confront such a choice is a choice *we* make, just as a disease epidemic would be implicitly our choice if we failed to provide vaccines and antibiotics. Such a choice—to tolerate the brutalization of children as we continue to do—is equally violent and equally evil, and we reap what we sow.

In the late spring of 1997, Lonnie Athens traveled to Northern California to visit his daughter, Maureen, a striking, self-confident eighteen-year-old. During their time together they walked the University of California campus where he had pursued his doctoral studies in criminology.

"Berkeley brought back memories," Athens wrote me when he returned east, "of sitting in Barrows Hall dreaming of solving the riddle of violent crime, of putting around in my VW bug from prison to prison talking with one violent criminal after another. I saw myself, foolishly, becoming the Darwin of criminology. Everything seemed possible back then." The work Athens accomplished in difficult circumstances is anything but foolish, nor was he foolish for dreaming that it might be fundamental. Having scored the soliloquy of the self, having identified and charted a deep human universal that reveals itself in ancient times and modern, in simple and complex societies, in every race and social class, in peacetime and in war, he has reached beyond criminology. If evil is the direct or indirect destruction of human beings, Lonnie Athens's rugged genius has been to strip away superficialities and expose the gears and levers of the very apparatus of evil itself.

Glade
May 1997–October 1998

Notes

Unreferenced quotations derive from tape-recorded interviews.
LA: Lonnie Athens

CHAPTER ONE: BRING IT ON

7 **Homicide rates; civilizing process:** Johnson & Monkkonen (1996), pp. 3–13; Elias (1939b).
10 **"I'm a hardworking":** Athens (1997), p. 56.
11 **"While I was walking":** Athens (1997), p. 123.
14 **"one need not actually":** Athens (1992), p. 20.

CHAPTER TWO: THOUGHTS FILLED WITH GHOSTS

21 **"for increasing the odds":** Athens (1992), p. x.
23 **"After a game":** Athens (1997), pp. 122–23.

CHAPTER THREE: HOW THE SYSTEM WORKS

30 **"Knowing that your major area":** LA to Marshall Clinard, May 11, 1970.
    "unique . . . very glad": Marshall Clinard to LA, June 9, 1970.
32 **American sociology:** This discussion follows Wiley (1986).
33 **"musty stacks":** Quoted in McKinney (1966), p. 71.
    "It has been the dream": Park and Burgess (1921), p. 15.
    "techniques of more precise": Clinard (1966), p. 402.
    "The opportunities provided": Clinard (1966), p. 405.
34 **Paper by Alfred Schutz:** Schutz (1954).
    "the world of nature": Schutz (1954), p. 266.
    "constructs of the second degree": Schutz (1954), p. 266.
    facts about such people: Cf. Wilson and Herrnstein (1985), p. 19.
    A book on method: Cicourel (1964).
35 **"While there are indeed":** Philips (1971), p. 7.
    "Thus, if mental health": Philips (1971), pp. 7–9.

35 **"If we are to go":** Philips (1971), p. 152. Philips's emphasis.
36 **"We can and":** Blumer (1969), p. 132.
    "direct observation": Blumer (1969), p. 41.
    "one of the world's greatest": Blumer (1969), p. 41.
    "from the position": Blumer (1969), p. 56.
37 **"After reading the works":** LA to Marshall Clinard, Dec. 18, 1978.

CHAPTER FOUR: THE FULL, UGLY REALITY

38 **Herbert Blumer's life and career:** Hammersley (1989), pp. 44, 86; LA (personal communication).
39 **"If I were handling":** Herbert Blumer to LA, Jan. 6, 1972.
41 **Inmate participation:** Athens (1974), n. 3.
    "I . . . believe that readers": Athens (1997), p. 41, n. 1.
    Case 2: Athens (1974), pp. 104–5.
42 **Three acknowledged crimes:** Athens (1974), p. 111, n. 4.
    Case 9: Athens (1997), pp. 66–67.
43 **"their relative lack":** Athens (1992), pp. 4–5. Athens's emphasis.
    Case 9: Athens (1992), p. 41.
44 **"When people look at":** Athens (1992), p. 6.
46 **"The Self and the Violent Criminal Act":** Athens (1974).

CHAPTER FIVE: TAKING THE ATTITUDE OF THE OTHER

49 **"I usually saw the inmates":** Athens (1997), pp. 102–3.
50 **Booty robber story and summary:** Athens (1997), pp. 135–36.
52–53 **Mead's and Blumer's model of human functioning:** cf. Mead (1934), Blumer (1981), Athens (1997), Brothers (1997), Swanson (1991), Cook (1993), Pfuetze (1954), Habermas (1991), Cronk (1987) and Lewis (1991).
53 **"the most original mind":** Dewey (1985), pp. 24, 25. Whitehead's concurrence: according to Pfuetze (1954), p. 102.
    "Human society": Mead (1934), p. 227.
53–54 **"young children experience":** Mead (1934), p. 135.
54 **"taking the attitude":** Mead (1934), p. 100.
    "Thus, individuals": Blumer (1981), pp. 137–38.
    bodily sensations: Brothers (1997), p. 101.
    "Mead saw the mind": Blumer (1981), p. 139.
55 **"Ideas . . . are simply":** Mead (1934), p. 99.
    "The self": Blumer (1981), p. 139.
    "To become an object": Blumer (1981), p. 140.
    "that the self": Blumer (1981), p. 140.
    "Mead proposes an": Blumer (1981), p. 140.
56 **"human group life":** Blumer (1981), p. 147.
    "Shown only a face": Bruce (1988), p. 31, quoted in Brothers (1997), p. 30.
56–57 **"individuals . . . may use":** Swanson (1991), p. 208.
57 **"This inner world":** Blumer (1981), p. 142.
    "The act of each dog": Mead (1934), pp. 42–43.
    "In having a self": Blumer (1981), p. 143.
58 **"The human actor":** Blumer (1981), p. 143.

CHAPTER SIX: BEAUTIFUL NARRATIVE

60–61 **"It is much more difficult"**: Athens (1997), p. 105.
61 **"seven inmates"**: Athens (1997), p. 104.
"The fact that the people": Athens (1997), p. 103.
62 **"In a library of"**: Polanyi (1958, 1962), p. 80.
63 **"since it would be"**: Polanyi (1958, 1962), p. 81.
"In the most general terms": Polanyi (1958, 1962), pp. 81–82.
"immediately we can read off": Polanyi (1958, 1962), p. 83.
64 **"Although one need not"**: Athens (1992), p. 20.
"The cultural diversity": Athens (1997), p. 102.
65 **"Dr. Athens's study"**: Athens (1997), p. 6.

CHAPTER SEVEN: CONSCIOUS CONSTRUCTIONS

66 **"*substantially* violent criminal"**: Athens (1997), p. 31. Athens's emphasis.
"That . . . the victim": Athens (1997), p. 31.
67 **"Thus, the data"**: Athens (1997), p. 32. Athens's emphasis.
"the true nature of": Banay (1952), p. 33, cited in Athens (1997), p. 33.
"ego-dystonic": Tanay (1972), pp. 815, 817, cited in Athens (1997), p. 33.
"real murderers are not": Lester and Lester (1975), p. 5, cited in Athens (1997), p. 33.
"passion crimes": Wolfgang and Ferracuti (1967a), pp. 140–41, 209, 263; (1967b), pp. 272–73, cited in Athens (1997), p. 33.
68 **Case 55:** Athens (1997), pp. 10–11.
69 **"The perpetrator forms"**: Athens (1997), p. 35.
70 **Case 18:** Athens (1997), p. 34.
70–71 **"The perpetrator forms"**: Athens (1997), p. 36.
71 **Case 49:** Athens (1997), pp. 37–38.
72 **Case 10:** Athens (1997), p. 38.
"The perpetrator forms": Athens (1997), pp. 38–39.
73 **"The perpetrator forms"**: Athens (1997), p. 40.
Case 21: Athens (1997), pp. 40–41.
74 **"Far more violent"**: Athens (1997), p. 53.
"It was believed that": Athens (1997), p. 13.
"After forming a violent": Athens (1997), p. 43.
75 **"*redefines* the situation"**: Athens (1997), p. 45. Athens's emphasis.
Case 55: Athens (1997), pp. 46–47.
76 **"he either momentarily"**: Athens (1997), p. 50.
Case 32: Athens (1997), pp. 50–51.
77 **"In short"**: Athens (1997), p. 52.

CHAPTER EIGHT: PHANTOM COMMUNITIES

80 **"A person is a personality"**: Mead (1934), p. 162.
"A child acquires": Mead (1922), pp. 161–62, quoted in Athens (1995), p. 253. Athens's emphases.
"When people take the": Athens (1994), p. 522.
81 **"the structure . . . on which"**: Mead (1934), p. 162.

81–82 **"we would be forced"**: Athens (1994), p. 523.
   82 **"phantom others"**: Athens (1994), p. 525.
       "we always converse": Athens (1994), p. 525.
       "following what another": Athens (1994), p. 524.
       "the people with whom we are": Athens (1994), p. 525. Athens's emphasis.
       "The people with whom we converse": Athens (1994), p. 525.
       "The phantom other is both": Athens (1994), p. 526. Athens's emphases.
   83 **"Most of the time"**: Athens (1994), p. 526.
       Emotions . . . are meanings: Athens (1994), p. 525; Brothers (1997), p. 117.
       "must be major": Athens (1994), pp. 526–27.
       "They tell us how": Athens (1994), p. 527.
   84 **"Although our conversations"**: Athens (1994), p. 528.
       "First, the actors": Athens (1997), p. 54.
   85 **"low rider"**: Athens (1997), p. 55.
       "I'm a man": Athens (1997), p. 57.
       "In contrast to people": Athens (1997), p. 57. Athens's emphasis.
       "definitely and genuinely": Athens (1997), p. 58.
   86 **Case 28**: Athens (1997), p. 58.
       "are not seen by": Athens (1997), pp. 58–59.
       Case 48: Athens (1997), p. 59.
86–87 **"In the fifty-eight cases"**: Athens (1997), p. 61.
   87 **Case 5**: Athens (1997), p. 62.
   88 **Case 57**: Athens (1997), pp. 63–64.
   89 **Case 29**: Athens (1997), pp. 64–66.
   90 **"interpret a wider"**: Athens (1997), p. 68.
       "These individuals must": Athens (1997), p. 71.
       "If violent crimes were": Athens (1997), p. 68.
       "a selective life history": Athens (1997), p. 69.
   91 **"When the perpetrators held violent"**: Athens (1997), pp. 70–71.
       Case 56: Athens (1997), pp. 75–78.
   92 **"the types of self-images"**: Athens (1997), p. 99.
       union leader: Athens (1997), p. 91 ff.
       "leads his present": Athens (1997), pp. 140–41.
   93 **"will commit violent"**: Athens (1997), p. 98. Athens's emphases.
       "Since human beings": Athens (1997), p. 118.
       "Those who hold violent": Athens (1997), p. 99. Athens's emphases.
   94 **"are at the heart"**: Athens (1997), p. 100.
       "an empirically grounded": Athens (1997), p. 144.
       "crime is a product": Athens (1997), p. 144. Athens's emphasis.
       "all or most criminal": Athens (1997), pp. 144–45.
   95 **"inhabit unmitigated"**: Athens (1997), pp. 145–46.
       "different types of violent": Athens (1997), pp. 146–48.

CHAPTER NINE: ACADEMIC CRACKERS AND CHEESE

   98 **"The first stated that"**: LA to Herbert Blumer, Nov. 15, 1976.
       "He's taken a topic": Undated three-page review of "Violent Criminal Acts,"
       signed "Howard S. Becker."
       "Ray stated explicitly": Hartung (1966), p. 162.
   99 **"While the reason may"**: Ray (1871), p. 215, quoted in Hartung (1966), p. 196.

99 **"almost the only proof"**: Ray (1871), pp. 257–58, quoted in Hartung (1966), p. 194.

"The question is asked": Hartung (1966), p. 194.

99–100 **"the recognition of the"**: East (1951), pp. 20–21, quoted in Hartung (1966), p. 199.

100 **"Human beings *acting* toward"**: Athens (1992), pp. 15–16. Athens's emphasis.

"The organization of": Hartung (1966), p. 155.

"[A person] identifies himself": Hartung (1966), p. 156.

101 **"one of our most"**: Memo "Re: Dr. Lonnie H. Athens," signed "Fred P. Wessels, Academic Services Officer," Dec. 14, 1978.

102 **"out in the field"**: LA to Norman Denzin, Oct. 18, 1982.

103 **"candidly admitted committing"**: Athens (1992), p. 22.

"was almost totally wrong": Athens (1992), p. 22.

"who had no known": Athens (1992), p. 24.

"half a dozen recent": Athens (1992), pp. 24–25.

105 *Sociological Quarterly* **paper**: Athens (1985).

"[display] to himself": Goffman (1967), pp. 184–85, quoted in Athens (1985), p. 420.

"provided a major source": Athens (1985), p. 420.

"On-the-spot agreements": Athens (1985), p. 423. Athens's emphasis.

"A character contest presumes": Athens (1985), p. 425 ff.

"Engaging in violence": Athens (1985), p. 429.

106 **"started a small consulting"**: LA to Norman Denzin, Sept. 18, 1986.

106–7 **"As you may recall"**: LA to Herbert Blumer, Mar. 24, 1987.

107 **"I do not expect"**: LA to Herbert Blumer, Mar. 24, 1987.

CHAPTER TEN:
THE CREATION OF DANGEROUS VIOLENT CRIMINALS (I)

109 **Case 16:** Athens (1992), pp. 2–3.

110–11 **"the elderly victim"**: Athens (1992), pp. 4–5.

111 **"that people are"**: Athens (1992), p. 18.

"consequential and": Athens (1992), pp. 18–19.

"the significant experiences": Athens (1992), pp. 20–21.

"it is far better": Athens (1992), p. 21.

"more discoveries have arisen": Beveridge (1957), p. 140, quoted in Athens (1992), p. 21.

112 **"the deceivingly simple"**: Athens (1992), p. 23.

"Each stage describes": Athens (1992), p. 25.

"three more elemental": Athens (1992), p. 27. Athens's emphases.

"a group characterized": Athens (1992), p. 28.

"bona fide or would-be": Athens (1992), p. 28.

113 **"Prior to the onset"**: Athens (1992), p. 29.

Case 19: Athens (1992), pp. 30–31.

114 **"The battery is continued"**: Athens (1992), p. 32.

"and sometimes even": Athens (1992), pp. 32–33.

115 **Case 38:** Athens (1992), pp. 35–36.

116 **"momentary submission"**: Athens (1992), pp. 36–37.

116–17 **"The subject does not"**: Athens (1992), p. 38.

117 **"some close relative"**: Athens (1992), pp. 38–39.

117 **"The wrath rapidly building"**: Athens (1992), p. 40.
118 **"The subject is now"**: Athens (1992), pp. 40–41.
    Case 22: Athens (1992), pp. 43–44.
119 **"The worst part of"**: Athens (1992), p. 44. Athens's emphases.
120 **"to instruct the subject"**: Athens (1992), p. 46.
    "Since many people": Athens (1992), p. 47.
    "Novices are taught": Athens (1992), p. 47.
    "is a *personal responsibility*": Athens (1992), p. 47. Athens's emphasis.
121 **"to operate upon"**: Athens (1992), pp. 47–48.
    "The plots in these anecdotes": Athens (1992), pp. 48–49.
    "The implication which novices": Athens (1992), pp. 49–50.
    Case 2: Athens (1992), pp. 50–51.
122 **"Some coaches threaten"**: Athens (1992), p. 51.
    Case 38: Athens (1992), p. 52.
123 **"The coach repeatedly rants"**: Athens (1992), p. 52.
    "A man should not back down": Athens (1992), Case 23, p. 53.
    "You can't depend on a man": Athens (1992), Case 37, p. 54.
    "derive a perverse": Athens (1992), p. 53.
    "potent combination of social": Athens (1992), p. 54.
    "A stepfather may take": Athens (1992), p. 55.
124 **"weeks, months or"**: Athens (1992), p. 56.

CHAPTER ELEVEN:
THE CREATION OF DANGEROUS VIOLENT CRIMINALS (II)

125 **"deeply troubled and"**: Athens (1992), p. 57.
    "Experiences as odious": Athens (1992), pp. 57–58.
    "his brooding is done": Athens (1992), pp. 58. Athens's emphasis.
126 **"generates relatively enduring"**: Athens (1992), pp. 58–59.
    "finally becomes fully": Athens (1992), pp. 59–60.
    "to attack other people": Athens (1992), p. 62.
127 **Case 9:** Athens (1992), p. 61.
    "Intentionally injuring another human": Athens (1992), p. 63.
128 **"purposely and cruelly"**: Athens (1992), pp. 63–64.
    "and becomes paralyzed": Athens (1992), p. 64.
    Case 13: Athens (1992), p. 65.
129 **Case 21:** Athens (1992), pp. 65–66.
    "In these performances": Athens (1992), p. 67.
130 **"especially several major"**: Athens (1992), p. 68.
    "Thus, bitter defeats": Athens (1992), p. 69.
    Case 21: Athens (1992), pp. 70–71.
131 **"*by itself* have any"**: Athens (1992), p. 72. Athens's emphasis.
132 **"The subject becomes conscious"**: Athens (1992), p. 73. Athens's emphasis.
    "now suddenly begin": Athens (1992), p. 73.
    "People treat him": Athens (1992), p. 74.
    "The subject must now": Athens (1992), pp. 74–75.
133 **"undergoes a drastic"**: Athens (1992), p. 75.
    "He now firmly resolves": Athens (1992), pp. 75–76.
    "The subject is ready": Athens (1992), p. 79.
134 **Case 33:** Athens (1992), pp. 78–79.

134 "**proverbial violent outcast**": Athens (1992), p. 76.
135 "**The mere entrance into**": Athens (1992), pp. 80–81.
135–36 "**people who commit**": Athens (1992), pp. 81–82.
136 "**Some very dangerous**": Athens (1992), p. 86.
      "**that we always have**": Athens (1992), p. 85.
      cataclysmic experience: Athens (1992), p. 83.
      "**just prior to their teens**": Athens (1992), p. 83.
      "**Just as people**": Athens (1992), p. 82.
137 "**Psychologists have been caught up**": Athens (1992), pp. 84–85.
      "**should they later reach**": Athens (1992), p. 85.
      Opiate Addiction: Lindesmith (1957).
138–39 **Lindesmith lecture**: Lindesmith (1979).

CHAPTER TWELVE: CHERYL CRANE

144 **Cheryl Crane memoir**: Crane (1988).
      "**I am lonely**": quoted in Crane (1988), p. 47.
      "**On one of Gran's**": Crane (1988), p. 86.
      "**people who simply**": Crane (1988), p. 82.
      "**thick reddish hair**": Crane (1988), p. 87.
145 "**She decided one**": Crane (1988), pp. 78–79.
      "**By age four**": Crane (1988), p. 78.
      "**obey[ing] authority so readily**": Crane (1988), p. 79.
      "**loveless**": Crane (1988), p. 80.
146 "**Papa had a low**": Crane (1988), p. 130.
      "**swallowed sleeping pills**": Crane (1988), p. 131.
147 " '**Y'know, Mother**' ": Crane (1988), p. 148.
      "**feared Mother's power**": Crane (1988), p. 150.
      "**some of them**": Crane (1988), p. 150.
      "**He was Tarzan**": Crane (1988), p. 151.
      "**I was growing rigid**": Crane (1988), pp. 152–53.
148 " '**Remember Mr. Rabbit**' ": Crane (1988), pp. 159–60.
      "**I was ten-and-a-half**": Crane (1988), p. 161.
      "**He was so confident**": Crane (1988), p. 175.
149 "**His forearm came up**": Crane (1988), pp. 180–81.
      "**She meant Lex**": Crane (1988), p. 189.
150 "**He was handsome**": Crane (1988), pp. 20, 198–99.
      "**After he lost**": Crane (1988), pp. 208–9.
      "**Two of the film's**": Crane (1988), p. 210.
151 "**the happiest time**": Crane (1988), p. 211.
      "**Mother says she lived**": Crane (1988), p. 212.
      "**he smashed a door**": Crane (1988), p. 213.
152 "**a fetal lump**": Crane (1988), p. 15.
      " '**Baby, things aren't**' ": Crane (1988), pp. 17–18.
153 "**She broke down**": Crane (1988), p. 19.
      " '**You damn BITCH**' ": Crane (1988), pp. 222–24.
154 "**heard [Cheryl's] version**": Crane (1988), p. 225.

CHAPTER THIRTEEN:
ALEX KELLY, PERRY SMITH, MIKE TYSON

156   *Saint of Circumstance:* Weller (1997).
       "Why would Alex": Weller (1997), p. 166.
       "People whispered": Weller (1997), pp. 36, 43.
157   **"Joe would come":** Weller (1997), p. 46.
       "used to be": Weller (1997), pp. 45, 201.
       "The other parents": Weller (1997), pp. 40–41, 42.
158   **" 'Alex went into' ":** Weller (1997), pp. 44–45.
       "noticed Alex grabbing": Weller (1997), pp. 47–48.
       "We were just fooling": Weller (1997), p. 48.
       "was aggressive though": Weller (1997), pp. 49, 69.
159   **" 'It was cold' ":** Weller (1997), pp. 61–62.
       "lasting and significant impact": Athens (1992), p. 72.
160   **" 'He grabbed me' ":** Weller (1997), pp. 76–80.
       " 'He was, like' ": Weller (1997), p. 114.
161   **"He put his hands":** Weller (1997), pp. 117–18.
       "Things were escalating": Weller (1997), p. 118.
       "feelings of exultancy": Athens (1992), p. 75.
       After that night: Weller (1997), p. 120.
       Vermont ski resort rape: Weller (1997), pp. 124–25.
       "rejuvenated": quoted in Weller (1997), p. 125.
162   **"He said I":** quoted in Weller (1997), pp. 5, 135–37.
       "He then forced": quoted in Weller (1997), p. 152.
       Bahamas rape, Kelly trial: Weller (1997), p. 303.
       In Cold Blood: Capote (1965).
163   **"I was born":** quoted in Capote (1965), p. 326.
       "had been presented": quoted in Capote (1965), p. 327.
164   **"In Frisco I was":** quoted in Capote (1965), p. 328.
       Smith told Capote: Capote (1965), p. 157.
       "The Black Widows": quoted in Capote (1965), p. 328.
165   **"When I was sixteen":** quoted in Capote (1965), pp. 329–30.
165–66 **Dr. Jones's evaluation:** quoted in Capote (1965), pp. 329–30.
166   **"See, Don—I did":** Capote (1965), p. 347.
167   **" 'Am I sorry' ":** Capote (1965), p. 347.
168   **"fairy boy":** Heller (1995), p. 7.
       "He would admit": Heller (1995), p. 9.
       "a bad-ass kid": Heller (1995), p. 10.
       "I wasn't sucked in": Heller (1995), p. 11.
169   **"I should have killed":** Heller (1995), p. 408.
170   **Jim Gray interview:** transcribed from live transmission.
170–71 **Steve Albert statement:** transcribed from live transmission.
171   **Tyson on "street fight":** paraphrased in Schouten (1998), p. 3.
       "issues related to": quoted in Schouten (1998), p. 5.
       Athens discussion of psychological traits: Athens (1992), pp. 84–85.
       "express[ing] an interest": Schouten (1998), p. 5.
171–72 **"during the early stages":** Athens (1992), p. 85.
172   **"Upon further exploration":** Schouten (1998), p. 5.
       "should be engaged": Schouten (1998), pp. 8–9.
       Hardick complaint: Richard Dale Hardick statement, District Court of

Maryland, Sept. 2, 1998, reproduced at
http://www.thesmokinggun.com/archive/tysonfight1.html.
173   **"I was irate, crazy":** quoted in Smith (1998a).
      "Everyone knows I'm on": quoted in Gurnick (1998).
174   **"He was butting me":** quoted in Smith (1998b).

CHAPTER FOURTEEN: LEE HARVEY OSWALD

175   **"She constantly reminded us":** Warren Commission (1964), vol. 11, p. 12.
      "outbursts": Oswald (1967), p. 34.
      "neglect": quoted in Warren Report (1964), p. 372.
      "adorable. . . . If you": Warren Commission (1964), vol. 8, pp. 160–61.
176   **"Mother came home":** Oswald (1967), p. 33.
      "All her life I": Oswald (1967), p. 22.
      "While John and I": Oswald (1967), p. 34.
      "you just couldn't": Warren Commission (1964), vol. 8, 102.
      "His salary was over": Warren Commission (1964), vol. 8, pp. 114, 117.
      "influenced in part": Warren Report (1964), p. 599.
177   **"He had white hair":** Warren Commission (1964), vol. 11, p. 21.
      "I think Lee found": Warren Commission (1964), vol. 11, p. 27.
      "She always wanted": Warren Commission (1964), vol. 11, p. 73.
      "they would have a fight": Warren Commission (1964), vol. 11, pp. 26–27.
      "and told me": Warren Commission (1964), vol. 11, p. 27.
      Ekdahl divorce: Warren Report (1964), p. 600; Davison (1983), p. 45.
      Marguerite testified: Warren Commission (1964), vol. 11, p. 29.
      "She lost": Warren Commission (1964), vol. 11, p. 29.
      violent subjugation: cf. Athens (1992), pp. 44–45.
      "was far more upset": Oswald (1967), pp. 38–39.
178   **"I should say":** Stafford (1966), pp. 30–32.
      "when we were just": Warren Commission (1964), vol. 8, pp. 77–78.
179   **"tirades . . . upset":** Oswald (1967), pp. 44–45.
      "They have these little": quoted in Posner (1993), pp. 9–10.
      "the picture it built": Warren Commission (1964), vol. 8, pp. 86–87.
180   **"Lee was nearly thirteen":** Oswald (1967), pp. 51–52.
      "Whenever there was": Warren Commission (1964), vol. 11, p. 37.
      "One afternoon John": Oswald (1967), pp. 52–53.
181   **"attempted to brush":** Warren Commission (1964), vol. 11, p. 38.
      "Mrs. Pic stated": Warren Commission (1964), vol. 22, exhibit no. 1382, p. 687.
      "I was never able": Warren Commission (1964), vol. 11, p. 38.
      "that while Lee": quoted in Davison (1983), p. 51.
      "He felt that they": John Carro, Warren Commission (1964), vol. 8, p. 211.
      "damn Yankee": Davison (1983), p. 49.
182   **"conflicting thoughts and":** Athens (1992), pp. 57–58.
182–83 **Renatus Hartogs report:** Warren Commission (1964), vol. 8, pp. 221–23.
183   **Evelyn Strickman report:** quoted in Davison (1983), pp. 52–53.
      "ponder[ing] the nature of": Athens (1992), p. 57.
      "I'm a Marxist": quoted in Warren Report (1964), p. 364.
184   **"In the early 1950s":** Oswald (1967), p. 47.
      "At fifteen": Warren Commission (1964), vol. 20, Johnson (Priscilla), exhibit
      no. 5, p. 300.

184 **"During the past two"**: quoted in Oswald (1967), p. 63.
185 **"watching the treatment"**: Warren Commission (1964), vol. 20, Johnson (Priscilla), exhibit no. 5, p. 299.
  New Orleans courtroom incident: Davison (1983), p. 169.
  "observ[ed] the treatment": Warren Commission (1964), vol. 20, Johnson (Priscilla), exhibit no. 5, p. 299.
  "ends with the subject": Athens (1992), p. 60.
186 **"They had a very bad"**: Warren Commission (1964), vol. 8, pp. 124–25.
  "because he was always": Bennierita Sparacio, quoted in Posner (1993), p. 15.
  "Several boys jumped": Oswald (1967), p. 68.
  "hit him in": Warren Commission (1964), vol. 8, p. 159.
  "Lee had a fight": Warren Commission (1964), vol. 8, pp. 2–3.
187 **"sympathy toward Lee"**: Warren Commission (1964), vol. 8, p. 3.
  "wouldn't start any": Warren Commission (1964), vol. 8, p. 5.
  "wanted a pistol": Warren Commission (1964), vol. 8, p. 9.
  "resort to more lethal": Athens (1992), p. 69.
188 **"The occurrence of restraining"**: Athens (1997), pp. 45–49.
  "Resourcefulness and patient": quoted in Warren Report (1964), p. 372.
  Oswald's first gun: Oswald (1967), p. 74.
189 **"Because we both enjoyed"**: Warren Commission (1964), vol. 22, pp. 710–11.
  Oswald as sharpshooter: Posner (1993), p. 20.
  "won the admiration": Kerry Thornley, Warren Commission (1964), vol. 11, p. 106.
190 **"lead[ing] an expedition"**: quoted in Davison (1983), p. 76.
  "started getting scared": quoted in Posner (1993), p. 29.
  "In general, our family": quoted in Warren Report (1964), p. 372.
  "I did not know": Warren Commission (1964), vol. 1, p. 10.
  Testimony Oswald beat Marina: Oswald (1967), p. 127; Posner (1993), pp. 93–96.
  Oswald's murder threats and rape: McMillan (1977), p. 257.
191 **"to attack people physically"**: Athens (1992), p. 75.
  Footnote: Warren Commission (1964), vol. 11, p. 120, 122.
  Priscilla McMillan judges: McMillan (1977), p. 258 ff.
  McMillan speculates: McMillan (1977), p. 267.
  "a very accurate weapon": quoted in Posner (1993), p. 104.
192 **"I told him that"**: Warren Commission (1964), vol. 1, pp. 16–17.
  "He had shot at": McMillan (1977), p. 299.
  "It was early in": Warren Commission (1964), vol. 1, pp. 388–92.
193 **"You'll have killed"**: quoted in McMillan (1977), p. 296.
  Lyndon Johnson: Posner (1993), p. 120n.
  "NIXON CALLS FOR DECISION": quoted in McMillan (1977), p. 295.
  "I asked him why": Warren Commission (1964), vol. 1, pp. 21–22.
  "Fidel Castro needs": quoted in McMillan (1977), p. 362.
194 **Oswald's reading**: Davison (1983), p. 148.
  Oswald talking grandiosely: McMillan (1977), pp. 342–43.
  "We are prepared to": quoted in Davison (1983), p. 22.
  "He engaged in": Warren Report (1964), p. 388.
  Footnote: cf. Schorr (1977), pp. 176–78.
  "The first time": quoted in Davison (1983), p. 213.
195 **"how completely relaxed"**: Oswald (1967), p. 143.

195 **"He struck me as"**: quoted in Davison (1983), p. 253.
"**I got the impression**": quoted in Davison (1983), p. 258.
196–98 **Jack Ruby's biography**: Warren Report (1964), pp. 688–711.
198 **"When people look"**: Athens (1992), p. 6.

CHAPTER FIFTEEN: MURDERS WITH MOTIVES

200 **"When the propensity"**: Isaac Ray, *A Treatise on the Medical Jurisprudence of Insanity*, 5th ed., 1871, p. 246, quoted in Hartung (1965), p. 162.
Satten et al.: Satten et al. (1960).
203 **"that he has been"**: Schouten (1998), p. 7.
205 **Lewis papers**: Lewis et al. (1980), Lewis et al. (1985), Lewis et al. (1988). Lewis book: Lewis (1998).
205–6 **Lewis et al. study of death-row juveniles**: Lewis et al. (1988).
206 **"the most striking difference"**: Lewis et al. (1980).
207–8 **Paper comparing nine boys to twenty-four**: Lewis et al. (1985).
208 **"It was believed that"**: Athens (1997), p. 137.
"multiple personality disorder": Lewis (1998), pp. 171–72.
210 **"Arthur Shawcross also experienced"**: Lewis (1998), p. 243.
211 **"the fraudulent construction of"**: Reuters (1998).
"material produced under hypnosis": Lewis (1998), p. 243.
calling violent criminals crazy: cf., e.g., Foucault (1975), p. 124 ff.
212 **"New views of serial"**: Jenkins (1994), p. 55.
"on patterns of murders": quoted in Jenkins (1994), p. 59.
Murder estimates: Jenkins (1994), p. 60, p. 22.
"current FBI estimates": Jenkins (1994), p. 60.
212–13 **"based largely on news"**: Jenkins (1994), pp. 25–26.
213 **"I mean, how many"**: quoted in Jenkins (1994), p. 71.
"It strains credibility": Douglas and Olshaker (1995), p. 348.

CHAPTER SIXTEEN: MONOPOLIES OF VIOLENCE

214 **"was much feared for"**: Fenton (1998), p. 22.
215 **"The young victim"**: Marder (1997), pp. 209–10.
Homicide statistics: FBI; Zimring and Hawkins (1997), pp. 53, 80.
215–16 **Homicides of black men, young men**: Currie (1998), pp. 24–25.
216 **Homicide rate, thirteenth-century England**: Johnson and Monkkonen (1996), p. 22.
Homicide rate, fifteenth-century Sweden: Johnson and Monkkonen (1996), p. 44.
Homicide rates, London, Amsterdam, Stockholm: Johnson and Monkkonen (1996), p. 9; Hannawalt (1979), p. 99.
Eighteenth-, nineteenth-century homicide rates: Johnson and Monkkonen (1996), pp. 9, 22.
U.S. homicide rate, 1900: Zimring and Hawkins (1997), p. 57.
"Every day, murders": Bloch (1940), p. 411.
"He spends his life": quoted in Elias (1939a), p. 194.
"fear reigned everywhere": Elias (1939a), p. 195.
217 **"I tell you that"**: Elias (1939a), p. 193.

217 **"By my troth":** Elias (1939a), p. 193.
"The fields": quoted in Given (1977), p. 33.
Case 35: Athens (1997), pp. 55–56.
"We should not be led": Pieter Spierenburg in Johnson and Monkkonen (1996), p. 68.

218 **"Violence was the normative":** Esther Cohen in Johnson and Monkkonen (1996), pp. 114–15.
"a society in which": Gurr (1981), p. 307.
"Thus, when people quarreled": Given (1977), p. 189.

218–19 **"So common was violent death":** Hanawalt (1979), p. 99.

219 *"Anne Ashmore":* Raine (1861), pp. 96–97.
"That, about 8 or 9 o'clock": Raine (1861), pp. 185–87.

220 **"in his politic and crafty":** Pitcairn (1833), pp. 473–75.

221 one historian remarks: Given (1977), p. 10.
"during the whole course": Pitcairn (1833), pp. 545–47.

222 **"The readiness of kinsmen":** Given (1977), p. 44.
"On September 25, 1205": Given (1977), p. 50.

223 **"The greatest triumph":** Stone (1965), p. 200.
"progressive shift of": Stone (1983), p. 23.
"The society of what": Elias (1939b), pp. 345–46.
"the precondition for": Elias (1939b), p. 353.

224 **"[Private] violence is only":** Given (1977), p. 200.
"Official justice was there": Soman (1980), pp. 20–21.
"most early modern homicides": Stone (1983), p. 28.
"the spread of education": Soman (1980), p. 21.
"cultural process of": Gurr (1981), p. 343.
"the stress on civility": Stone (1983), p. 29.

225 *The Spectacle of Suffering:* Spierenburg (1984).
"the emergence and stabilization": Spierenburg (1984), p. 10.
"Physical punishment was": Spierenburg (1984), p. 12.
"When medieval rulers": Spierenburg (1984), p. 54.

226 Spierenburg's partial list: Spierenburg (1984), pp. 72–74.
"The idea that the display": Spierenburg (1984), pp. 57–58.

227 **"The nation-state":** Spierenburg (1984), p. 205.

CHAPTER SEVENTEEN: THE HISTORY OF CHILDHOOD

228 **"Dominance is a social":** Athens (1998), p. 675.
"swaying the development": Athens (1998), p. 675.
"The norms that people use": Athens (1998), p. 676.
"the individual type that": Athens (1998), p. 678.

229 **"opposes taking serious":** Athens (1998), pp. 678–79.
"to overcome other": Athens (1998), pp. 679–83.

230 **"Conflict arises":** Athens (1998), pp. 683–84.
"The prevailing norm": Athens (1998), p. 682.
"Whatsoever therefore is consequent": Hobbes (1651), p. 186.

231 **"unpacified islands":** Spierenburg in Johnson and Monkkonen (1996), p. 94.
"war, rapine": Elias (1939b), p. 317.
"easily provoked to violent": Gurr (1981), p. 307.
Footnote: Given (1977), p. 53.

232 **Elias on money economy:** Elias (1939b), pp. 269–70.
"**forced by these**": Elias (1939b), p. 271.
"**[The prince] now possesses**": Elias (1939b), p. 352.
"**legitimated by**": Elias (1939a), p. 53.

233 "**the problem of behavior**": Elias (1939a), p. 73.
Erasmus's cautions: Elias (1939a), pp. 57–58, 130.
"**A wide-eyed look**": Elias (1939a), p. 55.
"**Restraint on the instincts**": Elias (1939a), p. 137.
Footnote: Elias (1939b), p. 480.

234 "**Civilization, and therefore**": Elias (1939b), p. 485.
"**The king succeeded**": quoted in Elias (1939a), p. 48. My emphasis.
"**Unlike the situation**": Elias (1939a), p. 50.

235 "**Family and school**": Ariès (1962), p. 413.

236 "**were unable to depict**": Ariès (1962), p. 10.
"**of over two hundred**": deMause (1974), pp. 40–41.
"**is a nightmare**": deMause (1974), p. 1.

237 "**All of this is not**": deMause (1974), p. 17.
"**When one actually reads**": deMause (1974), pp. 16–17.
"**The exclusive, absolute**": Gibbon (1995), pp. 808–9.

238 "**Medieval Europe believed**": Given (1977), pp. 194–200.

239 "**One thirteenth-century law**": deMause (1974), p. 42.
"**who had complained**": McLaughlin in deMause (1974), p. 131.

240 **Morelli diary:** quoted by James Bruce Ross in deMause (1974), pp. 183, 212.
"**It is only in**": deMause (1974), p. 42.
Jean Héroard diary: Soulié and de Barthélemy (1868).

241 "**The revival of religious**": Marvick in deMause (1974), p. 278.
"**after the gravest**": Hunt (1970), p. 133.
"**Various transgressions**": Hunt (1970), p. 135.

242 "**When he lost**": Hunt (1970), p. 137.
"**I have a complaint**": quoted in Hunt (1970), p. 135.
"**So [the dauphin]**": quoted in Hunt (1970), p. 146.

243 "**The rest of the day**": Hunt (1970), pp. 147–48.
"**When the dauphin**": Hunt (1970), p. 182.
"**Scarcely were his eyes**": quoted in Hunt (1970), p. 156.

244 "**I would rather do**": quoted in deMause (1974), p. 40.
"**he still awoke**": deMause (1974), p. 40.
"**a hunchbacked member**": Hunt (1970), p. 156.
"**As beatings began**": deMause (1974), p. 43.
"**in which the children**": deMause (1974), p. 14.
"**the enormous number**": deMause (1974), p. 49.

245 "**appropriate methods for**": May (1978), p. 151.
"**I, Pierre Rivière**": Foucault (1975), p. 54.
"**I did it to help**": Foucault (1975), p. 24.

246 "**of a very mild**": Foucault (1975), p. 24.
"**the father, very**": Foucault (1975), p. 29.
"**They had no wedding**": Foucault (1975), p. 57.
"**I was living with**": Foucault (1975), p. 61.
"**My uncle was more**": Foucault (1975), pp. 62–63.
"**My [grandmother] was**": Foucault (1975), pp. 66–67.
"**[Throwing out a tenant**": Foucault (1975), p. 74.

247   "**His father did tell**": Foucault (1975), p. 27.
      "**I knew Rivière when**": Foucault (1975), p. 27.
248   "**The child was weeping**": Foucault (1975), pp. 31–32.
      "**a flame that was drawing**": Foucault (1975), p. 32.
      "**I crucified frogs**": Foucault (1975), p. 104.
      "**I loved my father**": Foucault (1975), pp. 104–5.
      "**they were leagued**": Foucault (1975), p. 106.
      "**I conjured up Bonaparte**": Foucault (1975), p. 108.
249   "**I seized the bill**": Foucault (1975), p. 112.
      "**We found three bodies**": Foucault (1975), pp. 3–4.
      "**reduced to a mere**": Foucault (1975), pp. 5–7.
249–50   "**When reminded of his**": Foucault (1975), p. 123.
250   "**no signs of**": Foucault (1975), pp. 123–24.
      "**The basic assumption**": Athens (1997), p. 144.
      "**Since some people**": deMause (1974), p. 51.
      "**Specific childhood experiences**": deMause (1974), p. 3.

CHAPTER EIGHTEEN: PRIMITIVE VIOLENCE

251   "**Both men and women**": quoted in Langness (1981), p. 28.
      Indigenous homicide rates: table 2, Knauft (1987), p. 464.
251–52   "**Even anthropologists living**": Erikson (1950), p. 111.
252   "**stone-age cannibals**": Gajdusek (1978), p. 351.
      Micronesians: Gajdusek (1993), p. 110. Bligh: Zigas (1990), p. 6.
      "**long, relentless**": Gardner and Heider (1968), p. viii.
      Fore and warfare: Sorenson (1976), p. 41.
      "**enemies seem to have been**": Read (1965), p. 35.
253   "**the predominant motives**": Keeley (1996), p. 115.
      Sorcery accusations: Knauft (1987), p. 466.
      "**crushing of genitals**": Gajdusek (1968), p. 158.
      "**characteristic of all**": Langness (1972), p. 172.
      "**In the Bena Bena**": Langness (1972), pp. 173–74.
      "**Although rarely punished**": Langness (1972), p. 174.
254   "**A father early warns**": M. J. Meggit, *The Lineage System of the Mae-Enga of New Guinea* (Edinburgh: Oliver and Boyd, 1965), in Langness (1972), p. 174.
      "**It was considered necessary**": Margaret Mead, *Sex and Temperament in Three Primitive Societies* (New York: William Morrow, 1963), p. 242, quoted in Langness (1981), p. 15.
254–55   **Bena Bena initiation ceremonies**: Langness (1972), pp. 174–75.
255   "**New Guineans . . . are well aware**": Langness (1981), p. 29.
      "**The big men**": Langness (1972), pp. 179–81.
256   "**Their cruelty**": Erikson (1937), pp. 102, 107–8.
      "**To be permitted**": Erikson (1950), pp. 136–37.
257   "**It fell to the older**": Erikson (1950), pp. 143–44.
      "**Dakota children . . . describe**": Erikson (1950), pp. 161–62.
258   "**internal conflict is a good**": Ross (1985), p. 553.
      three variables: Ross (1985), p. 576.
      "**Our evidence is that gross**": Ross (1985), p. 564.
259   "**Most conflict situations**": Ross (1985), p. 564.
259–60   "**The Sioux girl was**": Erikson (1950), p. 144.

260 **"the importance of socialization"**: Knauft (1987), p. 457.
    "is affectionate rather": Knauft (1987), p. 457.
    "The opposite, negatively": Knauft (1987), p. 474.
    "a pattern of social life": Knauft (1987), p. 459.
    "nearly one-third": Knauft (1987), p. 462.
    "More aggressive, outspoken": Knauft (1987), p. 466.
260–61 **"little collective opposition"**: Knauft (1987), p. 462.
261 **"the violence that does"**: Knauft (1987), p. 460.
    Husbands . . . beat wives: Knauft (1987), p. 460, n. 4.
    "Any sign of adult anger": Knauft (1987), p. 475.
    "The exotic, unique": Gajdusek (1963), pp. 84–85.
262 **"We cannot cure their yaws"**: Gajdusek (1980), pp. 126–27.
    "When the world was half": Huizinga (1921), p. 1.

CHAPTER NINETEEN: DRAMATIC SELF-CHANGE

267 **"My own research"**: Johnson (1990), p. 295.
272 **"I still feel like I am hitting"**: LA to Norman K. Denzin, Dec. 17, 1996.
    "stop feeling sorry": Norman Denzin to LA, Jan. 2, 1997.

CHAPTER TWENTY: UNIVERSAL PROCESSES

273 **"The Self as a Soliloquy"**: Athens (1994).
    "Mead recognized": Athens (1994), p. 521.
274 **"The self should be viewed"**: Athens (1994), p. 524.
    Principle one: Athens (1994), p. 524.
    Principle two: Athens (1994), p. 524.
275 **Principle three**: Athens (1994), pp. 524–25.
    Principle four: Athens (1994), p. 525.
    Principle five: Athens (1994), p. 525.
    Principle six: Athens (1994), pp. 525–26.
276 **Principle seven**: Athens (1994), p. 526.
    Principle eight: Athens (1994), pp. 526–27.
    Principle nine: Athens (1994), pp. 527–28.
277 **Principle ten**: Athens (1994), pp. 528–29.
    Principle eleven: Athens (1994), p. 529.
    Principle twelve: Athens (1994), pp. 529–30.
    Principle thirteen: Athens (1994), p. 530.
278 **"soliloquizing is the key"**: Athens (1994), pp. 530–31.
    "Dramatic Self-Change": Athens (1995).
    "changes in the self": Tamotsu Shibutani, *Society and Personality* (Englewood Cliffs, N.J.: Prentice-Hall, 1961), p. 523, quoted in Athens (1995), p. 571.
    "At minimum": Athens (1995), p. 572.
    Stage one: Athens (1995), pp. 573–74.
279 **"Potentially traumatic experiences"**: Athens (1995), p. 584, n. 3.
    Stage two: Athens (1995), pp. 574–76.
280 **Stage three**: Athens (1995), pp. 576–78.
281 **Stage four**: Athens (1995), pp. 578–81.
283 **Stage five**: Athens (1995), pp. 581–82.

283 "the most insulated lives": Athens (1995), pp. 583–84.
284 *Young Man Luther:* Erikson (1958).
   "Luther himself never claimed": Erikson (1958), p. 94.
   "He had felt immediately": Erikson (1958), p. 92.
   "monkery": quoted in Erikson (1958), p. 67.
285 Levinson and Sheehy books: Levinson (1978), Levinson (1996), Sheehy (1984).
   "the gradual removal": Bohr (1958), p. 31.

CHAPTER TWENTY-ONE: THE GATES OF MERCY SHUT UP

286 "War is the business": Marshall (1947), p. 67.
   "a most significant contribution": Marshall Clinard to LA, Feb. 14, 1990, p. 2.
286–87 "Although I never originally": LA to Marshall Clinard, Feb. 21, 1990, p. 2.
288 "[Basic training] is": Dyer (1985), p. 103.
   "process of transformation": Ricks (1997), p. 37.
   "Everything is taken away": quoted in Ricks (1997), p. 43.
   "This is the point": Ricks (1997), p. 57.
   "a boot camp haiku": Ricks (1997), p. 62.
289 "I guess you could say": quoted in Dyer (1985), p. 105.
   "We're going to give": quoted in Dyer (1985), p. 111.
   "There's a love relationship": quoted in Dyer (1985), p. 104.
   "a tremendous volume": Grossman (1995), p. 149.
   "mutual surveillance": quoted in Grossman (1995), p. 150.
   "When they tell you": quoted in Ricks (1997), p. 222.
   "Just think of how": quoted in Dyer (1985), p. 102.
290 "The kids I trained": quoted in Ricks (1997), p. 50.
   "You want to rip": quoted in Dyer (1985), p. 121.
   "combat hitting skills": Ricks (1997), p. 75.
   "The pugil sticks themselves": Ricks (1997), p. 81.
   "are matched up": Dyer (1985), p. 120.
   "On the plane ride": Ricks (1997), p. 232.
   "Is surprised at how": Ricks (1997), p. 231.
291 "a black recruit": Ricks (1997), pp. 69, 235.
   "at night, Staff Sergeant": Ricks (1997), p. 242.
   "We found that on": Marshall (1947), p. 54.
   Battle experience no improvement: Marshall (1947), p. 57.
292 Marshall's infantry manual defense: Marshall (1947), p. 10.
   "A 1986 study": Grossman (1995), p. 16.
   "Of these, nearly 90": Grossman (1995), pp. 21–22.
   "possibly even mimicking": Grossman (1995), pp. 21–22.
   "Men working in groups": Marshall (1947), pp. 75–76.
293 "They were not malingerers": Marshall (1947), p. 59.
   "a result of a paralysis": Marshall (1947), p. 71.
   "The average, normal man": Marshall (1947), p. 78.
   "They found that fear": Marshall (1947), pp. 78–79. My emphasis.
294 Marshall Korean War investigation: Marshall (1947), p. 9.
   Vietnam firing rate: Grossman (1995), p. 35.
   "posturing": Grossman (1995), p. 181.
   "Ardant du Picq": Grossman (1995), pp. 9–12.
294–95 "Some of the most gallant": Marshall (1947), pp. 60–61.

295 "That the average man": Grossman (1995), pp. 30–31.
296 "We live among millions": quoted in Grossman (1995), p. 181.
   "will soon physically": Athens (1997), pp. 33–34.
   "is that the victim": Athens (1997), p. 34.
297 "the ruins of character": Shay (1994), p. 169.
297–98 "More than 40 percent": Shay (1994), p. 98.
298 "The specific content of": Shay (1994), p. 5.
   "Veterans can usually": Shay (1994), p. 20.
   "Walking point was an extremely": quoted in Shay (1994), p. 11.
   "indignant rage": Shay (1994), p. 12.
   "the mortal dependence": Shay (1994), p. 5.
298–99 "The vulnerable relationship": Shay (1994), p. 32.
299 "The U.S. Army": quoted in Shay (1994), p. 5.
   "My personal weapon": quoted in Shay (1994), p. 17.
   "The first deaths in": quoted in Shay (1994), p. 19.
   " 'Don't get sad' ": Shay (1994), p. 81.
300 "My clinical experience": Shay (1994), p. 98.
   "manic obsession": Shay (1994), p. 89.
   "[After my closest buddy": quoted in Shay (1994), p. 96.
   "After [my buddy] died": quoted in Shay (1994), p. 96.
   "[When an NVA": quoted in Shay (1994), pp. 78–79.
301 "I became a fucking": quoted in Shay (1994), p. 83.
   "Beastlike; godlike": Shay (1994), p. 82.
   "Betrayal of 'what's right' ": Shay (1994), p. 96.
302 "We were abused": Bilton and Sim (1992), pp. 70–71.
303 Calley admitted carelessness: Bilton and Sim (1992), p. 72.
   "When we first started": quoted in Bilton and Sim (1992), p. 74.
   "The voices of authority": quoted in Bilton and Sim (1992), pp. 76–77.
304 "It started with": Bilton and Sim (1992), p. 78.
   "Medina's dislike": Bilton and Sim (1992), p. 79.
   Old farmer incident: Bilton and Sim (1992), p. 79.
   "Rape?": quoted in Bilton and Sim (1992), p. 81.
   "a group within": Bilton and Sim (1992), p. 81.
   "The more successful": Athens (1992), p. 71.
   "I think if it ever": quoted in Bilton and Sim (1992), p. 80.
305 "reveling in thoughts": Athens (1992), p. 76.
   "came under heavy": Bilton and Sim (1992), p. 86.
   "Everybody was shaken": Bilton and Sim (1992), p. 85.
   "should resort to": Athens (1992), p. 69.
   "The idea that the villagers": Bilton and Sim (1992), p. 85.
306 "One of our platoons": quoted in Bilton and Sim (1992), p. 93.
   "[Medina] didn't actually say": quoted in Bilton and Sim (1992), p. 101.
   "We started to move": quoted in Bilton and Sim (1992), p. 114.
306–7 Dennis Conti episode: Bilton and Sim (1992), pp. 119–21.
307 "Neither eating, drinking": Elias (1939a), p. 193.
   "The greatest joy": Prawdin (1940), p. 143.
   "Several [men] became": Bilton and Sim (1992), p. 128.
308 "I didn't care whether": quoted in Alford (1997), p. 28.
   "Many Vietnam veterans": Shay (1994), pp. 84–85.
   "All of our virtues come": Shay (1994), p. 86.

308 "With this last development": Athens (1992), pp. 75–76.
     "I was eighteen years old": quoted in Shay (1994), pp. 32–33, 95.
310 "I never tried to": quoted in Shay (1994), pp. xvi–xvii.
     " 'I died in Vietnam' ": Shay (1994), pp. 51–52.
     "I think I don't have": quoted in Shay (1994), p. xvi.
311 "conversed regularly with a": Shay (1994), p. 51.
     "permanent state of": Athens (1995), p. 578.
     "I haven't really": quoted in Shay (1994), pp. xiv–xvi.
312 "These are the voices": Shay (1994), p. xix.
     "The character damage of": Shay (1994), p. 20.
     "the natural dominance": Gault (1971), p. 451.
     "If war goals": Shay (1994), p. 197.
     "tacitly becomes an": Athens (1992), p. 6.

CHAPTER TWENTY-TWO:
STRATEGIES OF PREVENTION AND CONTROL

313 "general prevention": Athens (1997), p. 155.
     "Although the community": Athens (1997), p. 156.
314 "how to fulfill": Athens (1997), p. 155.
     "a broad-based": Athens (1997), p. 156.
315 "The focal point": Greven (1991), p. 65.
     "breaking the will": Greven (1991), p. 69.
     "If the punishment": quoted in Greven (1991), p. 71.
     "The rod is to be": quoted in Greven (1991), p. 75.
     "Making stripes": quoted in Greven (1991), p. 80.
     "Crying quickly changes": quoted in Greven (1991), p. 78.
     "if the child repeatedly": quoted in Greven (1991), p. 77.
316 "Vaden said": quoted in Greven (1991), p. 26.
     "Since violent people": Athens (1997), p. 157.
316–17 "The mere entrance": Athens (1992), pp. 80–81.
317 "and consequently the entire": Athens (1992), p. 81.
     "outside the reach": Athens (1992), p. 157.
     "The predatory violent": Athens (1992), pp. 157–58.
318 "The telltale sign": Athens (1992), p. 158.
     "People are more likely": Athens (1992), p. 159.
319–20 Wilson on black male homicide rates: Wilson (1997), p. 40.
320 Public health improvements: cf. White and Preston (1996).
321 *H. pylori:* cf. National Institutes of Health (1994); Blaser (1996).

Bibliography

Acocella, Joan. 1998. "The Politics of Hysteria." *The New Yorker,* April 6, 64–79.

Alford, C. Fred. 1997. *What Evil Means to Us.* Ithaca, N.Y.: Cornell University Press.

Anderson, Elijah. 1990. *Streetwise: Race, Class, and Change in an Urban Community.* Chicago: University of Chicago Press.

Archer, Dane, and Rosemary Gartner. 1976. "Violent Acts and Violent Times: A Comparative Approach to Postwar Homicide Rates." *American Sociological Review* 41 (6): 937–63.

Ariès, Philippe. 1962. *Centuries of Childhood.* New York: Vintage.

Athens, Lonnie. 1974. "The Self and the Violent Criminal Act." *Urban Life and Culture* 3 (1): 98–112.

———. 1975. "Differences in the Liberal-Conservative Political Attitudes of Prison Guards and Felons: Status versus Race." *International Journal of Group Tensions* 5 (3): 143–55.

———. 1992. *The Creation of Dangerous Violent Criminals.* Urbana: University of Illinois Press.

———. 1994. "The Self as a Soliloquy." *Sociological Quarterly* 35 (3): 521–32.

———. 1995. "Dramatic Self-Change." *Sociological Quarterly* 36 (3): 571–86.

———. 1997. *Violent Criminal Acts and Actors Revisited.* Urbana: University of Illinois Press.

———. 1998. "Dominance, Ghettos and Violent Crime." *Sociological Quarterly* 39 (4): 673–91.

Aubrey, John. 1680 (1972). *Brief Lives.* Woodbridge, England: Boydell Press.

Baldwin, James Mark. 1895. *Mental Development in the Child and the Race.* New York: Macmillan.

Banay, Ralph. 1952. "Study in Murder." *Annals of the American Academy of Political and Social Sciences* 284: 26–34.

Beattie, J. M. 1974. "The Pattern of Crime in England 1660–1800." *Past and Present* (62): 47-95.

Becker, Howard. 1963. *Outsiders: Studies in the Sociology of Deviance.* New York: Free Press.

Beveridge, W. I. 1957. *The Art of Scientific Investigation.* New York: Vintage.

Bilton, Michael, and Kevin Sim. 1992. *Four Hours in My Lai.* New York: Viking.

Blaser, Martin J. 1996. "The Bacteria Behind Ulcers." *Scientific American Online.*

Bloch, Marc. 1940 (1961). *Feudal Society.* Translated by L. A. Manyon. Chicago: University of Chicago Press.

Blumer, Herbert. 1969. *Symbolic Interactionism: Perspective and Method.* Berkeley: University of California Press.

———. 1978. "Social Unrest and Collective Protest." *Studies in Symbolic Interaction* 1: 1–54.

———. 1981. "George Herbert Mead." In *The Future of the Sociological Classics,* edited by B. Rhea. London: George Allen & Unwin.

Bohr, Niels. 1958. *Atomic Physics and Human Knowledge.* New York: John Wiley.

Brothers, Leslie. 1997. *Friday's Footprint.* New York: Oxford University Press.

Brown, Keith M. 1986. *Bloodfeud in Scotland 1573–1625.* Edinburgh: John Donald Publishers.

Bruce, Vicki. 1988. *Recognizing Faces.* East Sussex, Eng.: Lawrence Erlbaum.

Butterfield, Fox. 1996. *All God's Children: The Bosket Family and the American Tradition of Violence.* New York: Avon Books.

———. 1997a. "Report Links Crime to States with Weak Gun Control." *New York Times,* April 9.

———. 1997b. "Crime Keeps On Falling, but Prisons Keep On Filling." *New York Times,* September 28.

———. 1997c. "Drop in Homicide Rate Linked to Crack's Decline." *New York Times,* October 27.

Capote, Truman. 1965. *In Cold Blood: A True Account of a Multiple Murder and Its Consequences.* New York: Modern Library.

Christie, Nils. 1997. "Four Blocks Against Insight: Notes on the Oversocialization of Criminologists." *Theoretical Criminology* 1 (1): 13–23.

Cicourel, Aaron V. 1964. *Method and Measurement in Sociology.* New York: Free Press.

Cleckley, Hervey. 1982. *The Mask of Sanity.* Rev. ed. New York: New American Library.

Clinard, Marshall B. 1966. "The Sociologist's Quest for Respectability." *Sociological Quarterly* (Fall): 399–412.

Cockburn, J. S. 1991. "Patterns of Violence in English Society: Homicide in Kent, 1560–1985." *Past and Present* 130: 70–106.

Comer, James P. 1988. "Educating Poor Minority Children." *Scientific American,* November, 42.

Cook, Gary A. 1993. *George Herbert Mead: The Making of a Social Pragmatist.* Urbana: University of Illinois Press.

Crane, Cheryl, with Cliff Jahr. 1988. *Detour: A Hollywood Story.* New York: Arbor House / William Morrow.

Currie, Elliott. 1998. *Crime and Punishment in America.* New York: Henry Holt.

Davison, Jean. 1983. *Oswald's Game.* New York: W. W. Norton.

deMause, Lloyd, ed. 1974. *The History of Childhood.* Northvale, N.J.: Jason Aronson.

———. 1980. "Our Forebears Made Childhood a Nightmare." In *Traumatic Abuse and Neglect of Children at Home,* edited by G. J. Williams and John Money. Baltimore: Johns Hopkins University Press.

Dewey, John. 1948. *Reconstruction in Philosophy.* Enlarged ed. Boston: Beacon Press.

———. 1985. "George Herbert Mead as I Knew Him." In *John Dewey: The Later Works, 1925–1953,* edited by J. A. Boydston. Carbondale: Southern Illinois University Press.

Douglas, John, and Mark Olshaker. 1995. *Mind Hunter: Inside the FBI's Elite Serial Crime Unit.* New York: Scribner.

Dyer, Gwynne. 1985. *War.* New York: Crown.

Easson, William M., and Richard M. Steinhilber. 1961. "Murderous Aggression by Children and Adolescents." *Archives of General Psychiatry* 4: 27/1–35/9.

East, Norwood. 1951. *Society and Its Criminals.* London: Blakiston's Sons & Co.

Elias, Norbert. 1939a (1978). *The History of Manners.* Translated by Edmund Jephcott. New York: Pantheon.

———. 1939b (1994). *The Civilizing Process.* Translated by Edmund Jephcott. Oxford: Blackwell.

Erikson, Erik Homburger. 1950. *Childhood and Society.* New York: W. W. Norton.

———. 1958. *Young Man Luther: A Study in Psychoanalysis and History.* New York: W. W. Norton.

———. 1973. "Observations on Sioux Education." *Journal of Psychology* 7: 101–56.

Fenton, James. 1998. "How Great Art Was Made." *New York Review of Books Online.*

Fine, Gary Alan, ed. 1995. *A Second Chicago School? The Development of a Postwar American Sociology.* Chicago: University of Chicago Press.

Fleming, Donald. 1967. "Attitude: The History of a Concept." *Perspectives in American History* 1: 287–365.

Foucault, Michel, ed. 1975. *I, Pierre Riviere, Having Slaughtered My Mother, My Sister, and My Brother . . . : A Case of Parricide in the 19th Century.* Lincoln: University of Nebraska Press.

Gajdusek, D. Carleton. 1963. "The Composition of Musics for Man, or Decoding from Primitive Cultures the Scores for Human Behavior." *Pediatrics* 31 (1): 84–91.

———. 1968. *New Guinea Journal, 2.x.61–4.vii.62, Part 1.* Bethesda, Md.: National Institutes of Health (NIH).

———. 1978. "Micronesians Adapt Easily to Change." *Ekistics* 272 (Sept.): 350–51.

———. 1980. *Journal of Further Explorations in the Kuru Region and in the Kukukuku Country, Eastern Highlands of Eastern New Guinea, and of a Return to West Guinea, 25.xii.63–4.v.64.* Bethesda, Md.: National Institutes of Health (NIH).

———. 1993. *Melanesian and Micronesian Journal: Return Expeditions to the New Hebrides, Caroline Islands and New Guinea, 29.vii.65–20.xii.65.* Bethesda, Md.: National Institutes of Health (NIH).

Gardner, Robert, and Karl G. Heider. 1968. *Gardens of War: Life and Death in the New Guinea Stone Age.* New York: Random House.

Gault, William Barry. 1971. "Some Remarks on Slaughter." *American Journal of Psychiatry* 128 (4): 450–54.

Gibbon, Edward. 1788 (1994). *The History of the Decline and Fall of the Roman Empire.* Vol. 2. London: Penguin.

Gillies, Hunter. 1976. "Homicide in the West of Scotland." *British Journal of Psychiatry* 128: 105–27.

Given, James Buchanan. 1977. *Society and Homicide in Thirteenth-Century England.* Stanford, Calif.: Stanford University Press.

Goffman, Erving. 1967. *Interaction Ritual: Essays on Face-to-Face Behavior.* New York: Doubleday.

Gold, Martin. 1957–58. "Suicide, Homicide and the Socialization of Aggression." *American Journal of Sociology* 63: 651–61.

Goldstein, Abraham S. 1967. *The Insanity Defense.* New Haven: Yale University Press.

Goldstein, Abraham S., and Joseph Goldstein, eds. 1971. *Crime, Law, and Society: Readings.* New York: Free Press.

Gough, Harrison G. 1948. "A Sociological Theory of Psychopathy." *American Journal of Sociology* 53: 359–66.

Greven, Philip. 1991. *Spare the Child.* New York: Alfred A. Knopf.

Grossman, Dave. 1995. *On Killing: The Psychological Cost of Learning to Kill in War and Society.* Boston: Little, Brown.

Gurnick, Ken. 1998. "A Relaxed Tyson Sets His Return to the Ring." *New York Times,* December 9.

Gurr, Ted Robert. 1981. "Historical Trends in Violent Crimes: A Critical Review of the Evidence." In *Crime and Justice: An Annual Review of Research,* edited by M. Tonry and Norval Morris. Chicago: University of Chicago Press.

Hagstrom, Warren Olaf. N.d. "Social Control in Modern Science." Ph.D. dissertation, University of California, Berkeley.

Hammersley, Martyn. 1989. *The Dilemma of Qualitative Method: Herbert Blumer and the Chicago Tradition.* London: Routledge.

Hannawalt, Barbara A. 1979. *Crime and Conflict in English Communities, 1300–1348.* Cambridge, Mass.: Harvard University Press.

Hartung, Frank E. 1966. *Crime, Law and Society.* Detroit: Wayne State University Press.

Helfer, Ray, and Ruth S. Kempe, eds. 1987. *The Battered Child.* 4th ed. Chicago: University of Chicago Press.

Heller, Peter. 1995. *Bad Intentions: The Mike Tyson Story.* Rev. ed. New York: Da Capo Press.

Herbert, Bob. 1997. "Connect the Dots." *New York Times,* August 24.

Herlihy, David. 1972. "Some Psychological and Social Roots of Violence in the Tuscan Cities." In *Violence and Civil Disorder in Italian Cities 1200–1500,* edited by L. Martines. Berkeley: University of California Press.

Hobbes, Thomas. 1651 (1968). *Leviathan.* London: Penguin.

Horowitz, Craig. 1997. "Show of Force." *New York,* September 27, 28–37.

Huizinga, Johan. 1921 (1996). *The Autumn of the Middle Ages.* Translated by Payton, Rodney J., and Ulrich Mammitzsch. Chicago: University of Chicago Press.

Hunt, David. 1970. *Parents and Children in History.* New York: Basic Books.

James, William. 1890, 1918. *The Principles of Psychology.* 2 vols. New York: Dover.

Jenkins, Philip. 1994. *Using Murder: The Social Construction of Serial Homicide.* New York: Aldine de Gruyter.

Joas, Hans. 1980. *G. H. Mead: A Contemporary Re-examination of His Thought.* Cambridge, Eng.: Polity Press.

Johnson, Eric A., and Eric H. Monkkonen, ed. 1996. *The Civilization of Crime: Violence in Town & Country Since the Middle Ages.* Urbana: University of Illinois Press.

Johnson, John M. 1990. Review *(The Creation of Dangerous Violent Criminals). Symbolic Interaction* 13 (2): 293–95.

Keeley, Lawrence H. 1996. *War Before Civilization.* New York: Oxford University Press.

Kempe, Ruth S., and C. Henry Kempe. 1978. *Child Abuse.* Cambridge, Mass.: Harvard University Press.

Knauft, Bruce M. 1985. *Good Company and Violence: Sorcery and Social Action in a Lowland New Guinea Society.* Berkeley: University of California Press.

———. 1987. "Reconsidering Violence in Simple Human Societies." *Current Anthropology* 28 (4): 457–500.

Langness, L. L. 1972. "Violence in the New Guinea Highlands." In *Collective Violence,* edited by James F. Short, Jr., and Marvin Wolfgang. Chicago: Aldine Atherton.

———. 1981. "Child Abuse and Cultural Values: The Case of New Guinea." In *Child Abuse and Neglect: Cross-Cultural Perspectives,* edited by J. E. Korbin. Berkeley: University of California Press.

Lawson, F. H., ed. 1969. *The Roman Law Reader.* Dobbs Ferry, N.Y.: Oceana Publications.

Lester, David, and Gene Lester. 1975. *Crime of Passion: Murder and Murderer.* Chicago: Nelson-Hall.

Levinson, Daniel J. 1978. *The Seasons of a Man's Life.* New York: Ballantine.

———. 1996. *The Seasons of a Woman's Life.* New York: Alfred A. Knopf.

Lewin, Tamar. 1995. "Parents' Poll Shows Child Abuse to Be More Common." *New York Times,* December 7.

Lewis, Dorothy Otnow. 1998. *Guilty by Reason of Insanity: A Psychiatrist Explores the Minds of Killers.* New York: Fawcett Columbine.

Lewis, Dorothy O., Ernest Moy et al. 1985. "Biopsychosocial Characteristics of Children Who Later Murder: A Prospective Study." *American Journal of Psychiatry* 142 (10): 1161–67.

Lewis, Dorothy O., Jonathan H. Pincus et al. 1988. "Neuropsychiatric, Psychoeducational and Family Characteristics of 14 Juveniles Condemned to Death in the United States." *American Journal of Psychiatry* 145 (5): 584–89.

Lewis, Dorothy O., Shelly S. Shanock, Jonathan H. Pincus, and Glibert H. Glaser. 1979. "Violent Juvenile Delinquents: Psychiatric, Neurological, Psychological and Abuse Factors." *Journal of the American Academy of Child Psychiatry* 2 (Spring): 307–19.

Lindesmith, Alfred R. 1957. *Opiate Addiction.* Evanston: Principia Press of Illinois.

———. 1981. "Symbolic Interactionism and Causality." *Symbolic Interaction* 4 (1): 87–96.

MacDowell, Douglas M. 1963. *Athenian Homicide Law in the Age of the Orators.* Manchester, Eng.: Manchester University Press.

Marder, T. A. 1997. *Bernini's Scala Regia at the Vatican Palace.* Cambridge, Eng.: Cambridge University Press.

Marshall, S. L. A. 1947 (1978). *Men Against Fire: The Problem of Battle Command in Future War.* Gloucester, Mass.: Peter Smith.

Matthews, Fred H. 1977. *Quest for an American Sociology: Robert E. Park and the Chicago School.* Montreal: McGill–Queen's University Press.

Matza, David. 1969. *Becoming Deviant.* Englewood Cliffs, N.J.: Prentice-Hall.

May, Margaret. 1978. "Violence in the Family: An Historical Perspective." In *Violence and the Family,* edited by J. P. Martin. New York: John Wiley & Sons.

McCord, Joan. 1979. "Some Child-rearing Antecedents of Criminal Behavior in Adult Men." *Journal of Personality and Social Psychology* 37 (9): 1477–86.

McKinney, J. C. 1966. *Constructive Typology and Social Theory.* New York: Appleton-Century-Crofts.

McMillan, Priscilla Johnson. 1977. *Marina and Lee.* New York: Harper & Row.

Mead, George Herbert. 1922. "A Behavioristic Account of Psychology and the Significant Symbol." *Journal of Philosophy* 19: 157–63.

———. 1934. *Mind, Self and Society.* Chicago: University of Chicago Press.

———. 1936. *Movements of Thought in the Nineteenth Century.* Chicago: University of Chicago Press.

———. 1964. *Selected Writings.* New York: Bobbs-Merrill.

Mitchell, G. Duncan. 1968. *A Hundred Years of Sociology.* Chicago: Aldine.

Morbidity and Mortality Weekly Report. 1998. "Suicide among Black Youths—United States, 1980–1995." *Morbidity and Mortality Weekly Report* 47 (10): 193–96.

N.a. 1997. "Biologists Cut Reductionist Approach Down to Size." *Science* 227 (July 25): 476.

National Institutes of Health Consensus Development Conference. 1994. "*Helicobacter pylori* in Peptic Ulcer Disease—Interim Draft Statement." *NIH Consens Statement Online* 12 (1): 1–23.

New York Times. 1994. "Murderer Put to Death in Virginia." April 28.

New York Times. 1997. "In 90's, Prison Building by States and U.S. Government Surged." August 8.

Osterberg, Eva. 1983. "Violence among Peasants: Comparative Perspectives on Sixteenth- and Seventeenth-century Sweden." In *Europe and Scandinavia: Aspects of the Process of Integration in the 17th Century*, edited by G. Rystad. Lund, Sweden: Esselte Studium.

Oswald, Robert L. 1967. *Lee: A Portrait of Lee Harvey Oswald by His Brother*. New York: Coward-McCann.

Panzram, Carl. 1996. "Autobiography." In *Lustmord: The Writings and Artifacts of Murderers*, edited by B. King. Burbank, Calif.: Bloat.

Park, Robert E., and Ernest W. Burgess. 1921. *Introduction to the Science of Sociology*. Chicago: University of Chicago Press.

Payne, George Henry. 1916. *The Child in Human Progress*. New York: G. P. Putnam's Sons.

Pfuetze, Paul E. 1954. *Self, Society, Existence*. New York: Harper Torchbook.

Philips, Derek L. 1971. *Knowledge from What?* Chicago: Rand McNally.

Pitcairn, Robert. 1833. *Ancient Criminal Trials in Scotland*. Vol. 3, part 2. Edinburgh: Bannatyne Club.

Polanyi, Michael. 1958, 1962. *Personal Knowledge*. New York: Harper Torchbook.

Posner, Gerald. 1993. *Case Closed: Lee Harvey Oswald and the Assassination of JFK*. New York: Random House.

Prawdin, Michael. 1940. *The Mongol Empire: Its Rise and Legacy*. New York: Free Press.

Raine, James, ed. 1861. *Depositions From the Castle of York*. Vol. 40, *The Publications of the Surtees Society*. London: Surtees Society.

Raushenbush, Winifred. 1979. *Robert E. Park: Biography of a Sociologist*. Durham, N.C.: Duke University Press.

Read, Kenneth E. 1954–1955. "Morality and the Concept of the Person among the Gahuku-Gama, Eastern Highlands, New Guinea." *Oceania* 25 (1–2): 233–82.

———. 1965. *The High Valley*. London: George Allen and Unwin.

Reuters. 1998. "Tapes Raise New Doubts about 'Sybil' Personalities." *New York Times*, August 19.

Rhodes, Ginger, and Richard Rhodes. 1996. *Trying to Get Some Dignity: Stories of Triumph over Childhood Abuse*. New York: William Morrow.

Rhodes, Richard. 1980. *The Last Safari*. Garden City, N.Y.: Doubleday.

———. 1990. *A Hole in the World: An American Boyhood*. New York: Simon & Schuster.

Ricks, Thomas E. 1997. *Making the Corps*. New York: Scribner's.

Roper, Marilyn Keyes. 1969. "A Survey of the Evidence for Intrahuman Killing in the Pleistocene." *Current Anthropology* 10 (4): 427–59.

Ross, Marc Howard. 1985. "Internal and External Conflict and Violence." *Journal of Conflict Resolution* 29 (4): 547–79.

———. 1986. "A Cross-cultural Theory of Political Conflict and Violence." *Political Psychology* 7 (3): 427–69.

Sampson, Robert J., Stephen W. Raudenbush, and Felton Earls. 1997. "Neighborhoods and Violent Crime: A Multilevel Study of Collective Efficacy." *Science* 277 (15): 918–24.

Satten, Joseph, Karl Menninger, Irwin Rosen, and Martin Mayman. 1960. "Murder without Apparent Motive: A Study in Personality Disorganization." *American Journal of Psychiatry* (July): 48–53.

Schouten, Ronald. 1998. "Independent Medical Evaluation of Michael Gerard Tyson for the Nevada State Athletic Commission." Boston: Massachusetts General Hospital.

Schutz, Alfred. 1954. "Concept and Theory Formation in the Social Sciences." *Journal of Philosophy* 51 (9): 257.

Sendi, Ismail B., and Paul G. Blomgren. 1975. "A Comparative Study of Predictive Criteria in the Predisposition of Homicidal Adolescents." *American Journal of Psychiatry* 132 (4): 423–27.

Shalit, Ben. 1988. *The Psychology of Conflict and Combat.* New York: Praeger.

Sharpe, J. A. 1985. "The History of Violence in England: Some Observations." *Past and Present* (108): 206–24.

Shay, Jonathan. 1994. *Achilles in Vietnam: Combat Trauma and the Undoing of Character.* New York: Atheneum.

Sheehy, Gail. 1984. *Passages.* New York: Bantam.

Simon, Linda. 1998. *Genuine Reality: A Life of William James.* New York: Harcourt Brace.

Smith, Timothy W. 1998a. "With a Warning, Nevada Lets Tyson Return to Boxing." *New York Times,* October 20.

———. 1998b. "Will Vargas Be Up to the Challenge?" *New York Times,* December 11.

Soman, Alfred. 1980. "Deviance and Criminal Justice in Western Europe, 1300–1800." *Criminal Justice History* 1: 1–28.

Sorenson, E. Richard. 1976. *The Edge of the Forest: Land, Childhood and Change in a New Guinea Protoagricultural Society.* Washington, D.C.: Smithsonian Institution Press.

Soulié, E., and E. de Barthélemy, eds. 1868. *Journal de Jean Héroard sur l'Enfance et la Jeunesse de Louis XIII.* Paris.

Spierenburg, Pieter. 1984. *The Spectacle of Suffering.* Cambridge, Eng.: Cambridge University Press.

Stafford, Jean. 1966. *A Mother in History.* New York: Farrar, Straus & Giroux.

Stone, Lawrence. 1965. *The Crisis of the Aristocracy 1558–1641.* New York: Oxford University Press.

———. 1983. "Interpersonal Violence in English Society 1300–1980." *Past and Present* (101): 22–33.

———. 1985. "A Rejoinder." *Past and Present* (108): 216–24.

Swanson, Guy E. 1991. "The Powers and Capabilities of Selves: Social and Collective Approaches." In *Philosophy, Social Theory, and the Thought of George Herbert Mead,* edited by M. Aboulafia. Albany: State University of New York Press.

Tanay, Emanuel. 1972. "Psychiatric Aspects of Homicide Prevention." *American Journal of Psychiatry* 128: 49–52.

Turner, Jonathan H., Leonard Beeghley, and Charles H. Powers. 1981, 1989. *The Emergence of Sociological Theory.* 2nd ed. Chicago: Dorsey Press.

Turner, Ralph. 1953. "The Quest for Universals in Sociological Research." *American Sociological Review* 16 (6): 604–11.

Warren Commission. 1964. *Hearings Before the President's Commission on the Assassination of President Kennedy.* 23 vols. Washington, D.C.: USGPO.

———. 1964. *Report of the Warren Commission on the Assassination of President Kennedy.* New York: McGraw-Hill.

Watson, Alan. 1970. *The Law of the Ancient Romans.* Dallas: Southern Methodist University Press.

Weller, Sheila. 1997. "The Making of a Serial Rapist." *New York,* November 3, 28–35.

———. 1997. *Saint of Circumstance.* New York: Pocket Books.

White, Kevin M., and Samuel H. Preston. 1996. "How Many Americans Are Alive Because of Twentieth-century Improvements in Mortality?" *Population and Development Review* 22 (3): 415–28.

Wiley, Norbert. 1986. "Early American Sociology and *The Polish Peasant.*" *Sociological Theory* 4 (Spring): 20–40.

Williams, Gertrude J., and John Money, ed. 1980. *Traumatic Abuse and Neglect of Children at Home.* Baltimore: Johns Hopkins University Press.

Wilson, James Q. 1997. "Hostility in America [Review of Franklin E. Zimring and Gordon Hawkins, *Crime Is Not the Problem: Lethal Violence in America,* Oxford University Press, 1997]." *New Republic,* August 25, 38–41.

Wilson, James Q., and Richard J. Herrnstein. 1985. *Crime and Human Nature.* New York: Simon & Schuster.

Wolfgang, Marvin. 1957. "Victim-precipitated Criminal Homicide." *Journal of Criminal Law, Criminology and Police Science* 48: 1–11.

———. 1958. *Patterns of Criminal Homicide.* Philadelphia: University of Pennsylvania Press.

———. 1969. "Who Kills Whom." *Psychology Today,* May, 54–56, 72, 74–75.

Wolfgang, Marvin, and Franco Ferracuti. 1967a. *The Subculture of Violence: Towards an Integrated Theory in Criminology.* London: Tavistock.

———. 1967b. "Subculture of Violence—A Social Psychological Theory." In *Studies in Homicide,* edited by M. Wolfgang. New York: Harper & Row.

Wong, M., and K. Singer. 1973. "Abnormal Homicide in Hong Kong." *British Journal of Psychiatry* 123: 295–98.

Wundt, Wilhelm. 1897 (1969). *Outlines of Psychology.* Translated by Charles Hubbard Judd. Leipzig: Wilhelm Engelmann.

———. 1973. *The Language of Gestures.* The Hague: Mouton.

Zigas, Vincent. 1990. *Laughing Death: The Untold Story of Kuru.* Clifton, N.J.: Humana Press.

Zimring, Franklin E., and Gordon Hawkins. 1997. *Crime Is Not the Problem: Lethal Violence in America.* New York: Oxford University Press.

Acknowledgments

After he recovered from the surprise of my descending on him, Lonnie Athens generously opened up his life and work to me in discussions, phone conversations, letters, e-mail and long days of sometimes painful interviewing. He guided me around Richmond, loaned me books, argued with me and answered my questions. He is indeed a Greek warrior. Any errors of biographical or technical omission or commission in this book are mine.

William Davenport, Warren Von Schuch, Elizabeth Bernhard and Father Constantine Dombalis graciously consented to interviews and made documents available. So did Stanley and Phyllis Rosenbluth, to whom I apologize for not including the story of the murders of their son and daughter-in-law, Richard and Rebecca Rosenbluth. They contributed significantly nonetheless by showing me the widening circle of lifelong suffering that violent crime leaves in its wake.

Jonathan Segal, my editor, and Sonny Mehta welcomed me to Knopf. Morton L. Janklow and Anne Sibbald ably represented me. I benefited from conversations with Maureen and Jennifer Athens, Dave Grossman, Priscilla Johnson McMillan, Eric Markusen and Edward O. Wilson. The Sterling Memorial Library at Yale and the Yale Medical Library were invaluable resources.

Ginger, my wife, flew us to Richmond, managed travel and interviews (which Helen Haversat skillfully transcribed), shared her own experience of murder and loss, read and debated and advised. Although an intimate member of my phantom community, she is never a phantom companion.

Index

Scribner: Excerpts from *Achilles in Vietnam* by Jonathan Shay, copyright © 1994 by Jonathan Shay. Reprinted by permission of Scribner, a division of Simon & Schuster.

Scribner and William Morris Agency, Inc.: Excerpts from *Making the Corps* by Thomas E. Ricks, copyright © 1997 by Thomas E. Ricks. Reprinted by permission of Scribner, a division of Simon & Schuster, and William Morris Agency, Inc., on behalf of the author.

Peter Smith Publisher, Inc.: Excerpts from *Men Against Fire* by S. L. Marshall (Gloucester, Mass.: Peter Smith Publisher, Inc., 1978). Reprinted by permission of Peter Smith Publisher, Inc.

Stanford University Press: Excerpts from *Society and Homicide in Thirteenth-Century England* by James Buchanan Given, copyright © 1977 by Stanford University Press. Reprinted by permission of Stanford University Press.

Sterling Lord Literistic, Inc.: Excerpts from *Lee: A Portrait of Lee Harvey Oswald by His Brother* by Barbara Land (New York: Coward-McCann), copyright © 1967 by Barbara Land. Reprinted by permission of Sterling Lord Literistic, Inc.

Lawrence Stone: Excerpts from "Interpersonal Violence in English Society, 1300–1800" by Lawrence Stone from *Past and Present*, copyright © 1983 by Lawrence Stone. Reprinted by permission of Lawrence Stone.

University of California Press Journals and Lonnie Athens: Excerpts from "The Self as Soliloquy" by Lonnie Athens (*The Sociological Quarterly*, 35/3, pp. 521–532), copyright © 1994 by The Midwest Sociological Society; excerpts from "Dramatic Self Change" by Lonnie Athens (*The Sociological Quarterly*, 36/3, pp. 571–586), copyright © 1995 by The Midwest Sociological Society; excerpts from "Dominance, Ghettos, and Violent Crime" by Lonnie Athens (*The Sociological Quarterly*, 39/4, pp. 673–691), copyright © 1998 by The Midwest Sociological Society. Reprinted by permission of University of California Press Journals and Lonnie Athens.

The University of Chicago Press and Bruce Knauft: Excerpts from "Reconsidering Violence in Simple Human Societies" by Bruce Knauft (*Current Anthropology*, 28:4, 1987, pp. 457–500), copyright © 1987 by The University of Chicago Press. Reprinted by permission of The University of Chicago Press and Bruce Knauft.

University of Illinois Press and Lonnie H. Athens: Excerpts from *The Creation of Dangerous Violent Criminals* by Lonnie H. Athens, copyright © 1992 by the Board of Trustees of the University of Illinois; excerpts from *Violent Criminal Acts and Actors Revisited* by Lonnie H. Athens, copyright © 1997 by the Board of Trustees of the University of Illinois. Reprinted by permission of the University of Illinois Press and the author.

Viking Penguin and David Grossman Literary Agency: Excerpts from *Four Hours in My Lai* by Michael Bilton and Kevin Sim, copyright © 1992 by Michael Bilton and Kevin Sim. Rights in the United Kingdom administered by David Grossman Literary Agency, London. Reprinted by permission of Viking Penguin, a division of Penguin Putnam Inc., and David Grossman Literary Agency.

Printed in the United States
by Baker & Taylor Publisher Services